END TIMES
for Beginners

Bible Prophecy Made Simpler

END TIMES
for Beginners

Bible Prophecy Made Simpler

M DAVID MCKILLEN

RITCHIE
John Ritchie Publishing

'Our brother David and his wife Helen have been our personal friends for many years and it was a privilege to watch both of them mature in their spiritual lives. They moved to live in the Kells area and joined the fellowship of the assembly here in 2003, from where they were heartily commended to the grace of God for 'full-time' service in 2004. We have followed their pathway and progress with prayerful interest, not only in all parts of Africa in which they travelled, but in other parts of the world as well. The Lord answered much prayer in restoring Helen from severe illness in 2014 and we have been blessed to have them back in fellowship with us in Kells since that time. David's interest, and increasing ability, in prophetic teaching, both formal and informal, on the platform and in Bible Class, has been a blessing to many.

Since his own illness and recovery in 2018 and the restrictions of 'Covid19', David has been blessed to be able to continue his work online and on various oral media. This led to a request for 'End Times' material to be put in print, and we rejoice that this was not only requested but has now been accomplished. We endorse his book, 'End Times for Beginners', as a source of sound of biblical answers to many questions that are being asked today.

We trust that the book will find wide acceptance and be a spiritual blessing to many who are seeking the truth concerning "things which must shortly come to pass" (Rev. 1:1).'

Robert Wilson, on behalf of Kells Assembly, NI.

'In recent times, books on prophecy have largely been based on a non-dispensational amillennial view of scripture. There has been a definite need for an entry-level book for beginners, setting out in clear language the scriptural case for a pretribulation rapture followed by the millennial reign of Christ on earth. David McKillen has provided us with such a book. Employing a literal, grammatical, historical method of interpretation, David brings together the prophecies of the Old and New Testaments, with special detailed emphasis on the Book of Revelation.

There are three main threads to prophesy: firstly, the Messiah; secondly, the Nation of Israel; and thirdly, the Gentile Nations. The prophecies concerning Christ's suffering and death were fulfilled literally. It follows, surely, that the prophecies concerning Christ's glory will also be fulfilled literally. David leaves us in no doubt that a consistent literal approach to prophecy is the correct one. I have known the author personally for many years and have benefitted often from his ministry. He has poured many years of study into this excellent book. We will all greatly benefit by it.'

John F Parkinson, Author, *'The Faith of God's Elect'*, Ballymena, NI.

'All believers should have a desire to be more familiar with the Scriptural teaching concerning the "End Times". The events leading up to and the fulfilment of the End Times are approaching ever nearer day by day.

David's timely book on this subject is written in an accessible style. It provides a comprehensive overview of prophetic studies and analyses different theories, clearly laying out the order of things to come. It will be of particular help to young believers seeking to study their Bibles with a view to developing their knowledge and understanding of future events.

I would commend this book to young and older believers alike as there is great benefit to be had in having a fuller awareness of what is yet to come as we prepare ourselves for these last days.'

Samuel W Jennings, Author, 'Alpha and Omega' (Revelation), Bangor, NI.

'David McKillen has given to all of us (not just beginners) a superbly penned, easy-read commentary on 'End Time Events'. His godly insights and exposition of various Bible passages are clear, concise, and contemporary. I have no hesitation in enthusiastically commending this book to you as a most helpful resource, especially for those who have an interest in prophetic truth and a passionate longing for the advent of Jesus Christ.'

Sam Gordon, Bible Teacher with Truth for Today,
Author 'All Hail the Lamb' (Revelation) 'Great God of Heaven' (Daniel), Bawtry, UK.

'Between 2004 and 2009 the Assembly in Francistown was privileged to have among us brother David McKillen and his dear wife Helen who were commended to the grace of God from Northern Ireland, United Kingdom. David, or 'Rra Anna', as he was affectionately known in the Assembly, soon distinguished himself as a very able teacher and gospel preacher whose knowledge of the Scriptures is profound and he was a blessing to all, not just in Francistown, but also in Zambia and South Africa, places he has continued to visit. With time we noticed he was very interested in Bible prophecy, a subject which I also had been studying for years since my early days as a believer. What a wonderful time I had, to have a brother like David who enriched me in this subject. As the Assembly in Francistown, we fondly remember those blessed days with David and his kind, gentle and hospitable wife, Helen.

Since the coming of Covid19 days, we have enjoyed his oral teaching on 'End Times for Beginners'. It is a great delight that this series is now going to be published as a book, and our prayer is that it will gain a wide readership and will be a blessing to many of the children of God.'

K. F. Mompati, Francistown Christian Assembly, Botswana.

'Time is irreversible, once it's gone into the past, we cannot call it back! It is now a little over sixteen years from when I met David and Helen McKillen first at a Conference in Serowe, Botswana. They had just come out as commended missionaries, into the Lord's work in southern Africa. What warm practical Christian fellowship in the Lord we have had since. Strangers to each other, different skin colours and different cultures, but one in the Lord. Was this coincidence? Not with the Lord. He was in the details blending us for our service for Him together! God is always in all the tiny details of our lives as believers, if we entrust them to Him.

David has a real comprehension of the Scriptures and is able to "rightly divide the Word". His ability to swiftly bring in everyday life experiences from his many outreach travels is most beneficial. I am amazed at the reservoir of information this brother has, firstly of the scriptures, but also of current happenings in our world, which he is able to blend together.

Recently there has been a deep interest among African believers for systematic teaching of the 'End Times' that our brother David has been so exercised about. I trust that this new literary work will be an encouragement and receive much exposure in every way possible, as has proved on the media already, where it has reached out to many thousands. May the Lord in His kindness continue to use our dear brother to bring sound doctrine to many more through this exercise.

I have followed his 'End Times' ministry often and have had real spiritual profit. Now that it will be put into printed form, may many others also enjoy the Word relating to the 'End Times for Beginners' as it will be accurately taught, and with depth and feeling.'

Daniel Nguluka, Evangelist, Maun, NW Botswana.

'I was privileged to work with, and make a dear friend of, the author in Botswana, Africa. I had known that David was working on an in-depth study of 'End time prophecy' for some time, but it was wonderful when he agreed to come to the small assembly at Selebi Phikwe for teaching on the subject.

David came with what was then a new "Revelation" Chart (now considerably updated) and we spent some blessed days in October 2012 going through these studies, their first outing in Botswana. All the believers in fellowship and some from other Christian groups in Phikwe came to those meetings, both in our little hall and in our home. All were enthralled with the teaching. I have copies of the 'Study Manuals' which we produced along the way. I am delighted that this book, 'End Times for Beginners', is being published, which will undoubtedly prove to be a blessing for the study of 'End times prophecy' and will help new students to get to grips, especially with the book of Revelation.

We pray that God will bless this work for His eternal glory.'

Bryan Jenkins, Cardiff, Wales.

'The Hermanus Assembly, and other Assemblies in the Overberg region, were introduced to brother David and his wife Helen by our late brother Eric McGrath. We soon learned that our brother and sister shared a common interest in the work of God, and we found them to be a loyal, committed, appreciative, spiritual and above all caring couple. With reference to teaching, we learned brother David had a deep interest in prophetic study, and we invited him for four weeks meetings, with his Chart, to be shared between the Hermanus, Hawston, and Stanford Assemblies.

Not only were the saints exposed to sound teaching (and also the fundamentals of sound personal Bible study, including 'burning the candle late', and the spiritual benefits thereof), but we were greatly encouraged in seeing restoration, and unbelievers coming to know the Lord Jesus. Our brother taught not only from the platform, but in house visitation, in personal Bible study, and by an example of personal determination and dedication to the Lord.

The teaching of the "End Times", leads us not only to the future, but also to foundational truths of the past. We acknowledge the contribution brother David's book will make to spiritual progress in others likewise, and the prayers of our assemblies follow to this end.

We, the Assemblies of the 'Overberg Region', are grateful for the spiritual investment of our brother and sister in this work.'

Dennis Hendricks, Hermanus Assembly, Overberg, W.C., South Africa.

'It was with great enthusiasm that our dear brother David McKillen and his wife Helen were received by the local assemblies in the Western Cape, more so when the subject of "End Times" was to be taken up. Normally brethren shy away from taking up prophecy especially from the books of Daniel and Revelation, which are often misunderstood, yet the truth was brought out so profoundly, making us as believers to realize our responsibility toward others, for we are now living in the very last days.

It is encouraging to see the dedication and commitment by our brother in expounding the scriptures, yet also the simplicity by which it is made easy for others to understand, both in spoken and now the written word. We, at Grassy Park Assembly, with our neighbouring assemblies, Retreat and Steenberg, will ever be thankful for such practical fellowship enjoyed in the Word, for it truly made us see our responsibility as a local assembly in these "End Times".'

Patrick Theunissen, Grassy Park Assembly, Peninsula, Cape Town, South Africa.

'It is a real privilege to write a commendation for our brother David McKillen and his book entitled 'End Times for Beginners'. We first got to know David, when he visited the assembly here in Kamloops, BC., and it was wonderful to see one of the Lord's own who not only knew his Bible but who also knew a close walk with the Lord. David's preaching not only brings honour to the Lord Jesus but exhibits a genuine love for people. This book he has written is focused on prophecy which is probably the second largest subject of the scriptures, following the subject of the Lord Jesus Himself. Of course, the subject of prophecy is also centered on the person of God's own Son.

This helpful and informative book will be a great asset for all who desire to grow in grace and in the knowledge of our Lord and Saviour Jesus Christ.'

John Eggers, Westsyde Assembly, Kamloops, B.C., Canada.

'A clear understanding of the fundamentals of Bible prophecy is vital to "rightly divide the word of truth" (2 Tim. 2:15). As the title suggests, this book provides a 'way-in' to this understanding.

David's exposition of 'End Times' has been a real help to us in the past in oral ministry. In fact, the first public use of this Chart (in a slightly more basic form) was during a series of meetings on Bible prophecy he had here with us in Sligo in 2016. We have very much appreciated our brother's care and exercise for us here, and I have no doubt God will use this book to guide and establish His people in prophetic truth.'

Stephen Goodwin, Collooney Assembly, Co. Sligo, Ireland.

'I have had the privilege of being taught by David on the topic of 'End Times' on many occasions: from the platform, in Bible class, to long discussions in carparks afterwards. His ability to teach clearly and link (at first) seemingly unrelated passages in relation to prophecy has helped me greatly in beginning to understand a fraction of what is happening in the world around us and how it relates to the scriptures.

This book deals directly with questions that I have found myself asking. Broad questions, such as 'What is prophecy?', and many more specific subjects. This book is a valuable resource for anyone seeking the truth about "things to come".'

Jack Aiken, Student, Kells, NI.

'Across our world the biblical truth of the 'End Times' is under attack. With no subject to compare in the controversy that exists around it and the opinions held on it, can we really find true answers to be assured in? The Apostle Paul wrote, "... the Lord shall deliver me from every evil work, and will preserve me unto His heavenly kingdom: to whom be glory for ever and ever. Amen." (2 Tim. 4:18). How could there be praise and unwavering faith from a man awaiting execution? Because he was grounded in the truth, and hope, of the 'End Times' ...

On this basis I heartily recommend David's scripturally based volume to a younger generation. The enquiring reader will find the book interactive and simple to understand and it will help to guide and teach us that regarding the many questions on the subject, God has made Himself crystal clear. The reader who is willing to share in the author's foundational principle of "What saith the scripture?" will find this to be a clear and simple exposition of God's Word on the subject of "things to come". May our hearts not miss the great climax that this subject will bring us to, with a victorious Lamb, in His Kingdom, and God receiving all the glory.'

Andrew Hutchinson, Student, Ballymoney, NI.

'Many Christians often perceive a book regarding Bible prophecy to be complex and confusing. This book is the antithesis of such a preconception. David McKillen has written an exceptionally readable and accessible introduction to the study of prophecy and eschatology; presenting a clear case for a literal, dispensational, futurist view of God's prophetic programme, which is essential for a proper understanding of scripture. David explains in meticulous detail God's prophetic programme, subsequently giving the reader a foundational understanding of concepts and events contained within. In an age where there exists many conspiracies and inaccurate ideas regarding prophecy that confuse and perplex the believer, it is valuable to own such a sound, well-written book introducing the subject of prophecy. I warmly commend it for any Bible student, whether they be well-versed in the subject of prophecy or perhaps approaching it for the first time.'

Tom Black, Student, Coleraine, NI.

What in the World is Happening?
M David McKillen

E: endtimesforbeginners@gmail.com

ISBN-13: 978 1 914273 08 7

Copyright © 2021 M David McKillen, Kells, NI.
Copyright © 2021 by John Ritchie Ltd.

www.ritchiechristianmedia.co.uk

Occasionally (O.T.) & (N.T.) abbreviations have been used: These apply to the Old Testament and New
Testament sections of the Bible.

NOTE: Scripture references in the text are written in full, for the benefit of any readers not familiar with
abbreviated Bible References. Where abbreviations do occur, the Book of the Bible is abbreviated to the
first three letters, then the chapter, and then the verse.
E.g. (Revelation chapter 1 verses 1 – 3) may appear as (Rev. 1:1-3).

All Scripture quotations have been "*italicised*", with double speech marks.
Other quotations with single speech marks.
Divine titles and personal pronouns referring to Deity have been capitalised.

Typeset & Cover Design by Brian Chalmers Design Services: www.brianchalmersdesign.co.uk
Printed by Bell & Bain Ltd., Glasgow.
Chart & Images Designed by MARTIN KENNY Design & Illustration Services, Belfast.
Copyright Photographs from Unsplash, Montreal, QC. or (as indicated) © J&H Fillis, Coleraine.

CONTENTS

PART THREE: The KINGDOM PERIOD ANTICIPATED

PART FOUR: The NEARNESS OF COMING EVENTS

PART FIVE: APPENDICES

Preface: *'The Author's Journey'*

As a person from a Christian background, when speaking of my early life I often say, 'I don't remember when I first learned that I needed salvation'. That is, to have my sins forgiven through faith in the death of Jesus on the Cross. I was *"born again"*, my spiritual birthday, on the 22nd of March 1967, during a gospel service in a rural mission hall. That very personal and conscious decision commenced my *"faith"* journey to heaven, which will continue until I die, or if I am alive when Jesus comes again for His Church.

In the same kind of way, I remember from as soon as I could read, having an interest in books of every sort. Books to be read sometimes even by torch light, long after Mum's official 'Lights out!' Two parallel interests grasped my attention from very early: books about missionaries, especially African stories, and more curiously books within the Bible about prophecy. If I ever became 'disinterested' during any kind of formal service, I turned in my Bible to the book of Revelation and started reading at chapter one. The fact that I understood next to nothing (nor of Ezekiel, Daniel or Zechariah either), did not lessen my fascination for the 'unseen' world of future events, as the Bible portrays them in the prophetic scriptures.

Little did I know, in those formative years, that the Spirit of God would bring both of these unusual interests together in an amazing manner. In 2003, after a period of deep spiritual personal thought and prayer, my wife Helen and I both accepted that God was calling us very specifically to leave secular employment and go to serve Him in Africa. We left our employment in 2004, in fellowship with our commending assembly in Kells, N.I., and dependent on our God to look after our needs. He has not failed, even though serious illness came the way of both of us. Much travelling was done in southern African countries in fellowship with other brothers and local workers too. Outreach in Namibia, encouraging small assemblies in Zambia, Botswana, and South Africa, kept me 'on the road' for weeks at a time during those early years.

In mid-2010 various circumstances led to a change in focus: Several assembly elders discussed with me at different times the ongoing problems of getting local people to come to in to hear the gospel. Traditionally the larger numbers attending from among the working classes of the Cape Town suburbs had shrunk, and interest seemed to have diminished. Their suggestion then was, 'Brother, could you not get a Chart made on the

Book of Revelation, or the End Times?' They explained, 'These are things that people are asking about when we visit round their houses.' This was a somewhat original idea, and my initial response was, 'That's not an easy request', but I promised to think and pray about it ...

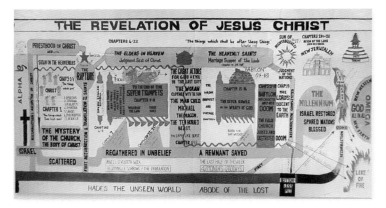

The original 'hand-painted' linen cloth Revelation Chart.

Helen's reaction was very encouraging, 'We must find a good Chart'. After much searching, and sketching, we settled on a black and white image, drawn for Dr H. A. Ironside in the 1930s. Colour was added on a trial and error basis, and a dear sister in one of the assemblies in the Western Cape was commissioned to turn it into something 'big scale'. I recall asking for 'double bed sheet size'. After a week or two (with a campaign date looming), we received a call to come and see the almost finished article. Esther's husband, Stephen, had put plyboard all along one wall of their garage and the chart, on linen cloth, was pinned up 14 feet long. She said, 'You will need it big enough for it to be seen from the back of a long Hall'. And the dear sister was proved to be right.

The introductory meetings started the following Sunday, with a full hall. God blessed in continuous preaching, from one set of meetings straight into another throughout the suburbs of the Cape, and into the outlying 'Overberg' area for almost three years without a break. A great many visitors heard the gospel message in a 'new' context for the first time. Many informal question and answer sessions were held in believers' homes afterwards, long into the night.

God was gracious in blessing both in restoration and salvation in many places and we often commented, 'The Holy Spirit is the real preacher using the images on the Chart. Not the missionary speaker at all.' That was often true and testified to be so by others.

The Revelation Chart in an Assembly Hall in N W Zambia.

Over the years since, that original hand painted chart has travelled 1,000s of kilometres, right up to the Angolan border and to many of the assemblies in the northwest of Zambia. The vision of the dear sister as to the size of the chart was no mistake.

In some locations many hundreds were present inside each night, and at times many listened through the windows outside and on public address broadcasts. God was gracious and blessed, in many different ways, and encouraged His servants too.

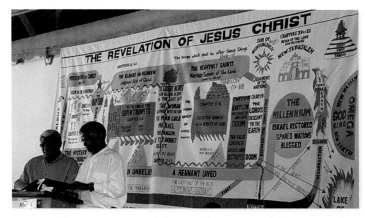

In some assemblies the preaching was in English and in others by parallel translation into a dialect with the help of a local brother or another

Bruce Mukwatu & Dan Nguluka at Loloma Assembly, N W Zambia.

national worker. Simple A4 handouts, which were requested, multiplied as time passed until a more complete 'booklet' was required. Many of the African saints in those days had rudimentary libraries and limited internet, and so an A4 'Study Manual' was put together. It was possible to carry the outer covers, even in airline luggage, and print the black and white text locally. In that way 1,000s of study books were printed in Zambia, Botswana, South Africa, and eventually back home in the U.K. and Ireland as well.

In 2013, Helen was unexpectedly diagnosed with acute Leukaemia. This was a difficult time for both of us and, due to her prolonged hospitalisation, the Lord brought us back home to be based once again in Ireland. In answer to the prayers of many, Helen made a good recovery and the Lord graciously opened new 'doors' for overseas travelling once again.

By this time the 'African Chart' was showing its mileage, and an update was clearly needed, even though the original had also been used in various locations for teaching series in our home province of Northern Ireland following on from our return.

With the help of two local Christian artists, Jonnie and Martin, a completely new chart was drawn up. A trial copy was used for outreach meetings with a small assembly at Collooney in the southwest of Ireland, and then a larger version was used with the assembly at Wick in the far north of Scotland. Following on from that came wonderful meetings with the Kirkwall assembly in the Orkney Islands. The interest from that local community confirmed again that the subject matter – though alien to many – would attract an audience that might not have otherwise attended evangelical meetings. The final version of this chart again extends to a large scale. Though a somewhat 'outmoded' concept in a day of digital projection, the panoramic aspect of a large print media chart is a real advantage in conveying 'graphic' truth across a broad timeline.

The onset of the global 'Covid 19 pandemic', and 'lock-down' in various parts of the world, has had an obvious impact on travel. The effects of the many different and difficult restrictions, and the speedy rollout of the various vaccines, have also put questions into the minds of many people, whether Christian or not. Requests were soon forthcoming, initially from New Zealand, for a video teaching series on 'End Times' topics targeted at young Christians and others with a lesser understanding of prophetic subjects ...

The original 'End Times' chart at Brae Gospel Hall, Shetland.

In early 2020, an 'overview' series was initially conducted via social media with the Kamloops assembly in the north of British Columbia, Canada, where I had been working in gospel outreach in previous years. Following on from that, the weekly video series, named '*End Times for Beginners*' continued for six months. The large response, and wide correspondence, was unexpected and deeply encouraging. After many requests for study notes we considered, prayerfully, committing something to print. Following on from that there came the request from John Ritchie's to put the series into book form. This, after much combined labour, is the finished product.

Dedication

I would like to dedicate this finished publication to my life partner, my wife, and mother of our four children, Helen. My true *"fellow labourer"* in the Lord's work. For all your love, support, advice, and patience during the long hours when I was totally committed to researching and writing. Thank you with all my heart. This book is a joint effort and with the Lord's help.

The Lord has brought us both through *"deep waters"* in the past few years. Helen's unwavering faith, support, positive critique, and encouragement has made this journey possible, thus far. Not only many days of willing separation when in the African 'bush', but in days for both of us in more recent times, asking the Lord 'Why?' Questions which, like many that are being asked by troubled people in these present times, we will not be provided answers for down here.

"It is not for you to know times or seasons", Jesus said, *"which the Father put in His own authority. But ye shall receive power ... and ye shall be witnesses ... unto the uttermost part of the earth."* (Acts 1:7-8 NRB). As William Tyndale said in his early translation, *"even to the end of the world"*.

We commend this book, a labour of love, to our God. May it be an awakening to spiritual truth, a confirmation that an eternal God is in control, and a blessing to all who peruse its contents, not only to the ends of our world, but to the end of the age: *"Amen. Even so, come, Lord Jesus."* (Revelation 22:20 KJV).

Acknowledgments

Special thanks are due to a great many – who assisted in the journey which has culminated in the publishing of this volume – who walked with us and encouraged, who worked and shared in many of the uphill battles and times of great spiritual joy that came through the quite specific path of *"End Times"* evangelism and ministry. (Many of those whom I would like to mention also have no desire to be highlighted. I know a full record is *"on high"*, so I will use first names only. All the brothers and sisters referred to know who they are.)

To Helen, my wife, I have already mentioned, but our children deserve mention too. Their sacrifices were real, and not necessarily voluntary, as ours were: Anna, Davy, Sarah, and Daniel; our thanks for your love and support, as well as our parents. To my Mum especially, who has made this book a matter of special prayer from its conception. Also our wider families over many years.

To the elders of the various 'Mitchell's Plain', 'Peninsula' and 'Overberg' Assemblies in the Western Cape, for planting a 'seed' which has led directly to this book. The concept of 'End Times Gospel', with a Chart, was their suggestion back in 2010 and the first such outreach meetings were in the Elsie's River Assembly. To Esther and Stephen, who provided the materials and drew the original Chart, well-worn now but still in use and widely travelled, our thanks also.

To Bryan, who not only arranged an *"End Times"* series for the Selibe Phikwe Assembly in Botswana, but who also assisted greatly in the original 'Study Manual', much of the material from which is contained in this book. To Jonnie, a source of real encouragement and a supplier of graphic material constantly at short notice. To Martin, my professional graphic artist: A perfectionist, and a supplier of artistic graphics of every size and sort. To Brian, for his excellent capabilities in graphic design and typesetting, without which (and the burning of a little 'midnight oil'), the book would not be presented as it is. Thank you.

To Bill, my father-in-law, to Gary, to Andrew, and others whose suggestions (and critique) helped to sharpen the edge and focus of the text. To Jim for his time in donating quality photographs and in discussion too. To David McGahie, my senior editor: A stickler for detail, but who deserves special mention for many hours of late-night labour which I believe is also reflected in the end product.

To Alison, Raymond, Leonard, Fraser, and others at John Ritchie Ltd., who requested the original media material to be put into print. They, and their printers, are deserving of thanks for the quality of the finished product and for its distribution.

Last, but by no means least, to Bobby and the other elders and members of our 'home' – and commending – assembly in Kells NI., a very sincere 'Thank you' from Helen and me for much love, care, continual contact, and support over the past years.

There are many more whom I could have mentioned, fellow companions along various branches of our journey, but I have focused on those who have contributed directly to this material coming into print. If I have accidentally left anyone out – in that context – I do apologise. The Lord Himself knows, and has a full and unbiased record for us to see in a day not too far off (2 Cor 5:10).

My humble record of appreciation is given with sincere thanks to all. Without each one, this book would not have been written, or would have been very different. May the Lord bless what is contained in the printed form for His glory. *"Maran-atha"* (1 Cor. 16:22).

M David McKillen

Foreword

The study of future events has occupied the Church since her earliest days. It is correct that it is so.

God has seen fit to unveil His prophetic programme in the Bible. Its study is intended not only to spiritually educate us (1 Thess. 4:13), but also comfort (1 Thess. 4:18), and change us (Romans 13:11). That is even more true today, for *"the time is short"* (1 Cor. 7:29).

The difficulty is that there is so much variety in prophetic teaching across Christendom that it is hard for the Bible student entering the arena for the first time to navigate his or her way through the big issues: What method of interpretation should be deployed? What is the relationship between the Church and Israel? What is the timing of the prophetic programme?

That the difficulty exists as it does is not least the case because of the comparatively recent explosion of teaching that belittles the literal method of Bible interpretation and a 'dispensational' understanding of scripture. Around us believers are being taught that God's Kingdom programme is only spiritual, and that Israel's promises are all fulfilled in the Church.

We remain convinced from scripture that a 'literal, pre-millennial, dispensational' understanding of scripture is the best way to approach a systemised study of prophetic matters. But that conviction is under attack and must be studied and taught rather than just asserted.

It was in part for those reasons that, in the summer 2016, David McKillen came to Wick for three weeks of sessions introducing prophetic teaching with the local assembly that meets here. David had lately returned from missionary service in Southern Africa, due to personal circumstances, and used various charts that he had developed there in prophecy-based outreach. The teaching was Biblical, simple, and the sessions were a great help not only to believers in the assembly but also to believers and unbelievers from elsewhere.

David's teaching has been repeated to profit in other locations and on various media and it is an encouragement to know that it will now be put into text introducing 'End Times for Beginners'. We are of course all beginners in the study of *"End Times"*!

In any significant book on future events, we will not agree on every last detail of interpretation. However, I am confident that this will be a helpful text introducing the study of prophecy in an accessible but Biblical way for new Christians, for non-Christians, and for those new to a literal approach to prophetic study.

We pray that it will be a blessing to the saints of God worldwide.

Eric Baijal, Wick Assembly, Scotland. August 2021.

PART ONE

AN OVERVIEW OF BIBLE PROPHECY

Chapter One
Introduction to Prophecy

This sounds like a strange title, and some will say, 'These are strange topics. Do we need to study them? Do we even need to consider them?' I think, prayerfully, the answer to those questions must be, 'Yes!' and for reasons which we will examine together. Some will also ask, 'Are there not enough books on prophecy already?' I might even answer, 'Yes' to that question myself! These studies would not have happened, in their original form, if they had not been requested, and the written form likewise only came to be by request.

So What's New?

Some who are looking into the book out of curiosity at this point might say, 'I don't believe in the kind of *"beginning"* that's talked about in the Bible, so why should I believe in an 'End Times'? Nothing has changed up to now, so surely nothing much will change?' There are three points to be addressed to that question straight off: Firstly, change is happening faster than it ever has before. The earth: its occupants, its nations, and its governments are spinning increasingly out of control. Who would deny that? Secondly, the Bible affirms that change HAS happened in the past. God judged wickedness in the past, even the geological evidence confirms past catastrophic events. The Apostle Peter argued that there was evidence of God's intervention in a past age, in a global catastrophe (2 Peter chapter 3). Thirdly, I would ask you to suspend your disbelief in what you cannot see. The Bible deals to a great extent with the 'unseen world'.

We will see, as we go forward, that these 'End Times' studies make sense of, and provide answers for, a great many of the 'darker questions' that often go unasked. Questions that are coming to the fore in many conversations today. You don't have to be a 'Church-going', 'Bible carrying', *"Jesus saves"* kind of person to know – even if you don't talk about it openly – that current events in our world are getting very strange indeed!

> **KEYNOTE: The Supernatural.** Is it not a strange thing that people who deny that God exists are much slower to deny that the Devil exists? Or that there are supernatural evil powers at work in our world? The 'paranormal' or 'supernatural' of which the Bible speaks with authority is very real.

Does the Bible Have Answers?

One of the reasons that this book has been titled 'End Times for Beginners' is that the very earliest requests came from young people (who had come to faith in Jesus Christ in the early days of the first 'Covid 19 lock-down', through what they already knew of the gospel and perhaps through some degree of concern for the things going on around them). They read their Bibles, they took in the truth of the Word of God, and they trusted in Jesus Christ as their Saviour. What a lovely thing! I do believe that God has been blessing through the recent pandemic and through things that the Holy Spirit has been putting into people's minds, turning them back again to the Word of God.

It would be our desire that this book on 'End Times' would cause many who don't know the Lord Jesus personally to come to an understanding, not only of what He has done for us through His death on the cross, but of where He is going to take those of us who have put their trust in Him as Saviour, and what He has prepared for us in the future. Those young people requested that 'End Times Studies' from the Bible would be done to make it simpler and easier to understand more about what is happening now, and future events which seem to be getting closer.

Are the 'End Times' important in relation to the study of the Word of God?

KEYNOTE: The First Prophecy. Search out where that is before we come to study the topic …

Absolutely so because the 'End Times' are not only found in the book of Revelation, the last book of the Bible. When we come to look at prophecy in the wider sense [in our third **Chapter**], we will discover that prophecy begins at the very start of the book of Genesis and the earliest prophecy in the Word of God is given in Genesis chapter three, perhaps even in chapter two. We will not say any more about that just now.

Let us examine a verse from the New Testament together (Matthew chapter 24 verse 3 ESV), *"As He* (that is Jesus) *sat on the mount of Olives, the disciples came to Him privately, saying,* (This was not a public question and what He told them was not a public declaration, it was given to those who already were believers in the Lord Jesus) *'Tell us, when will these things be, and what will be the sign of Your coming and of the end of the age?'"* If we had time to read the rest of Matthew chapters 24 & 25, we would find that what we have there is called 'The Olivet Discourse'. Jesus gave to His disciples a programme of signs of increasing intensity, that would be seen before He came back to earth. The early disciples, it seems, also wanted to know about the 'End Times', even while Jesus was still with them!

Why 'End Times for Beginners'?

Let us come back again now to our topic, 'End Times for Beginners'. Why have we picked such a title for this book? Chapter Two will be entitled 'Does God have a Programme?' and we will see that He does (from the beginning of time to the last days), and that much of His programme has been set out in advance. We must go back

KEYNOTE: Does God have a Programme? The answer to that question is, absolutely and definitely; 'Yes!' And God has revealed to us a great amount of detail in relation to His programme; for the universe, for planet earth, for mankind, for our salvation, our ultimate salvation, in the new heaven and the new earth that God will bring every saved person to, from every period of time. All of these topics will come up in later **Chps**.

to the beginning of time and forward to the end of earth time to fully answer that question. That is why we use the terms *"Alpha and Omega"* (Revelation chapter 1 verse 8 KJV), which you will see on the book cover, and also on the Chart. They indicate that God is the source of everything, from beginning to end.

In the second Chapter we will look at the subject of 'What is Prophecy?' That is not an easy question, but we will have to try and deal with it as simply as possible and after that we will come in further studies to look at 'the End Times' themselves; the study of prophecy in scripture that has not yet been fulfilled. [The technical word for that is 'eschatology'. You might have to look that up in a dictionary, but we are not going to use difficult dictionary terms in these studies.] We will focus on prophecies that have not yet been fulfilled and we will study in some detail 'end times prophecies' that we can prove from the Word of God. Things which are probably just about to be fulfilled in our time, and in our generation …

When we speak of 'End Times for Beginners' we are really suggesting that most of us know very little about 'End Times', and the true and humble answer to that is, 'Yes, we do know very little'. It may have been young people that requested the studies first, but when we come to these tremendous subjects of end time prophecy, pictures that God is painting for us in symbolic form in His Word and on the Chart, we see so many strange things that God is showing us that have not yet taken place or been fulfilled.

Check Out the Chart

KEYNOTE: The Chart. The 'End Times' Chart inside the front cover 'flips out'. It will be helpful to keep it in view because it will be referred to it a lot as we go forward.

If you look near the beginning of the Chart (where we are just now in time) you can see we are still in the 'Church Period', although that is not a Bible term. We are still in the 'Day of grace', the day in which Church testimony - corporate, individual, and gathered together in different places in this world in different forms - is ongoing and growing. We are not speaking of buildings, we are speaking of the greater building, the *"Church which is the body of Jesus Christ"* (Colossians chapter 1 verse 24 & Ephesians chapter 1 verse 23 KJV).

KEYNOTE: Left Behind. I remind myself often in prayer that this publication may never be completed because one of the first parts of 'the beginning of the end times' might take place before we have completed our studies. Jesus Christ could come for His Church, which would leave this book on these topics unfinished. He would have completed the first part of His promise *"I will come again, and receive you"* (John chapter 14 verse 3 KJV). Or someone could be reading this book, and other books like it, after Jesus has come for His Church, and all true Christians of the Church Age will have gone ...

The living part of the Church is still on earth and although the bodies of those who have died (who are still part of the Church) are in the grave, their spirits are in heaven with Jesus Christ and there will be a great day of resurrection. [Which we will come to in a future topic in **Chapter 6**.] The bodies of those saints and all who are still living belonging to the Church will all be joined together and changed and taken up to be with Jesus Christ forever (1 Thessalonians chapter 4 verse 17). That event has not happened yet.

Brothers and sisters in Jesus Christ, and some who still don't know Jesus Christ as their Saviour but have enough interest in their heart to investigate these pages; I trust the fear of God comes upon us all, especially any who are not ready for what God is going to do in judgment. There is a preparation that has already been completed when the Son of God said *"Finished"* on the cross at Calvary almost 2,000 years ago. There is no need for any person ever to finish up under God's judgment, or to be lost in Hell. There is sufficient in the death of Jesus Christ to cover every sin of every sinner who will come and put their faith in God's Son for salvation (John chapter 3 verse 16).

We are all beginners, we are all in God's 'kindergarten', we are all in the 'first grade' as we come to study with our Bibles and notebooks, something of the beginning of 'End Times' that have not happened yet. We are at the beginning of the end of the Church period; almost 2,000 years of Church history have already passed. A period which, since Pentecost and the birth of the Church (Acts chapter 2), we also call the 'Day of grace'. What a time we are living in! But we do not know how much of that grace period is left ...

KEYNOTE: The Church Period. What is called the 'Church Age' is the longest unbroken period in the history of mankind on planet earth during which God has not intervened, or rebuked man's rebellion, in judgment. We have been living uninterrupted in a 'day of grace' and gospel evangelism that is longer than any other single period in the Word of God.

Some will ask, 'Why are we speaking of 'End Times'?'

That is an easier question to answer because God's programme has a past, a present and a future, which has not yet all been fulfilled. The name *"Jehovah"* (which is a compound Hebrew phrase brought across into English) describes God as being 'in the future, in the present and in the past', and in that order. When we talk about the part of the programme of God that must still be fulfilled you might ask, 'Has God told us what He is going to do before it happens?' Yes, He has. He did often through the Old Testament prophets, predictions about events which came to pass, and some of which are still future yet.

Some will say, 'I am not interested in studying prophecy!'

That perhaps is a hasty comment because a quarter (25% if you are good at mathematics) of the Bible, from Genesis to Revelation, was given as 'prophecy' at the time of speaking or writing. Something that had not yet taken place, but God said it would surely happen. At the time it was either spoken forth by the prophets, or written down by those who were told it or heard it.

Another question people ask is, 'Are the 'End Times' really about us?'

Well, I am not sure what we should say in answer to that question! On one hand we could be very honest and very simple and say: 'No. A lot of the End Times prophecies are not about us.' 'Oh', some will say, 'That's very strange. Why then study them at all?' Every single person who is a believer in the Lord Jesus is going to be taken away and that will be near the beginning of the 'End Times'. Then the period that comes afterward, that fills the whole middle section of the book of Revelation (chapters 4 - 19), that period is not really for those of us who are believers in the Lord Jesus Christ today. 'Well then', you might say, 'That means we don't need to go through the book of Revelation, we don't need to go to those chapters in Matthew's gospel you have mentioned, or other hard prophetic passages that are often referred to ...'

'Can we not forget about the 'End Times' if we will not be in them?'

There are several answers to that question:

Firstly: God has given us detailed knowledge about the 'End Times' so that we do know, even in the worst of conditions that are already starting to cast their shadows, that God, not man nor the devil, is in control.

Secondly: And this is most important, no matter what Satan tries to do in influencing men behind the scenes, he cannot win. God and His purposes through the plan of salvation that was completed on the cross when Satan had his *"head bruised"* (Genesis chapter 3 verse 15) means that God must triumph. Satan must go to his final punishment. Satan cannot win, though a day will come in the period we are going to study when it looks as if the *"Dragon"* (another name for the *"Devil"*) has taken control. God will permit less *"restraint"* on evil (2 Thessalonians chapter 2 verses 5 – 7), but God will never lose control and God's purposes can never be defeated.

Thirdly: There will be a generation of people in the 'Tribulation period', at the start it will probably be mostly Jews, then there will also be Gentiles (those who are not Jews); they will come to faith in Jesus Christ through the preaching of the Gospel of the Kingdom. In that difficult period they will turn for comfort and help and encouragement, if they are going to live – or give – their lives for Jesus Christ, to these very passages that we find so difficult in the Word of God!

Fourthly: The Bible makes it clear that this period of End Times prophecy (that so many people find difficult to understand, and that so many people say we don't need to know about), this period while only seven years long in the programme of God in relation to mankind is most important. We can work it out in the Bible for ourselves: From Adam, who was made on the sixth day of creation, right through until the end of the future Kingdom period: That programme is somewhere around 7,000 years and if you are good at mathematics you will be able to see that seven years is only one-thousandth of that figure, a very tiny but yet hugely important period out of the vastness of the programme of God in relation to mankind. It is most important that we should study it, for it is the centre point and end point of much Old Testament (O.T.) and New Testament (N.T.) prophecy.

Fifthly: Perhaps the most important point of all; studying the 'End Times' should give us a great anticipation for the coming of the Lord Jesus, an appreciation of our accountability to Him (2 Corinthians chapter 5). If we are saved, it should spur on our testimony to those around us who do not yet know Jesus Christ as their Saviour, who could soon be under the *"wrath of the Lamb"* (Revelation chapter 6 verse 16 KJV) if they are not *"born again"* (John chapter 3 verse 7 KJV).

Some will ask, 'Who are the End Times about?'

Perhaps we have answered that already; the 'End Times' are about people on earth who will be saved, many who will be martyred, and about people who will follow Satan's 'Superman' [He will also appear in future topics]. The Bible calls him *"The Man of Sin"* and also *"The Beast"*, very strange titles but very suitable for a man that both Old and New Testament prophecy speaks about as a wicked person. They also tell us an awful lot about Satan, the Serpent, the Dragon, and the Devil (for he is all one and the same), his designs and his programme. His fall from heaven, his warfare with God's angels and with mankind, and about his end. [We will study that and fit all these topics together as we go forward.]

Some will be asking, 'Does this all end happily after all?'

KEYNOTE: Consecutive Reading. When I was a young fellow reading books, I used to skip forward, read the first page, and then jump forward to the last page. If I liked the end of the story, then I would be happy to buy the book and read all the pages in between. Try not to do that with this book! It will be much easier to understand the later **Chps.** if you carefully read all the early ones first.

If you go to the last page of the Bible (Revelation chapter 22), and read down through it to the end especially the last few verses - perhaps you have never done that before? - you will find it is one of the 'happiest' and most joyful paragraphs in all of the Word of God.

We shouldn't be frightened of the 'End Times'! We should <u>understand</u> and <u>learn</u> what the Bible tells us about them, those of us who are saved and have the Holy Spirit dwelling inside us, and Jesus Christ in heaven as our Saviour, waiting for Him to come for us. Those who will suffer persecution for Him now. And the believers who will suffer persecution in the tribulation period; we should all <u>learn</u> and <u>know</u> and <u>understand</u> that the ending is beyond happy, the end is a perfect Kingdom that Jesus Christ will bring to planet earth for 1,000 years and after that, the perfection of what the Bible calls the *"Day of God"* (2 Peter chapter 3 verse 12 KJV), to live with Jesus Christ and God His Father forever, in a new heaven and a new earth. No more sin, no more suffering forever, in what is called 'the Eternal State'.

That is the end of the 'End Times' subject: Not just a period of 'tribulation' but a period of perfect happiness for every person who has begun, at some point in their life, a journey of faith in Jesus Christ. From Abel (in Genesis chapter 4) through to the last person born, who believes in the Messiah, during the Millennial Kingdom which is still in the future. What a tremendous encouragement for God's people in present times of difficulty!

> **KEYNOTE: Hard words ...** Many of these difficult terms and expressions – which may be completely new to some readers – will be fully explained, in their context, as we develop the various topics in the **Chapters** which follow.

Q&A >

Chp. 1 — 'Introduction to Prophecy'

Q1. How much of the Bible is prophecy? (a fraction or percentage). If you don't remember, look back and note it, because a great part of the Bible was given as prophecy!

Q2. Where does prophecy start? Look for the first promise and the first prophecy in the Word of God. Note down the Bible reference and remember it.

Q3. How much of the Bible is already history? How long a period, approximately, does the Bible cover? If you draw a 'timeline', where are we on it just now?

Q4. We come to the period in which we live, what is it most often called? There are three or four answers, write down as many as you can.

Q5. Why should we study 'End Times'? There is more than one answer to that question!

Chapter Two
Does God have a Programme?

In the previous chapter, we looked at the meaning of the question, 'What are the End Times?' Why should we call ourselves 'beginners' in relation to 'End Times' study? I trust that we are all humble enough to accept and understand now that when it comes to the purposes of God, especially in relation to the concluding events, we all are just beginners in God's 'kindergarten' class.

Does God have a Programme?

We have put a question mark at the end of the title because we need to satisfy our hearts that God's interactions with mankind are not random. Is our God (although He is a great God, a loving God, a giving and forgiving God, a saving and a Saviour God, a gracious God and an eternal God), only a God who is reactionary?

Does He respond only to things down here when they happen? Is God just a 'heavenly super first responder'? Does He have to wait until people have done something bad, something unsafe? Until mankind down here on earth has had some sort of spiritual 'accident', and then God responds and does something to help? The answer is, absolutely, NO!

> **KEYNOTE: God is Proactive.** God is not just 'reactive'. He is 'proactive'. He knows the end from the beginning. (Unlike the nurses, the police force, the fire service and everybody else that is involved in those activities.) The emergency services must wait until something goes wrong. A phone call is made, an alarm goes out, and then they rush as fast as possible to the incident scene to help and to save. That's why they are called 'first responders'. Is that what God is? 'No, He is not.'

God has a programme which has been in place *"from the foundation of the world"* (Revelation chapter 13 verse 8 KJV). God's programme is fixed and certain. We can even put dates on some parts of it and God had His programme planned from before He began to work on the creation of mankind, whom He put in charge of the government of planet earth, back in the Garden of Eden long ago.

Let us examine a key passage, right at the beginning of our Bibles (because before we can understand anything of the book of Revelation, we need to understand something of the 'Book of Beginnings', the book of Genesis), and look at what God did at the beginning of the creation of our world. We must understand that before we can appreciate what God will do at the end of our age, and at the end of the world.

Genesis chapter 1 verses 1 – 3 reads, *"In the beginning, God created the heavens and the earth. The earth was without form and void* (empty) *and darkness was over the face of the deep. And the Spirit of God was hovering over the face of the waters. And God said, 'Let there be light', and there was light."* We can look at another verse towards the end of the creation programme, *"Then God said* (this is now Day Six of the creation week), *'Let us make man in our image* (that's plural)*, after our likeness. And let them have dominion over the fish of the sea and over the birds of the heavens and over the livestock* (that is domestic animals)*, and over all the earth and over every creeping thing that creeps on the earth'. So God created man in his own image, in the image of God He created him; male and female He created them."* (Genesis chapter 1 verses 26 – 27 ESV).

God and His Programme

When we come to study the programme of God, as revealed in His Word, we can see divisions in it, especially as we are looking from our standpoint backwards at a good part of it, though it is not completed yet: Some of the most significant parts are still future. We can probably divide God's dealings with humanity into eight sections*, including our final destiny in a *"new heaven and new earth"* (Revelation chapter 21 verse 1). It has often been said, 'Distinguish the times and seasons and all scripture will be in harmony with itself'. We should be like the *"children of Issachar, men that had understanding of the times"* (1 Chronicles chapter 12 verse 32). The word *"understanding"* here in Hebrew is a compound of two words, 'to be discerning' and 'to know': In these 'last days' which we find ourselves in, if we have knowledge of what the scripture says, relative to our 'times', we will have the greater spiritual 'discernment' to understand how to respond.

*KEYNOTE: Ages & Stages. The scholars who hold to a series of 'divisions' in God's programme often refer to them as 'Dispensations', a phrase taken from Paul's words, *"... the dispensation of the grace of God"* (Eph. 3:2). The Greek word here is *'oíkonomía'* which means 'management' or 'stewardship' especially in relation to administration of property. C. I. Scofield (1843–1921), a leading 'dispensationalist' of his era, said a dispensation is *'a period of time during which man is tested in respect of obedience to some specific revelation of the will of God'*, Scofield Reference Bible (1917) Pg. 5. An excellent presentation of 'Dispensationalism' vs. 'Reformed Theology' is given by David Dunlap in, *'The Glory of the Ages'* (Ontario, Canada, Gospel Folio Press), 2008.

We will see that a great many of those sections end in human failure, and then God reveals something more of Himself and of His purposes. He picks mankind up again and says, 'Let's go forward in fellowship and in faith ...' God works in goodness as well as in government, all the way through the history of humanity. We will look at these stages of God's working with mankind just on their surface and bring them all to a simple conclusion.

Period One: which we have read about, is the creation of the universe; the earth, the sun and the moon, and the stars and the planets. We didn't read the verse, but it is one of the most amazing phrases in the whole of the Book of Genesis: *"He made the stars also."*

(Genesis chapter 1 verse 16 KJV). Astronomers are still, with bigger and bigger telescopes, trying to count them all but the Bible just puts it down in a tiny little phrase; just the finger of God touching the darkness of the inky sky and every time He does so another star shines brightly and thousands of years later it is only part way through its life, *"He made the stars also ..."*

God said, *"Let there be light"* and there was. *"Let there be dry land and sea ..."* We can work the whole way down through the creation story, 6 literal days of 24 hours. Light and dark, day and night, waters above and below (we don't have time to study that just here). Dry land, earth and seas, lights greater and lesser; sun, moon, and stars. On Day five, fish and birds; on Day six, the creeping things, domestic animals, the rest of the animal creation and then the very pinnacle of God's creation: He made man (and woman) and He put the man in charge of everything in the world that He had made.

> **KEYNOTE: Creation Week.** The creation took place in one week of six days of 24 hours each. Do not let anyone tell you anything different, because at the end of each of the first six days the Biblical record says (counting time as the Jews still count today, because the Jewish day starts at 6 o'clock in the evening), *"evening and morning day first"*; *"evening and morning day second"*; *"evening and morning day third"*, and so on, until all was complete.

How Long was Adam in Charge?

We are not actually told. If we read in Genesis chapter 5 where the genealogy and the timeline with man's ages begin, we can probably work out that Adam and Eve could have been in the garden of Eden (a real place), in fellowship with God for a period of, at the maximum, 100 years. Certainly not any more than that, and probably much less. Then Satan came into the garden, because he had already fallen (we are told that in the Old Testament, in Isaiah chapter 14). His original name was *"Lucifer"*, he was the highest of all created angels. He rebelled from the position that God had given him, he was filled with pride and a desire to exalt himself, and God cast him out of His inner presence.

After his *"fall"* (we are not told how long after) Satan came into the garden, taking the serpent's form, to test the highest of all created beings on earth, mankind. He found similar thoughts of pride and rebellion in the heart of the woman, Eve. She listened to him and not God, she was deceived, she ate the fruit and she sinned. Her husband Adam took it along with her willingly and both 'fell'. They sinned. That first period of innocence and peace and happiness and all the other things that were there in the garden came to a sudden end. Instead of that came *"thorns and thistles"*, sweat, shame, separation, and sin (The sad story is told in Genesis chapter 3).

This is where prophecy starts, but it is also where the promise of two separate and divergent themes begin: The ultimate fulfilment of the promise of a *"Saviour"*, and the ultimate fulfilment of the punishment of Satan who became the *"Serpent"*.

> **KEYNOTE: Two Prophetic Themes.** These two statements are key 'spines' that run the whole way through all the prophecies of the Word of God. God MUST send a *"Saviour"* because He said He would, and the Saviour MUST finally defeat the *"Serpent"* because God said that He would as well.

What Happened After the Fall?

Period Two: When we come to the second period in our Bible, we find something very interesting. We can move very quickly through what seems to be a hard chapter, but it is also fascinating, that is Genesis chapter 5: We can see that men lived very long lives before they died, and the length of years they lived; the average age of all these people, ten generations from Adam to Noah, was about 900 years. Methuselah was the oldest. He lived 969 years *"and he died"*. His name is very strange because it translates as 'When he has gone it will come'. What does that mean?

We can see in the context; it tells us that God's judgment was not sent in a hurry. He was waiting to give time for men, who were wicked and evil and idolatrous and immoral, to repent of their rebellion against Him. But instead, they got worse and corrupted themselves totally, again provoked by the Devil and his agents. God only found one man Noah (that is a true story as well) who was *"pure"* and *"just"*; morally, spiritually, and perhaps even genetically, such was the corruption before the Flood (Genesis chapter 6). It is amazing that so many different cultures in our world, even secular cultures, go back into their history where they have a story of a flood that covered the whole world and one family that was preserved in a wooden box, or *"Ark"* as we know it. We have the root story and the true story in the Word of God (in Genesis chapters 6 – 9), the story of Noah and his family and the global flood. Failure once again, the increasing sin of man and yet God came in and preserved that family and brought them safely through the flood to a cleansed earth ... What a lovely picture of salvation by faith in God's word (Hebrews chapter 11 verse 7).

What Happened After the Flood?

Period Three: Following that we come, after the flood, to another short section of earth time. It doesn't take very long until rebellion starts again. You say, 'Did they not learn a lesson?' No, obviously not. God told them to spread out and populate the whole earth again and behave themselves. Instead of that there came a very strange man (we can't say any more about him here) whose name was *"Nimrod"* and he was a *"mighty man"*, but he was also a mighty rebel and he lived in a place called *"Babel"* or Babylon (it is now quite a famous place in modern politics today, in southern Iraq). He built a great city and a great tower. The people said, 'Let us make a religious kind of tower, in the middle of our city, and let's examine the heavens from the top of it'. We don't have time just here to look into all that was involved; astrology, star worship and other things. It was a great monument of rebellion against God. [We will look at this in more detail in **Chapter 18**

'*The Fall of Babylon*'.] God came down, the Bible uses lovely pictorial language, "*And the Lord came down to see the city and the tower, which the children of man had built*"; God said, 'They're rebelling. This is only the beginning!' "*Nothing that they propose to do will now be impossible for them.*" (Genesis chapter 11 verses 1 – 9 ESV).

Did God Judge Man's Rebellion?

God worked in government again. (What a story. I loved to imagine it as a young boy; God changed their language, just like that!) They all spoke one language in the morning and by lunchtime the plasterer couldn't speak to the bricklayer, who wasn't able to speak to the barrow boy, who wasn't able to speak to the foreman. They were all speaking different languages, nobody understood each other. I suppose they probably found a little group that they could make sense with, and then that made a little bubble, a little family group because they could understand each other, and so they moved off. What was the point of living beside people when you couldn't understand what they're saying? And so, in little family pods, they did, what they should have done at the start, what God told them to; they moved out across the continental land-bridges and populated the world. We see that God came again in government and judgment because, once again, mankind had rebelled.

What Happened Next?

Period Four: We come next to another lovely section of the Old Testament (It begins in Genesis chapter 12 and it goes right through to the end of the book of Genesis in chapter 50). That is the story of what we call "*The Patriarchs*"; Abraham, Isaac, Jacob and Joseph. Beautiful stories in the second part of the book of Genesis. God called Abraham out of a place of rebellion and idol worship, called "*Ur of the Chaldees*" (Genesis chapter 12). God called him to a place that he didn't know then where it was, but he moved in faith and followed God. What a lovely example to us today (Hebrews chapter 11 verses 8 – 16).

God was working in grace again, showing unworthy mankind His favour that is unmerited. God was calling people, sinful people, to come out of an idolatrous place, to follow Him and move in faith. The interesting thing is that when we get to Genesis chapter 12 some things change quite significantly. Abraham lived to be 175 and Isaac lived to be 180, Jacob lived to be 147 and Joseph, (at the end of Genesis chapter 50), lived to be 110. Something strange must have happened after the flood. Noah (who came through the flood and had lived 600 years on the old earth), lived to be 950 years old before he died. By the

KEYNOTE: Timeline. If we are talking about timelines, how far do you think we have come already through the Old Testament story? The O.T. is 4,000 years long at least. You might say, 'Genesis chapter 12 is not even halfway through the first book'. Yes, but don't forget about the long ages of all the men that lived before the flood: Genesis chapter 12 is halfway through the time period of the Old Testament. It is 2,000 years along the 4,000-year timeline from Genesis to Matthew, with a 400-year time gap between the end of the O.T. and the beginning of the N.T.

time we get to the end of Genesis, Joseph was just about living the same length of time as an older person in our world today ... I wonder what changed? What happened? Men went from living almost 1,000 years to living just 100 years inside a few generations, and having children in their thirties, like today. Why? We don't really know. God changed the conditions of our world, after the Flood. Perhaps God will change some of those conditions back in the future Kingdom Age?

This period begins with the call of Abram (or Abraham as he became), who went out *"by faith"* as we are told in Hebrews chapter 11. And the same record of faith tells us that Isaac, Jacob (who became *"Israel"*), and Joseph who became the Prince of Egypt and the saviour of his generation, all walked by faith. This period finishes in Egypt, but the end of the book of Genesis is not the end of the period. That is not the end of the whole story, for Egypt was not their promised home, and God must keep every one of His promises ...

What About Moses and the Law?

Period Five: When we come to the book of Exodus, we can see that *"the Children of Israel"* had now become a people in bondage. They were beaten with whips, they were made to make bricks, they had to go and find the straw first, and yet they still had to make as many bricks as they did before when the straw was given to them ... Their baby boys were drowned in the river Nile. 'Oh', you say, 'Genocide and murder and the people are going to be deliberately wiped out!' God intervenes again. Jehovah is going to save His people, and this time He's going to teach them the lesson of *"redemption"* through the blood of a slain lamb. What an amazing picture we discover in Exodus chapter 12. The story of the plagues, followed by the story of the *"Passover"*. The story of the Exodus and then the story of the giving of the Law to Israel, the *"Ten Commandments"* (Exodus chapter 20 right through to chapter 32).

KEYNOTE: Covenants. God will keep the promises that He has given to His people, especially if – like the promises to Abraham – they are without conditions. But, in His grace, He has kept certain conditional promises even though His people broke their side of the covenant. However 'unconditional covenants' were given deliberately, so that God could not break them, even if those on the other, receiving, side, did. More of that in later **Chps**.

Moses led the people out to the mountain of Horeb and God gave them the 'Decalogue' or *"Ten Commandments"* written on two Tables of Stone. Mind you, they broke the Law the day they got it, that is a serious rebellion is it not? (Exodus chapter 32). Yet God gave them promises, because often the promises of God in the Old Testament were prophecies and God gave both, and kept His side of them, even though in many cases the people of Israel broke the conditions that He attached to them, and suffered the penalties which had been set out in advance. God is always righteous, and fair.

God had promised a Saviour. He promised them a Messiah, one who would come to deliver them. They didn't understand that, but at the end of that period (which goes right through the whole of the Old Testament, through the Kings period, Saul, David, Solomon, and the rest; through the first captivity in 720 BC, the second in 606 BC (2 Chronicles chapter 36), the carrying away into Babylon. Big subjects that we cannot develop right now), we can see how the Monarchy and the Kingdom also ended in failure and judgment.

What Happened After That?

You might ask, 'Wasn't there a period when God never spoke at all?' Indeed, there was. At least not in public utterance (or in written prophecy). A period of 430 years, from Malachi the prophet until John Baptist the prophet, during which God never gave a new message. This is the 'gap' period of approximately 400 years between the end of the Old Testament and the beginning of the New Testament record: Then John preached between Jerusalem and Jordan down in southern Judea. John said, *"He's coming, the Promised one"*, (the one who was promised first in Genesis chapter 3) 'He's coming, you will see Him, He'll soon be here'; the one who is *"Mightier than I"* (Luke chapter 3 verses 16 – 17 KJV). But we know what happened next; the greatest failure of all! They refused the one whom God sent. They rejected Jesus, their Messiah. They said, 'We don't want this kind of King, we don't want the kind of kingdom He is offering us, and we don't want this man to be our Saviour'. *"We will not have this man to reign over us."* (Luke chapter 19 verse 14 KJV), *"We have no king but Caesar"*. They handed Jesus over to the Romans and they put the Son of God, who had come to save them, on the cross at Calvary and they watched Him die ...

Were the Purposes of God Spoilt?

'Were the promises of God broken, and the power of the Devil manifest? Were God's plans and purposes all brought to a crashing conclusion because Jesus died?' Well might you ask. 'No!' is the answer. The purposes of God were being fulfilled. *"The Son of Man must be lifted up"*, Jesus said to Nicodemus (John chapter 3 verse 14 KJV), and when He said *"Finished!"* on the cross (John chapter 19 verse 30), He had fulfilled everything in God's programme that God had given Him to do in relation to the provision of salvation, just as it had been promised at the 'fall of man' (Genesis chapter 3).

Where Does the Church Begin?

Period Six: Now we come to the next period, after the resurrection of the Lord Jesus. His interaction with His disciples *"during forty days"*, His going back to Heaven (Acts chapters 1 & 2) and the commencement of the period that we call the 'Church Age'. You might ask, 'How long is this period going to last?' It has lasted for almost 2,000 years already. God is still saving, God is still calling a people, from all nations, to trust in Jesus Christ. This period will finish when Jesus comes

KEYNOTE: The Church Period. This is often referred to as the 'Day of Grace' and the 'Church Age'. These are not strictly biblical titles. The scriptural title is *"The Acceptable Year of the Lord"* (Isaiah 61:2). This is a slightly longer period of time, but includes all of the 'Church Age'. We will look at that in more detail in **Chps. 5** & **6**.

again and takes every single person who is waiting for Him, living and dead, from this period since *"Pentecost"*, home to be with Himself forever (1 Thessalonians chapter 4 verses 13 – 18).

Some will be asking, 'Are we at the end of God's programme when the Church goes?' No. There is much more after that. There will be a short period of judgment, only seven years long in total. But Jesus said in Matthew 24 (we read there previously), it will be the worst period of judgment that has ever been and if God did not set a bound, a time limit, upon it no one would survive …

At the end of that period the *"Messiah"* will come back to earth the second time. Rebellion will be ended, Satan will be put in prison for 1,000 years, the earth will be cleaned up, and Jesus will reign as *"King of kings and Lord of lords"* from Jerusalem in Israel, and over the whole world. Exactly how long until that future stage of God's programme commences, we don't know. We know for sure that it hasn't started yet, because the Church, the saved people from the 'Church Age', has not been taken away, nor has the *"Man of Sin"* been revealed [Those are all subjects for future **Chapters**]. Sometimes God gives us dates, and times and periods, and sometimes He doesn't.

What Happens When Jesus Returns?

Period Seven: The 'Kingdom Age' is just as real as the story of Adam and Eve in Genesis chapters 1 - 3, and the story of the Patriarchs, and the gap between Malachi and John the Baptist. We can date those past periods, and we can also tell the length of the literal future kingdom as being 1,000 years. Those who are saved are going to be part of it, we are going to be part of the government. We will serve Him happily for 1,000 years. What a lovely thing to look forward to. But we cannot date the end of the 'day of grace …' That makes the gospel message which we proclaim very urgent!

Will that be The End?

Period Eight: No, there is going to be another stage (if we count the stages numerically, 1,2,3 etc., then the final stage will be the 8th). There was 'eternity' before creation in Genesis chapter 1, and there will be 'eternity' after Revelation chapter 22. We know that God lives in *"Eternity"*. Eternity is not a period, it is a place, it is where God lives (Isaiah chapter 57 verse 15). The 'Eternal State' is going to be an 'age' that will never end. Satan will never be able to contaminate it, sin will never come there. The heart of man will never be rebellious, because every person there will be saved, cleansed, righteous and

> **KEYNOTE: *'Alpha - Omega'.*** If you look at the Chart inside the book covers, there is a strange word there that says *"Alpha"* at the beginning, and at the end of the Chart is another strange word *"Omega"*. These are the first and last letters of the Greek alphabet. They mean in pictorial terms, 'the beginning and the end of everything that can be known and learned and understood about our God'.

perfect. What a wonderful endless period in the programme of God to look forward to; for those who are *"born again"*.

There is also an alternative destination; banishment from God and degrees of punishment, for all who have not believed, who will share the doom of Satan and his fallen angels forever. That is why there is an urgency with the message of the gospel. Heaven is for the *"redeemed"*, for those who have trusted in the sacrifice of Jesus – just as was promised – on the cross at Calvary. The *"seed of the woman"* (Genesis chapter 3 verse 15) did crush the head of the Serpent. Satan's destiny is sure.

The substitutionary death and miraculous resurrection of Jesus Christ, the Son of God, has provided a choice for every living individual to make, regarding their own destiny, forever.

Q&A >

Questions and Answers for Chapter Two – 'Does God have a Programme?'

Chp. 2 – 'Does God have a Programme?'

Q1. We looked at periods in God's Programme, in which mankind behaved in different ways – quite often in rebellion – and God brought different judgments. Yet He also worked in grace.
Can you list at least SIX of those periods?

Q2. Can you list some of the judgments God brought on those who rebelled?

Q3. Can you find at least one promise of God that He must keep?
A promise that cannot be removed because it had no 'conditions' attached to it?

Q4. What is meant by an 'unconditional promise'?

Chapter Three

What is Prophecy?

Let us turn again to the Word of God, to introduce this third topic: 'What is prophecy?' *"The Lord God said to the serpent, 'Because you have done this, cursed are you above all livestock and above all beasts of the field; on your belly you shall go, and dust you shall eat all the days of your life. I will put enmity* (strife) *between you and the woman, and between your offspring (seed) and her offspring; He* (seed of the woman) *shall bruise your head, and you* (the Serpent) *shall bruise His heel."* (Genesis chapter 3 verses 14 – 15 ESV).

What is Prophecy?

If we look in a dictionary, we will find that different definitions are given. One American dictionary says, 'Prophecy is what a prophet says, so prophecy comes from someone who is a prophet'. The second point is, 'Prophecy is a prediction, a telling forward of something that is to come, something that has not yet happened'. Then the third and most important thing connected with the other two is, 'It is a declaration of the mind of God'. Before the scriptures were complete, even in the early Church period *"prophecy"* was also a 'telling forth' of God's truth.

Perhaps we should say, in the context of our studies, 'A declaration of the purposes of God about things that are shortly to happen, things that still have not happened yet'. We will discover that a prophecy can sometimes be <u>very short</u>, fulfilled in just a few days. Or prophecy (as we have read in Genesis chapter 3), can be <u>very long</u>; in that case, not fulfilled until around 4,000 years later. There are 'prophecies', 'promises' and 'pictures': we will connect these three things together as we go forward in our studies.

> **KEYNOTE: Prophecies.** We are going to examine some of these <u>prophecies</u> and <u>promises</u>, because in many senses they are both. A prophecy can be a promise, and a promise that comes from God is often a prophecy. God also, at times, connects <u>pictures</u> together with His promises. More of that shortly.

How Prophecy Works

Let us have a simple illustration as to how prophecy works:

If I said to you, 'Look out the window and you will see a blue car going past in two minutes time', you would say to me, 'A good percentage of cars are blue, it could just be chance

that among the white ones and the red ones there will be, in a couple of minutes, a blue one'. But if I said to you, 'In two minutes exactly, past your yard or out the window will come; first a police vehicle, then an ambulance, then a fire engine. They will be going to the first junction down the road, or the first traffic circle, because a man who is 70 years old on his birthday, riding a red motorcycle, has been knocked down by a blue car, and the man on the motorcycle was wearing an orange crash helmet'. You would say, 'There is no possibility of knowing those details before they actually happened. Chance alone could not make that happen'.

That's exactly how prophecy works. God gives <u>specific details</u>, not generalities. When God gives a prophecy, He gives it with amazing detail, in some cases including miraculous aspects of it, that could only be worked out by the will and purpose of God Himself. The fulfilment is beyond human capability, and sometimes the prophecies come to pass at very specifically defined times as well.

> **KEYNOTE: What Prophecy is Not.**
> Young believer, or any reader, be very beware of 'horoscopes' and 'astrological predictions'. Example: *'You're going to meet a handsome person at a party and you're going to fall in love with them'*. That could be anybody or anything and you could make that happen by yourself. That is called 'wish fulfilment'. 'Horoscopes', 'astrological predictions', 'star signs' etc. are dangerous, and are things that no Christian should allow themselves to be influenced by.

Where does Prophecy Begin?

That is a good question! We have read of that in our Bible passage. It begins in Genesis chapter 3. The first person that a prophecy was given to was also the first person in our world, and it is in the first period in our Bible, the period that begins with the creation of mankind, and that leads up to the 'fall' of man and woman. Even the Devil, the Serpent himself, was included in that first prophecy!

God put Adam and Eve, our 'fore-parents', in a perfect environment. He gave them every opportunity to be obedient, with only one prohibition. God said, *"In the day you eat of it* (the forbidden tree)*, you shall surely die"*. That also was a prophecy. We didn't focus on that because we wanted to major on the positive side. Prophecy, as well as being <u>long</u> or <u>short</u>, can also be <u>positive</u> or <u>negative</u>. God had said, *"If you eat of the forbidden tree, you will die"*, and so they did. Not just 'right there'. They died spiritually, but they did begin to die physically also. That was a <u>negative prophecy</u>, and it came true many years later, because they had disobeyed God.

The Promise to Adam & Eve

God also gave them a positive prophecy after that. He said, 'I am going to send someone who can fix the problem that you have created. I'm going to use woman'. The Serpent used her when he deceived Eve and he then used her to attract her husband. God said, 'I will take woman up again', it will not be the same lady, but it will be a woman. 'I will use her to bring in the promised seed.' The one who will be able to crush the Serpent and put down all his rebellion and deceitfulness and activity in the background. Since his fall from heaven, Satan has been fighting against the purposes of God being fulfilled and he did that in the garden of Eden too. Here is a prophecy that took more than 4,000 years to be fulfilled. But it was, and as we will see later, it was fulfilled to the very exact day specified in other prophecies that came afterwards.

God keeps His word to a place and a point in time, to work out His divine purpose, and in most cases for the blessing of you and me, and for the blessing of mankind. God said, 'I will send deliverance by a Saviour who will come'. God said, 'I will bring about the defeat of the Serpent' who had become the deceiver of mankind. As we have seen, almost all prophecies in the Word of God fit around those two points; the defeat of the Serpent, and the deliverance by the Saviour who would come. It was not obvious at the time that both would be fulfilled at the Cross, but in the resurrection of Jesus we see the basis for all enemies to be destroyed, *"through death He might destroy the one who has the power of death, that is, the Devil; and deliver all those who through of death were subject to lifelong slavery."* (Hebrews chapter 2 verses 14 – 15 ESV).

God is going to bring every single person who has believed in Jesus, either looking forward, or like the Christians of today looking back, into blessing in a future Kingdom of 1,000 years. Then we will go into what is called the 'Eternal State' (Revelation chapter 21 verses 1 – 7). This is not really a Bible term, but we use it to mean the final period of God's rule, which will have no interruption or end. God is going to bring a total deliverance from sin and Satan. Forever. From even the contamination of sin in this world. God will bring that about through a Saviour, Jesus Christ, and the total complete and final defeat of Satan also, because God prepared the *"eternal fire"* for the Devil and his angels who rebelled with him (Matthew chapter 25 verse 41 ESV).

The first prophecy we have looked at is in Genesis chapter 3 and it concerns Adam and the 'fall of man'. God used a picture even there to help Adam to understand the prophecy. He made, to cover their nakedness, a coat of skin each. The Bible says very little more about it at that point in time, but as we learn about the principles of sacrifice later, we understand that an animal must have been killed, blood must have been shed, and the skin must have been removed. Then that animal in giving its life, (like Abel's sacrificial lamb in Genesis chapter 4), provided a covering for the shame and the nakedness of our first parents. There is a <u>picture</u> that relates to the <u>promise</u> and the <u>prophecy</u> that we have been considering.

The Promise to Noah and the Symbol

Come now to Period Three, to a man called Noah. He lived for 600 years and then with his family came through a terrible year of flood inside his self-built boat, trusting God, who had promised him He would bring him through the 'deluge'. He came out safely on the other side and he lived for 350 years more. I suppose every time he saw dark clouds come over, he would have wondered, 'Is it going to rain like that again, is there going to be a flood and will I have to go back to the boat and hide again?' God understands the weakness of our heart and mind far better than we know ourselves.

The Covenant Sign – A Rainbow

God's 'Rainbow' unchanged. North Antrim NI. (MDM)

God said, 'I'm going to give you a lovely picture, I'm going to give you a sign of My covenant'. Jehovah linked this first *"covenant"* to a promise and a picture; a picture which we still have in our world today.

God said, *"Never again shall there be a flood to destroy the earth"*. Even though the coming rebellion and sinfulness of mankind, Jesus said, would be again *"like the days of Noah"* (Matthew chapter 24 verse 37), Jehovah said, *"This is the token of the covenant ... between Me and the earth ... I do set My bow in the cloud"* (Genesis chapter 9 verses 12 – 13 KJV). When the dark clouds come, do we not often see the rainbow against the darkened sky? It takes the darkness of the cloud to show the beauty of the rainbow shining over the land or shining over the sea. The beauty of the rainbow and the promise of God are linked. Noah could look up and say, 'God promised never to destroy the world again by a flood. Every time the clouds come, every time the darkness comes, every time I'm fearful, I will look up and remember God's promise'. Is that not a wonderful thought?

> **KEYNOTE: The Rainbow.** It is a great pity that the *'rainbow'* symbol in our world today has been connected and associated with other things that are contrary to God's order. Sometimes even the colours are altered from how God created it. The purity and the perfection of the rainbow in the sky and, as we will see later, in heaven is linked with God Himself. It tells of a Divine unbroken promise.

The Covenant with Abraham

We move now to Period Four about a man called Abram, or Abraham as he became. God called him out of a place called *"Ur of the Chaldees"*. God said, *"Go to a land that I will show you"*. He must go in faith. God said to Abraham, *"I will make of you a great nation,*

> **❝**
> **...when Messiah did come, there could be no mistake as to who He was, where He came from, where He came to, and what exactly He came for.'**

I will ... make your name great ... I will bless those who bless you" (Genesis chapter 12 verses 1 – 2 ESV). God also said to Abraham (here's a negative part), *"Him who dishonours you, I will curse"*. Then God said to Abraham (here's the most beautiful part of all), *"In you, all the families of the earth shall be blessed"*.

You say, 'How could that come true?' Because Jesus was a son of Abraham, He came from one of Abraham's grandson's tribes. We will look at that in a later Chapter; the tribe that was chosen to be the royal tribe and another promise that was given to another person; that from his branch of the family would come the Messiah, Jesus Christ. In addition to the promise that was given in the Garden of Eden (Genesis chapter 3 verse 15), God is now beginning to make specific detail known ... (You remember the illustration not just about the blue car, but all the details that we could not really have known in advance), God is going to narrow the prophecy down, that when Messiah did come, there could be no mistake as to who He was, where He came from, where He came to, and what exactly He came for.

The Birth of the Nation

Let us now look at another person in Period Five. We looked at a man called Moses and we also touched on a man called David. That period was long. It ran from the *'Exodus'* out of Egypt, the giving of the Law, the 'Torah', at Sinai, right through the 'Judges period' and what we call the 'Monarchy period'. The Kings of Israel and Judah, the captivity period in Babylon, through until the end of the Old Testament, and across into the beginning of the New Testament. That is a very long period, yet it was not as long as the period in which we are living (which we are calling for now, 'the Day of Grace').

Look at a very short prophecy that God gave at the beginning of that period. God appeared to Moses in the burning bush, and Moses came close, for he said, *"I will turn aside to see this great sight, why the bush is not burned"* (Exodus chapter 3 verse 3 ESV). He discovered that Jehovah was speaking to him from the bush and God said, 'Leave the sheep and go back to Egypt. I'm going to use you to set the people free and bring them out of bondage'. The whole nation every single one of them, and their flocks as well. *"Not a hoof shall be left behind"* (Exodus chapter 10 verse 26 ESV).

Someone will ask, 'How long did that prophecy take to be fulfilled?' Just weeks ... God said to Moses (Exodus chapter 3 verses 21-22), 'When you come out, the Egyptians will be so glad to see you go, that your neighbours the Egyptians will give you gold and silver and jewels and garments. You will be able to spoil them without a fight. They will just give you all their good things that you can carry away with you. You shall plunder the Egyptians'.

You say, 'That's impossible, how could that come true, they were helpless hated slaves?' But it did, and in Exodus chapter 13 we read, in the night in which God brought His people out, the Egyptians sent them out. They said, 'Please go!' and they gave them clothing and jewels of gold and silver, just as God had told Moses when he was sitting by himself as a shepherd, far away at Horeb, in the wilderness.

The Law Given

We cannot stay much longer with the story of Moses because we must move on. We could have looked at the Law: The Law was also prophecy, and the Law also contained promises, both positive and negative. Jehovah said, in summary, 'If you keep it, you will be blessed, and if you don't keep it then there will be curses that will come upon you for not keeping it'. Those were conditional promises, and the people said, *"All that the Lord has spoken we will do"*, (Exodus chapter 19 verse 8 ESV). Moses went up the mountain and God gave him *"The Ten Commandments"*. The Law written by Jehovah on stone. God promised them blessings if they would keep them. But they didn't, they broke the Law the very day it was given! (You can read that story in Exodus chapter 32.)

A Royal Family Line

We will come now to King David. We must single him out because he was the king that God chose. The people picked their king, his name was Saul. They picked him from the wrong tribe (he wasn't from the promised tribe of Judah), they picked him for the wrong reason, because he was big and tall and strong. They were looking on the outside, but God said, *"The Lord looks on the heart"* (1 Samuel chapter 16 verse 7 ESV). God sent Samuel to Jesse's house in Bethlehem (that's a significant place). From the tribe of Judah and from an insignificant family, God picked the youngest son. Those things were all in God's purpose, and David became the king, the second king, God's chosen King of Israel. God gave to him a very special promise. Jehovah said, *"I will raise up your offspring after you"*, (that is the same *"seed"* word as Genesis chapter 3) *"who shall come from your body, and I will establish His kingdom ... Your house and your kingdom will be made sure forever before Me. Your throne shall be established forever."* (2 Samuel chapter 7 verses 12 – 16 ESV). That sounds very literal and is not a promise that can easily be 'spiritualised' or made to have anything to do with the Church.

> **KEYNOTE: Literal & Future.** We will look at the balance between 'spiritualising' prophecies, and taking certain prophecies as still future and having a literal fulfilment, in **Appx. II**.

You say, 'Israel doesn't have a king today, and before the end of the Old Testament period were they not put out of their Land and they were out of it for a very long time?'

But we are going to discover now, in the promise that God gave, away back in Genesis chapter 3, that He was going to bring the seed of the woman through David's family and David's line. Jesus, who is David's son, is going to reign not only for 1,000 years in the future Kingdom, but Jesus will reign forever. So David's son, who came from Bethlehem, and the tribe of Judah, *"Messiah"* who is also David's greater Son, will one day sit upon David's throne, not only for 1,000 years, but will reign forever.

Messiah's First Coming

Let us come now to Period Six. It begins, as we saw in our previous chapter, with the public ministry of the Lord Jesus and His death, and extends forward into the period in which we are today. Can we bring together the prophecies that must

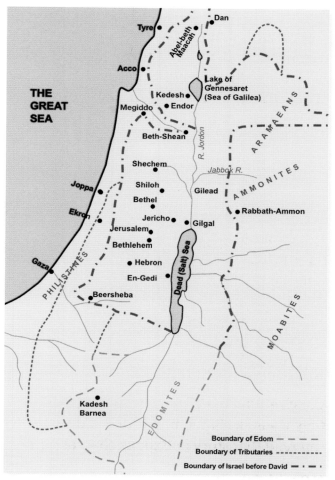

The Land of Israel in the Time of David & Solomon
(c. 1050 – 970 BC)
This is the largest territory the Nation occupied. The 'Millennial Kingdom' will be larger still.

be fulfilled in relation to the first coming of Messiah, the seed of the woman? Firstly, He wasn't coming as an angel, and He wasn't coming as a spirit. He was coming in a body. He was coming as *"seed of the woman"* (Genesis chapter 3 verse 15). That promise must be fulfilled. He must come as a <u>son of Abraham</u>. He must come as a Jew, to use modern language. That promise is given in Genesis chapter 12 verses 1 – 2. He must come from <u>Judah's tribe</u>, to be a <u>son of David</u> from <u>Bethlehem</u> (that promise was given in 2 Samuel chapter 7 verse 12).

He must come from Bethlehem, He must be born there in the district of *"Ephrath"*, in the southern part of Judah. (We can find that promise in the prophecy of Micah in chapter 5 verse 2.) Here is a seemingly impossible part of the prophecy and the promise; He must be *"born of a virgin"*. You might say, 'Biologically that's impossible!' When Isaiah spoke in chapter 7 of this prophecy, people may have thought, 'That must be picture language, that must be symbolic': But it came true. We know that. Jesus was born in Bethlehem, of the virgin Mary, from the tribe of Judah, descended (as Luke and Matthew's Gospels both tell us), from David and Abraham and Adam. And God.

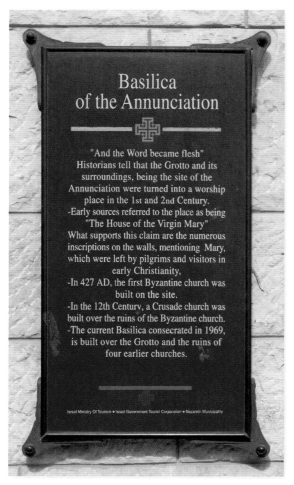

"And the Word became flesh"
Historians tell that the Grotto and its
surroundings, being the site of the
Annunciation were turned into a worship
place in the 1st and 2nd Century.
-Early sources referred to the place as being
"The House of the Virgin Mary"
What supports this claim are the numerous
inscriptions on the walls, mentioning Mary,
which were left by pilgrims and visitors in
early Christianity,
-In 427 AD, the first Byzantine church was
built on the site.
-In the 12th Century, a Crusade church was
built over the ruins of the Byzantine church.
-The current Basilica consecrated in 1969,
is built over the Grotto and the ruins of
four earlier churches.

Plaque at the 'Church of the Annunciation' in Nazareth, where Mary grew up. (JHF)

He was also born to fit into something we haven't touched on at all in our studies as yet; the 'timeline of Daniel chapter 9'. There is a '490 year timeline'* in Daniel's prophecy that said exactly (because sometimes God does give dates, and exact numbers of years) when the date for the rejection and crucifixion of Messiah, Jesus Christ, would be. His birth then must be 30 or 40 years before His death, to allow Him to grow to be the *"Son of Man"* who would be *"cut off"*, rejected by His own people the Jews (John chapter 1 verse 11).

Here are seven points, some of them humanly impossible, which we have examined that must have been fulfilled literally or else Jesus Christ, the son of Mary of Nazareth when He came, could not have been who He claimed to be. Without them being fulfilled, He could not be the promised one. He could not be the Son of God, and He could not have become the *"seed of the woman"* that was promised in the garden of Eden (Genesis chapter 3 verse 15). Yet, all these prophecies, and a great many more, were fulfilled in exact detail in the life, death, and resurrection of Jesus Christ.

He truly is who He said He was, the Son of Man who must *"be lifted up, that whoever believes in Him may have eternal life."* (John chapter 3 verse 14 – 15 ESV).

*KEYNOTE: Daniel's Timeline. Some of the more difficult prophetic topics have been dealt in more detail in the 'Appendices' at the end of the book. This is one of them. **Appx. I** *'Daniel's 70 Weeks'* will discuss more of Daniel's prophecy of the 490 years.

Questions and Answers for Chapter Three – *'What is Prophecy?'*

Chp. 3 – 'What is Prophecy?'

Q1. What is prophecy?
Can you give a definition of the term?

Q2. What is the first prophecy in the Bible?
(There might be more than one answer.)
Don't forget, prophecies can be positive
OR negative.

Q3. Can you give the detail of a short prophecy
– fulfilled within a short time period?

Q4. Prophecies are often also promises. And
pictures or symbols as well.
Can you give an example of where a
prophecy is also a promise and a picture?

Q5. Can you draw out a 'Timeline', beginning
from Creation (Genesis 1), to the lifetime
of Jesus, including the 'Church Age' and
also the 'Kingdom Age' still to come?

KEYNOTE: Timeline. The O.T. is approximately 4,000 years long. So far 'The Church Age' is almost 2,000 years long, and continuing (2,021 – 32 years). The 'Tribulation Period' will be 7 years long. After that 'The Kingdom Age' will be for 1,000 years.

JOTTINGS

Chapter Four

The First Coming of Jesus

We have seen how the long and short prophecies of the Old Testament were absolutely fulfilled in every single detail, including things that were humanly impossible, to prove that Jesus Christ who came and was rejected, died and rose again, truly was the *"promised seed"* and also the Son of God from eternity. Let us look now at Luke's story, *"Now there was a man in Jerusalem, whose name was Simeon, and this man was righteous and devout, waiting for the consolation of Israel, and the Holy Spirit was upon him. And it had been revealed to him by the Holy Spirit that he would not see death before he had seen the Lord's Christ."* So, Simeon came by the Spirit into the Temple and when the parents brought in the child Jesus, he took him up in his arms and blessed God and said, *"Lord, now You are letting Your servant depart in peace, according to Your Word; for mine eyes have seen Your salvation that You have prepared in the presence of all peoples, a light for revelation to the Gentiles, and for glory to Your people Israel."* (Luke chapter 2 verses 25 – 32 ESV).

Prophecies as Proof

Our previous study concluded by looking at seven very important prophecies which had to be fulfilled if Jesus Christ was to be the promised one. He must be *"seed of the woman"*, He must be *"a son of Abraham"*. As a Jew in His own time, He must be *"son of David"*. He must come from the tribe of Judah. He must be born in Bethlehem and in the district of Ephrath in Judea. He must be born of a virgin (Isaiah chapter 7), He must be born to fit into the timeline of Daniel chapter 9, where there was an exact date given for the *"cutting off"* of Messiah. Those looking for Him could work back from that a little bit to estimate the time of Jesus' birth, because the date of His death was given in prophecy. Not only that but He was born to be rejected, He was born to die. These are seven key prophecies given in the Old Testament that must be fulfilled in relation to the first coming of Jesus, and in reality there were hundreds more. All of which were fulfilled exactly, according to Divine order.

> **KEYNOTE: The Second Coming.** Let me challenge you, perhaps a reader who is not a believer in the Lord Jesus as the Saviour of mankind: If the prophecies and promises connected with the First Coming of Jesus Christ have all been accurately fulfilled; what about the promises in relation to His Second Coming that we are going to consider? Jesus Himself said, *"If I go ... I will come again"* (John 14:3).

Let us look at some key questions, just to help us through this particular study. We have read of Simeon who had it confirmed to him by a prophecy from the Holy Spirit directly, that he would not die until he saw the promised one. He had with him his friend Anna, who was also looking for the coming of Messiah. These two old people came every morning to the Temple, expecting to see their Messiah.

Why did they not go to Bethlehem?

Excavations on the outskirts of Bethlehem – dating back to the 5th Century AD.

'They were sure that the promised one was to be born there, were they not?' That is a good question. They couldn't tell the exact day of His coming, but they could read in the book of Daniel and could work out on a timeline the date of His death. *"Messiah the Prince"*, who was going to be rejected and *"cut off"* in manhood (Daniel chapter 9 verses 25 – 27), would have to be born thirty or forty years before that date. I'm sure these old people had worked out that maybe God would be gracious enough to let them see the evidence of His birth, if that time was close. And because it was near, God gave Simeon the promise that he would see the birth of Messiah.

Why did they go to the Temple?

That brings us back to our question, 'Why did they go to the Temple?' In the Old Testament Law (in the book of Leviticus chapter 12), one of the requirements was that when a baby boy was born, after forty days, the parents must bring him to the Tabernacle or the Temple and offer a sacrifice of thanksgiving. For a girl it was eighty days, but for a boy it was forty. Simeon and Anna knew that once the baby would be born in Bethlehem, after His 'naming' and 'circumcising' at 8 days, whenever He was 40 days old His parents must bring Him to the Temple.

If they had been a family who had some wealth or animals, they would have come with a lamb for a sacrifice to celebrate the birth of their son. But Jehovah said (back in Leviticus chapter 12 verse 8 ESV), *"And if she cannot afford a lamb, then she shall take two turtledoves or two pigeons"*. That shows us that Joseph and Mary were poor, for it was birds that he brought (Luke chapter 2 verse 24). Mary, as well as being a young woman, now his wife and still a virgin, was poor too.

God evidently intended that Jesus would be born in a very poor home. Just to show that He would know poverty. More than that; God loves His pictures and His symbols. God did not want Joseph and Mary to come to the temple with two lambs. But you say, 'No, it was one lamb or two birds?' Yes, but Mary was carrying in her arms 'God's Lamb', and so God determined that Joseph would not bring another lamb, he would just bring the two birds. Jesus, even as a newborn-child, fulfilled the 'picture' of the *"Lamb of God"*. As soon as they saw the child Jesus it was identified to Simeon, by the Holy Spirit, that this is the right one. He went forward and took the child and he lifted Him up, as if the child Himself was being offered in a kind of sacrificial manner. Simeon said, 'I can now die satisfied. I've had Your promise fulfilled. I have seen the Lord's Christ. I have seen Jehovah's Anointed.'

KEYNOTE: Temple Model. This detailed, and long-forgotten, replica of the Temple Mount and Herod's 1st Century Temple in Jerusalem's Old City was the handiwork of Conrad Schick, a German architect and archaeologist. In 1872, Schick became one of the only Westerners ever allowed to investigate the subterranean spaces under the Islamic shrines on the Temple Mount, and recreated in miniature what he saw from below ground level. The – until recently – lost model was built by Schick for the Vienna World Trade Fair in 1873 (Photo: Times of Israel Feb. 2012).

Herod's Temple on Temple Mount – 1ˢᵗ Century AD.
– A Model by Conrad Schick (1822 – 1901)

The Prophecy of Simeon

You remember all those prophecies that must be fulfilled? Now Simeon is adding something that we have not heard before. He is speaking as a Prophet. He said, *"My eyes have seen Your salvation that You have prepared in the presence of all peoples, a light for revelation to the Gentiles, and for glory to Your people Israel"* (see Luke chapter 2 verses 29 – 32 ESV). People who are not even Jewish by birth. Remember in Genesis (chapter 22 verse 18) there was the promise that God gave to Abraham, *"In your offspring shall all the nations of the earth be blessed"*. Simeon is saying that again by the Holy Spirit, not only Jewish people in the land of Israel, but Gentiles and every nation in the world would be blessed by the coming into the world of the promised Messiah.

Why did Joseph & Mary go to Bethlehem?

Let us now ask this question and answer it from the details in the Word of God. Mary and Joseph didn't live in Bethlehem. Mary lived in Galilee, away up in the north-east, in a poor village that didn't have a very good reputation, a place called Nazareth. 'Why was Mary chosen, if she was from Nazareth?' And 'What made them go to Bethlehem?'

The answers lie in a revelation from the angel Gabriel. He is a famous angel, one of the few angels of all the millions of them, that in the Bible we are given his name. We know about Michael because he is the head of all the angels. We know about Lucifer because he was the highest angel of all, but he failed because of pride, and became Satan. Gabriel seems to be God's special angel for bringing messages to chosen people. When God wanted to send a very important message down to earth He quite often used Gabriel. He was sent first to Daniel, who lived in a Palace. He was a Prince, he was a Prophet, he was a servant of great Kings and lived in two empires in the past. Gabriel when he was sent from heaven came down to a palace to give a prophet a prophecy.

Gabriel came again, a second time, we find that in Luke's Gospel. He came to the Temple, to a Priest, not a Prophet this time; a man called Zachariah. Gabriel said, 'You're going to have a son even though your wife Elizabeth is old. He will be the 'forerunner' of Messiah. You will call him John'. Zachariah said, 'I can't really believe I'm going to have a son. We're both far too old' (That story is told in Luke's Gospel chapter 1.) Gabriel said, 'Because you have not believed my message you will not speak again, until the day the boy is born'. That was a <u>negative</u> prophecy that was to last for nine months. Elizabeth did get pregnant, even though she was very old, and the day that the child was born they got Zachariah to write on a wax tablet (because he couldn't talk). They were probably discussing, 'Will we call him Zachariah the second?' But Zachariah wrote *"His name is John,"* and his tongue was loosed, *"and he spoke, blessing God"* (Luke chapter 1 verses 59 – 66 ESV).

The 'Church of the Annunciation' at Nazareth in Galilee. (JHF)

Gabriel was sent a third time. He had come to a palace to talk to a prophet. He had come to the Temple to talk to a priest. 'Where did he come the third time?' you might ask. He came to Nazareth. An unclean village in the north of Israel, away up in the land of Galilee that others looked down on. He came to a poor virgin, doing her day's work. Gabriel came and said, *"Do not be afraid, Mary, for you have found favour with God. And behold you will conceive in your womb and bear a son, and you shall call His name Jesus."* (Luke chapter 1 verses 30 – 31 ESV).

What a blessing, and she truly is blessed. There are many people in this world today and they put Mary in the wrong place. But we should not make the mistake of going to the other

> **'God fulfils His prophecies to the very day, to the exact moment.'**

extreme. She is blessed above all women, because God gave to her that precious possession to be born of her. The promised Son who was also David's son, for she came from David's family (Luke chapter 3). And Abraham's son, for they were descended from Abraham. Adam's son for they came from Adam. But most blessed of all, the Son of God because He was born of the Holy Spirit.

Nazareth to Bethlehem

Perhaps you are asking, 'I get that part, but why Nazareth? The baby was born in Bethlehem how do you connect those two places together?' Here is a very interesting thing. We are told in Luke chapter 2, that there was a King whose name was, *"Caesar Augustus"*. He was on the throne in Rome. Not even in the same continent, thousands of kilometres away. Yet he decreed, 'We will make every single person in the Roman Empire fill in a census. They will also have to complete it in their hometown, where they come from. It doesn't matter how far they have to travel, the census will not be properly completed unless they go from here to wherever in order to hand it in.'

While Mary was almost at the stage of having her child, the word came to Nazareth that Joseph and Mary must both go to Bethlehem, because that was their hometown, to fill in the census form. They had no choice. Joseph took his donkey (it's not in the Bible but it is most likely that he did) and they would have put Mary, almost ready to have the baby, on the donkey very gently and walked very slowly. They arrived in Bethlehem, and because of the crowds, were only able to find shelter in a shepherd's feeding place. Perhaps even a small cave? (The Bible story does have a manger, but it does not a stable.)

> **KEYNOTE: God's Timing.** God is never behind, and God is never in front in His timing. God fulfils His prophecies to the very day, to the exact moment. There are so many illustrations of that truth in the Bible record. Joseph and Mary arrived in Bethlehem just in time, but it was heaven's time too.

An angel came to shepherds in their night watch. They may have been Temple shepherds, guarding lambs for the sacrifices. The angel said, 'Leave your sheep in the field and go into Bethlehem village just now, and you will see an amazing thing that has happened. You will find a baby that has been born *"wrapped in swaddling clothes and lying in a manger"*. They left their sheep; they ran into Bethlehem and found that the prophecy had just been fulfilled. They bowed down and worshipped the baby who had been *"born this day in the city of David a Saviour, which is Christ the Lord"* (Luke chapter 2 verses 8 – 18 KJV).

Why did Jesus Come the First Time?

That brings us to our last question, 'Did Jesus come just to live a good life and then die accidentally, as a Jewish martyr?' Daniel said He must die: *"Messiah will be cut off"* (Daniel

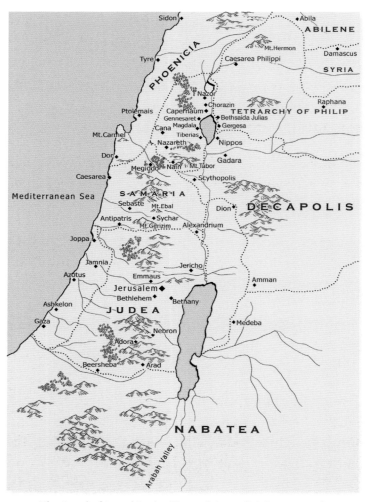

The Land of Israel in the Time of Jesus (1ˢᵗ Century AD)

chapter 9 verse 26). But His death was no accident. Peter said, *"You crucified Him, but God delivered Him over"* (Acts chapter 2 verse 23).

Jesus told Nicodemus (John chapter 3 verses 14 – 16 NASB), *"Even so must the Son of Man be lifted up (on a cross); that whoever believes may in Him have eternal life. For God so loved the world that He gave His only begotten Son, that whoever believes in Him should not perish (come under God's judgment), but have eternal life."*

The Acceptable Year of the Lord

Jesus stood up one day in the synagogue in Nazareth on the Sabbath. He took up the scroll of Isaiah and He opened it (at what we know as chapter 61) and He read, *"The Spirit of Jehovah is upon Me; because Jehovah anointed Me … to proclaim <u>the acceptable year of the Lord</u> …"* He then stopped in the middle of the verse and said, *"This day is this scripture fulfilled in your ears"*. The second part of the verse, which He did not read, says *"… and the <u>day of vengeance of our God</u>."* (Isaiah chapter 61 verse 1 – 2 Newberry Reference Bible 'NRB'). That *"day"* (a short period in prophecy) still has not been fulfilled yet, almost 2,000 years later. But it surely must be. We are approaching the end of what Jesus called, *"the Acceptable year of the Lord"*.

Jesus the Messiah Rejected!

Do you know what happened next, in the synagogue, in His hometown? He was rejected by the people of Nazareth. That very day they said, 'Let's throw him over the brow of the hill, because he cannot be who he says he is'. But they could not touch Him, for it was not the time for Jesus to be delivered over (Luke chapter 4 verses 18 – 30).

> **KEYNOTE: Prophecies Divide.** Here is an important point. A prophecy can sometimes divide in two, so that it will have its fulfilment in two different time periods. Even if that was not obvious to the prophet himself, or to the original hearers. If it was not so, it would become clearer later. We will see more of the concept of '<u>divided fulfilment</u>' as we go forward.

After just more than 3 years in which *"Jesus went about all Galilee, teaching in the synagogues and preaching the gospel of the kingdom, and healing every manner of sickness and every manner of disease among the people ... they brought unto Him all the sick ... and He healed them."* (Matthew chapter 4 verses 23 – 25 NRB), He came again to Jerusalem for the Passover Feast. Jesus *"knowing all things ..."* kept the 'Passover Supper' for the last time, with the eleven apostles in the 'upper room' in Jerusalem.

After giving what we know as the 'Upper Room Ministry' (John chapters 14 – 17), *"He went forth with His disciples over the brook Kidron, where was a garden into which He entered with His disciples ..."* (John chapter 18 verse 1).

The 'Garden of Gethsemane' across the 'winter-brook' Kidron, at the foot of Olivet.
One of the few 'Holy Sites' which is most probably authentic. The older trees are reputed to be c. 2,000 years old. The Lord may indeed have wept under their branches (JHF)

The *"hour"*, God's time for Jesus to be *"delivered over"*, had come. He was betrayed by Judas. He was arrested and rejected by the rulers and the Pharisees in the temple. He was rejected by the people, who had shouted *"Hosanna"* on the very same week that He had come into Jerusalem riding on the colt (Another prophecy fulfilled in detail, Zechariah chapter 9 verse 9 & Matthew chapter 21 verses 1 – 9.) At the last they took Him to Pilate, the Roman Governor in Jerusalem. They said, in the words of Jesus' parable, *"We will not have this man to reign over us"* (Luke chapter 19 verse 14 KJV). The one that God promised, the one that God sent, the one that was born of Mary. That part of Daniel's prophecy had now been fulfilled. Messiah was *"cut off but not for Himself"*. He was cut off to become the Saviour of mankind.

Satan is Defeated!

What is known as 'Gordon's Calvary' – The possible site (outside the Old City) of 'Skull Hill' – where Jesus was crucified. No site today is totally certain. Identified as such by Maj. Gen. C. G. Gordon (1833 – 1885) in 1883. (JHF)

Did Satan think that he had won a victory over God's purposes again? As he thought he had in the garden of Eden? Did he think when Jesus said *"Finished!"* that God was defeated? Satan does not seem to give up, and will not until his defeat and his destiny is final. When Jesus said *"Finished!"* on the cross it was a cry of victory. Three days later, as He had prophesied to His disciples that He would, He rose again from the dead (John chapter 20 verse 19).

Jesus had told the people in the Temple, at the very beginning of His public ministry, *"Destroy this temple* (the Temple of His body), *and in three days I will raise it up."* (John chapter 2 verse 19 - 21 KJV). Even His enemies remembered that prophecy, three years later. After He was put to death and after He was put in the grave. They came and asked Pilate for a guard, to protect the tomb where Joseph and Nicodemus had put His body, *"Lest His disciples come by night, and steal Him away."* (Matthew chapter 27 verses 62 – 65 KJV). But just as He had promised that He would, three days later, Jesus arose!

A 'Garden Tomb' in Jerusalem. Not necessarily the "new Tomb" of Joseph, but of similar style and antiquity. The 'bricked up' section would have been the wider circular "mouth", and the stone channel (bottom centre) was where the round stone rolled back. In this case to the right side. (JHF)

'Up from the grave He arose,
With a mighty triumph o'er His foes;
He arose a victor from the dark domain,
And He lives for ever with His saints to reign;
He arose! He arose!
Hallelujah! Christ arose!

(Robert Lowry 1826 – 1899, Plainfield NJ.)

Q&A >

Questions and Answers for Chapter Four – *'First Coming of Jesus'*

Chp. 4 – 'First Coming of Jesus'

Q1. Who were the two old people at the start of the chapter who came to the Temple, to see the baby that God had promised they would?

Q2. Why were they looking in the Temple and not in Bethlehem?

Q3. What were they looking for?

Q4. Why did Joseph and Mary have to go to Bethlehem? (You might want to write out a sentence or two to answer that question.)

Q5. Why did Jesus come?
There are various answers to that question.

Q6. What happened to Jesus, at the end of His period of teaching?

Q7. Remember the 'Timeline' that you have previously started; are there any new dates or details that can now be added to it?

Chapter Five

The Church Period

In this Chapter we will be looking at when the Church began, and in our next Chapter we will look at when the 'Church period' will come to an end. Then we will examine in detail what will happen after the Church has gone. The verses we will focus on, just now, are found in Matthew's Gospel (chapter 16 verses 13 – 18 ESV): *"When Jesus came into the district of Caesarea Philippi, He asked His disciples, 'Who do people say that the Son of Man is?' And they said, 'Some say John the Baptist, others say Elijah, and others Jeremiah or one of the prophets.' He said unto them, 'But who do you say that I am?' Simon Peter replied, 'You are the Christ, the Son of the living God.' And Jesus answered him, 'Blessed are you, Simon bar-Jonah! For flesh and blood has not revealed this to you, but My Father who is in heaven. And I tell you, you are Peter* (a small stone), *and on this* (bed)*rock I will build My Church; and the gates of Hades shall not prevail against it.'"*

Our previous chapter finished on the high note of the resurrection of the Lord Jesus. Not only did Jesus prophesy His resurrection He also prophesied His *"going away"* (John chapter 14 verses 1 – 20) and His eventual coming back again. He also prophesied the much sooner coming down of the *"Comforter"* or *"Helper"*, who is the *"Holy Spirit"* to be *"with you and in you"*. That 'alongside you' and 'within you' and the *"baptism in Holy Spirit"* that John the Baptist spoke of (Matthew chapter 3 verse 11) were all fulfilled at *"Pentecost"* when the Church came into existence. We have referred quite often to the 'Church Age', but that is not strictly a Bible expression. Do you recall the occasion when Jesus stood up in Nazareth and read from Isaiah's prophecy and said, *"This day is this scripture fulfilled in your hearing"*? That was the beginning of *"The acceptable year of the Lord"* (Isaiah chapter 61 verse 2 KJV).

That was not, however, the beginning of the Church Age. The *"Acceptable year of the Lord"* is not strictly the same length as the Church period. The *"Acceptable year of the Lord"* includes the period of the public ministry of Jesus when He preached and taught, and His disciples who believed in Him also preached the *"gospel of the kingdom"*. There were many believers before the Church was born. Paul tells us (in 1 Corinthians chapter 15 verses 3 – 8) that there were more than 500 believers who saw the Lord Jesus all at once, after His resurrection. This company of Christians all predated the birth of the Church.

Is the Church in Prophecy?

Or, to ask a slightly different question, 'Is the Church in the Old Testament?' We need to answer both of those questions before we go forward. 'Is the Church in prophecy?' The answer is: Yes. 'Is the Church in the Old Testament?' The answer is: No. The Church is neither in the Old Testament, nor is it prophesied in the Old Testament, though we might see (looking back) some 'pictures' or illustrations of the Church, and her relationship to Jesus Christ.

> **KEYNOTE: Past or Future?** The idea of all prophecy having already been fulfilled historically is called *'preterism'*. A Latin term which means 'in the past'. That is a mistaken idea, because there are a great many prophecies in the Old and New Testaments which have not had their fulfilment yet. If they had been, then Jesus would also have had to return as well. Many centuries ago! Some of those terms and theories are examined in **Appx. II**.

'But', some will say, 'if the Church is in prophecy and the Church is not prophesied in the Old Testament then how do we find the Church in prophecy?' That is a very interesting question, because there are those who think that future prophecy is something that was contained in the Old Testament only. When we come to the New Testament prophecy is not for now, it is not for today, and everything to do with prophecy (even the book of Revelation) has already been fulfilled in the past.

Some of the prophecies Jesus gave were fulfilled in His own lifetime, proving that He was a true prophet. There are not as many prophecies in the New Testament as in the Old. The New Testament is shorter and some of the books don't contain much in the way of prophecy. On the other hand, some books written by the apostles and others, after the ascension of Jesus, contain much prophecy. [Many of these key New Testament prophecies we will be examining as we go forward in later **Chapters**.] What we are saying is: The Church is in prophecy, but the Church was not revealed in the Old Testament. It was prophesied by Jesus Himself, <u>for the first time</u>, in the passage we have read in Matthew's Gospel chapter 16 in the New Testament.

What Is 'The Church'?

The Church is the complete *"Body of Christ"*. (We are told that in 1 Corinthians chapter 12 verse 27, also in Romans chapter 12 and verse 5) Paul says, *"We are one body in Christ"*. The Church has only ever been seen, by human eyes, in its totality on the day in which it was born. A few days after that many of those who were new believers went home, for they were Jewish pilgrims, visitors to Jerusalem for a Feast Day. Following that (in Acts chapter 8), the Jerusalem-based believers, because of persecution in Judea, were also scattered to different parts of the world and they told out the gospel, and the *"Apostle's doctrine"*. Little local churches were eventually established all over the Greek and Roman world. People who were believers in the Lord Jesus, who were baptised, who were *"gathered together"* in local fellowships to remember Jesus in the ceremony of *"the breaking of bread"*, just as Jesus had instructed.

God the Father, and the Lord Jesus Christ, who are in heaven sent down the Holy Spirit at *"Pentecost"* (Acts chapter 2 verses 1 – 47) not only to *"baptise"* the early believers into one body, but so that the same Spirit would indwell every single believer in the Lord Jesus. We cannot 'see' the whole of the Church; nor all the *"born again"* believers in the world (never mind the twenty centuries of thousands and thousands of Christians, all part of the church, who have already died). That presents another question that some people will asking in their mind, 'How can the whole Church ever come together again?'

[We will deal with that in the next **Chapter** *'The Church Removed'*.]

So, 'Is the Church in prophecy?' Yes. But the church was prophesied in the New Testament not in the Old. We saw in our earlier reading (in Matthew chapter 16 verse 18 ESV), that Jesus told His disciples *"I will build My Church (and when I do), the gates of Hades (the powers of darkness) shall not prevail against it."*

Is the Church in the New Testament a Replacement for Israel in the Old Testament?

That question will be answered in full as we go forward, but for now, the answer is: No. The Church is not 'the new Israel' and the Church is not a 'replacement' for Israel. The nation of Israel was, and is, an earthly people with a future in the purposes of God. A future that is still linked to 'Eretz Israel', their land, and their capital city Jerusalem: An earthly inheritance and a literal Kingdom. The Church is heavenly, where Jesus our *"Head"* is, and we are not looking for any earthly inheritance at all, *"you joyfully accepted the plundering of your property, since you knew that you yourselves had a better possession and an abiding one"* the writer to the Hebrews reminded the early first century Christians (Hebrews chapter 10 verse 34 ESV).

The nation of Israel was promised – in Abraham – a literal and future inheritance of an actual land with boundaries. To David it was also promised that not only would the nation be a monarchy, but his Son would rule forever. Although the Church will one day be *"the Bride, the wife of the Lamb"* (Revelation chapter 21 verse 9 ESV), and share in the Kingdom glory, she will be distinct in relationship and role to Israel throughout the Kingdom Age.

Pictures of the Church in the New Testament

The beginning of the Church is foretold in Matthew chapter 16 verse 18 (When we read there, we should remember again that the prophecies in the Bible can be divided into short and long). That was a short prophecy; it was going to begin to be fulfilled in less than three years. In Matthew chapter 16 Jesus called the Church 'a building'. When we go to other parts of the New Testament (Acts chapter two; 1 Corinthians chapter 12 & Ephesians chapter 5 for example), we find the Church is pictured as a *"Body"*, and then when we come towards the end of the book of Revelation, we find that the Church is also called a *"Bride"*.

Those three titles are all significant; the Church is a <u>Building</u>, the Church is a <u>Body</u>, and the Church is also a <u>Bride</u>. 'Can she be all three things at once?' you might ask. Yes, she

> **KEYNOTE: Marriage.** That is why the marriage of man and woman together is so precious and so important in the eyes of God. It points to the relationship between Jesus Christ, who is our heavenly Bridegroom, and every single saved person down here in this age, who is going to be in a future day part of the *"Bride, the wife of the Lamb"* (Rev. 21:9 ESV).

can, we will explain the meaning of them all as we go. Remember that the very first bride who was ever in this world was also called a *"building"*. Are you confused? Away back in the beginning (Genesis chapter 2 verse 22), God put Adam to sleep, God opened up his side, and from his side He took the flesh, and from the flesh he <u>made</u> *"woman"*. The word in Hebrew is *"He built ..."*. God built a bride for the first man, and whenever Adam and Eve were brought together, she understood that she had been made from his flesh and she was part of his *"bone and flesh"* (Genesis chapter 2 verse 23). He had been 'wounded' for her as well.

Is the Church Pictured in the Old Testament?

Let us come now to another question that some students of their Bible sometimes ask, 'Is the birth of the Church pictured in the Old Testament, even if it is not prophesied?' We have mentioned that already, but to answer that question in detail, we need to examine the calendar of Jewish Feasts (We find that laid out in Leviticus chapter 23). The first Feast on the Jewish calendar was *"Passover"*, they kept it on day fourteen of the first month. It came very early in the year, and it was a reminder of the first *"Passover"* when they came out of the land of Egypt (Exodus chapter 12).

The second Feast was *"The Feast of unleavened bread"*, kept from the fifteenth to the twenty first day of the same month. The next Feast came just a few days after that, depending on how the calendar worked, it was called *"The Feast of Firstfruits"*. This Feast was to commemorate the very beginning of their harvest. When one sheaf had come up out of the ground, out of the grain that had been sown before the winter season, it was plucked as a *"first fruit"* and was taken into the Tabernacle or the Temple and waved before Jehovah, before the Lord. It was a promise, a picture, a kind of tiny 'prophecy', that all the other sheaves and all the other harvests would also spring up and be brought in, to be ground for meal and bread for the whole year. This Feast was the day after the Sabbath immediately after Passover.

After that they kept what was called *"The Feast of Weeks"*. A strange title, but so called because it was seven weeks between the *"Feast of Firstfruits"* and the *"Feast of Weeks"*. Fifty days (or forty-nine days), depending on whether you count from the *"Sabbath"* (Saturday) or whether you count from the day after Sabbath, which is our Sunday.

Those four 'Spring Feasts' are very important, because when we come to the death of the Lord Jesus, we find a very interesting parallel: The day the Lord Jesus Christ died was the 14th day of the first month, the Gospels are very clear that it was Passover Day. Not only was He the fulfilment in His death of all the Passover pictures, but He died between the beginning and the end of Passover day. Three days later, early on a Sunday morning, the day after 'Shabbat', the Jewish Sabbath, Jesus rose from the dead. He also fulfilled the picture of the Feast of first fruits, and the day on which He rose from the dead was the same day that the priests kept the Feast of first fruits in the Temple. Forty-nine days after that, the priests kept another feast *"the Feast of Weeks"*. Two little fresh loaves, from the first barley harvest, were ceremonially taken in before Jehovah (Leviticus chapter 23 verses 17 – 18).

What Happened at the Feast of Weeks?

Something else happened on that day, forty-nine days after Jesus' resurrection (50 days from the Sabbath); that was the day that the Spirit came down and the Church was born. In John chapter 14, while talking to them in the *"Upper room"* just before He went to His arrest in Gethsemane, Jesus told His disciples some very important things. They were all prophecies, some of them were very short, and some of them were very long. He said, *"If I go away* (and He did), *and prepare a place for you* (in My Father's house), *I will come again and receive you to Myself ... I will not leave you as orphans; I will come to you."* (John chapter 14 verses 3 & 18 NASB). The words *"receive you"* here are also translated *"will take you"* (ESV). They come from two compound Greek words *'para-lambanō'* which really mean 'lay hold of for official reasons' and 'bring alongside'. The 'to take' verb can be used both negatively and positively in scripture, and the context is needed to confirm which is the case. Here the meaning could not be more positive, nor joyful. We have not seen the fulfilment of that prophecy yet. But Jesus also said, *"I will ask the Father and He will give you another Helper, to be with you forever, even the Spirit of truth ... you know Him for He dwells with you and will be in you."* (John chapter 14 verses 16 – 17 ESV). That promise, and prophecy, was fulfilled as well just a few days later (in Acts chapter 2).

> **KEYNOTE: Take Away ...** There are scholars who suggest that the 'rapture' or removal of the Church is found in the 'Olivet Discourse' passage, in the story of the two together, where *"one shall be taken, and the other left"* (Matt. 24:36-44). The context argues for a removal for negative purposes, not positive, and compares to the *"the days of Noah ..."*. So removed for judgment is in view, as a warning. Not removed for blessing. The word *'lambanō'* is used for Pilate taking Jesus to be scourged (John 19:1), and also of Joseph and Nicodemus taking down the body of Jesus from the cross (John 19:40), two entirely opposite activities.

What Happened at Pentecost?

'So, where do we get the word *"Pentecost"* from?' It is really a Greek word that has just been brought into English without being translated. There was no '*Feast of Pentecost*' in the Old Testament either, the Jews called it *"The Feast of Weeks"* as we have seen. The word we have in English just means 'the fiftieth of ...', so it is the fiftieth day, counting from Saturday (the Jewish Sabbath), and forty-nine days counting from the Sunday.

It was on a Sunday Jesus that came into Jerusalem riding on his *"colt the foal of an ass"* (Matthew chapter 21 verses 1 – 9 KJV), He presented Himself to the nation. (On certain calendars it is called 'Palm Sunday'.) The rulers rejected Him, and delivered Him to the Romans to be crucified, on the evening of *"Passover"* in the middle of the week. Three days after His crucifixion and death, Jesus rose again from the dead on a Sunday morning. It was on another Sunday seven weeks later that the Spirit came down and the Church was born …

All Together in One Place

An "upper room" in an older two-storey home in Jerusalem.

In Acts chapter 2 verse 1 it tells us that the disciples were *"all together in one place"* ten days after Jesus went back to heaven. Perhaps by this time they had seen the parallels with their Jewish Feasts, and they were expecting that something was going to happen to fulfil the picture of the next feast on their calendar, the *"Feast of weeks"*? Luke's record says, *"Suddenly there came a sound out of heaven as of a rushing mighty wind"* (Acts chapter 2 verses 1 – 4 NRB).

The word in the original language means *'breath'*. You might say, 'That doesn't really make sense, because if it is rushing and mighty, how can it sound like a breath?' But this was God's breath. That links us back again to the beginning, when God made Adam before He made Eve, *"The Lord God … breathed into man's nostrils the breath of life"* (Genesis chapter 2 verse 7), and man became a living person; body, soul and spirit. At Pentecost it was as if God, in His Holy Spirit, stooped and *"breathed"* again, and the whole room they were sitting in was filled with the sound of the rushing mighty wind.

What they Heard & What they Saw

Each of them heard the wind, and they also saw *"divided tongues as of fire"*, resting upon each one of them *"and they were all filled with Holy Spirit, and began to speak with other tongues, as the Spirit gave them utterance"* (Acts chapter 2 verses 3 – 4 NRB). The *"tongues"* were not to glorify the speakers, those who had been in the upper room. Nor were they to give glory to the *"Holy Spirit"* who had come down.

KEYNOTE: **Tongues.** These were not languages that were unintelligible, nor ungrammatical. They were recognisable languages, and dialects, that the disciples themselves had never learned to speak. It was a miracle of speaking, and it was the beginning of the *"sign"* of speaking in tongues, so that every single person who was on the street, mostly Jewish pilgrims who had come to the Feast from *"out of every nation under heaven"*, might be able to hear (without any interpreter) in their own language and in their own dialect, the gospel (Acts 2:1-13). There is no record anywhere in the N.T of *"tongues"* being 'unintelligible', or 'uninterpretable'.

They were a sign to the Jews that God was doing something new, and also that this new message being preached was for the ears of everyone, Gentiles included, from every part of the world.

On the day of Pentecost, the day on which the Church was born, on the streets of Jerusalem, people from Europe, Asia, and Africa heard in their own dialects and the accent of their home village *"the wonderful words of God"*. They heard too 'the wonderful works of God': Peter stood up with the disciples and he preached the first sermon of the Church. He preached the first open air message of the 'Church Age' and he told the people *"that whosoever shall call upon the name of the Lord shall be saved"*. Many of the visitors when they heard the message asked, *"What should we do?"* They were told to *"repent and to believe"*, and we are told that more than 3,000 people were saved on that day on which the Church was born (Acts chapter 2 verses 37 – 42).

The Lord Added to The Church

A 'colonnade' against the outer wall of Temple Mount. A modern rebuilding, but reminiscent of what was known – in the time of Jesus – as 'Solomon's Porch'. Said to have been able to hold 3,000 people it was not only a teaching place for Jesus Himself, but a gathering centre for the early Church. (JHF)
"And they were all with one accord in Solomon's Porch" (Acts 5:12)

Not only did they receive the Word, but the narrative also tells us they *"were baptised"*. Peter must have included that in his preaching. To prove outwardly that you have received the Word inwardly, you should be baptised. And they were. All baptised with no exceptions. They were all added to the church that was the testimony in Jerusalem, but more importantly they were all added to the Body of Christ. Many of them didn't stay in Jerusalem long, for most of them were pilgrims and after a few days of fellowshipping together (probably in the porch of the temple with the other local Christians), they left, and they took the message with them far away to other parts of the world.

We (those of us today who are geographically far from Jerusalem) have received the message in our part of the world as well. The *"apostles' doctrine"*, the truth of fellowship, the truth of being gathered together to *"break bread"*, the truth of coming together to pray, to keep the commandments of Jesus and the teaching of the apostles. Some *"come together"* in little groups of testimony; sometimes in houses, sometimes in out-buildings, sometimes in the open air, and some even in hiding. We don't need to have a building to be obedient to the Word of God in our testimony to Him.

Before He went back to heaven, just before the Church commenced, (John chapter 14) Jesus told His disciples, *"If I go away, I will come again."* He has not come back yet almost 2,000 years later. But He will come quickly (we will see that later in our studies). He will most likely come shortly, for the 'Church Age' will soon be over, and the time of the judgment period cannot be far away.

The old Sunday School chorus went something like this …

> **'Say, will you be ready when Jesus comes?**
> **Are you sure you're born again?'**
> *(Frank Jenner 1903 – 1977, Kogarah, NSW.)*

Questions and Answers for Chapter Five – *'The Church Period'*

Chp. 5 – 'The Church Period'

Q1. Is the Church to be found in the Old Testament?

Q2. Is the Church foretold in prophecy?

Q3. Can you give one reason why the Church is different to Israel?

Q4. Which Jewish Feast was Jesus' death a fulfilment of?

Q5. Why do we know this?

Q6. Which Jewish Feast was Jesus' resurrection a fulfilment of?

Q7. How many days after the resurrection was the Church born?

Q8. What did the "Holy Spirit" do on the day of Pentecost?

Q9. If you have been drafting out a 'timeline', you should have some more new events and dates to add to it.

JOTTINGS

Chapter Six

The Church Removed

This chapter is titled 'The Church Removed' which will take us forward in our thinking into the near future. To the end of the 'Church Age' and into the 'Judgment Period'. Almost 2,000 years forward, since *"Pentecost"* and the birth of the Church, where we were in the previous Chapter. The birth of the Church was a 'short prophecy', fulfilled in just over three years from

when it was first foretold by Jesus Himself (Matthew chapter 16 verse 18). The end of the Church period, and her removal is also a prophesied event, but it is a 'long prophecy'. We have already seen this link between 'short' and 'long' prophecies: The shorter predictions of what God will do, and those which have already been fulfilled, are in themselves confirmation that the long predictions will come true as well. The end of the Church Age is just as sure as was the commencement. As we have seen in our prophetic (looking forward) and historic (looking back) timeline, the 'Church Period' is the longest 'Age' without a break in the calendar of God. This period cannot continue forever. There are other 'ages' still to come in God's programme. We should be prepared for, and very aware of, what is going to come next ...

Is Jesus Coming for Us First?

In a key Bible passage on this subject Paul is writing to a newly planted Church in a place called Thessaloniki, where he had preached for a few months. They have come back to him afterwards with questions about 'last days' and particularly about Christians who had already died. 'Would they miss out on the promised return of Jesus? Would His coming only be to take away believers who were living at the time?'

Here is how Paul replied, *"I would not have you to be ignorant, brethren, concerning them which are asleep (died in Christ), that ye sorrow not, even as also the others which have no hope. For if we believe that Jesus died and rose again, even so them also which sleep through Jesus will God bring with Him ... For the Lord Himself shall descend from heaven with a shout, with voice of archangel, and with trump of God: and the dead ones in Christ shall rise first: then we which are alive and remain shall be caught up (snatched away) together with them in clouds, to meet the Lord in the air: and so shall we ever be with the Lord. Wherefore exhort one another with these words."* (1Thessalonians chapter 4 verses 13 – 18 NRB).

You will remember that Jesus said to His disciples in the *"Upper Room"*, before He went to Calvary, *"If I go ... I will come again, and receive you unto Myself"* (John chapter 14 verses 1 – 4 KJV). We have looked at that word *"receive"* previously. It means, 'take you to be with myself to be joined to me, to be at my side'. It is not so much the idea of Him coming <u>here</u> to be with us, it is of us being taken <u>there</u> to be with Him. We will find another word in this study that reinforces and emphasises that very same thought.

The Church or Israel?

We have seen that certain of the key *"covenant"* promises of the Old Testament still have not yet been fulfilled. We cannot 'spiritualize' the prophecies given to Abraham and David and roll them over into an application to the Church. The Bible clearly teaches, both in the Old Testament and in the New Testament (Romans chapters 9 – 11), that God has a future for the nation of Israel, not only spiritually but literally. And God has a future for the Church which is a building, a body now, and which will be the Bride of Christ in that future Kingdom. The *"Bride, the Lamb's wife"*, and the nation of Israel, over which He will be King, will be seen together in that Kingdom period of 1,000 years. Jesus is coming back. He is coming back to take away the Christians of the Church period; He is also coming to judge wickedness and rebellion during the 'Tribulation Period'. He is coming to reign, to fulfil His promises to David, in the 'Kingdom Period'. He is coming to sit upon His throne in Jerusalem, with the tribes of Israel gathered into their Land. But He is coming for His Church first.

> **KEYNOTE: The Second Coming.** The N.T. does not present Jesus as having 'Three Comings'. His 'First Coming' is in the past. His birth, life, death, and resurrection (Approximately 4 BC – 32 AD). His 'Second Coming', is still future. It will be in stages, as was His first. A 'silent' part, a 'legal' introduction, and a 'public' part. His 'Second Coming' will be in the same order of events. It will have 'stages' but it will all be one *"Coming Again"*.

Why is Jesus coming for the Church?

'Does the Church need to be removed?' These are big questions, and 'Why should the Church be taken away first?' We won't go into all the detail of that now, that would be too much for this section. We will find out (as we move into our next study) that one of the reasons the Church will be removed first is that the Holy Spirit who dwells within the Christians in the Church, and the true Church herself, are functioning as a 'resistance movement'. God is using our influence, through the Holy Spirit, to hold back the full 'manifestation' or flood of total wickedness that is going to come when all restraint has been removed. There is a *"mystery of lawlessness"*, total rebellion against God and moral order, which is already building up in our time, but it has not been fully let loose yet.

At the head of this 'tsunami' of evil will be two men who will be head of all of it. This passage of scripture, written to the same Church as in our previous reading (2 Thessalonians chapter 2 verses 3 – 12), speaks of *"The Man of Sin"*, who appears on the scene first, and it is made very clear that his controlling power comes, not from God, but from Satan. The full exposure of what he represents, his *"revelation"* as *"The Man of Sin"*, can only happen after the resistance of the Church and the indwelling presence of the person of the Spirit of God have been removed. The other personality is called the *"False Prophet"*. In this passage the Bible calls him *"The Lawless one"*, which matches the mindset of *"lawlessness"* which will be prevalent in those days.

What about Dead Christians?

Contrasting cemeteries: The Jewish 'Silwan Necropolis' (c700 BC) & outside the 'Eastern Gate', the Muslim cemetery. The Eastern or 'Golden Gate' was bricked up by Sultan Suleiman in 1541 AD. (JFH)

Here is an interesting problem which was probably in the forefront of the minds of the early Christians too. Their question was, 'What about Christians who have died, and have been buried? Will they miss out on Jesus' return?' God has not given us a day, or a date, for when Jesus Christ will come to take us to the Father's house. He wanted every generation of Christians to be watching and waiting for that coming. We are waiting, as we should be. But what about Christians who have already died, and their bodies have been put in the grave?

Are they going to miss out? In other words, will it only be the generation of Christians who are living who will be taken up in their changed bodies, when Jesus comes again?

Paul answers that question by explaining that all the saved ones who have died will hear the voice of Christ

> **KEYNOTE: *'Fallen asleep in Jesus'.*** This is just a biblical picture to minimise the impact of death and burial, and to emphasise eternal security in Christ. The Scriptures do not ever speak of 'soul sleep'. When Christians die they are *"absent from the body and … at home with the Lord"* (2 Cor. 5:8 NASB). It is only the *"body"* which *"sleeps"* and goes to dust in the grave.

first, and rise first. To emphasise his point (as inspired by the Holy Spirit), Paul calls them *"the fallen asleep in Jesus."* He says that we should think of brothers and sisters who have died as just asleep in their graves, waiting to hear the *"shout"* of Jesus Christ. Then we, the Christians who are still alive, will join them in the air (having our bodies changed) and be 'snatched up' to be with the Lord Jesus.

Just as the word *"receive"* in the Upper Room teaching in John chapter 14 means to 'take to be with Himself', so the words *"caught up"* in our passage mean 'snatched away', before the *"lawlessness"* comes. It is a very strong word, 'snatched by an outside power' away from danger. We know now what the danger is, though much more detail will come in our later studies. We know who will be *"caught up"*, who will be *"received"*; the Christians of the Church period, both living and *"sleeping in Jesus"*.

> **KEYNOTE: 'Rapture Event'.** After almost 2,000 years of global evangelism: We have no concept of how many *"born again"* living people will disappear (perhaps in our generation), in a moment. Nor how many millions more are in the Church, the *"Body of Christ"*, from generations past. We have little understanding of the impact of the *"Rapture"* event on our present world.

Perhaps today?

From the first-generation disciples, who were there in the Upper Room, to those at Pentecost when the Church was born, to the dead saints of the church in Thessaloniki in the first century, right through until ...

Until the very moment that Jesus comes to the air. Perhaps in our generation? Perhaps today?

What about the 'Rapture' word?

Some will say, 'We have read all through the prophecy passages of the New Testament, and we can't find it at all!' That is not a problem. The first part of the answer is, 'Yes, you are correct!' The 'rapture' word is not found in our English Bibles. But let us remember that after the New Testament was first written in Greek, it was gradually translated into Latin (which was the everyday language of the Roman Empire). The Latin 'Vulgate', or 'common language' version of the Bible, continued until almost 1,500 AD, when William Tyndale translated and published the first printed English New Testament, directly from Greek. If we could read Latin, we would find the *'rapture'* word right there in our passage. Because the words *"caught up"* in our Bibles are in the Latin Bible as one word: *"rapture"*.

> **KEYNOTE: 'Rapture Truth'.** We are not debating here the 'timing' of the Rapture, but the 'truth' of it. No serious student of N.T. prophecy can deny that Jesus will come again to 'take away' His Church. He will not just arrive here to join us! We will examine that in more detail in **Appx. II**.

Another key word, which adds another piece to our picture, is also found in Paul's letter to the church in Thessaloniki (This young church must have had a wonderful appetite for 'End Times' study). Paul reminds them that, when they heard the gospel, *"ye turned to God from idols to serve a living and true God, and to await His Son from the heavens,* *whom He raised from among the dead, Jesus, our <u>deliverer from the coming wrath</u>"*. (1 Thessalonians chapter 1 verses 9 – 10 JND). This word *"deliverer"* includes the thought of '<u>drawing to Himself</u>', but also the additional idea of 'rescuing in a hurry'. Jesus is not just coming for us because He said He would. When He does come it will be an urgent 'rescue mission' because great danger is coming here too. What is meant by *"the coming wrath"* will be examined in later chapters. This is not the judgment of Hell, nor even the *"lake of fire"*. This is a *"wrath"* which the prophets, and Jesus, foretold is coming here to our world.

We have looked at the question, 'Who will be *"received"* or *"caught up"* to be with Jesus?' We have seen something of the reason, 'Why will Christians be taken up?' One of the prime answers is (as we have seen so often in our studies) God must keep His promises. We have seen a little of the answer to the question, 'When will we be caught up?' The answer to that is at the end of the 'Church Period', and before the full *"revelation"* of the *"Man of Sin"* and total lawlessness. 'Where will we be taken to?' That is not such a hard question. The answer was found in our reading at the beginning. We shall be *"forever with the Lord"*, and in that hope we should encourage each other every day.

What will Happen After the Church is Taken up?

Much of the rest of our studies will be looking at that question in detail. But it is not all doom and gloom, even for this old world. There is coming a terrible period of judgment, on the *"Man of Sin"*, on the *"False Prophet"* (we have only mentioned him), on the *"Dragon"* who is Satan, and on all who follow them in rebellion against God: fallen angels, demons, and mankind all included. This will be the *"wrath of the Lamb"*, as we will discover later in our studies in the early chapters of the book of Revelation.

After That?

Is it not a great thought that God always has an *'after that …'*? The Devil cannot win. Jesus must reign. The Kingdom Age must come. The covenant promises must be fulfilled. 'And after that? What then?' you ask. After that will come what we call the 'Eternal State'. And there is no subsequent 'after that …' What a terrible thing not to be ready when Jesus comes. To miss having Him as Saviour, as our King in the Kingdom, and to have to look forward to an 'after that' of banishment and pain forever. Before we move into the next part of our studies, it would be a wonderful thing now to have the assurance of Jesus Christ as your Saviour, and the true hope of being *"received up"* when Jesus comes for His Church. Never to experience the *"wrath which is coming here"*, nor the awfulness of the *"lake of fire"*, which will never be quenched, and banishment from God's presence forever.

KEYNOTE: The Eternal Kingdom. This will be forever, a new heaven and new earth which will be without end. It is entirely separate from the 'Kingdom Age', which will be on this earth. It will include every true believer in Messiah, in Jesus the Saviour, from Abel (Genesis 4), through until the end of the Kingdom. The 'Kingdom Age' is for a fixed period, the 'Eternal State' is forever. We will look at those subjects in more detail in **Chps. 21-23**.

Questions and Answers for Chapter Six – *'The Church Removed'*

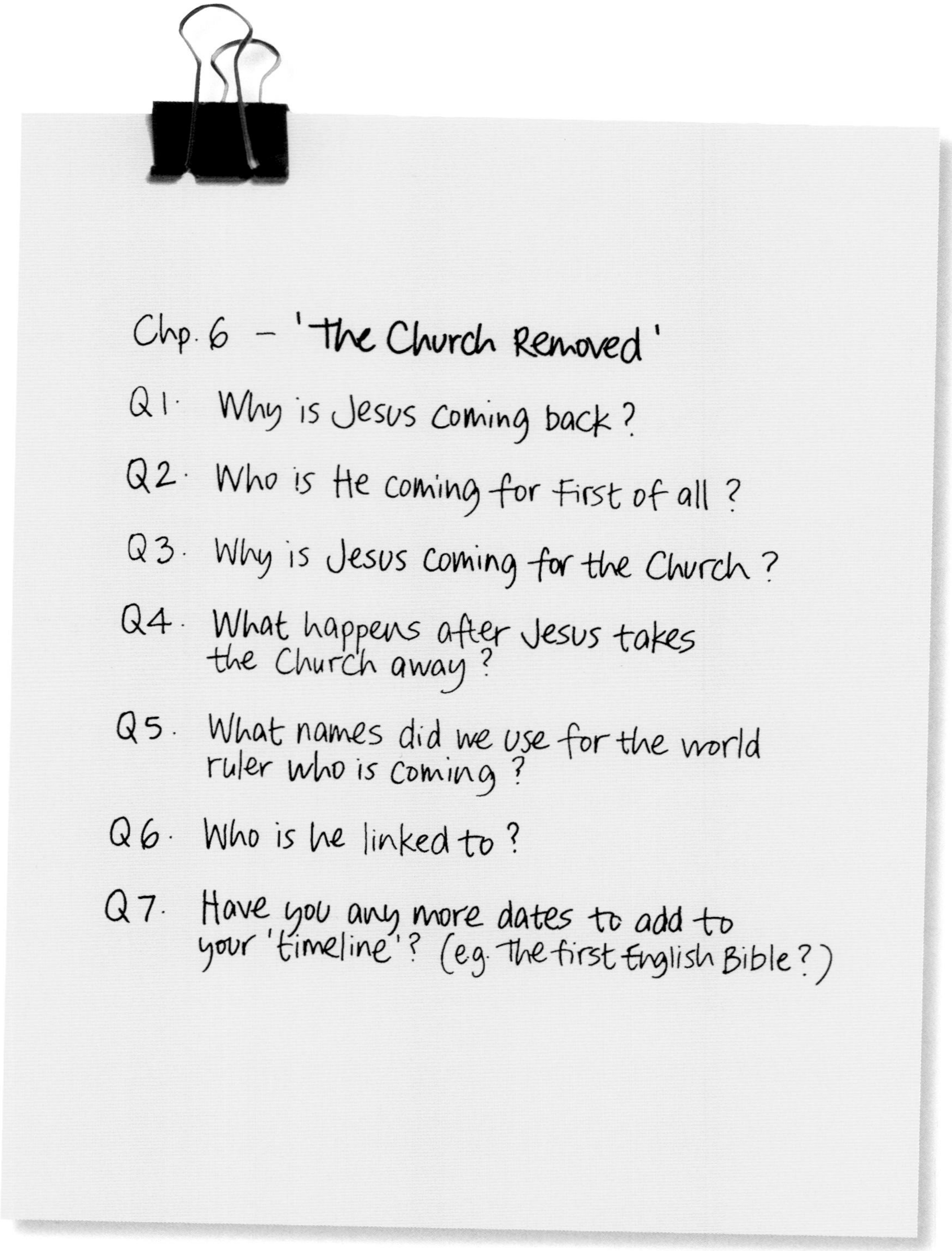

Chp. 6 – 'The Church Removed'

Q1. Why is Jesus coming back?

Q2. Who is He coming for first of all?

Q3. Why is Jesus coming for the Church?

Q4. What happens after Jesus takes the Church away?

Q5. What names did we use for the world ruler who is coming?

Q6. Who is he linked to?

Q7. Have you any more dates to add to your 'timeline'? (e.g. The first English Bible?)

PART TWO

THE JUDGMENT PERIOD EXAMINED

Chapter Seven

The Symbols Explained

We are now at the stage in our studies where we will be moving into the book of Revelation. Almost the whole book is one entire prophecy of 'End Times' and *"last days"* events, a pulling together and concluding of those prophecies, still unfulfilled, of the Old and New Testaments (Revelation chapters 4 – 22). The author is the Apostle John, known as *"the disciple whom Jesus loved"* (John chapter 21 verse 20 KJV). The last survivor of the twelve apostles, a prisoner on an island called Patmos, where he received the first part of this series of visions which is the conclusion of all prophecy, and of the Word of God.

Before we get into the detail of the Chart (which is a graphic depiction of John's visions), let us have an 'overview' of all that we will be looking at, and the key 'symbols' upon the Chart.

> **KEYNOTE: The 'End Times' Chart** inside the book covers flip out, you can keep it open from now on if you want to refer to it throughout the rest of the studies in the Book.

The Last Revelation

Let us start at the beginning of the book of Revelation, *"The revelation of Jesus Christ ..."* (This is the last time the *"revelation"* word is used in the Bible. The whole of the book of Revelation is one great 'revealing' of Jesus Christ. 'Apocalypse' in Greek means an 'unveiling'. It is not a 'disaster' word at all, as the media sometimes use it.) *"The revelation of Jesus Christ, which God gave unto Him, to shew to His servants things which must shortly come to pass; and He sent and made it known by signs through His angel unto His servant John: who testified of the word of God, and the testimony of Jesus Christ, and all the things that he saw. Blessed is he that readeth, and they that hear the words of this prophecy, and keep those things which are written therein: for the time at hand."* (Revelation chapter 1 verses 1 – 3 NRB).

There is a special blessing for reading and studying prophecy. Remember, way back at the beginning of our journey into these subjects, we encountered some who said, 'Why study prophecy?' Here is another great answer given at the very start of this difficult book: <u>There is a blessing for all who do study prophecy</u>. In fact, we will find as we go on that there are seven 'blessings' in this book; all of them for God's people down here, and they are spread right through the book to the very last page!

The 'Alpha & Omega'

The first symbol that we must touch on, before we move forward, is one that we have studied already, that is *"the Alpha and the Omega"*. The first and the last letter of the Greek alphabet. Their meaning in this context is; all that which can be written, all that which can be calculated, all that which can be known of, and revealed in, Jesus Christ. John, the same writer said, *"In the beginning was the Word, and the Word was with God, and the Word was God."* (John chapter 1 verse 1 KJV).

KEYNOTE: 'Eternality'. Before there was knowledge of God, there still was God. Before there was an Adam in the garden, there was God, who is the Creator, originator and sustainer of all things that do exist: *"All things were made by Him; and without Him was not any thing made that was made."* (John 1:3 KJV).

"Omega", by contrast, does not mean the ending or the cessation of matter and existence. We need to be very careful that we understand that is not what it means in a biblical sense. The Bible does not teach 'annihilationism'. It does not mean before God there was nothing, and at the end there will also be nothing, except God. It means that everything will have its conclusion, its *'terminus'*, in God. Every single person who has ever lived will have their everlasting existence determined within the will of God and Jesus Christ. [It will take until the very end of this Book to expand on that subject.]

The 'Acceptable Year of the Lord'

The second item we want to look at is something that you will find down at the bottom of the Chart (if you look back inside the front cover.) It is called *"The Acceptable Year of the Lord"*. We have already met that title in our studies. It connects with the first coming into the world of Jesus, specifically the very beginning of His public ministry. He stood up in the synagogue in Nazareth, where He was brought up, and He read from Isaiah chapter 61 verses 1 – 2 (NRB), *"The Spirit of the Lord God is upon Me; because Jehovah* (the LORD) *hath anointed Me to preach good tidings* (the gospel) *unto the meek ... To proclaim the acceptable year of Jehovah"*. The second half of the same verse reads, *"and the Day of vengeance of our God* (Elohim)*"*. But Jesus broke the verse up into two parts.

He didn't read the second half, and He said (Luke chapter 4 verse 21 KJV), *"This day is this scripture fulfilled in your ears"*. Jesus applied that <u>only to the first half</u> of the verse, to *"The Acceptable year of the Lord"*.

This is of real vital importance. It helps us in our interpretation of many difficult prophecies:

Firstly, it teaches us that Jesus was, as we read in our passage at the beginning of the Chapter, the *"revelation"* of God to man.

Secondly, it tells us that Jesus' first coming was not about judgment, but about freedom and 'good news', the gospel of the grace of God.

Thirdly, it tells us that *"the Day of vengeance of our God"* is also under the authority of Jesus, but it has not happened yet. We are still in *"the Acceptable year of the Lord"*, and the message we preach is one of good tidings!

Fourthly, and fundamentally for accurate interpretation of scripture, it also tells us that Old Testament and New Testament <u>prophecies can be divided in two</u>.

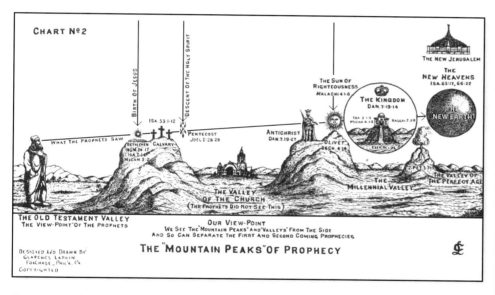

> **KEYNOTE: Time-Gaps.** The prophets themselves may not have seen the time 'split' in their prophecies, but looking back from New Testament times, we can see other prophecies that divide with a 'time gap' inside them, which was not obvious from far in advance. Clarence Larkin entitled this, 'The Mountain Peaks of Prophecy'. C. Larkin, 'Dispensational Truth' (Glenside PA: Larkin Est., 1920) 6-7.

The 'Church Age'

The next three symbols on the Chart are all connected. We have covered them already in some detail. They represent the death, the resurrection of Jesus, and the 'Church period'. We have seen that this is not really a scriptural title, and that *"the Acceptable year of the Lord"* includes the 'Church Age' that we are in today. This 'Day of Grace', we have also seen, will come to a sudden end (the gap in the prophecies of Isaiah and Daniel will be closed) and the next event that we are looking forward to is what has been called 'The Rapture of the Church'. The taking away of that which is the resistance against evil, along with removal of the *"He"* who is holding back lawlessness and wickedness, the indwelling Holy Spirit, who is in each born again person (2 Thessalonians chapter 2).

Daniel tells us* (in a very difficult part of his book, chapter 9 verse 26 NRB) that at a time which could be specifically dated *"shall Messiah be cut off, but not for Himself* (and have nothing)"*. He would be put upon a cross (David described that prophetically in his Psalms), He would be rejected by the nation, but on the third day He would rise again from the dead. The timeline of Daniel's prophecy paused at the point of Messiah's rejection, with 7 years out of a total of 490 years still unfulfilled (Daniel chapter 9 verses 24 – 27). The '490 years' is given in Daniel as *"seventy sevens"* (which does not have to mean 'years'), but calculating backwards, from the death of Jesus to the decree referred to in Daniel's prophecy, the 'sevens' must be seen as literal years). The first event in that 'prophecy gap' is that *"the people of the Prince that shall come shall destroy the city and the sanctuary"* (Daniel chapter 9 verse 26 KJV). Jesus also said as He taught in the Temple that, *"there shall not be left one stone upon another"* (Mark chapter 13 verse 2 KJV).

Those two prophecies were given 500 years apart, but the destruction of Jerusalem happened only 38 years after Jesus said so, in 70 AD. The generation who saw Messiah rejected was the same generation who saw the nation rejected by Jehovah: The Temple torn down, and the nation of Israel scattered for 1,900 years. Even though Israel is in their land today, they have no Temple, no Priesthood, and no sacrificial worship, and they have still a *"blindness"* as to what they did to their Messiah: *"blindness in part is happened to Israel, until the fulness of the Gentiles be come in"* (Romans chapter 11 verse 25 KJV).

After the Church will be taken away (a date which is not revealed in prophecy), then the remainder of God's programme will run its course. A programme of judgment, which will be contained within the last seven years of the 490 years of Daniel's 'timeline'. The detail of that we will come to later, but as well as seeing a gap in Isaiah chapter 61, we will also find there is a gap in Daniel chapter 9. After *"Messiah the Prince"* was *"cut off"*, there was a short break until the Temple was destroyed, just 38 years. But the longer 'gap' continues until now, even though Israel has been back in their land since 1948 AD. The last seven years of the 490 years of Daniel's 'timeline' does not begin until the other person *"The Prince that shall come"*, the one who is called the *"Man of Sin"*, the *"Antichrist"*, facilitates a seven-year peace treaty with Israel and her neighbours *"He shall confirm a covenant …"* (Daniel chapter 9 verse 27 NRB).

> ***KEYNOTE: Daniel's '70 weeks' Timeline.** Topic examined in greater detail in **Appx. I**.

The 'Day of the Lord'

We cannot be sure exactly when the *"Day of the Lord"* (spoken of by the prophet Joel, chapter 2 verse 31) begins. Possibly it will not even be known at the beginning which *"covenant"* with Israel will be the critical one? For even in recent days there have been many covenants, some even called 'Abraham Accords'. But none of them have been for "*seven years*", and none of them with the correct number of former enemies of Israel, as suggested in the prophecies of Daniel.

Nevertheless, these things in prophecy 'cast a shadow forwards' and we are moving very rapidly towards the 'End Times'. It is possible that the "*Day of the Lord*" will not begin with judgment. Paul said, writing again to the Church in Thessaloniki (1 Thessalonians chapter 5 verses 1 – 3 KJV), that the "*Day of the Lord*" will commence as "*a thief in the night*". Perhaps we can line up the beginning of the Day of the Lord, the signing of the 'Peace Covenant' for seven years, and most importantly, the opening by Jesus Christ of the 'Seven Sealed Scroll' (Revelation chapter 5 verses 1 – 8 ESV), as all happening at the same time.

The Seven Sealed Scroll

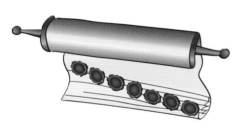

This is the next symbol on the Chart to be considered, the 'Scroll' and the 'Seven Seals' which are opened in order by "*The Lamb*", who is "*The Lion of the tribe of Judah, the Root of David*" (Revelation chapter 5 verses 5 – 7 KJV). In some translations it is called a "*book*", but the word really is a 'rolled book', a scroll, as the Jews still use for their holy writings and Old Testament books even today.

It is very much a legal picture. The scene is set in the throne room of God, His 'law chamber' and it is the Lamb, who was slain and rose again, Jesus who is now in heaven who is opening the Scroll. The day of His judgment and the beginning of "*the wrath of the Lamb*" will commence, once the first seal is broken open. (Revelation chapter 6 verses 16 – 17 KJV).

KEYNOTE: The Sealed Scroll. A scroll is opened differently from a book. One end is unrolled to open it. The other end, at the same time, is rolled up so that only a small portion is seen at once, and you read from it a little at a time. And in Hebrew, from right to left. The first seal would be broken to open the scroll, and each seal must be opened in turn to access the next section of the book.

The Four Horsemen

The next symbol on the chart is one that many people already know something about. It is often referred to, and sometimes the media use it as well. They speak of the 'Four Horsemen of the Apocalypse'. The Bible doesn't call them that, but there are four riders on four different coloured horses who appear as the first four seals are opened. The reason why the first horse is white is that this man who will have his "*revelation*", or 'unveiling', the "*Prince who shall come*" (of Daniel chapter 9), will present himself as a 'peacemaker'. He will "*confirm*" a peace treaty for a declared period of seven years. He will have a European and middle eastern

Kingdom, and will also have global influence, though he will not rule the whole planet. Even so, he will be the greatest ruler in the world, and he will come as a false Christ.

Will He Bring Peace?

No. Only *"Messiah"* can bring peace, at His second coming. The Bible calls this man an *"Antichrist"*. That means 'against Christ', but it can also mean 'instead of Christ'. He will come as a pretend Messiah, and he will come with a pretend promise of peace. We will see that these horses are each of a different colour: He truly is a false Messiah, because he does not bring lasting peace, he brings war. With war comes death. With war famine follows. And with famine also comes disease and more death. These are all the judgments of God on a world which has rejected Messiah, Jesus Christ the Saviour.

Our political world today is looking for a global leader of any sort, seemingly as anti-God as possible, who will take charge of problems that are on a global scale. What the world desires God will (in His judgment) allow them to have. Just as, back at the commencement of the Kingdom of Israel, Jehovah allowed the people to choose a *"Saul"*, before He sent them His chosen one, David the shepherd King, from Bethlehem in Judah.

The Seven Trumpets

The next symbol that we see on the Chart are *"The seven trumpets"*. They overlap the 'Seven Seals Judgments'* a little bit. It is the Lord Jesus who opens the seals, and it is He who oversees the trumpet judgments also, although this time the trumpets will be blown by angels. When the early Roman readers of the book of Revelation read of *"trumpets"* they would think of it as a military picture. It is like God's 'parade ground'. Don't forget; the heaven where God dwells in *"Eternity"* is a real place. It has rooms and furniture, a throne, and great space. Here the thought is of His 'marshalling yard' for the army of His angels, trumpets being blown, and angels being prepared to intervene in the affairs of this world, and to eventually go to battle with the *"Dragon"* and his fallen angels.

*KEYNOTE: Seven Seals etc. These subjects are examined in more detail in the studies at the examining of the 'Seal Judgments' and the *'Trumpet Judgments'* individually in **Chps. 9** & **11**.

The Dragon & His Two Beasts

That brings us directly to another symbol on the Chart: *"The great red Dragon"*, and what is called (right in the centre of the seven-year period) the *"War in heaven"*. If the seven years of the *"Day of vengeance of our God"*

divide exactly in two parts, then here in the middle are two equal periods of 1,260 days and 42 months, dividing into two halves. We will see more of that in later studies as well. The *"Dragon"* has two 'front-men' who will control and orchestrate politics, commerce, religion and at last fierce persecution against all the worshippers of *"The Lamb"*.

[We will study these *"Beasts"* separately, and the period of their rule in **Chapters 13 – 15**.]

The 'Mark of the Beast' – '666'

At this time will appear another symbol, one which is being talked about more and more today; the *"Mark of the Beast"* and the number *"666"*. We are not in that time period just yet, so we cannot be seeing the *"mark"* in things that are happening around us. But these 'End Times' are not far off, and in God's 'timeline' things could be allowed to happen very quickly indeed. We may be seeing not only 'shadows' but also the preparation for things which are just over our horizon …

The Seven Bowls

The next symbol on the chart is the *"Bowl Judgments"*. This is the third set of judgments; each set gets more prominent, each becoming more obvious that it is God at work, not random global changes! The first set, the *"Seals"* are silent, a legal picture, set up in heaven. The second set, the *"Trumpets"* are a military picture, and more obvious. The third set of judgments, which happen towards the end of the second half of the seven-year period, are the most severe. The picture is of God's *"wrath"* like something 'boiling' in a great pot, and the bowls filled from there and poured out by angels, wherever God instructs them to be targeted on this earth. What a very solemn picture indeed.

Babylon Destroyed

After that on the Chart we see the *"Fall of Babylon"*. There are two separate pictures, and two separate systems. Both judged by God. There are some difficult questions on these subjects, but we will come to both of them in time.

KEYNOTE: Mystery Babylon. That study will be in two parts [**Chps. 17** & **18**]. One part is about a world religious system. The other part is about a newly built capital city and a commercial centre. Both are judged by God, before the conclusion of the seven year period.

What is Symbolic, and what is Literal?

That is one of the hardest questions in relation to prophecy. It may be, as in many of the prophecies of the Old Testament, that things which appeared 'symbolic' and even humanly 'impossible' when the prophecy was given (especially long prophecies) turn out to be very literal when the time comes for them to be fulfilled. We must remember that God can do anything that He chooses. And events which were described as far off in the future can be difficult to understand with the knowledge of that day, or even today.

Someone will be asking, 'You didn't mention the battle of Armageddon?' No, we didn't. Strictly speaking, there is no battle! That might surprise you, but we will deal with that when we get there. That will come after the judgment of Babylon, at the end of the Tribulation period, at the *"Coming in Power"* of the King (Revelation chapter 16 verse 16 & chapter 19 verse 11).

The Coming in Power

Now the end of the Chart is in sight. 'What is left?' you ask. Another rider on another white horse! Some people get the two white horses (Revelation chapters 6 and 19) confused, and some even think that it is Jesus coming on the first white horse, at the beginning of the Seal judgments. That cannot be true! The rider on the second white horse is the real Messiah. The rider on the first white horse (Revelation chapter 6 verses 1 – 2) is the impostor, a false Messiah, a self-declared 'peace-keeper' in the Middle East.

The rider on the white horse (in chapter 19) is Jesus, the true Messiah, coming as was promised in the Old Testament, and as He Himself also promised in the New Testament. This is His *"Coming in power"* (Matthew chapter 24), His coming with the saints and with the armies of heaven. Coming to set up His Kingdom, *"the Year of My Redeemed"* as God calls it prophetically (in Isaiah chapter 63 verse 4). The 'Millennial Kingdom', as we will find in Revelation chapter 20, is a literal period of 1,000 years.

The Messiah is going to clean up planet earth; no more plastic problems, no pollution problems, no global warming. He will regulate the temperature. Possibly all the world will be 'sub-tropical' like the garden of Eden was? He will regulate the farming, and the crops. He will rule and reign from His new throne in the rebuilt city of Jerusalem for 1,000 years. What an amazing

> **KEYNOTE: 'Millennium'.** The word *'millennium'* means a period of 1,000 years. It is another Latin word (like *'rapture'*). It means 'a 1,000 of ...' something and we are told in Rev. Chp. 20, six times over, that it is *"years"* that are being spoken of.

Kingdom that is going to be. And all the saved, from all the ages, will be part of it. You and I too. If we are truly *"born again"* and awaiting His Second Coming.

What next, Peace Forever?

You would think so. But Satan, who will be imprisoned for the 1,000 years, will be let loose at the end. And despite the glory of the King, and the beauty of the Kingdom, Satan will find rebels to side with him for one last attack against the people of God and the city of Jerusalem! God will destroy them all in an instant. Then will come the final judgment. All the unbelieving dead will be raised. The picture on the Chart is of *"The Great White Throne"* set in space. What a fearful judgment that will be, and what an awful sentence for all unbelievers: *"Cast into the Lake of Fire"*, the place that was prepared for the Devil and his fallen angels (Matthew chapter 25 verse 41 KJV).

The New Jerusalem

'And what then?' some will ask. Last of all we have a lovely description of the *"New Jerusalem"*, the *"Holy City"*. That will be a wonderful study when we get there. We will have to decide, is the city literal? And is it within the '1,000 year Kingdom' as well as in the 'Eternal State'? Those are hard questions too. Not everyone will agree on every detail, but we will see that the *"Holy City"* can have a place both in the *"Millennial Kingdom"* and on the new earth, in the 'Eternal State'. We will try and sort all of these details out [In **Chapters 21** & **23**] before we get to the end of our Studies.

The End ...

The most wonderful thing is, for those who are believers there is no 'End' to our blessing. The book of Revelation is not a storybook. It is not fiction with a 'happy ending'. We are often disappointed when we get to the last page and there is nothing more to read. But the last pages of the Bible will take us into *"Eternity"*, where God has always lived, before earth and earth-time began. Never ending, never changing, and best of all, never sinning. What an 'endless ending' that is going to be for the redeemed people of all ages.

> **KEYNOTE: The Seven Churches.** We will not deal with the detail of John's vision of and the letters to the 'Seven Churches in Asia' (Rev. 2-3). They refer to the period we are in today, 'the Church Age'. We will begin our more detailed study of John's visions at the point where he was taken up into heaven (Chp. 4:1-2). We will start there in the next Chapter. An excellent study of the 7 Churches and the Letter to each is found in: S. Jennings, *'Alpha and Omega'* (Belfast, NI: Ambassador, 1996), 41-166.

Questions and Answers for Chapter Seven – 'Symbols Explained'

Chp. 7 – 'Symbols Explained'

Q1. What do the two symbols which come at the beginning and end of the Chart mean?

Q2. What is the phrase (in Isaiah 61), which describes the time we are in now?

Q3. What is the phrase, in the same verse, which describes the judgment period?

Q4. What is the next event on God's programme?

Q5. How long is the whole of the Judgment Period?

Q6. What are the three sets of judgments pictured as?

Q7. Can you suggest any difference in time between the Seals and the Bowls?

Q8. How long is the Kingdom Age?

Q9. What do we call the last period, after the kingdom on this earth has finished?

Chapter Eight

The Sealed Scroll

In this study we are going to step with John (who was writing down all that he saw for our benefit) right into heaven! We won't look, just yet, at the detail of the *"Sealed Scroll"* being opened. We will keep that to the next Chapter. We must get ourselves 'adjusted', like John, to seeing heavenly things. And to seeing earthly things from the viewpoint of heaven. That is not easy. For even we who are saved are still 'earth dwellers'. We don't have heavenly bodies, yet. We don't fully have the mind of Christ, yet. And we struggle to see ourselves, and our degenerate world as God sees it. So, just as John took some time to adjust his mind to seeing *"heavenly things"* so we will too, even in our study of this book of Revelation.

Key Phrases in Revelation

We are going to look at what John saw whenever he was *"caught up"* and so we will look at Revelation chapter 4 verses 1 - 3. John begins this section with, *"After these things ..."* (one of the most important phrases in the book). Even though John saw it nearly 2,000 years ago as one set of visions, there is a period across the vision programme of at least 1,007 years of literal time, ALL of which is still in the future. John is moved in his visions forwards and backwards, along this timeline. We will see as we move through Revelation that John's visions were <u>not</u> all chronological in time. At certain points he was taken 'backwards' to review in greater detail things that he had already seen.

Some other very important phrases we should underline in the book are the words: *"I looked"*, *"I beheld"*, and *"I saw"* (In the original language they are all the same word). When you find them, underline them, for they highlight important details that John was often instructed to pay attention to. They occur, on average, twice in every chapter of the book.

> **KEYNOTE:** *"After these things".* This is a phrase that if you are reading in the book of Revelation you should <u>underline.</u> When we find this phrase repeated it indicates a 'shift in time'. It is a moving forward in the <u>chronology</u> of the timeline of the book. It is also worth noting or underlining everywhere in the text of Revelation where you find, *"I looked"*, *"I saw"* and, *"I beheld".* They are 'pointers' to KEY things that John was shown, and told to look out for, in his visions.

There was so much for John to take in, and so much to see that he didn't understand, it must have been very difficult. But understanding was not the most important thing. Getting it written down as he saw it was. That it might be recorded here for us, and even more importantly here for the tribulation saints, who will more fully understand the contents of this book, in a day that's not very far away, much more clearly than we can understand it today:

> **KEYNOTE: Thomas Newberry** in his 'Newberry Reference Bible' (NRB) uses older English pronouns, e.g. *"thou"* and *"thine"*, which are not in common usage today. But his translation is very accurate in many key places. Here, for example, he highlights the double *"after these things"* in one sentence, at this point in John's vision, which few other translations do (Rev. 4:1-2). Newberry Reference Bible (1886) Kregel Publications.

"After these things I looked, and behold, a door was opened (standing open) *in heaven: and the first voice which I heard as it were of a trumpet talking with me; which said, 'Come up hither, and I will show thee things which must be after these things. And immediately I became in Spirit, and, behold, a throne was set in heaven, and one sat on the throne ..."* (Revelation 4 verses 1 – 2 NRB). As we discovered in a previous study, there is a blessing for reading and studying prophecy, and John got that blessing too. He was in a prison on an island called Patmos, off the coast of Turkey today. He was a 'religious prisoner' (we read that in Revelation chapter 1), the year was about 95 AD, all the other Apostles had died, and John was left alone. Now he had been imprisoned for his faith, by an Emperor who persecuted Christians (most probably Domitian), and so we find John, at the beginning of the book, in prison and isolated. Yet it says he *"became in Spirit on the Lord's Day"* (Revelation chapter 1 verse 10 NRB). His circumstances did not deter him from having fellowship with his Lord and worshipping Him.

Here is another important phrase in the book, *"in the Spirit"*, or *"in Spirit"*. It indicates, not a time movement for John, but a location movement. So firstly, he is in the prison *"in Spirit"*. This is where he sees the first part of his vision (chapters 1 – 3). Then where we had our present reading, we see he was *"in Spirit ... in heaven"*. What a change! Just in a moment. In response to a voice, and a power that took him up, straight into God's heaven.

> **KEYNOTE:** *"in Spirit"*. We will find John in two more *"in Spirit"* positions later. **Chp. 17** 'The Scarlet Woman' & **Chp. 23** 'The New Jerusalem'.

John Called Up

Some of you will say, 'Is John being taken up a picture of the 'catching up' of the Church?' Yes, I think it is. Not perhaps a verse we would go to for the doctrine of the *'rapture'*, or as a 'proof-text' for its timing, but perhaps a picture, nonetheless. And probably quite significant in where it is placed in the order of the book of Revelation. *"After these things"*, as we have seen occurring twice here in one sentence, moves John on and up, not only from his position in the cell, but also from the position of the *"lampstands"* of testimony on earth that we are told about in Revelation chapters 2 and 3. John in his writings is often guided to say important things twice, close together, *"Verily, verily"* for example, or *"You must be born again"* (cf. John chapter 3 verses 3 & 7).

We can see John going up as a tiny picture of the Church saints going home to the *"Father's house"* before the Tribulation. Jesus promised, *"Because you have kept My word about patient endurance, I will keep you from the hour of trial that is coming on the whole world, to try those who dwell on the earth. I am coming soon ..."* (Revelation chapter 3 verses 10 – 11 ESV).

What John Saw

The first thing John sees is a throne, and one that is sitting on it. There is not a clear description given of the person on the throne, which is in keeping with how Jehovah is seen, even in visions in the Old Testament. Only the person of Jesus Christ will be visible to us, even in heaven. Jesus said, *"If you knew Me, you would know My Father also"* (John chapter 8 verse 19 ESV). All we ever need to know, or see, of God we will see in the person of Jesus in His glorified body. But still with visible wounds from His suffering. In just a few verses' time John will tell us he saw *"a slain Lamb standing"* (Revelation 5 verse 6 KJV).

The one thing that John could see clearly round about the throne was a *"rainbow"*. How wonderful. This takes us back in our minds to Genesis chapter 9, and the *"covenant"* promise God gave to Noah after the flood. God is a promise-keeper, and is it not beautiful that 1,000s of years after Noah saw the rainbow in our world for the first time, the first thing John sees around the throne of God in heaven is a rainbow? The heavenly purity of this miracle of light can never be tarnished up there.

'Well, John', you might ask, 'What did you see next?' John says, 'There were 24 elders, wearing crowns, and they fell down before the throne and they said', *"Thou art worthy, O Jehovah, to receive glory and honour, and power ..."* (chapter 4 verse 11 NRB). We should take note of the number of, and the increase in the content of, the songs or 'doxologies' in the Book of Revelation. There are more than we might expect! They begin in chapter 1, and they get longer as they go on. In most cases the number of people singing them increases as well. We are going to find that Revelation is much more than just a book of judgment. It is also a book of songs, of singing, and of *"Hallelujahs"* too!

> **KEYNOTE: Songs.** Here is something else to highlight or underline in your Bible (To go with the *"after these things"*, and the *"I saw"* etc.) Note the number of, and the developing content of, the *"songs"* in the book of Revelation. The first one is in Chp. 1:5b-6. There are many more ...

Who are the Elders?

Someone will ask, 'Who are the 24 elders?' The best answer is: We don't know, because we are not told. They may represent the Church in heaven as *"kings and priests unto God"* (Revelation chapter 1 verse 6 KJV). They are certainly representative of redeemed saints, for they are often connected with praise to the Lamb. Some think they are a picture of the

Old Testament saints, because the priests had twenty-four *"courses"* or divisions. Some think they represent the Old Testament saints (as the 12 tribes) and also the Church saints (as the 12 apostles) combined. We cannot be certain, but they are redeemed ones, who worship the Lamb and lead His praise. There is a difficulty with seeing the *"twenty four elders"* as a picture of the Church, because John himself was an *"apostle"* and part of the *"foundation"* of the Church. Clearly, he was not a part of what he was seeing in his own vision.

John next saw *"seven lamps of fire"* before the throne. Way back in the book of Isaiah chapter 11 we are told about seven different characteristics of the Spirit of God, so that helps with the description here, as being a representation of the Holy Spirit who will still be active in the world in the Judgment Period. We are not specifically told that He is *"indwelling"* believers, as He does in the Church Age, but the Holy Spirit did not 'permanently' indwell in the Old Testament. He 'remained' and empowered, but He sometimes left a person, if they turned away from God, as did King Saul.

> **KEYNOTE: Symbols.** Sometimes 'symbols' in prophecy are explained in their context, sometimes from various other places in the Bible, as most of the Revelation symbols are. But sometimes we will just have to wait to have all these things fully explained in a future time, and all of them finally when we get to heaven.

Four Living Creatures?

There were also around the throne *"four living ones"*. Some translations have *"beasts"* which creates a problem with our mental picture, especially as the False King, the *"Antichrist"*, and his *"False Prophet"*, are both described as *"Beasts"* throughout the later chapters of Revelation. The words in the original language are not the same. Here, in Revelation chapter 4, the Greek word 'zōon' means 'a living creature' (our word 'zoo' comes from the same root), whereas the word used later for the *"Dragon"* and his two *"Beasts"*, which is 'thērion', means 'a ferocious wild beast'.

When we go back to Ezekiel chapter 1 and Isaiah chapter 6 in the Old Testament, we see descriptions of four very strange created heavenly beings called *"Seraphim"*. They seem to be able to change their shape, they have four faces, and they can move in any direction without turning round! They seem to be a very special group within the angel family, and they are responsible for guarding the throne, and the glory of God. It is most likely that they are the *"four living ones"* here (Revelation chapter 4 verse 6 NRB).

Who Will Take the Scroll?

John tells us that the next thing he saw was a *"rolled book"*, a scroll, *"on the right hand"* of the one sitting on the throne (Revelation chapter 5 verses 1 – 4 NRB). John could see the closed scroll, and the attached seals, seven of them in all. John was able to count the seals, and probably see that there was a 'summary' of the contents written on the outside. Someone will ask, 'What was in the Scroll?' That is a good question. We are not told exactly.

The scroll is probably the 'title deeds' of creation, the proof of ownership, with penalties written in for false claims or for rebellion against the rightful owner.

> **KEYNOTE: Title Deeds.** What are the contents of the Sealed Scroll? Probably the 'title deeds' of all of the created universe. Look up a story back in Jeremiah chp. 32 in the O.T. and you will see there a good illustration of a legal 'scroll' being prepared as a 'title deed' to transfer ownership from one person to another.

John saw a *"strong angel proclaiming with a loud voice, 'Who is worthy to open the book, and to loose the seals thereof?'"* (Revelation chapter 5 verse 2 KJV). God waited and heaven waited. John says nobody came forward. A search was made but no one in heaven, on the earth, or under the earth was found who was able even to look at the scroll. 'What does this mean? Is there an angel who would dare to challenge God's authority?' (There was in the past.) 'Is there a man, who thinks he has the right?' (There was one who had delegated authority in the past, he lost his position too.) 'Is there a fallen angel, a demon, who thinks he might dare?' No. Not even Satan with all his pride dare come close to God's glory, or even look on the scroll. John says, *'I began to weep'* (Revelation chapter 5 verse 4 ESV). He thought that there was going to be a problem, the purposes of God might be spoiled by all the rebellion and sin of the past, in heaven and in our world. No one would be *"found worthy"*.

The Lion and the Lamb

One of the elders said to John, *"Weep not: Behold, The Lion which is of the tribe of Judah, the Root of David, hath overcome to open the roll, and to loose the seven seals thereof"* (Revelation 5 verse 5 NRB). These are strange titles! But again, Old Testament pictures help us in our understanding. The *"Lion of Judah"* goes way back to a picture Jacob used in describing one who would come from Judah's family (Genesis chapter 49). The *"Root of David"* title comes from the covenant promise God gave to David, that his son would sit upon his throne forever (2 Samuel chapter 7). The one who was born in Bethlehem, who died on Calvary, who rose the third day, who ascended back to heaven forty days later: HE is the Overcomer. He has prevailed. He has overcome every obstacle, He has paid redemption (the buy-back price), and He is worthy to take the scroll and to open the seven seals.

John turned to see the Lion, but what a surprise: John tells us, 'I saw a standing Lamb with the wounds of His death upon Him'. The Lamb who was slain, of whom the other prophet John the Baptist said, *"Behold, the Lamb of God, who takes away the sin of the world"* (John chapter 1 verse 29 NASB). He, the risen Lamb, came and took the scroll. And the *"four living creatures and the twenty-four elders fell down before the Lamb ... and they sang a new song, saying; ... Worthy is the Lamb who was slain, to receive power and wealth and wisdom and might and honour and glory and blessing!"* (Revelation chapter 5 verses 8 – 14 ESV). What a wonderful song - in which the angels now join - and what a wonderful prospect to be part of that choir forever!

The Lamb is now in control, the Scroll is in His hand. The Seals are about to be opened, one by one. The judgment of God on the rebellion of Satan and sinners is about to begin. On earth – at first – this will hardly be noticed. In fact, it will seem at first to be a time of peace and less war. But things where the Devil is concerned are very deceptive, and God's time for judgment to begin has commenced. The gap in Isaiah's prophecy, after at least 2,700 years from when it was given, will finally be closing. The *"Acceptable year of the Lord"* will then be over. The *"Day of vengeance of our God"* will have arrived. The first seal is about to be broken. God's programme of judgment will be moving towards the *"Day of His wrath"* (Revelation 6 verse 16 – 17 KJV).

How wonderful to be sure of our salvation, the impossibility of being deceived by the Dragon, never to come under the judgment of God, and the full assurance of our names written in another scroll, which we will discover further on in the Book of Revelation; *"The Book of Life of the Lamb"* (Revelation chapter 13 verse 8).

> **KEYNOTE: Days of Persecution?** Although things may get much worse in the very near future, though days of persecution may come in parts of the world where persecution has not been seen for 100s of years … Though many of our comforts and liberties (in western societies) may soon be lost, for we are not promised to escape *"persecution"*, yet we are promised to be kept from the *"wrath which is coming here"* (1 Thess. 1:10 NRB). The true Church cannot be under the *"wrath of the Lamb"*.

Questions and Answers for Chapter Eight – *'The Sealed Scroll'*

Chp. 8 – 'The Sealed Scroll'

Q1. Where was John when we are introduced to him first?

Q2. Why was he there?

Q3. What did John see first in Chapter 4?

Q4. What did John see round the throne?

Q5. Who do you think are the 'Four living ones'?

Q6. What was the challenge of the strong angel?

Q7. Why did the challenge go out in heaven, earth, and under the earth?

Q8. Who took the Scroll?
[More than one name was mentioned.]

Q9. Why is the Lamb worthy?

JOTTINGS

Chapter Nine

The Four Horsemen

 This study has been called: 'The Four Horsemen', rather than the 'Sealed Scroll Opened', because they are one of the best-known sets of symbols of the book of Revelation. We have already learned that they should not really be called 'The Four Horsemen of the Apocalypse', because that phrase is not a Bible one, though it does make some sense as we shall see. The true meaning of the *'apocalypse'* word is 'unveiling'. It is applied to the *"Man of Sin"*, and the *"Lawless One"* (probably two different men), three times over in 2 Thessalonians chapter 2. The *'apocalypse'* word is also used, for the last time, of the person of Jesus Christ right in the first sentence of the book of Revelation, as we have seen (Revelation chapter 1 verses 1 – 2).

We have noted that *"the Prince that shall come"*, as Daniel called him, will appear first as a peacemaker who will *"confirm a covenant"* with the Jews, possibly that is the first part of his 'unveiling'. We will see, as we continue with our studies, that his role as a 'peacemaker' is not his real ambition. He will not desire peace. He will desire ultimate power. His true 'unveiling' will come later in his career, and further on in the book of Revelation, but we haven't got to that part just yet ...

We are going to look specifically at the opening of the Seals on the Scroll and see what happens when they are broken open by Jesus who is the *"Lamb"* of John's visions. We saw the scene being set in heaven in our previous study. We saw John getting adjusted to being *"in spirit"* (most probably outside the limitations of his earthly body). He was also outside the limits of earth time, able by the Spirit of God to be moved forwards (and backwards) and to see things in heaven from when and where God wanted him to.

The Lamb in Control

We will see now that it is *"the Lamb"* who will take the book. The time has come for the seals to be opened. God's authority has been rebelled against at every level, by Satan and his angels in the heavens, by mankind down here in our world, by the very demons, some of whom are *"under the earth"*. Every part of creation has been affected by this rebellion, *"For we know that the whole creation has been groaning together in the pains of childbirth until now."* (Romans chapter 8 verse 22 ESV), and all that rebellion must be judged, before the problems can be corrected and restoration begins.

KEYNOTE: Daniel's Timeline. On the subject of Daniel's 'timeline' of 490 years, is it a literal time frame? When did it commence? How much of that period has already been fulfilled? How much is still future? Those questions are looked at in more detail also in **Appx. I**.

We have suggested (though we cannot be totally sure) that: the *"Day of the Lord"* (the beginning of the judgment programme), the *"confirming of a covenant"* (Daniel chapter 9 verse 27), and the opening of the first seal in heaven (Revelation chapter 6 verse 1), will all happen at the same time on God's calendar. That is, they may all be 'concurrent' events but controlled from heaven.

Men on earth will not understand any of these things, at that point. They will not know that God's judgment programme has commenced. They will not know anything about a sealed scroll being opened in the throne room of heaven. And they will not know that the *"Prince"* who makes his appearance on the media of this world is an imposter, and controlled by the *"Dragon"*. They will come to know this much later, and men will also know later that the judgments are part of the *"Day of the ... wrath of the Lamb"*, but they will not repent of their rebellion, not even then (Revelation chapter 6 verse 16 and chapter 9 verse 21).

John says, *"I watched when the Lamb opened one of the seven seals, and I heard one of the four living creatures saying with a voice like thunder, 'Come!' And I looked, and behold, a white horse! And its rider had a bow; and a (victor's) crown was given to him, and he came out conquering, and to conquer."* (Revelation chapter 6 verses 1 – 2 ESV).

Three Sets of Judgments

We are about to commence in our studies looking at the first of these three sets of seven judgments. We have seen already that there will be:

> **1.) Seven Seals Broken.**
> **2.) Seven Trumpets Blown.**
> **3.) Seven Bowls Poured out**.

These judgments are not a repetition of the same events. Nor do they all happen at the same time. They are not a 7 + 7 + 7 in a row either, like 21 unconnected judgments. The link between them, as to timing, is not easy to work out. We will explain more of that as we go forward. Perhaps we should say here that the 'Seal Judgments' begin at the beginning of the seven years, they are concentrated mostly in the first three and a half years, but they do stretch out to conclude at the very end of the seven year period as well.

The 'Trumpet Judgments' commence later than the 'Seal Judgments'. They probably begin around the middle of the seven-year period, but they also stretch right to the end. The 'Bowl Judgments' are concentrated towards the end of the second half of the seven years, and they are very much the concluding, 'climactic' judgments. The technical word in relation to the end of the three sets of judgments is 'coterminous'. Like railway lines coming into a marshalling yard, they all end up in the <u>same place</u> and at the <u>same time</u>. And of course, the

END will be a place, as well as a point in time. This place is called in Hebrew *"Armageddon"* (Revelation chapter 16 verse 16), but we will not get there for some time yet …

Something else we should put emphasis on is that the seven-year period, the last

KEYNOTE: Prophetic Year. When we compare these numbers of: Years, Months, & Days, we can calculate that a prophetic year has 360 days, not 365.24 as our present calendar. That is important in Revelation, and also very important when we will look at Daniel's 'timeline' in **Appx. I**.

or 70th *"week of years"* of Daniel's prophecy, is <u>divided absolutely in the centre</u>. We have seen how prophecies can divide, and although here there is no time gap in the centre there is a split exactly down the middle; 1,260 days, which is 42 months, or three and a half years each on either side of the division.

The Seal Judgments Commence

We have been connecting the three sets of judgments together in order that we get an 'overview' of their relationship. That is necessary, but some will be asking, 'What about the four horsemen? Where do they fit into all this?' When we come back to the start of the 'Seal Judgments' in our passage, we see straight away there is a great contrast which we should examine closely.

Here we see a rider on a white horse, and in Revelation chapter 19 verse 11, there is also a rider on a white horse. Just as in chapter 4 verse 1 – 2 there was "a *door open in heaven*", and in chapter 19 verse 11, there is *"heaven open"*. Someone might ask, 'Are these pictures connected?' The answer is: 'Yes. But they are not the same!' We have already seen that some people get the interpretation of the symbols of Revelation mixed up, and some even think (just because the horse here is white) that the rider must be Jesus in both cases. That is not so, as we have already seen.

KEYNOTE: Context. That brings in another important point in the study of prophecy, in fact in the study of all scripture: The idea of '<u>context</u>'. We should never look at a word by itself, or even a verse, or a paragraph by itself. We should 'pull back' and look at the wider focus of what the writer is 'getting at' and compare with other relevant Bible passages too.

If we have got our interpretation correct in relation to any passage of scripture in its own 'context' (without being dogmatic, for we cannot be sure of every picture in prophecy), then all other pictures and passages will fit together as well. We sometimes call that a 'helicopter view', or maybe nowadays a 'drone view' would provide a better mental picture!

We can see a connection between the two white horses and their riders. One is the 'counterfeit Messiah', the *"False Christ"*; the other is Jesus, the *"King of kings and Lord of lords"*. We will see how much the Devil will be allowed to <u>counterfeit</u> as we go through this book. Satan has never been the originator of anything, except for his original sin. Since then (for he has a great knowledge of God's programme, though not the timing) Satan has been counterfeiting many of the truths of God's Word and when his *"restraint"* is removed, he will counterfeit even more!

Are the Horses Literal?

Someone will no doubt be asking, 'Are they literal horses?' That is a good question. Distinguishing between the 'symbolic' and 'literal' in prophecy is not easy. We may not be sure about the actuality of the four different coloured horses here (we are coming to the others just now), but it is possible this first one is real. The rider is a real person: Since he is the *"Coming Prince"*, why should he not have a coronation ceremony? The British Monarchy have many horses and carriages and they often, in what we call 'pageantry', ride in procession through the streets of the city of London.

When Jesus came formally into Jerusalem the first time, at His public presentation, He was riding on a *"colt"* (the foal of a donkey and a horse). He was not a crowned King but that was a very literal procession, and a literal fulfilment of prophecy too (Zechariah chapter 9 verse 9; Matthew chapter 21 verses 1 – 11). When Jesus rides into Jerusalem again, as *"King of kings"*, at the beginning of His '1,000 year Kingdom', it may be that He will be on a literal *"white horse"* as well (Psalm 24 verses 7 – 10; Revelation chapter 19 verse 11).

> **KEYNOTE: Literalist Interpretation.** As we have said before, things which look symbolic from far away often become very literal when seen close up, at the very point in time of their fulfilment. We will say more about 'context', 'literality' and other principles of interpretation in **Appx. II.**

The White Horse

It appears, to continue with the contrasts, that this man on the first horse is an imposter. He is not identified as such at his first appearing on the 'stage of the world'. Perhaps he will not even be recognised in advance for who he is: Remember that the one *"Coming in Power"* (in Revelation chapter 19) has many names. His identity can never be mistaken. He is the *"King of kings"*. But the rider on the first white horse (in Revelation chapter 6) has no name.

Perhaps some have imagined that the *"Antichrist"* will appear as a wicked man, a dictator, a warlord, a terrible person? A 'Genghis Khan', a 'Hitler' or a 'Pol Pot'? He will be all of that and more for sure, but he will appear firstly as a 'peacemaker', a charismatic figure with solutions to many of the world's greatest problems. Telling huge lies but making them sound like great solutions! (Daniel chapter 7 verses 8 & 25.)

White is not only the colour of peace, but it is also the colour of surrender. You remember war stories where the white flag being raised meant, 'No shooting anymore: we are surrendering'. This coming King doesn't have to make war, for other kings will give their power and authority to him. He will get *"a victor's crown"* without fighting. He has a bow, but does not seem to need arrows, he conquers without bloodshed. At least, not just at the start …

When he appears at the beginning he will say, 'Let me prove my power to make peace: Where is the least peaceful place in the world?' We might say, 'The Middle East, among Israel and her Arab neighbours'. Imagine a treaty with all of Israel's enemies, for seven years, and all weapons put to the side? Imagine peace between Israel and the Arab nations, between Judaism and Islam? Peace for the Jews to worship on Temple Mount; to have a Sanctuary and sacrificial ceremonies once again. This man will be given as much power as he desires. But it will be a short-lived peace indeed. (We already know that from Daniel chapter 9.) The peace will be broken, deliberately, in the very middle of the seven years!

> **KEYNOTE: The 'Coming Prince'.** He will not display his true character, as the *"Man of Sin"*, until the centre point of the seven year period has arrived. That is the moment when Satan will be permitted to go 'full throttle' with his deception of humanity through his two Leaders. The 3 ½ years, the 42 months, and the 1,260 days are all counted off for us later, in context, showing the exact length of the latter part of the period.

The Red Horse

Let us continue with the other horses in the order in which John saw them called out … Again, on the second horse its rider is indistinct and has no name. But this picture is not so hard to explain. The symbol really explains itself. The white horse has given way to a red one, and the bow (without arrows) changes to *"a great sword"*. Power from God is given to the rider to take away peace and allow war to begin again. This will be well before the halfway point of the seven years has arrived. The peace that was promoted by the *"Prince"* himself will be broken, and most likely deliberately so, perhaps by himself as well.

War, worse than ever, will return especially in other regions of the world around Israel. And true peace of any kind will be gone, until the real *"Prince of Peace"* (Isaiah chapter 9 verse 6) comes, to bring war to an end and to bring in a lasting peace for 1,000 years.

The Black Horse

The third horse, again with a shadowy un-named rider, is very different. Not white, nor red, but this time black. And neither a bow, nor a sword (both of which are war weapons), but, strangely enough, carrying a pair of 'weighing scales', the old-fashioned kind with weights on one side and grain or vegetables on the other. Some will ask, 'Is this a famine picture, following war?' That may be so, but it also may be a rationing picture. It does not have to be scarcity

KEYNOTE: Rationing. Starvation does not have to come because of famine. It can be artificially induced, by control mechanisms. Rationing by various 'statist' means. The poor can be kept at starvation levels, and the rich can still have their luxuries. This would fit with another picture we will come to later in our studies, in connection with the *"666"* subject in **Chp. 15**.

only from famine. But in our passage here it says, *"Three measures of barley for a denarius ... and hurt not the oil and the wine."* (Revelation chapter 6 verse 6 NRB).

Three measures of barley would have made a loaf of coarse bread to feed a family in John's time for a day, and a Roman *"denarius"* was a labourer's wage for a day. So, there will be nothing left over! No other food stuff, no rent money nor anything else. Just 'bread and water' for a full day's work. Starvation levels among the manual labourers, yet the *"oil and wine"* are not rationed; the rich can have their table full of luxuries, even in the artificial famine times. Global war will also probably affect the food production levels, but what is available will be kept for the elite. Those who are 'connected' to the upper circles, and the rulers associated with the supreme leader. Marked out as his supporters. That is nothing new from a historical perspective and may not be far off in the future, even in this generation.

The Fourth Horse is the Worst

The fourth and last horse is different again. Most modern translations call it a *"pale horse"*, but Tyndale's translation (the first one from Greek to English, back in 1525 AD) called it a *"green horse"*. This is closer to the true meaning. The original word translates to English as '*cholera*', an old disease which used to follow war, displaced persons in refugee camps, and poor sanitation. Here the rider has a name; he is called *"Death"*, and *"Hades"* follows him. He is given authority to kill; with war, hunger, death from disease, and from the wild beasts. Not necessarily the 'Big Five' of Africa. There are the 'little five' as they are known: mosquitoes, tsetse flies, house flies, ticks etc. The passage says *"a fourth part of the earth"* will be killed. This will be a massive loss of life and the centre point of the seven years, which brings the worst part of the judgment, has not even been reached yet ...

KEYNOTE: Death Toll. This initial death toll is (at today's figures), approximately 2,000,000,000 people or 2 billion out of 7.8 billion. Though we don't know what the world population will be at the timing of the *"fourth seal"*. The *"rapture"* event will already have removed millions. And there may be a significant war <u>before</u> the *"Prince"* comes to power and brokers the Middle East Peace Covenant. Perhaps major war will come again in our time in the Middle East, or even the Far East?

Seal Five – From the Midpoint to the End

When the Lamb opens the fifth seal, John sees the souls of those who had been slain for the Word of God. Martyrs of the first half of the seven years, for not only has peace broken down but religious tolerance has too. These are not Church age saints we can tell, for they are crying for vengeance: *"O Sovereign Lord, holy and true, how long before You will judge and avenge our blood on those who dwell on the earth?"* (Revelation chapter 6 verse 10 ESV.)

They are told that they should wait a little while until *"their brothers should ... be killed"* (chapter 6 verses 9 – 11 ESV). This refers to the many more who will be martyred for the testimony of Jesus in the second half of the seven years; the *"Great Tribulation"*. Jeremiah called it: *"The time of Jacob's Trouble"*, for the Jews will once again be targeted for world-wide slaughter (Jeremiah 30 verse 7).

Seal Six

When we come to the sixth seal, we are moving into the latter stages of the tribulation period. Heaven is disturbed, mountains and islands are moved, the sun and moon are blackened, and there is a great earthquake. The kings, and mighty men; those who were friends with the False Prince, those who weren't affected by the food shortages. Those who survived war because they did not go to fight. Those who claimed to be 'atheist' and said there is no God: Now they are calling on the rocks to fall on them *"and hide us from the face of Him who is seated on the throne, and from the wrath of the Lamb."* (Revelation chapter 6 verses 15 – 17 ESV).

One of the amazing and sobering things about the judgment period is this: People will not repent, many will openly worship the Dragon, but <u>all</u> will acknowledge the existence of the God they formerly denied, and that the one who is in control of the *"wrath"* being poured out is the *"Lamb"* who was rejected and slain, at His first coming.

Seal Seven

The seventh seal is not opened until the beginning of Revelation chapter 8, and when it is opened, all of heaven observes silence for half an hour. Before that silence is observed John will be shown a very special company of people. We noted before that John has gone 'outside' of time as we know it, and can be moved forwards and backwards in his viewpoints. Having come to the end of the Seals, and having had a little glimpse of the end of the Tribulation, now John is going to be taken back, to a time just before the judgments commence. To see a different kind of *"Seal"* altogether; and one that the Devil will also counterfeit later in the seven-year period.

> **KEYNOTE: 144,000.** Before we look at the last 'Seal Judgment', and the '7 Trumpet Judgments' which follow (which will be our study in **Chp. 11**), we will take a short look at something very interesting in Revelation chapter 7. A *"Sealed Company"*. That will be our study in **Chp. 10**. It will also introduce us to the concept of a *'parenthesis'* in the narrative. A '<u>gap</u>' in the story (with additional detail), but in most cases, for John, a time difference as well.

Questions and Answers for Chapter Nine – *'The Four Horsemen'*

Chp. 9 – 'The Four Horsemen'

Q1. Can you note down the colour of the horses, and in the right order?

Q2. How many Seals are opened in total?

Q3. Why is the first horse white?

Q4. Why are the 2nd, 3rd and 4th horses different in colour from the first?

Q5. What do the 'balances' represent?

Q6. What percentage of people will be killed by the wars and famines etc.? Or how many?

Q7. Who are the 'souls' seen at the opening of the fifth seal?

Q8. What are the kings and great men hiding from?

Q9. What happens at the 7th Seal?

Chapter Ten
The Sealed Company

We have seen that the *"seventh seal"* does not get mentioned until Revelation chapter 8 verse 1. Not only are the 'Trumpet Judgments' linked with it, but there is also a gap in the narrative between the descriptions of the sixth and seventh seals. This is interesting, as there are several 'gaps' in the flow of the book of Revelation. A break in the story (to put something in that is additional to the narrative) is called a *'parenthesis'*. It is common in writing, and the Holy Spirit uses it to show John additional detail, that is not in the main flow of the visions.

When we compare the three sets of judgments, we can see there is a 'parenthetic gap' between the sixth and seventh seal (in Revelation chapter 7), a break between the descriptions of the sixth and seventh trumpet (chapter 10 verse 1 through to chapter

> **KEYNOTE: Demonic Imagery.** We have learned that Satan is a master of counterfeiting. He does not produce anything original (except for his original sin). He only copies things which God has already done or has planned to do, and which he already knows about. Satanic imagery often <u>inverts</u> or <u>reverses</u> biblical symbols as well. That is something young Christians should be very careful of. Such imagery can be 'interwoven' into jewellery etc., without the wearer being aware. And very much so in 'body-art' or 'inking', which all true followers of Jesus should avoid.

11 verse 14), and a very short break between the sixth and seventh bowl (in chapter 16 verses 15 – 16). In fact, in quite a few translations, these two verses in chapter 16 are put inside brackets to show that they are a short parenthesis. The contents of the 'gaps' in the narrative between the sixth and seventh seal, and the sixth and seventh trumpet are linked. Both sections (chapters 7 and chapters 10 – 11) deal with Jewish witnesses, with the emphasis being on the first half of the seven-year period. The two very special *"witnesses"* we will look at in the narrative 'gap' between the sixth and seven trumpet judgments.

A Marked Out Company

We will look at the first group of 'witnesses' in a little more detail now, for they are very interesting. We are aware in our world that the 'actual' must come before the 'copy'. The $50 bill must be examined and handled before a 'good copy' or counterfeit can be made. Not the real thing, but close enough that we can be deceived, and only a close comparison of the genuine and the fake will show the difference! Satan works like that. He knows God's purposes, even some of the things that have not taken place yet (but not the timing). Things that God has not revealed to us fully.

Satan has greater understanding than we do, and sometimes God allows him to produce the 'counterfeit' even before God unveils the real thing. This will happen on several occasions during the Tribulation period.

A Counterfeit Christ

We know Satan will have a 'False Messiah', an *"Antichrist"*: Who himself will have a counterfeit death and resurrection. We know he will have a *"False Prophet"*, a counterfeit Holy Spirit. Satan himself, *"the Dragon"*, will be worshipped as a counterfeit god. He will also have a false system of worship, a false kingdom, a false capital city and, as we shall see, a false *"mark"* to identify and unite all his followers. These will not be new ideas. They are counterfeit, a reversal, a turning upside down of things God has already done.

Back in the prophecy of Ezekiel (who like Daniel and John was a prophet who had visions), he saw in one of his visions a man with a *"writer's inkhorn"* marking people in Jerusalem. God was marking them for preservation. They were true worshippers of Jehovah, and they were marked so that they would not be killed by the invaders (Ezekiel chapter 9 verses 1 – 11 KJV). The Devil will copy that in a future time, but he will invert the picture. He will mark people, whom God will then judge (Revelation chapter 14 verses 9 – 11). Here in our gap-story we can see another 'sealing'. Not seals of judgment, nor the *"mark of the beast"*, but a mark from God, upon a very interesting group of people whom He will preserve from Satan's hatred, right through the seven-year judgment period until the end, and allow them to enter alive into the Millennial Kingdom.

John says that he saw, *"four angels standing on the four corners of the earth, holding the four winds of the earth, that the wind should not blow … and another angel … having the seal of the living God: and he cried … to the four angels … saying, 'Hurt not the earth, neither the sea, nor the trees, till we have sealed the servants of our God in their foreheads.'"* (Revelation chapter 7 verses 1 – 3 KJV). A very strange picture indeed! The *"winds"* are often linked to God's judgment, the *"earth, sea and trees"* will all be affected by both the trumpet and bowl judgments later. God is holding the judgment back for a reason. He has a very special company to mark out first.

Who are the 144,000?

'Is the Church not already in heaven?' you might ask. At this point the answer is most likely: 'Yes!' John seems to be going back in time here, probably to near the beginning of the seven-year period. Just as later in the chapter he is moved forward again where it says, *"after these things …"* (Revelation 7 verse 9 NRB). John says, *"I heard the number of them which were sealed: a 144,000 of all the tribes of the children of Israel."* (chapter 7 verse 4 – 8 KJV).

> **The sealed company are Jews: Not just any Jews, but 12,000 from each tribe.'**

The sealed company are Jews: Not just any Jews, but 12,000 from each tribe. We will have to pause and take a closer look at what is going on here! The Devil hates the Jews*. We know that. History has taught us that Jews are hated, despised, persecuted, and condemned. On the one hand, Jehovah must chastise them for rejecting their Messiah. They do not believe He has already come the first time, and they said back then, *"His blood be on us, and on our children."* (Matthew chapter 27 verse 25 KJV). How terribly that statement has come true! On the other hand, Satan continues to persecute them because he hates the fact that Abraham's children survived to produce the *"seed of the woman"*, who was promised in Eden. That was the *"Messiah"*, who at His Second Coming will bring about Satan's final downfall.

> ***KEYNOTE: 'Anti-Semitism'.** A term which sadly we hear increasingly today is 'Anti-Semitism'. This is a 'negative' term, and normally describes opposition to Jews or Jewish political identity. It is taken from the name of Noah's son Shem, who was the ancestor of Abraham. The word *"Hebrew"* is linked with Abraham (Genesis 14:13), it means 'one who is not from here'. The name *"Israel"* is linked with Jacob (Genesis 32:28), *"Prince with God"*. The word *"Jews"* is linked with Judah. All the significant names for the Jewish people have early O.T. roots.

During tribulation times, days that are called prophetically the *"time of Jacob's trouble"* (Jeremiah chapter 30 verse 7 KJV), Satan will try to wipe out the Jews if he can. If he could destroy even one tribe, then the promises of God to Abraham, Isaac, and Jacob would be damaged. He would do it if he could. But he can't! Here is why. God will *"seal"* a fixed number from each tribe, before the time of *"great tribulation"* begins. They may even be the earliest 'evangelists', the gospel preachers of this persecution period. Even during the false peace at the start of the seven years of the *"covenant"* period, they may proclaim the true identity of the 'Imposter Prince' and preach the gospel of the *"Coming King"*. We are not sure if that is their purpose, but they are linked with a huge number of saved people whom we will view later in this same chapter of Revelation.

The Twelve Tribes as Listed

When we look at the list of the tribes of Israel, we can see there a few unusual details. Right away someone will say, 'Judah wasn't firstborn, why is he before Reuben?' Someone else may ask, 'Where is Dan?' And someone else may even ask, 'Why is there a tribe of Joseph. He isn't usually listed as a tribe?' Those are all very good questions. Perhaps we should check out the birth order of the *"tribes"*, or the *"sons of Jacob"* as they were called back then, for they are very seldom listed in the order in which they were born. We know that Jacob married Leah and Rachel, and he had two *"maids"* who were not his wives but were his wives' servants. From them he had twelve sons, and daughters too.

The family progression went like this: Leah had Reuben first, then Simeon, Levi, and Judah. Rachel was upset that she wasn't having sons, so she gave her maid Bilhah to Jacob, who had Dan and Naphtali. Leah copied Rachel with her maid, Zilpah, who had Gad and Asher. Leah had another son called Issachar, then Zebulun, and a daughter Dinah. Last of all Rachel had Joseph, and a few years later Benjamin. Twelve sons and at least one daughter. Reuben (in those days) should have been family head and got twice the inheritance of his brothers. He should also have been family 'priest', as the firstborn was back then. He lost all of these *"blessings"* because of moral sin. Jacob made Joseph the family priest (Genesis chapter 37), Judah became the family head (Genesis chapter 49), and in Genesis chapter 48, Joseph's sons, Ephraim and Manasseh, got the 'double portion' of land inheritance.

This explains why, in the possession of the Land of Canaan, there was no tribe of Joseph; Ephraim and Manasseh were both there as 'adopted' sons of Jacob. Levi, whom Jehovah made the priestly tribe (Numbers chapter 3 verse 11), had no land possession either. The Levites were provided for from their portion of all that was brought to the Tabernacle, and later on to the Temple.

When we come back to our passage, we can see that we have now answered a question or two, but perhaps raised a few more. We can see why Judah is first. His is the Kingly tribe, prophesied as such by Israel (Genesis chapter 49 verses 8 – 12), from whom David and Messiah came. Levi appears as well, for this is not about possession in the Land, this is preservation in the Tribulation. 'But', someone will be asking, 'Why no Dan?' and for that matter, 'Why a Joseph but not an Ephraim?' Those are difficult questions!

> **KEYNOTE: Jewish Identity.** Today most of the people of Israel, and Jews worldwide, do not know their true tribal identity. Many of the records have been lost (except for a few whose family background was Levitical). Some Jews have been absorbed into Gentile families, and some even covered their Semitic background by changing their names; yet God knows the true tribal roots of every Jew alive, and the tribes will <u>all</u> have a marked-out possession in the Land, from Dan down to Gad, in the Kingdom Age (Ezekiel 48). See *'Israel in the Kingdom'* Map **Chp. 21**.

Again, Joseph doesn't have a personal tribal possession in the Millennial Kingdom (Ezekiel chapter 48), but he is listed here. The reason for the omission of Dan and Ephraim is harder to pin down. However, Dan and Ephraim were both linked with, and leaders of, idolatry in the nation (Judges chapter 17; 1 Kings chapter 12). Israel (Jacob's spiritual name) said some very strange things about Dan in his *"latter days"* prophecy just before he died (Genesis chapter 49 verses 16 – 17). He links him with the *"serpent"* and the *"adder"*, and Dan appears to attack his own brothers by deceitful means. Is it possible if the *"False Prophet"* is a Jew (as we shall consider later), that perhaps he comes from the tribe of Dan? There are twelve tribes sealed here (there are usually twelve mentioned), but God Himself knows why Dan and Ephraim are not among the marked-out number.

The 144,000 Plus

John says, *"after these things"*, the phrase which again indicates a time-shift, *"I beheld, and, lo, a great multitude, which no man could number, out of all nations, and kindreds, and people, and tongues, stood before the throne and before the Lamb, clothed with white robes ... and cried with a loud voice, saying, 'Salvation to our God which sitteth upon the throne, and unto the Lamb.'"* (Revelation chapter 7 verses 9 – 10 NRB).

One of the elders asked John, *"Who are these?"* John doesn't know. We could guess wrongly too. A great multitude which no man could count: Are they Old Testament saints in heaven? Are they Church saints in heaven? Neither of these, John is told. They are the *"Great Tribulation"* saints (not necessarily all martyrs). All their persecution, hiding on the run, and suffering hardship passed. Safe in God's presence forever, after the tribulation time has ended.

Is it not an amazing thought, as we recommence our journey further into the judgment period, to the blowing of the trumpets and the pouring out of the bowls, to the persecution of Christians and the compulsory worship of the Beast, that millions will be saved in such a short and terrible time?

Satan can never triumph. Even when he seems to be in control, God will still prevail. From every age that there has ever been, until the end of the Kingdom Age itself; the Coming Messiah, the rejected Saviour, the Slain Lamb, the King of kings, will have His true followers, in numbers only God Himself can count.

What a blessing to be also part of that company, those whom, *"the Lamb which is in the midst of the throne shall feed ... and shall lead ... unto living fountains of waters"* (Revelation 7 verse 14 – 17 KJV). Not only into the 1,000 year Kingdom Age. But forever ...

Q&A >

Questions and Answers for Chapter Ten – 'The Sealed Company'

Chp. 10 – 'The Sealed Company'

Q1. Why were the four angels holding back the four winds?

Q2. How many Jews are sealed in total?

Q3. Why does God seal them before the Tribulation?

Q4. Why does Satan hate the Jewish people?

Q5. Why is the tribe of Judah put first?

Q6. Why do you think there is no tribe of Dan?

Q7. Why is Joseph listed as a tribe?

Q8. Who are the multitude before the throne?

Q9. What do we have in common with this Company of people?

Chapter Eleven

The Trumpet Judgments

When we were studying the Seal Judgments, we saw three things of note towards the end: Firstly, that there is a 'gap' between John's vision of seal six and seven (just as there will be between the sixth and seventh trumpet, and as there will be between the sixth and seventh bowl also). Secondly, there is something different, but interesting, happening in the gap each time.

KEYNOTE: Time Periods. It is probable that this is a literal time period, as many of the specific times in the book of Revelation are. When 'quantities' are added to days, months or years (like *"42 months"*) they generally become literal time periods in scripture and in prophecy. An *"hour"* is a short period of time. A *"day"* is relatively longer, but still unspecified. A *"year"* is longer still. But when a 'denominator' is attached, the figures become literal time periods.

Thirdly, the seventh seal leads into the Seven Trumpet Judgments. Before the trumpets are sounded John writes, *"there was silence in heaven for about half an hour"* (Revelation chapter 8 verse 1 ESV).

Thirty minutes is a long time to be still and silent! There used to be, in some countries, a 'one minute silence' to commemorate the end of the First World War, at the eleventh hour, of the eleventh day, of the eleventh month. (It seemed a very long time to a small school child, to stand at his desk for 60 seconds!) 'Why half an hour of silence?' you might ask. Possibly because the angels and the redeemed saints, all of those in heaven, have a sense of awareness of how awful the final part of the *"Tribulation"* judgment, which is just about to begin, will be.

The Censer Angel

John saw the seven angels with their seven trumpets, ready to sound, but before they do so, he sees another strange sight: *"Another angel came and stood at the altar with a golden censer, and he was given much incense to offer with the prayers of all the saints on the golden altar before the throne … Then the angel took the censer and filled it with fire from the altar and threw it on the earth, and there were peals of thunder, rumblings, flashes of lightning, and an earthquake. Now the seven angels who had the seven trumpets prepared to blow them."* (Revelation chapter 8 verses 1 – 6 ESV.)

What does this picture represent? It relates to prayers, which are often linked to *"incense"* in the Bible. Remember that in the middle of the seal judgments (in Revelation chapter 6),

> ❛ *Even unbelievers will acknowledge that the Lamb on the throne is in control.* ❜

there were the prayers of the martyrs, who said *"How long, O Lord?"* They were waiting for vengeance from God on their enemies. Now the vengeance of God is about to be shown; the censer (a container which held coals and incense, and could be carried in a priest's hand, on a chain) being cast down is a picture of God's wrath on the enemies and persecutors of His people. Their time of judgment, while still on earth, has come.

The Seven Trumpet Angels

We are coming now to angel 'messengers' who will be blowing trumpets. This is a military picture. There is a greater awareness from mankind down here and a closer link between what is happening in the courts of heaven and what is happening on the environment of our earth. Men will now realise, and admit, that these are not 'climate change' disasters, nor 'global warming' events. They are divinely-controlled judgments. There is an increasingly obvious link, as the judgments progress, between what is happening in heaven and what is happening on earth. Even unbelievers will acknowledge that the Lamb on the throne is in control. The *"day of His wrath has come"*.

Trumpet One Sounds

The first angel blows his trumpet, and there is the judgment of the 'burning storm'. Hail, fire mixed with blood are poured out on the ground. You might say, 'It sounds like the plagues in Egypt way back there in Exodus chapters 7 to 12?' Indeed, it does! Many of these judgments of God are magnified versions of the judgments on the nation of Egypt long ago. They had persecuted Jehovah's people for up to 400 years, before God set them free and brought them out. God was able to make a separation in those judgments. Even though some of the plagues fell from heaven they weren't allowed to touch the people or the cattle in the land of Goshen, where the Israelites were. Remember in the previous seal judgment the figure was a quarter (25%) of things which were destroyed? Now God is increasing the percentage to 33%; a third of trees are burned up and *"all green grass"*.

KEYNOTE: Divine Control. God's judgments are always measured and targeted and determined in degree, by the extent of rebellion of those that they fall on. His judgments are never random, nor are they ever out of control.

Do you recall back in the seal judgment the *"Black horse"*, which represented famine, and scarcity? We thought then about restrictions on food. Bread and water on the table, no mention of meat. *"Oil and wine"* reserved only for the very rich. There was no mention of milk, cheese, and other products. Now God will destroy the green grass, so even dairy products will disappear. Our earth, even the previously fertile zones, will begin to resemble vast barren deserts.

Trumpet Two Sounds

The second angel now sounds his trumpet. The sea is made to boil, for a *"great mountain burning with fire was cast into the sea"* (Revelation chapter 8 verse 8 KJV). This is what John saw. Why make his vision anything other than literal? Some interpret this as the 'sea' equalling the nations, and the 'mountain' a major government, so they say, 'A great government must collapse'.

It is true that the *"Man of Sin"* will destroy some of his minor monarchy supporters to consolidate his power (Daniel chapter 7 verses 7 – 8) but the rest of the description here must make sense as well. John is told that one third (33%) of sea-life dies, and one third (33%) of shipping is destroyed. This cannot relate to 'governments' or 'nations' and can only be taken consistently (and literally) as being connected with the sea and sea-life as we know it.

> **KEYNOTE: Literal vs. Symbolic.** There are a variety of views on the 'literality' of future prophecy. There are some who view prophecy as having ALL been fulfilled in the past. And some who see prophecy as ALL symbolic, none of it literal. And quite a few other views in between. We will deal with this topic in more detail in **Appx. II**.

John may or may not have been shown all the world's oceans in his heavenly visions. As far as his real world was concerned in the first century, he would only have known the eastern part of the Mediterranean. Certainly not the global shipping across all the oceans of the world as we know it. At today's figures there are around 90,000 commercial shipping vessels on the sea. More than three quarters (80%) of everything that is consumed in our world - from motor cars to bicycles, computers and phones, goods of so many different categories - are all moved by sea in shipping containers. As well as crude oil, and gas, and other fuels. Imagine 30,000 ships destroyed in one 'tsunami', directed by God?

The Ring of Fire

Could it possibly be that one of the great volcanic islands of the Pacific (an area known as the 'Ring of Fire' where there are over 160 large volcanoes, some of them islands and some of them mountains on the shore) will explode? God could begin this judgment with the greatest of them falling into the sea, to create a massive tsunami, perhaps even other volcanoes erupting as well. We live in days of increasing volcanic activity. Experts speak of long dormant volcanoes 'coming awake'. God is getting His instruments of judgment within His creation ready. Back in 1815 a Pacific Island called 'Tamboro', did blow up. Such was the devastation in the lower atmosphere that 1816 was called historically, 'The year of no summer and no harvest'. The sun did not shine properly, nor the moon at night for six months. God could magnify these things, which He has stored in His creation, to be 'weapons' of His mass destruction at His own timing and to divinely-determined degrees.

A Falling 'Fallen' Angel?

The third angel sounds his trumpet. The judgment seems very strange but let us examine the detail: *"There fell a great star out of heaven, burning as it were a torch, and it fell upon the third part of the rivers ... and the name of the star is called 'Wormwood' ... many men died of the waters, because they were made bitter"* (Revelation chapter 8 verses 10 – 11 NRB). What does this mean? It cannot be an actual star, for even small stars are many times larger than our earth.

Quite often in the Bible angels (and fallen ones too) are referred to as *"stars"*, because they do come down from heaven. This star has a name. In the original Greek language it is *"Absinthos"*, which means 'bitterness'. Perhaps he is a fallen angel whom God permits to poison a third part of all fresh water? There are some who think it could be a meteorite, or a comet, which falling down the sky 'looks' like a star. This may be possible, but in context of what is about to follow (in the trumpet judgments) a fallen angel is a stronger possibility. We will see other fallen angels, also with names, before we go much further. And the greatest of all 'fallen angels' was *"Lucifer"*, who became the *"Serpent"*, who is now *"Satan"*, the *"Dragon"* and the head of all the fallen-ones.

KEYNOTE: A Falling Star. The smallest star, closest to earth, is 'Proxima Centauri' 4.2 light years away. It has a diameter of 200,000k. Even a star this small cannot fall on the *"third part of ..."* things on earth. Our planet has a diameter of 12,740 kilometres, so even this tiny star is about 16 times bigger than earth. It would wipe our planet out if it even came close.

Trumpet Four Sounds

When the fourth angel blows his trumpet, *"the third part of the sun was smitten, and the third part of the moon, and the third part of the stars"* (Revelation chapter 8 verse 12 KJV). In many parts of the world the hours of daylight do not change much. Some places not at all; 12 hours day and 12 hours night, summer and winter alike. It seems here it is not the sun itself that is affected, but the light coming to earth *"the third* (part) *of them might not shine"*. It is interesting that some of the most fertile parts of the world are places where daylight does vary. In northern and southern latitudes, it does, but not in the tropics. A one third reduction in light, as well as the superstition and fear that it will bring to many, those who looks for signs in the sky, will also affect the growth of what vegetation and trees are still left.

KEYNOTE: Space Debris. A 'satellite', or similar object, falling to earth does not really fit the picture. Although we can see many of them as tiny 'pin-pricks' of light in the night sky, they are quite small. They are only visible because they reflect star and moonlight, and they seem bigger than they are because they are only between 100 and 500 kilometres up. Just above the edge of 'space'.

It is possible that this fourth judgment is linked to the previous one. Perhaps the volcanic explosions are so severe that the earth shifts on its axis and daylight hours are altered? Or perhaps – as certain astronomers have been searching for – there is a 'dark star' which is presently invisible within our solar system? God could have such a thing already in place and He could move its orbit to block part of the light out, in a permanent eclipse. Some of these things we do not know, and we should

A 'Solar eclipse' in June 2021 AD.

not speculate too much in advance. Either way, God is in control of His creation, He has put elements there to use in further judgments (even from creation) and the stars and planets must move as He directs them. *"When I look at Your heavens, the work of Your fingers, the moon and the stars, which You have set in place …"* (Psalm 8 verse 3 ESV).

Three 'Woes' Pronounced

If it sounds like conditions are now getting bad, the next event in heaven is another angel announcing three *"woes"* on the inhabitants of the earth which come with the remaining three trumpet judgments. These three *"woes"* are all linked to the demonic and spirit world. God is going to allow the powers of darkness (which some have been dabbling with for many years) a level of freedom which they have not had before. The first *"woe"* is linked with another falling *"star"* and the opening of the *"pit of the Abyss"*, from which a demon army will be let loose. The second *"woe"* is linked with the *"Beast out of the Abyss"* (Revelation chapter 11 verse 7), and the third *"woe"* is linked with the final fall of Satan from heaven to earth (Revelation chapter 12 verses 7 – 12).

Trumpet Five Sounds

When the fifth angel sounds his trumpet, John says, *"I saw a star fall out of heaven unto the earth: and to him was given the key of the pit of the Abyss."* (see Revelation chapter 9 verses 1 – 10 NRB). When the inner chamber of the *"Abyss"* is opened, there will come out an army which defies description. John could only write down a depiction of what he saw; beings which looked like locusts crossed with scorpions, but as large as horses. A

KEYNOTE: A Demon Army? There are many suggestions as to what John actually saw. Don't forget, he was looking 2,000 years into the future. Some have suggested he saw 'helicopter gunships' (which if you look at some pictures of modern aerial military aircraft is not so fanciful). In the context it seems most likely that God is removing a restraint again and <u>demons</u> undisguised, by the million, will be let loose. We cannot speculate beyond what John saw and wrote, from his 1st Century viewpoint.

> ‘ **God will allow the "Beast out of the Abyss" to kill the two witnesses.**’

terrifying picture, and all too possible if they are demons in bodily form. They have a *"king over them"* (they cannot be normal locusts, for the Bible says locusts have no king). His name is *"Apollyon"*, which means destroyer. Some think it is another name for the Devil, but it is probably not. This may be another senior demon in Satan's terrible army, many of whom are bound up now (Jude 6), whom God will let loose in these final days of His judgment.

Trumpet Six Sounds

When the sixth angel blows his trumpet, a second demonic army is loosed. Not from the *"Abyss"* into the air, but an earth army, which seem to come from beyond the river Euphrates. Not men, though a great army of men will come later from the east, and it is possible both events are close together. Here is another fraction, *"the third part of men"* are killed. We have already seen today's figure of around 8,000,000,000 reduced to less than 6,000,000,000 in the seal judgments (not counting the 1,000,000s of Christians who will be 'raptured'). One third of this remaining number is something like a further 2,000,000,000. Possibly much more? The population of the world will have been more than halved, in well under seven years! Some clever men are looking for ways to control and manipulate world population today; but not like this. This is God at work in judgment and using natural disasters and infernal agents to do His bidding. What terrible days are ahead for those who are rejectors of Jesus Christ.

The Two Witnesses

At this point we have the 'gap story' between the sixth and seventh trumpet that we mentioned earlier. John has a strange meeting with an angel, who gives him a *"little scroll"* to eat, a small book, which represents things that John heard and was told not to write down. Some of the details of God's judgments, and some of the blessings too, will only be known when they happen.

Next, in the same 'parenthesis', we have the story of the *"two witnesses"* who will prophesy in Jerusalem for 1,260 days (which is three and a half prophetic years, and probably the first half of the seven-year period). They are in the character of Old Testament prophets. They dress in *"sackcloth"* and they are capable of doing the kind of miracles that Moses and Elijah did. Some will ask, 'Who are they?' There have been various suggestions about their identity: Enoch and Elijah because they went up to heaven and never died? Or Moses and Elijah, because they appeared with Jesus on the Mount of Transfiguration (Matthew chapter 17)? And there is a strange passage in Jude about Michael, the archangel, and the Devil and the recovery of the body of Moses. The best answer is, we don't know. It may be two of these three, or perhaps none of the above.

It may be two previously unknown men on whom God will pour out His Spirit for three and a half years, and they will not only do miracles, but they will also be invincible. The *"Beast"* will wish to kill them, but he will not be able to. Then when he himself comes back *"out of the Abyss"*, God will allow the two witnesses to be killed. Wicked men will rejoice that God's witnesses are silenced, and the Beast won't allow their bodies to be collected for burial for four days. (I wonder why?) But after three and a half days they will come alive, and God will call them to *"Come up hither"*. There will be another great earthquake, and a tenth part of Jerusalem will collapse. This is the *"second woe"*, and the third woe is still to come.

Back to the End

Now the seventh angel gets to sound his trumpet, and once again we arrive at the end of the tribulation period. Heaven announces, *"The kingdoms of this world are become the kingdoms of our Lord, and of His Christ; and He shall reign until the ages of the ages"* (Revelation 11 verses 15 – 19 NRB). What a wonderful thing to be on the side of Christ; not only the winning side, but the position of security and hope forever. The Devil and his wicked leaders may touch the lives of many, but they can never take one soul out of the grip of Jesus or His Father, *"I give unto them eternal life; and they shall never perish, neither shall any man pluck them out of My hand ... I and My Father are one"* (John chapter 10 verses 28 – 30 KJV).

> **KEYNOTE: 'Parenthesis'.** We are now going to examine another large 'parenthesis' between the Trumpet Judgments and the Bowl Judgments. It is as if John himself is being given a 'break' from viewing and writing on increasingly terrible judgments. In this 'gap story' the focus will change. John will have his vision widened out, to look back and forward, and to see 'Seven Great Personalities' who will have participated in the 'Conflict of the Ages' (some from the beginning of time itself) through until the conclusion of the Kingdom Age. That will be our study in **Chps. 12-15**.

Q&A >

Questions and Answers for Chapter Eleven – *'The Trumpet Judgments'*

Chp. 11 – 'The Trumpet Judgments'

Q1. What happened before the angels blew their trumpets? And why?

Q2. What did the first trumpet judgment affect?

Q3. What did the second trumpet judgment affect?

Q4. What did the fourth trumpet judgment affect?

Q5. What came out of the 'pit of the Abyss' at the 5th trumpet?

Q6. Who was the King over the demons?

Q7. How many are in the demon land army?

Q8. What did the voice from heaven say, at the 7th trumpet?

Q9. What is the main reason for God's judgments in this period?

Chapter Twelve

The War in Heaven

We are going to look now at the centre point on the middle section of the Chart. The 'Seven Seals' have been broken open; the '144,000 Jews' have been sealed; the 'Seven Trumpets' have been blown; two of the *"woes"* are past, the 'demon armies' have been released. John has been taken, in vision, to the 'end point' of the Tribulation period in relation to the last of the Seals, and in relation to the last of the Trumpets. Here, in what we have already referred to as a long 'parenthesis', John is taken back in time to the midpoint of the seven year period (after the first 1,260 days), before he sees the 'Bowl Judgments' poured out. Not only are we at the midpoint of our Chart, but we are also at the midpoint of the book of Revelation. We will see in Revelation chapter twelve as we progress, the very middle paragraph of the whole book!

The Central Parenthesis

As we have said, this is another of the '<u>parentheses</u>' of the book. (Interestingly enough this English word is two Greek words, imported or 'transliterated'. They mean 'put alongside', in addition to the main content.) There are quite a few 'parentheses' in Revelation. We may not highlight all of them, but the longest is right here. It is quite easy to identify this one, for it is bracketed between two verses which are almost the same: *"The Temple of God was opened in the heaven, and there was seen in His Temple the ark of His covenant"* (Revelation chapter 11 verse 19 NRB). This parenthetic passage runs through to chapter 15 verse 5, where we have another *"after these things"*, and then the expression we have had about God's *"inner Temple"* being opened is repeated (Revelation chapter 15 verse 5).

It is possible that something literally takes place *"in heaven"*. God may open the veil of the heavens, and a glimpse of His inner Sanctuary may be seen, accompanied by *"lightnings and voices, and thunderings, and an earthquake, and great hail"* (Revelation chapter 11

> **KEYNOTE: The Revelation Chart.** If we look at the Chart (inside the front and back cover), it will be apparent that it is not drawn to scale. The *"Acceptable Year of the Lord"*, which includes the 'Church Age' (in the left-hand corner), has now run for around 1,990 years. The *"Year of My Redeemed"* (Isaiah chp. 63:4), which is the 'Kingdom Age' (on the right-hand side) is exactly 1,000 years long. The 'Judgment Period' in the centre is only seven years long. It is called by various titles, but the one which most closely matches the two already mentioned is *"The Day of Vengeance of our God"* (Isa. chp. 61:1-2). The centre section of the Chart has been increased in size to accommodate the detail of the seven-year judgment programme, which divides evenly in two.

verse 19 KJV). These things are all characteristic of God's judgments upon men who have rebelled against Him, even *"hail"* (not the kind we see often in parts of our world but hail stones large enough to kill) is an element of God's judgment (Joshua chapter 10 verse 11; Job chapter 38 verse 22; Revelation chapter 16 verse 21).

The Seven Personalities

Although this chapter has been called 'War in Heaven', when we combine Revelation chapter 12, chapter 13 and into chapter 14, we will also see 'Seven Great Personalities' who represent, in different forms, the 'Conflict of the Ages' between the purposes of God and the opposition of the Devil. What an amazing panorama John is just about to see, and from the vantage point of God's throne room as well. Any of these different titles could be put over this amazing section.

The 'personalities' appear in a particular order, but perhaps not as we would expect: *"There appeared a great sign in heaven; a woman clothed with the sun ... and being with child"* (Revelation 12 verse 1 NRB). The next personality to appear is very different: *"Another sign in heaven, a great red dragon ... and his tail drew the third part of the stars of heaven, and cast them to the earth"* (chapter 12 verses 3 – 4 NRB). Now we go back to the woman: *"She brought forth a male son, who is about to rule all nations with a rod of iron"* (chapter 12 verse 5 NRB). Some will ask, 'Why is the Dragon put between the woman and her son? Why are they not together?' Those are very important questions. We will come back to them shortly.

Let us move on quickly. The next personality group seen by John is *"Michael and his angels"* (chapter 12 verses 7 – 9), and they are at war in heaven with the Dragon and his angels! Michael is the *"archangel"*. (We will say a little more about him shortly as well.) When we cross over to chapter 13 (John didn't have any chapters or verses in his manuscript originally), John sees two more personalities appear: *"A Beast rising out of the sea"* (chapter 13 verse 1 ESV) and: *"another Beast rising out of the earth"* (chapter 13 verse 11 ESV). If you have been counting, that makes six personalities, and perhaps this sixth one is the worst. 'Who is the seventh?' you ask, 'Is seven not a special number in the Bible?' Indeed it is. The seventh personality is seen in chapter 14 verses 1 – 5 (ESV), *"Behold, on Mount Zion stood the Lamb, and with Him 144,000 who had His name and His Father's name written on their foreheads"*, a very significant picture indeed.

KEYNOTE: Two Beasts. The two *"Beasts"* are examined individually in **Chps. 13-15**, but here we can see that they are very closely connected with the *"Dragon"*. They are like him in character, and he will control their activities. Much more will be said about them in the **Chapters** that follow.

When we go back to the *"woman"* at the beginning of this panoramic picture, we will have to establish her identity. It is easier to do so if we scan across the other personalities first, which we have already partly done. The Dragon is identified for us as *"the great Dragon ... the old Serpent, called Devil and Satan, which deceiveth the whole world"* (Revelation 12 verses 7 – 9 NRB).

Michael, we know, is the foremost angel. Not only is he head of the lower angels, but the prophet Daniel tells us he is the angel *"Prince"* of the nation of Israel and is in conflict in the heavens with other enemy angels (Daniel chapter 10). It is possible (though we cannot really prove it) that God has put an angel in charge of every nation in the world; and Satan, who has one third of fallen angels on his side, has done likewise. There are possibly more angels than people, and 'guardian angels' is not just a wistful expression. Jesus said that *"little ones"* had *"their angels"* who were looking on: *"the face of My Father which is in heaven"* (Matthew 18 verse 10 KJV). What an amazing thought! On occasions in the Old Testament, when people were in difficulty, God allowed them to see the angel hosts which protected them.

> **KEYNOTE: Extreme Caution!** The powers of darkness are very real, and we should have a respect for them. They are much greater than we imagine. Peter says, *"Be watchful. Your adversary the Devil prowls around like a roaring lion, seeking someone to devour"* (1 Peter 5:8 ESV). John when writing of the *"spirit of antichrist ... in the world ..."* reminds us, *"Ye are of God, little children, and have <u>overcome</u> them: because <u>greater is He that is in you</u>, than he that is in the world"* (1 John 4:4 KJV). There are many things in today's world linked to the powers of darkness that young Christians should avoid at all costs.

Two Opposing Groups

We can now see that our 'Seven Personalities' divide into a four and a three. (This 4:3 ratio is very common in scripture whenever 7 things are grouped together. Right from Genesis chapter 1.) Three of the personalities are essentially evil: the *"Dragon"*, and the two *"Beasts"*. The other four we expect to be on the opposite side, the side of God and of good. That should be so, and we will see that it is. *"Michael"*, we have already covered. He is the *"archangel"* and the protector of the nation of Israel. So, we are left with the *"woman"*, the *"male son"* and the *"Lamb on Mount Zion"* (Revelation chapter 14 verses 1 – 5 ESV).

Again, working backwards helps us in our deductions as to who they are. The *"Lamb"* can only be Jesus Himself, for He is pictured as a *"Lamb"* more often in Revelation than in any other book in the Bible. John is getting a look forward (remember this is a 'panorama') to the end of the Tribulation period. The Lamb is seen *"on Mount Zion"* which is not heaven. It is the mountain of Jerusalem and the *"144,000"*, whom we saw *"sealed"* in a previous study (at the beginning of the Tribulation), are now shown with Christ at the beginning of his earthly Kingdom.

The *"Lamb"* we can connect back with the *"male son"*, or as some versions put it, *"a man child"* (in chapter 12 verse 5 KJV). The son, whom the woman brought forth, John was told *"is about to rule all nations with a rod of iron"* (This picture of 'ruling with an iron rod' is one that has come across into our ordinary language and many a school principal of a past day was so described). It is found four times in the Bible, and each time the meaning is the same. It speaks of Messiah in His coming Kingdom, who will break the power of rebellious nations (Psalm 2 verse 9; Revelation chapter 2 verse 27; chapter 12 verse 5; chapter 19 verse 15). So, by the description of what He will do, and is just about to do as John is told, we can establish who the *"male son"* is. He is *"Messiah"*, the coming King.

There is an interesting prophecy in Isaiah which amplifies (but changes) the 'birthing' analogy, *"<u>Before</u> she was in labour she gave birth; <u>before</u> her pain came upon her she delivered a son. Who has heard such a thing?"* (Isaiah chapter 66 verses 7 – 8 ESV). Jesus spoke of *"the beginning of birth pains"* in His 'Olivet Prophecy' (Matthew 24 verse 8 ESV). So, the *"male son"* is the Messiah. But the *"birth pains"* (which normally come before the birth) are prophetically connected here with the *"Tribulation"*, which will produce the spiritual 'rebirth of Israel', after they accept that their *"Messiah"* has already come, the first time. The nation of Israel will have her 'tribulation pains' after the Child has been born! They must accept that to be true. The one they are expecting to 'deliver' them, was born more than 2,000 years previously. At which point Old Testament prophecies (which have sections written in the past tense, like Isaiah 53) will be finally and completely fulfilled. As has often been said, the Jews are presently in their Land in unbelief.

Why Birth and Ascension Only?

'But' you might ask, 'If it is Jesus who is spoken of at the time of His birth, why is His life and death not mentioned?' That is an excellent question, and we should think about it. The promises contained in the covenants to Abraham, and to David, spoke of a descendant who would rule the nation that God would bring from the children of Abraham, a nation which would be *"the head and not the tail ... above and ... not be beneath"* (Deuteronomy 28 verse 13 KJV). David was promised a son who would sit upon *"the throne of His kingdom for ever"* (2 Samuel 7 verses 12 – 16 KJV).

Although David prophesied in his Psalms the death of Messiah on a cross (Psalm 22), yet even David probably did not understand, nor Abraham either, that the one who would rule the nations would be the one who would also die for the nation. Caiaphas the High Priest at the time of Jesus' death *"prophesied that Jesus would die for the nation"*. Caiaphas was an unbeliever, and a blasphemous priest, but God put those words in his mouth (John 11 verses 46 – 53 ESV), prophesying that the death of Messiah would be on behalf of others. As Daniel had also prophesied, 500 years earlier.

In the 'panorama' picture that John is being shown here (Revelation chapters 12 – 14), it is not the death of Messiah that is in view. That which was hidden from the understanding of the prophets is now passed over; He was born to rule. His glory days are near. The *"Son of Man coming in power"* (Matthew chapter 24 verses 29 – 30) is getting very close. John is told, *"the male son is about to rule ..."* (Revelation 12 verse 5 NRB).

Who is the Woman?

'If the *"male son"* is Jesus, then the woman must be the virgin Mary. Is that correct?' Another good question, and a fair deduction too. But we are in a 'panorama' picture here, and we need to keep our focus very wide (like a 'wide angle' lens on a camera), not a microscope! There are four 'woman' pictures in Revelation. John saw each one of them from four different vantage points:

1. The rebellious *"Jezebel"* in the Church in Thyatira (Revelation chapter 2 verse 20), which was a part of his vision that John saw while still on Patmos Island, and in his prison cell.

2. The *"woman clothed with the sun, and the moon under her feet, and upon her head a crown of twelve stars"* (chapter 12 verses 1 – 2 KJV), whom John saw in the heavenly part of his visions.

3. The Scarlet Woman, *"the Great Whore ... Mystery, Babylon the Great"* (chapter 17 verses 1 – 6 KJV), whom John saw after he had been taken *"in Spirit into a wilderness"*.

4. Lastly *"the Bride, the Lamb's wife"*, whom John saw in the Spirit on *"a great and high mountain"* (chapter 21 verses 9 – 10 KJV), after the Kingdom part of his visions was past.

We can see straight away that two of these *"women"* are representative of something wicked, and two of them something good. So, there are comparisons and contrasts between them, which John was meant to identify [Some of these we will see in more detail as we go forward]. The big question is, 'Are these actual individual women?' Here we get some clarity. The answer in each case is, probably not. The first and third represent systems of false religion, and at different stages of their development, although it is possible an actual 'woman' functions as a figurehead in both cases.

If the fourth woman represents the *"Bride of the Lamb"*, a future title for the *"Church"*, then can we suggest that the woman, that we are looking at in chapter 12, represents Israel, God's earthly nation? The two separate companies who both have a future in the Kingdom. Is that a sound supposition? Someone will still say, 'But the picture looks like the virgin

> **KEYNOTE: O.T. Analogies.** So often, especially in the 'End Times' prophecies of the book of Revelation, we must go back to the O.T. prophecies for help. Although there are no direct 'quotations' from the O.T. in Revelation, there are over 400 references or 'allusions' to prophecies or pictures that have already been given. Many of them shed light on the 'pictures' and 'symbols' within the book of Revelation.

Mary, does it not?' Well, we may have seen statues and icons of the virgin Mary with, 'stars on her head ... and the moon under her feet', but that does not make it biblically correct. In fact, EVERY image is wrong, even pictures of Jesus. God forbad every *"image ... or likeness"* even of Himself (Exodus chapter 20 verses 4 – 7).

END TIMES for BEGINNERS

Joseph's Dreams

Do you remember Joseph's dreams? Back when he was a teenage shepherd with his wicked brothers. Why did he share his strange dreams when he knew it would increase their jealousy? If he had not, they would not be on record as being fulfilled. Even Jacob his father was upset at the second one! *"Behold I have dreamed another dream"* Joseph said, *"... The sun, the moon, and eleven stars were bowing down to me"*. Jacob replied, *"Shall I and your mother and your brothers indeed come to bow down ourselves to the ground before you?"* (Genesis 37 verses 5 – 11 ESV). Look at this comment closely: Firstly, the dream is a prophecy, which Joseph himself didn't understand. Secondly, Jacob, though he objects to the picture, interprets part of the dream. Thirdly, it is (once again) a <u>divided prophecy</u>. The part about Joseph's actual brothers bowing down came true less than twenty years later; they *"bowed down themselves before him with their faces to the earth"* (Genesis chapter 42 verse 6 KJV), not once but many times!

'But' you ask, 'What of, *"the sun and the moon and the stars"*? Jacob interprets the stars as his sons, and the sun as himself, and interestingly, the moon as Joseph's mother Rachel, even though she had been dead for about fourteen years. The overall picture is 'Messianic'. Joseph is seen in the long prophecy (remember prophecy can be both short and long, and can also divide in two) as Jacob's descendent, the Messiah, who would rule the nation of Israel in the future kingdom. Some of this is further pictured in Joseph's reign as Prince in Egypt, and in his Gentile bride (Genesis chapter 41 verses 41 – 45).

Why is the Dragon between the Woman and her Male Son?

Back to our 'panorama' in Revelation chapter 12: We can now see more clearly that the *"woman"* is Israel, from whom, out of the tribe of Judah, Messiah came. One last question remains, 'Why are the woman and the male son not put side by side? Why is the Dragon put between them?' We should be able to work that out now without too much difficulty. The Spirit of God, who is in control of John's visions, wants us to see the historic hatred of the Devil for Israel, and his opposition to the Son being born.

> **KEYNOTE: Satan Cannot Win.** The Devil failed to prevent the first coming of Messiah. Before we reach the end of the Book of Revelation, it will be seen that he cannot prevent Messiah's Second Coming either. And Satan will have his final failure at the end of the Kingdom Age. We will study all of this in **Chp. 21**.

Did he not put it in the mind of Herod to *"slay all the male children that were in Bethlehem ... from two years old and under"*? (Matthew 2 verses 16 – 18 NRB). Such a wicked and callous slaughter could only be provoked by devilish thoughts. Yet the *"male son"* was safe, for God had instructed Joseph to take Him to Egypt, where they stayed until Herod died. The purposes of Satan, from the first promise in Eden [which we looked at in the early Chapters], through the promises to the Patriarchs, through the occupation of the Land, and the promises to David and Solomon; all the way through the Dragon was opposing the coming of Messiah.

One last detail in the 'panorama' which will confirm that the *"woman"* is the Nation of Israel, and not Mary herself, is the *"remnant of her seed"* mentioned later (chapter 12 verses 13 – 17). The remnant goes into hiding in the wilderness, to be protected for *"a time and times and half a time"*, an expression taken from Daniel (chapter 12 verse 7 KJV), and which here refers again to three and a half years, that is the second half of the seven year period. Where this 'refuge' place will be we don't know. Some think it may be in an old area of *"Edom"*, where the hidden city of Petra was a refuge in the past. Or possibly some secret valley that God will close at the time, where the *"remnant"* who escape from direct persecution in Israel and Jerusalem will flee to. The Dragon will be angry, but he cannot touch that remnant of believing Jews whom God will miraculously protect.

The ancient hidden rock city of 'Petra' in the deserts of Jordan – the 'Edom' of the Old Testament – which some scholars believe will again be the 'place in the wilderness' of the Jewish remnant in the days of the 'Great Tribulation' – This is not stated in scripture.

The War in Heaven

'What about the *"war in heaven"*? When does it happen?' someone will ask. Another good question. Though the angel who was *"Lucifer, son of the morning"*, the shining one (Isaiah 14 verses 12 – 15 KJV), *"the anointed cherub"* was cast out of God's presence, because of his pride and desire to be as God (Ezekiel 28 verses 12 – 19), and was followed by other angels in his rebellion, this is not what is being described here. This battle between Michael and God's angels, against the Dragon and his angels, takes place probably at the mid-point of the seven years, as is referred to in this chapter.

The Devil becomes even angrier. He has *"great wrath"* not just at his defeat (which he never admits), but because he understands the time-periods of prophecy and knows he has now only three and a half years left to deceive the nations, before the *"Coming in Power"* of Messiah. This is what was referred to as the third *"woe"* on the earth dwellers (Revelation chapter 12 verse 12). The Devil knows how short a time he has left, and his anger is concentrated on earth and on mankind, for he has been finally cast out of the heavens for ever.

When God opens a window into the spirit world, and allows us a glimpse within, so often we see Satan coming further and further <u>down</u>. Never does he rise, and never can he come close to his original position. He himself knows his final confinement is the *"lake of fire"* (Revelation chapter 20 verse 10). It is an amazing display of divine symmetry that right here, the very pivotal point of the book, *"there came a war in heaven ..."* (chapter 12 verses 7 – 9). Small wonder the loud voice from heaven says, *"Now is come salvation, and strength, and the kingdom of our God, and the authority of His Christ."* (chapter 12 verse 10 NRB).

KEYNOTE: Centrepoint. This short paragraph (Rev. 12:7-9) is the very centre of the book of Revelation. Counting the verses inwards from both ends, you would meet here. Though that would take a lot of counting! In many ways it is meant to be seen as a great spiritual climax at the centre of the Book, and at the exact centre of the seven year period as well.

Questions and Answers for Chapter Twelve – *'The War in Heaven'*

Chp. 12 – 'The War in Heaven'

Q1. This 'parenthesis' is the middle section of the book, where does it begin and end? Can you give the chapter and verse for both the beginning and end?

Q2. There are seven 'personalities' in this centre section (Two we have not yet examined). Can you list the five that we have studied, and in the order in which they appear?

Q3. Why does the Dragon come between the 'woman' and the 'man child'?

Q4. How many names does the Devil have in this Chapter?

Q5. Who are the leaders of the armies who fight a war in heaven?

Q6. Why is the Dragon angry at this point?

Q7. What lessons can we learn from this 'panoramic' study in the middle of the book?

JOTTINGS

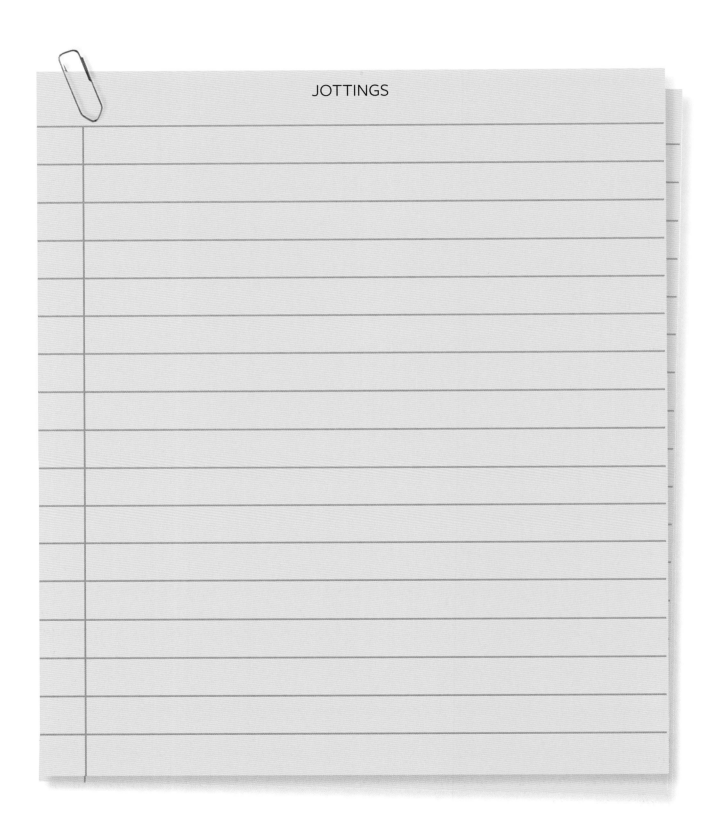

Chapter Thirteen

The Beast out of the Sea

We are not moving any further forward in the 'Judgment Programme' just yet. (We are still in the 'parenthesis' between Revelation chapter 11 verse 19 & chapter 15 verse 5.) We have seen that the *"third woe"* is the confinement of the Devil to the surface of the earth, and also his awareness that he has *"a short time"* (Revelation chapter 12 verse 12) and his resultant increased anger. Satan will be aware of the '1,260 day' timeframe until the end of the judgment period and the *"Coming in power"* of Messiah. We have searched out the identity of the 'Seven Personalities' in this section; the woman, the male son, Michael the archangel, the Lamb on Mount Zion (four who are connected), and the *"Dragon"* and his two *"Beasts"* (all three of them connected), whom we are going to look at individually in the next two chapters.

The first personality is the *"Beast out of the Sea"*, and the second personality, possibly appearing a little later in time, is the *"Beast out of the Land"*. They are connected to each other and to the Dragon their master, but their roles are as distinct as their origins, very different indeed.

The Beast out of the Sea

John says, *"He* (that is the *"Dragon"* of chapter 12 verse 17) *stood upon the sand of the sea, and I saw a beast rise up out of the sea, having seven heads and ten horns, and upon his horns ten crowns, and upon his heads the name of blasphemy. And the beast which I saw was like unto a leopard, and his feet as the feet of a bear, and his mouth as the mouth of a lion: and the dragon gave him his power, and his throne, and great authority. And I saw one of his heads as it were wounded to death; and his deadly wound was healed. And in all the earth there was wonder after the beast. And they worshipped the dragon which gave authority unto the beast: and they worshipped the beast, saying, 'Who is like unto the beast? Who is able to make war with him? ... and authority was given unto him to continue forty-two months."* (Revelation 13 verses 1 – 5 NRB).

Who is this 'Sea-Beast'?

'Is the Beast a person? Why is he described in this way?' Those are good questions. He is not the Dragon, but it is surprising how like the dragon his description is! If you read and compare with chapter 12 verses 3 – 4, you will see that the only real difference between them is that the Dragon has his crowns on his *"seven heads"*, but the Beast has his crowns on his *"ten horns"*. The *"seven heads"* may represent the historic kingdoms which have been inveterate enemies of Israel, from Egypt onwards. The future kingdom of the Beast is the *"seventh"*. This Beast, who appears out of the sea, has his crowns on his horns, ten of them: the kings who will be his confederates.

KEYNOTE: Enemies of Israel.
In biblical history these 7 kings or kingdoms would be, in chronological order: Egypt, Assyria, Babylon, Medo-Persia, Greece, Rome and lastly the confederate kingdom of 'Antichrist'.

The 'ten' here are not historic kingdoms, but the future kingdoms of Europe and the Middle East who will give their support to the Beast, and get their authority from him. They will *"receive authority ... one hour with the Beast"* (Revelation chapter 17 verse 12 NRB). A possible interpretation is that some of these are actual *"kings"* who have no present 'authority', that is current monarchies with no governmental role (different to the British monarchy, for example). Some of these will be given authority because they have supported the Beast in his rise to power, possibly initially behind the scenes.

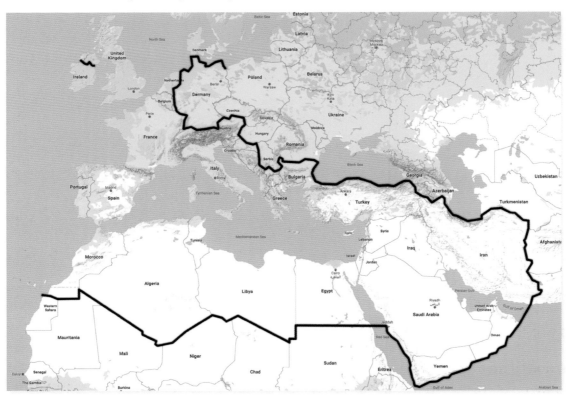

Southern Europe, Middle East, and N. Africa – marking off countries (within the boundary) which have 'Royal Houses'. Many are not in prominence; some are in exile. But – in contrast to most of the others – these countries still have monarchies, many of which are of the same bloodlines.

Why does He come out of the Sea?

That is a very good question as well and, of course, contrasts with the second Beast we will look at later, who comes *"out of the Land"*. The *"Sea"* to John would have been the Mediterranean, and he saw the Dragon standing on the shore. The Dragon is looking westwards and overseeing the rise of his 'Superman' who will come from the Latin nations, from the territory of the old Roman Empire. His kingdom does not have to be the 'Revived Roman Empire' (the Bible doesn't say so). We should remember the Roman Empire had two parts; a European and a Byzantine, the latter part of which continued much longer than the western part. In fact, half of his support may be from the Middle East, the Arab nations south and east of Israel, but, as Daniel foretold, the *"Coming Prince"* himself will be ethnically linked with the people who destroyed Jerusalem in 70 AD. (Daniel chapter 9 verses 25 - 27), which historically was the Roman general Titus, and the Tenth Legion of the Roman army.

> **KEYNOTE: Modern Monarchies.** Many western democracies and even some countries which are republics have 'royal houses' in their background. Some in exile, but very much connected to one another biologically in one extended family tree. Some are very wealthy, and with great commercial power even if not outwardly political. This man may well go to some of these 'royal houses' for support, as well as to the formal governments of the world for political position. His *"Ten kings"* may well be two groups, one western and one eastern, just as the *"toes of the feet"* of the image in Nebuchadnezzar's dream (Dan. 2:42-43).

We should also remember that in our day of emigration and global movement, a man may have more than one set of roots. This man may 'come from' southern Europe, as Daniel appears to indicate, but his origins may be further east (from the old Byzantine part of the Roman empire, not necessarily the European part). He may even be Islamic in his origin, or possibly even in his faith, yet present a very cosmopolitan and 'western' front. We can see these things clearly in the leading personalities of some western governments today.

Is He the White Horse Conqueror?

'Is he the same man as the rider on the white horse in Revelation chapter 6?' some will ask. That is an important question. There cannot be much doubt that he is the same person. In Revelation 6, we see him from a 'political worldview' perspective, coming in peace as a covenant facilitator. A 'False Messiah', bringing peace to the Middle East and Israel, where there has been no peace for centuries. But God sees him very differently, and here John is seeing things from heaven's standpoint; a 'heavenly worldview'.

Does the Beast Really Die?

'What does it mean that he had a head *"wounded to death"*?'* That is a very difficult question, but as we go further into our studies in Revelation the meaning will become clearer. Since he has seven heads (which are kingdoms), and he is the seventh, it is the seventh that is *"wounded"*. It seems there will be an assassination attempt at the very centre point of the seven years (whether genuinely successful or not). Has he not already been called *"the Beast out of the Abyss"* (Revelation chapter 11 verse 7 KJV)? If he is truly assassinated, and recovers from death, it is no surprise that in all the world there is awe and wonder about this man. But, more terribly, we are told that men will acknowledge that his 'reappearance' is linked with the Dragon and *"they worshipped the Dragon"* (chapter 13 verse 4 KJV).

One thing we do know, Satan does not have the power to raise the dead (he does have demons who can impersonate dead people, a very serious and dangerous subject indeed). But will God allow such a thing to happen? He did with Saul. The *"witch of Endor"* was apparently expecting a demon to impersonate Samuel and to speak with Saul, but she was terrified when Samuel himself appeared! (1 Samuel chapter 28). The question is not, 'Can God bring people back from the dead?' We know that He can and did in the days of Jesus' earthly ministry. The question rather is, 'Will God allow such a thing to be seen to be done by the power of Satan?' It is probable that the answer to this question is also, 'Yes.'

> ***KEYNOTE: Assassination.** Here is one of the great difficulties of the book of Revelation. 'Is this Beast-man really assassinated, and does he rise from the dead?' A hard question, and one on which many of the scholars have been divided down through the years. There are two main points of view (assuming that we are talking about a person):
> **The first view:** His 'assassination' is staged, he is wounded but not killed. To make him appear more 'god-like' the story is 'spun' that he has come back from the dead.
> **The second view:** The Beast is really assassinated (possibly even by one of his own guards). He does truly die, but God permits him to come back *"out of the Abyss"* (Chp. 11:7). He is the *"Beast that was, and is not, even he is the eighth"* (Chp. 17:10-11 KJV). Mark Hitchcock writes, *'I believe the Antichrist will truly die and come back to life – in a striking parody of the death and resurrection of Jesus Christ'. 'Who Is The Antichrist?'* (Eugene, ON: Harvest House, 2011), 143.

The Biggest Lie of All

We are not told what *"THE Lie"* (in 1 Thessalonians chapter 2 verse 11) actually is, or when that *"lie"* is broadcast. Many have thought in the past that *"the lie"* would be about the 'whereabouts' of the Christians who will disappear at the *"rapture"*. Though Satan will have plausible lies (probably about aliens, parallel universes, black holes and such like) ready for that event, those may not be the greatest lie of all. *"THE Lie"* may be that this man, who has come back from the *"Abyss"*, is a god and the Dragon, who has performed the deed, is the greater god: The greatest of all gods. That may explain why, even though men will acknowledge *"God"* in tribulation times, they will still worship the Dragon. What awful days of demonic delusion will that be? And those days are not very far away ...

We live in a day, not only of social media, and global news, but of instant news as well. Seconds after an event takes place – whether by official means or not – the news has travelled to millions of devices around the world. The focus of all the world will be increasingly on this man, and after three and a half years of his rule, and increasing unrest as well, such an event as an assassination will shock and paralyse the world, including the places where he doesn't officially rule. The stage will be set for the beginning of *"signs, miracles and wonders"*, which will be performed by the second *"Beast"*.

[We will study him in the next **Chapter**, *'The Beast out of the Land'*.]

The Beast and His End

Some will ask, 'Who gives him his authority?' Is it the Dragon? There is no doubt that the Dragon is behind him and his deceptions. But as we look at the remaining verses of the passage, we will see that it is God who sets the limits and boundaries on what Satan can do. God permits, but God also limits. Nothing happens outside the 'permissive will' of our God, and when boundaries He has set are approached, or rebelled against, God always 'pushes back' in judgment. And it will be so here, *"He that gathereth into captivity he shall go into captivity: he that killeth with the sword he must be killed with the sword. Here is the endurance and the faith of the saints."* (Revelation 13 verse 10 NRB).

What does this mean? John is still speaking of the first Beast. You remember the promise given to Abraham, way back in Genesis (chapter 12 verse 2 KJV), *"I will bless them that bless thee, and curse him that curseth thee"*. The blessing is for many who have a right attitude to the descendants of Abraham, not only today, but especially in the Tribulation time as well. But the *"curse"* is on individuals.

It is on a *"him"*. Do we not see, even from history, that the greatest attacks and hatred against Jews often began with one individual leader? So it will be here: This *"Beast"* ruler will hate the Jews as much as his father the Devil. And for his persecuting of the Jews, here in our passage we have the *"curse"* of God pronounced upon him. His end is prophesied, it is 1,260 days away.

> **KEYNOTE: The Last Battle.** At the 'Campaign of *"Armageddon"'* where the two *"Beasts"* make their last stand, they will be cut down by the word of the *"King of kings"*, whose spoken word is as a sword itself (Rev. 19:11-21). How true to the last detail are the prophecies of the Word of God. From Genesis through to Revelation! We will look at *"Armageddon"* as a separate topic in **Chp. 19**.

The First Beast – A Summary

Let us summarise our study about the *"Sea-Beast"*:

We have seen he is supervised by the Dragon. He rises from southern Europe, connected with the old Roman or Latin nations (though perhaps with wider roots). He closely resembles the Dragon his master, at least from heaven's viewpoint, where he can have no disguise. He will be supported by *"ten kings"* (Revelation chapter 17 verse 12), some of whom have no monarchical *"authority"*, but he will allow them to share his ceremonial position for as long as they suit his purposes. He will destroy <u>three</u> of them at some point in his reign (We are told this in Daniel chapter 7 verse 8. The *"little horn"*, who rises unexpectedly, will *"pluck up"* three of the ten horns). All the prophetic pictures must fit together, or else we have got our interpretation wrong, and we need to adjust our thinking. The Word of God must 'harmonise', and no more so than in our present prophetic studies.

At some point in the seven-year period (possibly the very mid-point), an assassination attempt will take place. This man will have more enemies than friends, no matter how powerful he is, and someone will cut him down. We will look at that again when we come to the *"Second Beast"*. It is possible traditional weapons will be used in the battles and fighting in Revelation. A *"sword wound"* (Revelation chapter 13 verse 14 KJV) is not surprising, and many ceremonial guards today still carry swords and bayonets.

The Dragon takes credit for the 'reappearing' of the King from *"out of the Abyss"*, as we have seen (Revelation chapter 11 verse 7 KJV), and much worship will be given to both the man, and the *"Dragon"*. With his renewed power, the *"Beast"* will now throw off the last of his 'peace-maker' disguises, and he will begin a programme of intense persecution against Jews, and any who worship God, or look for a coming Messiah. To take his programme to the next level, the Dragon needs another man, a second *"Beast"*. Though he may have been in the shadows for some time, now when Satan is on earth and angry (at the midpoint of the seven years) is the time for him to make his appearance and bring the last part of Satan's programme to a climax.

Terrifying times lie ahead. The choices will be stark: Worship *"Anti-Christ"* and live for a time until Jesus returns in judgment. Or worship *"the Lamb"*, and most probably be martyred, but live again in the Kingdom with the *"King of kings"* for ever.

Many, sadly, will make the wrong choice and be damned. For all eternity.

Questions and Answers for Chapter Thirteen – *'The Beast out of the Sea'*

Chp. 13 – 'The Beast out of the Sea'

Q1. Where does the first Beast come from?

Q2. What and where does this 'sea' represent?

Q3. How many heads does the Beast have?

Q4. How many horns does he have?

Q5. Who is he like?

Q6. Is there any difference between the description of the 'Dragon' and the 'Beast'?

Q7. Which animals, in the passage, is he compared to?

Q8. Who does he receive his power from?

Q9. Who sets his limits, and his final judgment?

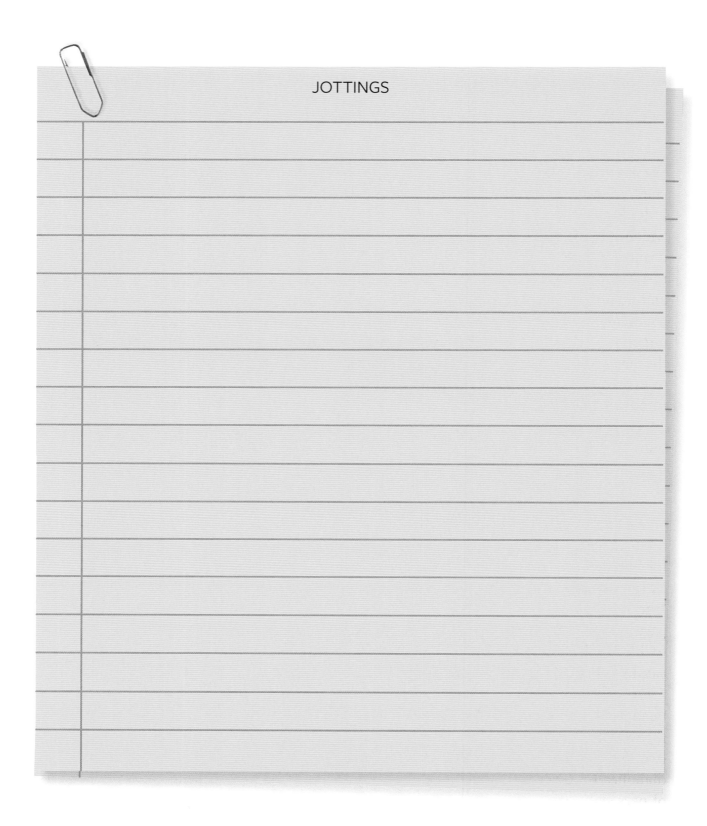

JOTTINGS

Chapter Fourteen

The Beast out of the Land

We are still in the 'gap' or centre parenthesis (Revelation chapter 11 verse 19 through to chapter 15 verse 5). God has hit the 'pause button' on what He is showing John of the judgment programme, after his visions of the Seals and the Trumpets. The focus has been widened and John is being shown the 'Conflict of the Ages' and the key players in that great drama. It is the *'Unfolding Drama of Redemption'* as W. G. Scroggie titled it. The final result is not in doubt; the Lamb will be victorious, Satan and his angels will be defeated, and finally condemned. But right here, in the centre section, John is being shown the new characters that the Dragon will move to 'centre stage' ready for the very last days. The *"Beast out of the Sea"* (chapter 13 verse 1 KJV) will make his appearance towards the beginning of the seven years. He may be moving in the background before that, in commerce, politics, or even nobility, we do not know (he may be alive now). At God's time when restraint is removed, Satan will empower him and he will appear – the rider on the white horse – with great charisma and rhetoric, to sway millions, billions even, of the world's population with his appeal.

But only for a short time. God is working above and beyond the powers of darkness. The *"Sealed scroll"* is being opened, and judgment for human and demonic rebellion is underway. In the mid-point of the seven years, following *"the war in heaven"*, Satan is cast down to earth. From that moment he can count the days to his final conflict with Messiah (which he cannot win). His days are literally numbered: 1,260 of them exactly. He no longer has any need for a disguise, and all false pretences are thrown off like a cloak. His two key 'front men' (we are coming to the second one now), are diabolically inspired, and the worst days ever of persecution and judgment are approaching. Small wonder Jeremiah called it *"the time of Jacob's Trouble"* (Jeremiah 30 verse 7 KJV),

> **KEYNOTE: More Counterfeiting.**
> We already know Satan is a master counterfeiter. He presents himself as a counterfeit God. His first Beast will be a counterfeit *"King of kings"*. His death and resurrection will be a counterfeit of what took place at Jesus' first coming. He will have a counterfeit covenant with the Jews. A counterfeit peace and a counterfeit religion. (The subject of 'Religious Babylon' in **Chp. 17**.) He will have a counterfeit prophet, a miracle worker like Moses, who *"doeth great signs, so that also he maketh fire come down from heaven unto the earth in the sight of men, and deceiveth them which dwell on the earth by means of signs which he had power to do in the sight of the Beast."* (Rev. 13:13-14 NRB). It is worthwhile listing the things that you are aware of that Satan will be permitted to 'counterfeit'.

a *"day of which there is none like it"*, just as Jesus confirmed in His 'Olivet Discourse' (Matthew chapters 24 – 25).

The Beast out of the Land

Let us look now at this second Beast, *"out of the Land"*. His appearance and his role are very different from the first, but Satan needs them both to work together for a total deception. John says, *"I beheld another beast coming up out of the earth; and he had two horns like a young (male) lamb, and he spoke as a dragon. And he exerciseth all the authority of the first beast in his presence, and causeth the earth and them which dwell therein to worship the first beast whose deadly would was healed."* (Revelation chapter 13 verses 11 – 12 NRB).

Trinity of Evil

> ***KEYNOTE: Which Beast is Anti-Christ?**
> Some scholars have considered the second Beast to be the *"Anti-Christ"*, because he looks like a 'ram-lamb' with two horns, which is often a picture of Jesus, even in the book of Revelation. Others feel, author included, that the context of the chapter leans towards a 'trinity of evil', in which case the 1st Beast, following the Dragon, would represent The Anti-Christ. The word *'anti'* in the original language carries both meanings, 'against' as well as 'instead of'. Both *"Beasts"* and the *"Dragon"* likewise are against God. The 1st Beast is instead of Christ, as a 'false-Messiah'.

The infernal trinity will then be complete:

- **The Dragon is 'Anti-God'.**
- **The Sea-Beast is 'Anti-Christ'.**
- **The second Land-Beast is 'Anti-Spirit'.**

The 'Lamb-like Beast' directs worship to the first Beast, which Jesus said the Holy Spirit would do in relation to Him (John chapter 16 verse 13)*. Though there is a sense in which both Beasts are *"Anti-Christs"*, we should remember that the word *"Anti-Christ"* in the singular is only found once in the Bible (1 John chapter 2 verse 18 NRB), but John says, *"we know it is the last hour, for there are many anti-Christs"*. So, although both Beasts (and the Dragon) and other false prophets and false teachers too are 'anti-Christ' (as in 'against Christ'), it would appear that the first Beast (whom we have seen in different forms from Revelation chapter 6 onwards), and who has many names in the Old Testament prophecies, is *"The Anti-Christ"* of whom John speaks in the singular. He is not only 'against Christ', but he is also 'instead of' Christ.*

The Second Beast looks very Different?

Some will ask, 'If the first Beast looks like his master the Dragon, why does this Beast look like a Lamb?' That is a good question. There is no doubt the 'lamb-like' appearance is meant to be Messianic. He looks at first sight like a returning Jesus, though he is an arch-deceiver, for he has a 'dragon voice'. We should remember that Jesus, when He returns as *"Messiah"* for remnant Israel, as the *"Bridegroom"* for the Church, and as *"King of kings"* to rule the world, will fulfil all three of these roles at the same time. Satan in his counterfeiting can only come as close as he is permitted by God. No counterfeit is perfect, or else it would become the 'real thing'. Satan, the *"Serpent of old"*, desires world rule and has the authority to give it, for a time, to the man who will worship him. Though Jesus could not fail in His temptations, what the Devil offered Him was a genuine offer of 'world rule' (Matthew chapter 4 verses 1 – 11), and in God's time Satan will make the same offer to a man who will accept it, and the worship of the Devil which goes with it.

Satan will then have a man who has bowed to him, to become the political and commercial leader of much of the world. But he needs a second man to bring the 'Messianic' personality into the relationship. Is it possible, because Satan knows God's programme but not His timetable (the *"times and seasons"* we looked at earlier), that he will have had key men ready in EVERY generation, since the beginning of the 'Church Age'? When God's programme begins to move again, the 'clock of prophecy' will move forward, and God will begin to remove restraint: Satan will have his men ready, waiting in the wings. It is not likely that he will want, or need, a further generation of many years to bring his 'front-men' to maturity.

The Jews will make a <u>political</u> and <u>territorial</u> covenant for seven years with the first Beast, *"a covenant with Death and with Hades …"* (Isaiah chapter 28 verse 15 NRB) but the second Beast will convince many of the Jews to worship a false Messiah (the *"signs"* may be primarily for Jews), and the wider religious world to worship a unified single false god. Every other false religion, as well as true Christianity, will be banned. Satan needs both men to accomplish his infernal purposes; that of global control and world-wide worship. A counterfeit Messianic Kingdom, which he cannot achieve, but his incorrigible hatred and anger will never allow him to admit his defeat. What an awfully perverted being the high angel who fell from heaven has become!

A Beast 'Out of the Land'?

Another question some will be asking is, 'Why does this Beast come out of the 'earth', or 'land'. What does that mean?' Just as the *"seas"* in the Bible speak of the Gentile nations, so the word for *"land"* (which is the same word as for *"earth"* in Hebrew) often refers to Israel* and their promised territorial possession.

> ***KEYNOTE: The Land.** Though the Jews had no 'Land', while they were in Egypt, nor while they were in the wilderness (Ex. 1 to Jos. 4), nor while they were in 'exile' from 606 BC. (2 Chron. 36), nor from the destruction of Jerusalem in 70 AD. through to 1948 AD, yet Jehovah had promised Abraham a *"Land"* and a *"nation"*, and to David a *"king forever"* on the throne. (Gen. 12:1-3; 2 Sam. 7:11-12). These unconditional *"covenants"* must have a literal conclusion.

It is most likely that regarding the *"Beast out of the land"* pictured here, the *"<u>land</u>"* refers again to Israel's geographical territory. This second Beast will most probably not be a Gentile, but an Israeli born Jew. We suggested earlier that he may even be from the most northerly tribe of Dan and from the Syrian border area. This combining of a cosmopolitan multi-ethnic westerner (perhaps of Islamic origin), and an Israeli born Jew would be a very potent combination, at least for Western and Middle Eastern supremacy. It would appear from certain scriptures (Ezekiel chapters 38-39; Daniel chapter 11 verse 44; Revelation chapter 16 verse 12) that their control will not extend into the far north of Russia, nor to China, nor possibly beyond northern Africa. But for these final three and a half years their control commercially, politically, and religiously over their sovereign territory will be absolute.

Israel in the Land

The Sign of the Fig Tree's Leaves

Since the 15th of May 1948 the State of Israel, '*Eretz Israel*', has occupied part of their ancient territory west of the Jordan Valley. The commonly used term 'Occupied West Bank', implying illegal settlement, has no foundation in scripture. The boundaries were set out by Jehovah to Abraham hundreds of years in advance, *"from the river of Egypt unto the great River … Euphrates"* (Genesis chapter 15 verse 18 KJV). Though their present territory is small, a 'dagger at the heart of humanity', a past President of Iraq has said, referring to the shape of the modern map, yet many prophecy scholars believe that the regeneration of the Nation State – even though in disregard for Jehovah or Messiah – is that which was *"cursed"* now having come back to life. Political life that is. This is why the illustration and parable were regarding a *"fig tree"*, not an olive tree or a vine.

The fig tree with no spiritual fruit (Matthew chapter 21 verses 18 – 20 ESV) was cursed by Jesus and *"withered at once"*, fulfilled in 70 AD. Now, the *"fig tree putting out its leaves"* (Matthew chapter 24 verses 32 – 35 ESV) is seen in the rebirth of the Nation. Jesus said, *"This generation will not pass away until all these things take place"*. That is, not the generation which slew Messiah and saw Jerusalem razed, for that took place inside the <u>same</u> generation, but the generation which will see Israel reborn politically – see the *"Great Tribulation"* – which shall be reborn spiritually, and *"see the Son of Man Coming"*. That also will take place inside a generation. The key to interpreting these combined parables is this; scripture <u>does not</u> define a generation. God can (and will) lengthen or shorten as He pleases.

KEYNOTE: Date-Setting! Scripture does not say that a generation is 'fixed' between 70 and 80 years (Psalm 90 verse 10). Those who add '80 maximum' years to 1948 AD = 2028 etc. are guilty of 'date-setting'. So to were the Rabbis, who added 70 years and expected 'big events' in 2018. ALL who set dates will be disappointed, and discredit prophetic teaching. Jesus said, *"Concerning that day and hour knoweth no one, no, not the angels which are in heaven, neither the Son, but the Father"* (Mk. 13:32 NRB).

The False Prophet Acts

The political link, followed by the religious idolatry of their association with the 'Land Beast', will draw Israel into the very last days of her *"Trouble"*. What – by political expediency – she seeks to avoid, that is her annihilation, will come closer than ever before. The desires of Satan would be fulfilled, but for the unalterable purposes of God.

We have seen that this second and final period of 1,260 days begins with the assassination of the first Beast. He is cut down, and returns mysteriously *"out of the Abyss"* (Revelation chapter 11 verse 7; chapter 17 verse 11). The second Beast, who is called the *"False Prophet"* (Revelation chapter 16 verses 13; chapter 19 verse 20), will surely make tremendous media capital out of this event. For such a prominent man to be cut down will be a world-shaking event. Most of our readers will not remember the assassination of President J. F. Kennedy of the USA, but some will remember the shock of the assassination of the Israeli Prime Minister, Yitzhak Rabin, on 4ᵗʰ November 1995. Or even the attempted assassination of President Ronald Reagan of the USA on 30ᵗʰ March 1981. President Reagan did not die, thankfully, for bodyguards and policemen took some of the bullets intended for him. This assassination event, regarding the 'Beast-Ruler', will stop the world in its tracks. The news will be conveyed in an instant, and his many enemies will rejoice. Perhaps even persecuted Christians too? The increasingly unpopular and demagogic leader will be gone …

Will the *"False Prophet"* be wounded too? It is possible. The first Beast will have a 'sword wound'. We will see that in more detail now. There is a strange passage in Old Testament prophecy which speaks of, *"The idol shepherd … the sword shall be upon his arm, and upon his right eye: his arm shall be clean dried up, and his right eye shall be utterly darkened"* (Zechariah chapter 11 verse 17 KJV). The word *"idol"* here is not 'lazy'. It is 'a false god'. Perhaps this foremost Man-Beast is indeed killed, and his main supporter is also wounded in the attack and carries his wounds afterwards? The Israeli Defence Minister, Moshe Dayan (1915 – 1981), lost an eye in battle, and wore a black eye patch as a trademark afterwards as a politician. Keep these physical deformities in mind as we move forward into the latter part of the chapter; the *"right arm and right eye"* may be very significant.

Shock and Awe

The shock and awe of the assassination will be nothing to that which will follow. We don't know if a great funeral will be arranged, but it is very possible. 'Where will it be?' you might ask. Either in his new capital city Babylon, or in the old Jewish city of Jerusalem. It is possible, if such an event takes place, that it will be in Jerusalem, where the media may gather for the event and possibly a time of enforced global mourning. 'Will it be on the third day?' someone asks. It would not be surprising if it was. Perhaps even during his funeral preparations, the *"Beast out of the Abyss"* will reappear. Will there also be a change in his character, more closely linked to the Dragon, more demonic? We do not really know.

The eastern approach to 'Haram al-Sharif (the Noble Sanctuary) the Muslim name for Temple Mount. (JHF)
A possible location (the Jews having shared right to worship) of the appearance of the "Beast out of the Abyss".

It is possible he will appear in the very *"holy place"* of the newly built Temple Court and Jewish Sanctuary, just as Jesus prophesied in His Olivet Discourse, *"When ye therefore shall see the* <u>*Abomination of Desolation*</u>*, spoken of by Daniel the prophet, stand in* <u>*the holy place*</u> *..."* (Matthew chapter 24 verses 15 - 22 KJV). The *"False Prophet"* will now take charge. This is now his greatest *"sign"*, and the greatest deception.

The Devil's 'spin-doctor' (perhaps 'witch-doctor' would be a better label) will reveal the true purpose of his position. The miracle event and this miraculous person must be commemorated. No one can doubt his claim to supremacy, and his demand for worship any longer. *"Make an image of the Beast"* (Revelation chapter 13 verse 14), will be the command, just as Nebuchadnezzar did, back in Daniel chapter 3. He alone must be worshipped, as the only God. The Beast, the Image, and the Dragon. All the false gods of all religions will have become one infernal trinity.

A Living Statue Speaks

Worse is yet to come. Now the *"Image"* (probably a literal statue), set up in the Temple court (where all Jewish worship which was permitted under the seven-year covenant will now be banned), will come to life. It will have *"breath"* or *"spirit"*. 'What does this mean?' you ask. 'Artificial intelligence?' (A.I.) 'Demonic possession?' Or an actual 'living statue'? We do not really know. Every picture is terrifying, and those who will be there will understand the implications, for the full detail of Jesus' warnings in His last teaching to the Jews, the 'Olivet Discourse', will now come true. *"Flee into the mountains"* (Matthew chapter 24 verse 16 KJV), 'Don't even go home to get a bag!' The greatest days of Tribulation ever will be just about to begin. The whole world appears damned ...

Is the World Doomed?

Is it really? Not so. The Devil can never have 'full control'. God is supreme. *"Blessed are the dead which die in the Lord from henceforth"* (Revelation chapter 14 verse 13 KJV), the Lord Jesus said. There are seven *"blessings"* in the book of Revelation, but this one is addressed directly to those who will be martyred for their faith during the Tribulation. Remember the story of the three Hebrew young men, *"Shadrach, Meshach and Abednego"*, in Daniel chapter three. What did they say? *"O Nebuchadnezzar, we have no need to answer you in this matter. If this be so, our God whom we serve is able to deliver us from the burning fiery furnace, and He will … But if not, be it known to you, O King, that we will not … worship the golden image that you have set up."* (Daniel chapter 3 verses 16 – 18 ESV). The penalty for not worshipping this Image is not death by fire but by beheading (with an *"axe"* as the original meaning in Revelation chapter 20 verse 4 tells us).

The choice is stark. Side with Christ or with Anti-Christ: Believe in the *"Coming King"*, who is Jesus the *"Lamb of God"*. Own Him as Lord and denounce the Lie. Suffer the death penalty, physically endure a martyr's death, and live forever spiritually. Or, alternatively, worship the Dragon, deny Christ, live on for a short time. But die spiritually forever. *"This is the second death"* (Revelation chapter 20 verse 14 KJV). Lose your head or lose your soul. That is how stark the choice will be. Yet millions will bow willingly to the Dragon, and to his icon. For they will already have joined with the Beast and the False Prophet in a terrible union, from which there is no escape. An association to begin with. Then a commercial permit, lastly prohibitions and compulsory religious identification.

'What is the *'Mark of the Beast'*?

That is a subject by itself, and not an easy one either. We will look at that in some detail in our next Chapter …

Q&A >

Questions and Answers for Chapter Fourteen – *'The Beast out of the Land'*

Chp. 14 – 'The Beast out of Land'

Q1. Where does the second Beast appear from?

Q2. What does the 'land' usually represent? And why?

Q3. Why is this Beast so different looking?

Q4. What is his role?

Q5. Who is he a counterfeit of?

Q6. What key event happens at the mid-point of the 7 years?

Q7. What, at that point, does the False Prophet propose?

Q8. What is the final choice, and between which two opposites?

Chapter Fifteen

The Mark of the Beast: 666

This Chapter may be a little different, and some parts of it will be a recap for those who have been reading all the way through the book. But there will be some who will arrive at this Chapter first. Before they have read anything else. They will have scanned the Chapter Index, and come straight here. That is no surprise, and you are most welcome at this point!

KEYNOTE: Overview. It might be helpful, even if you don't want to read the whole book just now, to have a look at, *'Does God have a Programme?'* (**Chp. 2**). *'The Symbols Explained'* (**Chp. 7**) and at the two previous *'Beast'* Sections (**Chps. 13 & 14**). That would provide a backdrop to where we are here. But even that is not essential. Do please continue with this Chapter first if it is your prime interest or concern.

A New World Order?

Many in our world right now are concerned about things they don't understand, the possibility of a 'behind-the-scenes' agenda (many have heard the phrase 'Agenda 2030' or the '2045 Initiative'), and incoming systems of control that, once put in place, will never be reversed. In one sense all of that is credible and harmonises with a biblical 'End Times' worldview. *'Coming Events Cast Their Shadows Before Them'*, as the poet Thomas Campbell wrote back in 1802. Events that are going to happen often give 'signs' that they are on the way. Like earth tremors building up to a mighty eruption, so things that are about to happen, in God's programme, will likewise have their 'shadows' cast in front.

[We will look at the build-up of *"signs"* in, *'Things That Could Happen'* **Chp. 25**.]

There is no doubt that a generation growing up today, and even mature adults too, are seeing things that they have never seen before. 'Unprecedented' is a much over-used word in the global media, yet it can be applied more and more to things we are seeing in our times. Global *"pestilences"* (to use a Bible word) are on the increase. Global travel helps to spread a 'virus' in a way that could not have happened 100 years ago. The 'Spanish Flu' of 1918-20 (the original 'H1N1' virus) is estimated to have affected one third of the world's population; about 500,000,000 out of 1.5 billion back then, and over 50,000,000 died, making the mortality rate 1:10. There is no one left alive who remembers that 'pandemic', truly an event of 'biblical proportions' (another term beloved of the media). Is it not strange how people refer to the *"plagues"* of the Bible, but on the other hand often deny the God of the Bible?

Though many of these *"pestilences"* had natural causes, the 'Spanish flu', for example, became rapidly global not from jet travel, for such a thing didn't then exist, but from the large numbers of 'demobbed' soldiers returning by ship to every corner of the British Empire. The First World War (1914 - 18), and the 'Spanish Flu' (1918 – 20) were early global events at the entry to the twentieth century. 'Globalisation' has not slowed since, and many of the events we have been studying will be global in effect. The Second World War (1939 – 45), closely following the First, was even more global and in a great many respects our world changed hugely and permanently in the years of rebuilding after WW2.

The gradual collapse of the 'British Empire', the creation of the 'United Nations' (U.N.G.A.), the rebirth of the State of Israel (1948), the dissolution of the U.S.S.R. (1988 – 91), the rise in economic power of the U.S.A., the might of the dollar and the 'Federal Reserve', the growth of the 'European Union' (E.U.), the emergence of China as an eastern 'Superpower' have all set the stage for a world that is different in many ways, but has now become familiar to the present generation …

The 'millennials', those coming into their thirties, born in the entry to the twenty first century, and the global student-age generation (who make up 40% of global population) see our present world through very different eyes than any generation before (except perhaps the generation that lived before the Genesis Flood, but that is another story altogether). Though birth rate is falling in the west, it is increasing in Sub-Saharan Africa and Southern Asia. Most of the world's youth today are Asian or African, not Caucasian. This 'multi-ethnic' generation lives in a connected 'techno-world' which was foreign to previous generations, and still is to many older people. Social media has relevance and connectivity, and apparent 'truth' that mainstream media is deemed not to have. All these factors have changed our world for ever, but not necessarily for 'good'.

We are connected by hardware, and disconnected socially. The increasing monitoring of our activity; our movements, our health, our wealth, and our opinions are generally accepted. Even considered a good thing by some. The '5G' and '6G' technology rollout will take us further and further into an unimaginable cyber-age. All of this 'casts a shadow' in relation to what prophetic pronouncements say about the world in the soon coming *"seven years"* which is the 'back-bone' of all unfulfilled Bible prophecy (Daniel chapter 9 verses 24 – 27).

Literal Prophecy – Must be Fulfilled

Some Bible scholars (let us review things a little) tell us that 'prophecy is history'. The technical term is 'preterism' (a Latin word which means 'in the past'). They say that all the trouble and terrors of the *"Seal Judgments"*, the *"Four Horsemen"*, the *"Trumpets"*, the *"Bowls"*; the war, famine, death and pestilence, were all fulfilled as far back as 70 AD when Jerusalem was burned by the Romans. The greatest rebuttal to that argument is: If all 'future event' prophecy was fulfilled in the first century, why did Jesus not return then? All 'End Times' prophecies, Old Testament and New, are linked with that singular event: The <u>Second Coming of Messiah</u>. But He has not come back. Not yet ...

Some other scholars, following largely from a teacher called 'Augustine of Hippo' (354 – 430AD), taught that no future prophecy or 'End Times' predictions were literal. <u>All were symbolic</u>. There is no doubt that some prophetic pictures are symbolic, but many are not. And have we not seen already that some that seemed symbolic, when they were given, became very literal at the time of their fulfilment? The *"white horse"* in Revelation 6 may be symbolic (maybe not). The *"Beast with seven heads"* (Revelation chapter 12 & 13) may be representative of both an evil man and the Devil, not a literal animal. That may be true.

But the return of Jesus for His Church? Is that not a literal event? If not, then what He told His disciples before He went away was only a myth. The future Kingdom, promised to the Patriarchs, and a monarchy promised to David? (Genesis chapter 12 and 15; 2 Samuel chapter 7). Are these only 'heavenly pictures'? Does this world – our world – which we are polluting and contaminating; does it not have a future cleansing and restoration and a 1,000 year period of peace to look forward to? Does Israel have no long-term future, as Abraham and David were promised? Were they also deluded over 4,000 years ago? Is the return of Israel to the world map in 1948 of no significance? Is the *"Holy City ... New Jerusalem"* not a city at all? Such things <u>must</u> be true, or all scripture becomes fanciful in its interpretation.

> **KEYNOTE:** We will look at a short summary of each of the different 'views' on prophecy, and the subject of 'literality' in **Appx. II**. It is sufficient to say here that the position taken within this book is what is known as; 'Literal, futurist, pre-tribulational & pre-millennial'. Some of these terms will become clearer as we proceed.

Numbers in Scripture

Here is another problem, once you begin to make numbers in the Bible symbolic; that *"seven"* for instance does not mean 7, or *"one thousand"* does not mean 1,000. That *"42 months"* does not mean *"1,260 days"*: Then *"the third day"* in relation to Jesus' resurrection is questionable as to its reality as well. To use the Latin term, *'reductio ad adsurdum'*, this argument when reduced to a basic level makes no sense at all. We have seen before that when scripture attaches a number to a period, then that period becomes literal and measured. For example, *"a day"* prophetically is an undefined short period, but *"six days"* is specific, and means six literal days of 24 hours each (as in Genesis chapter 1).

We have also found, further back in our studies, that when dealing with prophecy we can see that as the fulfilment time comes closer so the 'focus' becomes clearer, and things which seemed symbolic from far away, such as *"a virgin shall conceive, and bear a son"* (Isaiah chapter 7 verse 14 KJV), can come true totally and literally, 700 years later. It did not matter if the prophet did not fully understand what he foretold, often he did not. But he, and his hearers were expected to believe that if God said He would do something, anything, then He would fulfil it. When the specified time came.

The Devil's Agenda

That brings us back to our key subject here: *"The Mark of the Beast"*. 'Is there a literal future time of statist control and totalitarianism in which this scene is set?' The answer is, 'Yes.' 'Will there be a Gentile political ruler and a religious Israeli 'spin-doctor' who will assume control of all commercial and religious freedoms?' The answer again is, 'Yes.' 'Will this mega-lock-down period begin in the middle of a seven-year period, which will begin apparently peacefully?' 'Yes, and yes.' 'Will there be huge deception? Will people walk into this scenario with their eyes closed?' 'Yes, and no.' Those answers are the core of our subject here.

Let us get the context and timing right. What we are dealing with here, the *"Mark of the Beast"*, and the *"666"* brand (Revelation chapter 13 verses 14 – 18), are set in the middle of the seven-year period, and run from then for 42 months to the conclusion of that same period.

Even when this 'Peacemaker', the covenant-broker, the Gentile western ruler comes to the fore, even then these things do not 'go to the bad' straight away. There must be *"a covenant with the many"*; between Israel and her neighbours (Daniel chapter 9 verses 25 – 27). Possibly ten western and middle eastern signatories, as well as the representatives of the state of Israel, and perhaps the *"Coming Prince"* will sign too. Twelve signatures in all. This may include (as a condition of the agreement) a standing down of the armed forces of Israel. And a period of stability in the Middle East, between Jew and Arab which has not existed for 1,400 years, or perhaps in a biblical context not for 3,900 years since the days of Isaac and Ishmael, Abraham's sons.

Where does the Peace Plan go Wrong?

Some might ask, 'Does the seven-year peace plan go wrong?' 'No, it doesn't!' At least not from the perspective of Satan, the arch-deceiver, the master counterfeiter, the 'Power behind the Throne' in this Kingdom, who will be working out his own agenda*. An 'anti-God' plan in which

Jew and Arab together again in peace? Not this time. Not in a *"covenant"*, for that will have been already broken. Satan, the *"Dragon"* has another dimension to his plan altogether. A global false religious system.

everyone and everything (even his Key-Men) are expendable, so long as he can achieve his goal. 'What is that?' you ask. Revenge. Against God. Nowhere in scripture is the Devil recorded as acknowledging his errors. Neither his original sin nor otherwise. He will hate and oppose, lie, and deceive, until his final judgment. Even his 'confinement' during the future '1,000 year Kingdom' will apparently teach him nothing. He will emerge, at the end, a bigger rebel than when he was locked up. And at this point, which we are discussing here, he will have a clear timetable which he himself will be aware of to work within (Revelation chapter 12 verse 12).

A Counterfeit 'Monotheistic' Religion

False Christianity (the true Church will already be gone), the Church of Rome, Jewish Temple worship, Islam with its billions of adherents in every corner of the globe. 'Chrislam' as has already been propagated in parts of the west, all coalescing together. The old 'Babylonish' religions of 'God-Woman' worship, the pagan religions of 'earth, wind and fire', the polytheistic religions of the east, animism and spiritism and ancestral worship … All combined into one blasphemous, devilish contract: 'Worship the Image or die':

- The *"Dragon"* will claim to be the supreme god.
- The *"Beast"* his human representation.
- The *"False Prophet"* his worship leader.
- The *"Image"*, the physical object of veneration: 'Bow, or be beheaded'.

On the other hand, the Devil will give the global religious masses the end point for which their own religions have been seeking: The Jews will receive this man, by the convincing of the *"signs"* of the *"False Prophet"*, as the kind of *"Messiah"* they have desired. Eastern mystical religions are seeking for 'The Maitreya', the one who will identify the 'Lord of the World'. The 'World Teacher' that many esoteric orders are seeking for too. The 'Imam Al-Mahdi', the 'Twelfth Iman', that both branches of Islam have been seeking for 1,400 years. A *"false Christ"*, as Jesus prophesied (Matthew chapter 24 verse 24). False-Christianity, mega-churches of 'pseudo-saved', but looking for a 'Christ' in their own image, when their world is ready for him to come … All of these will be convinced by the deception of the Dragon, the Beast, and the False Prophet (Revelation chapter 16 verses 13 – 14) that the 'One True God' has come. *"The Lie"*, which will be God's judgment on those who rejected the gospel of Jesus Christ will have come to pass (2 Thessalonians chapter 2 verses 11 – 12 NRB). Millions will be deceived into believing the credentials of deity of this demonic trinity, *"that they should believe the lie: that they all might be damned who believed not the truth."*

Satan will have the millions fully convinced, for the deception will be complete. His *"Beast out of the Abyss"* will have accomplished the greatest miracle of all; he will have come back from the 'other side'. The *"Image"* of this man, his statue, will have 'come to life' as well. The *"False Prophet"* will call down fire from heaven, as a further sign. Who would not be convinced to be associated with such a powerful combination?

Identification with Evil

'Identification' is the key word. Following on from the shock of the assassination of this man, a vulnerability that will be unexpected, along with the failure of his 'peace treaty' and the war and famine and disease, many may be saying, 'He is not as god-like or as invincible as we thought'. Then will come this massive reversal of events. The totally unexpected. Especially for those who today deny any form of 'after life'. This 'god-man', whom the Bible describes as *"the Beast out of the Abyss"*, will return to life. Possibly (as we have suggested) at his own funeral, and certainly appearing in the newly rebuilt Temple Court in Jerusalem.

Disbelief and disaffection turn to adulation, and the *"False Prophet"* takes full advantage, with a pre-planned strategy of infernal guile. John says, *"He causeth all both small and great, and rich and poor, and free and bond, to receive a mark on their right hand, or on their foreheads: and that no one should be able to buy or sell, save he that had the mark, or the name of the Beast, or the number of his name."* (Revelation 13 verses 16 – 17 NRB).

The Mark of The Beast!

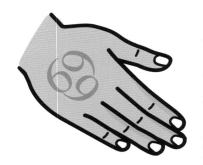

Here is strange language indeed. 'What is the Mark of The Beast?' Many of you will be asking that. And, 'We want to know because we don't want it!'

That is a hugely important. A very pertinent fear; and growing increasingly relevant in the minds of many every day. And yet … Here is one incredible fact to grasp hold of: Today, even as you read this, most people do NOT want this *"Mark"*, whatever it is. The *"666"* brand. People today are cautious, even of vaccines and the like, in case … In case of what? Of the unknown, the accidental, or even the irreversible …

In that coming day (from the middle of the seven-year period onwards), despite the failure of his peace-programme, and the breaking of his *"covenant"* with the Jews, in the adulation of a 'god-man' surrounded by miracles of every evil kind, many will want the insignia which identifies them with him. There will be no holding back. Except by those who will not worship the 'False Trinity'.

What Is the Mark?

'But what is the 'Mark of the Beast'?' you ask. The answer is twofold: Firstly, we don't know. Secondly, it is more than one thing. The *"Beast"* has a fourfold insignia or 'iconography'.

Let us examine that:

1. **The *"Image"*.** Probably an actual statue (not just his 'image' projected on TV as many used to imagine years ago). A statue, larger than life, like that designed by Nebuchadnezzar (Daniel chapter 3), and set in the place of the Jewish altar in the newly erected Temple Court. That is why it was called the *"Abomination of Desolation standing in the Holy Place"* by Jesus in His Olivet Discourse (Matthew chapter 24 verse 15 – 22). He expanded prophetically on what Daniel said in chapter 9 of his prophecy. This will be the 'Mecca' of the *"Beast's"* new religious epicentre. 'Come to Jerusalem, and prostrate yourself before the Image.' East meets West in religious superstition, genuflection, and prostration.

2. **The *"Mark"*.** Three things are important here: Firstly, though all three 'insignia' are linked, it is not called 'The Mark of the Beast'. That is our short-hand terminology. It is referred to firstly as *"a mark"*, then after that as *"the mark"*. Secondly, it is initially offered (by the spin-doctor who is the *"False Prophet"*) as a 'free gift'. That is the meaning of the word *"receive"* in our passage. It is not initially enforced. It is offered. Thirdly, the word *"mark"* itself means 'cutting in'. It may possibly be a 'tattoo' of some kind, for all who want to have an 'identifier' with this person. 'Inking' has become the norm, even in our times, across all generations. A progression towards the very days we are looking at here. Desecration of the *"image"* is a delight to the Devil. Not the *"Image"* of Revelation, but the *"image"* of Genesis chapter 1; man made in God's image from the beginning.

3. **The *"Name"*.** This carries the thought of 'character' and reputation. What he stands for, and who is his power source. Whatever god he acknowledges, people will want to be associated with that. No deception here about thinking this is worshipping the God of the Bible, and an accidental worship of the Image, the Beast, and the Dragon. Satanic worship by accident? Not at all, this is deliberate and identifiable association. Humanity, despite God's judgments and God's warnings, will be 'queued round the block', world over, to receive a loyalty mark with this trinity of evil.

4. **The *"Number"*.** This is very difficult to interpret. *"Here is wisdom,"* John says, *"Let him that hath understanding calculate the number of the Beast: for it is the number of a man; and his number is six hundred, and sixty, and six."* (Revelation 13 verse 18 KJV). We should remember that Greek and Latin, the languages John would have been familiar with, did not use numerals as we do. The numerals 1 to 9 (which are all we need for any size of number) did not begin to be used until about 1000 AD, and 'numerals' came from Hindu in India. Roman 'numbers' some of us are more familiar with, for they still appear on traditional clock faces today. (V being 5, IX being 9, X being 10, XI representing 11, and of course XII equalling 12 o'clock, and so on.)

Greek was different. They wrote numbers as 'phrases'. The English number *"666"*, which is not really what it appears to be here, is a short sentence in Greek which includes the words *"Chi, Xi, Stigma"* and the three numbers are distinct. This carries no significance to us as English speakers, but most strangely this phrase is a 'palindrome'. It makes sense, in Arabic, read from right to left, just as it does in Greek, read from left to right! We have seen hints of 'East meets West' not only in covenant, government, and territory; now we are seeing the same concept again in religious affiliation. This is very strange to our minds, but all will become clear in *"those days"*, which are coming closer and closer.

Can Anyone Take the 'Mark of the Beast' by Accident?

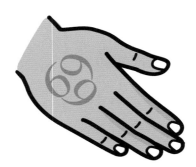

This is possibly one of the most important questions of our time, and of all 'eschatology' (all prophecy still to be fulfilled). We should be able to see now, even in the process of thinking and deduction in this passage so far; the answer must be a definite and scriptural: **NO.**

The *"mark"* may possibly be introduced as an 'identifier'. Not only will it be offered free initially, the *"mark"* will then be used as a 'permit' for buying and selling. Trading in general will gradually become possible only with the *"mark"*. Possibly not only 'permission' to buy and sell, but the very capacity to purchase anything. (A 'cryptocurrency' linked microchip implanted and remotely scanned? RFID technology is just about there already. We can only speculate as to where current technology will lead.) Probably given out to the 'elite' initially. Remember the wealthy associates of the *"Prince"* who were not affected by the 'rationing', back in the days of the third Seal? (Revelation chapter 6.) Oil and wine aplenty when the underclasses could only get bread and water to survive? Here may be another link, privileged by association to get the 'trading permit' free, right from the start, for the friends of the *"Prince"*.

After the changes at the mid-point of the seven years, with the 'deification' of the *"Beast out of the Sea"*, whose Master is the Dragon, the *"mark"* takes on a new dimension: Even if it has existed before that as an 'identification', a 'loyalty symbol', it will then move to a 'permission', and then to a 'prohibition'. *"No man might buy or sell"* unless they have the *"mark"*. All who do not take the *"mark"*, nor bow down to the *"Image"*, are cut off from society. And if they are exposed, and refuse to *"bow"* they must be killed. Probably mass beheading, as we saw in a previous study.

But the Bible is clear that the 'mark' cannot be Received by Accident?

That is still a burning question for many. And the answer: The *"mark"* cannot be received by accident, or unknowingly. God Himself will make it clear, even announcing publicly by angelic messengers (for those will be unprecedented times), not only the *"everlasting gospel"* of *"fear God and give glory to Him"* (Revelation chapter 14 verses 6 – 8 KJV), but also a warning against those who *"worship the Beast and his image, and receive his mark on his forehead or on his hand"* (chapter 14 verses 9 – 10 NRB). Those who take the *"mark"* will have identified themselves with the Beast and the Dragon (chapter 13 verse 4). There will be no secret as to the source of power, and the object of worship. *"The Lie"* is in the belief that Satan is greater than Messiah, and able to overcome the one true eternal God.

KEYNOTE: Not Yet … We are seeing 'coming events casting shadows before them'. Newly publicised methods of vaccination using 'mRNA' has caused concern in the minds of many. Strange 'Patents' may be talked about, which have been registered for reasons we cannot fully comprehend. Though '5G', and the not so far distant '6G', technology will change not only the means of our communication, but also our supervision for the rest of our time. Though 'blockchain' technology and 'cryptocurrency' will change how we *"buy and sell"*. Though our world is changing daily as we speak. Yet, the *"mark of the Beast"* is neither here, nor available. Much prophecy has still to be fulfilled before the *"Beast"*, his *"mark"* and his *"worship"* are revealed.

What Actually is the Mark?

'What does the *"666"* represent?' Those are questions we cannot fully answer. 'Coming events cast their shadow in front' as we were reminded at the start of the discussion. Such is the fading legacy of Christianity in the west: A sense of fear in the hearts of many, yet they do not fully understand what they fear. So many are no longer clear as to the timetable of the fulfilment of God's programme, and of His promises to His own, given in His inerrant Word.

Here are some Key Scriptural Fundamentals to hold firmly onto in our minds:

1. **God is in Control**.
   His programme is set in heaven, Satan cannot move it forward by one second. He will not have freedom to legislate, until God permits.

   And that is within a very rigidly established timeframe (as we have seen in Revelation chapter 13 and in Daniel chapter 9).

2. **The Promises and Prophecies of Jesus must be Fulfilled**. He must return to set up His Kingdom on earth, but He must come for His Church first. He has promised to keep her (all truly *"born again"* ones), *"from the wrath which is coming here"* (1 Thessalonians chapter 1 verse 10 NRB).

3. **The Church must be Taken Away**. The part which is alive in this world, and the person of the Holy Spirit who indwells each Christian, both must be removed before full *"lawlessness"*, the *"Man of Sin"* and the *"Lawless One"* can have their *"revelation"* (2 Thessalonians chapter 2 verses 3 – 9). The Church and the Spirit

are the *"restraint"* and the *"restrainer"* against Satan bringing his key men, and his schemes to the fore.

4. **The Dead Christians must be Raised**. The *"sleeping in Jesus"*, who will be raised and changed first, so that the complete Church departs together. This is what is often called the *"Rapture"* (a word from the Latin New Testament). This event, the instantaneous disappearance of millions of Christians (from every denomination) world over, must happen before the events of this topic take place. And that event will cause massive shock waves of huge social and commercial

> **KEYNOTE: Retribution.** We do know that a deliberate association with the *"Beast"* and worship of the *"Dragon"* will bring not only eternal punishment on all who *"receive the mark"*, but also terrible pain and punishment on them during the latter part of the second half of the seven years. The *"Day of Vengeance of our God"* which will climax as the *"Wrath of the Lamb"* (Rev. 6:15-17). We will study that in more detail in *'The Bowl Judgments'* **Chp. 16**.

upheaval, especially in countries with a significant Christian population. (It has been estimated that the 'born again' percentage of the population of America is greater than the total population of Canada. The Christian population of China may be greater than the population of England etc.)

5. **The Introduction of the *'mark of the Beast'*** and the *"666"* events <u>cannot</u> happen while the Church is present here on earth. (Regardless of what strange technological or pharmacological advances are announced, and there will be many at an astonishing rapidity in the coming days.)

6. **Being Identified with BOTH Christ and Antichrist Cannot Happen**. For any person, in this day or in Tribulation days, this is spiritually impossible. Even in those awful days, refusing the Devil's identifier and being identified with Jesus as the Coming Messiah will still be possible, even if it comes with an immediate death sentence upon a refusal to bow to the *"Image"*.

Is there No Escape?

<u>There is now</u>. But there is no time to delay! The shadows of coming events are getting darker each day. There is a Saviour for all who will come to Him. Jesus Himself says, *"Come unto Me, all ye that labour* (are worn out) *and are heavy laden* (over loaded), *and I will give you rest. Take My yoke upon you, and learn of Me; for I am meek and lowly in heart: and you shall find rest unto your souls. For My yoke is easy* (to wear), *and My burden is light* (to bear)" (Matthew chapter 11 verses 28 - 30 NRB). The one who bore *"our sins in His own body on the tree"* (1 Peter chapter 2 verse 24 KJV) is the one who understands every secret fear, and every secret burden. You can find true rest, and peace, in Him right now. He is waiting for you to come.

Worship Jesus Christ today, and have no fear of the worship of *"Anti-Christ"*, in a day that is not far distant.

Questions and Answers for Chapter Fifteen – *'The Mark of the Beast: 666'*

Chp. 15 – 'The Mark of the Beast : 666'

Q1. Who are the 4 personalities linked on the side of 'good'?

Q2. Who are the 3 personalities linked on the side of 'evil'?

Q3. What does the 'False Prophet' make compulsory?

Q4. What is introduced first, and why?

Q5. What can you not do without the 'Mark'? (There may be more than one answer).

Q6. What 4 things are linked to the 'Beast' (We used 'iconography' as a general term)

Q7. What is the 'Number'?

Q8. What is God's verdict on those who have the 'Mark'?

Q9. How can we be sure that the times of the 'Mark' have not arrived?

JOTTINGS

Chapter Sixteen
The Bowl Judgments

We have come now to the other side of the 'parenthesis' (which we saw extends from Revelation chapter 11 verse 19 through to chapter 15 verse 5). Inside the parenthetic section, John is shown the 'Conflict of the Ages', the *"War in Heaven"* and the 'Seven Great Personalities' involved in this conflict down through the centuries of time and the ages of the Bible.

Recap the Parenthesis

We have looked at each of those personalities in turn; the *"Woman"*, the *"Male Son"*, the Jewish *"remnant"* and the *"Lamb on Mount Zion"* (Revelation chapter 12 verse 1 to chapter 14 verse 5). We have studied the opposing 'Trinity of Evil'; the *"Dragon"*, the *"Sea-Beast"*, and the *"Land-Beast"* or the *"False Prophet"* as he is also called. And we have seen the diabolical agenda of *"Satan"*: his desire to have as much of this world as possible take the *"mark"*, worship the *"Beast"* and the *"Image"*, and of course worship himself, the *"Dragon"*, and ultimately share his destiny in the *"eternal fire"* forever (Matthew chapter 25 verse 41 ESV).

Now this parenthetic vision is closed up. John's familiar 'time-shift' phrase, *"after these things"*, occurs again and John is introduced to the prelude of the third set of judgments; the seven angels with the *"seven plagues"* in *"seven golden bowls full of the wrath of God"* (Revelation chapter 15 verses 5 – 8 NRB).

Recap of the Judgments

When we were studying the 'Seal Judgments' (Revelation chapter 6), we saw three things of note towards the end:

Firstly, the seventh of the first two sets of judgments lead into the next set. That is, the *"seventh seal"* leads into the *"seven trumpets"* (chapter 8 verses 1 – 2) and the *"seventh trumpet"* leads into the *"seven bowls"* (chapter 11 verse 15, chapter 15 verses 6 - 8). If you recall that a 'parenthesis' is additional information, set alongside the main discussion or 'text', then you will see that you can read from the *"seventh angel sound(ing)"* the 'seventh trumpet' directly through to the *"seven angels ... having the seven plagues, and ... the seven golden bowls"* (chapter 8 verse 1 to chapter 15 verse 7). The opening of the scroll by the Lamb on the throne controls, not just the 'Seal Judgments', but ALL the judgments that will follow after in their order.

Secondly, there is a 'gap' between John's vision of the sixth and seventh seal (just as there is between the sixth and seventh trumpet, and as there will be between the sixth and seventh bowl).

Thirdly, there is something different, but most interesting, happening in the gap each time.

The Timing of the Judgments

We noted [in **Chapter 8** of our studies] that the 'Seal Judgments' introduce the *"white horse"* and its rider (Revelation chapter 6 verses 1 – 2), whom we have identified with the *"Prince that shall come"* (Daniel chapter 9 verse 26 KJV), and we have suggested that the seven year period, the *"70th week"* of Daniel's 490 year prophecy (Daniel chapter 9 verse 24) commences at this point. The seven year period begins peacefully with an accord, *"a covenant"* between Israel and her neighbours. This peace will soon break down, giving way to war, and the treaty itself will be broken by the *"Prince"* at the very centre point, when he is revealed in his true identity as the *"Man of Sin"* (2 Thessalonians chapter 2 verses 3 – 4).

Even if Israel as a national entity has been protected by the *"covenant"*, and by her association with the 'False Prince', from trouble brewing in other parts of the Middle East, this 'false peace' cannot last. There is no true peace for Israel until she acknowledges, not only her need for *"Messiah the Prince"* to come, but also her rejection of Him when He came the first time. Until then Jesus said, *"Jerusalem shall be trodden down by the Gentiles, until the times of the Gentiles be fulfilled (completed)."* (Luke chapter 21 verse 24 NRB). The 'peace' will be shattered, even for Israel, at the centre of the covenant period. The remaining 'Seal Judgments', after the appearing of the four horsemen, take us past the 'mid-point' [where we have been in 'parenthesis' in the last 4 **Chapters**], and on to the conclusion of the 'Judgment Period'.

The 'Trumpet Judgments' commence close to the mid-point, as we have suggested and also continue to the end of the seven year period. The 'Bowl Judgments' – which we are coming to – appear to commence later in the second half of the seven years, and continue with increasing intensity and rapidity to the culmination of the 'Judgment Period'. The second half, the latter 42 months of the seven years, was called by Jesus, *"the Great Tribulation"* *(Matthew chapter 24 verse 21), and also prophetically in the Old Testament, *"The time of Jacob's Trouble"* *(Jeremiah chapter 30 verse 7). Though the <u>focal point</u> of each set of judgments is different, yet – as we have seen – all three sets finish at the same <u>end point</u>, at the 'Campaign of *Armageddon*' (Revelation chapter 16 verse 16), and the *"Coming in Power"* of Messiah (Revelation chapter 19 verse 11). We have referred to this framework in relation to the three sets of judgments as being 'coterminous'; that is ending at the same time and the same place.

---

* Capitalisation by author, to emphasis 2nd half of 'tribulation period', the whole of which is 7 years, but the second – intensified and determined – section is 3.5 years.

Overview of the Bowl Judgments

Come now to the commencement of the third set of judgments, the pouring out of the *"Bowls"*. Some translations have *"vials"* but that gives a wrong mental picture. The 'receptacle' which contains each portion of 'God's wrath' is not like a chemistry 'vial', it is a broad dish. The precision of the *"bowls"* being *"poured out"* directly onto their 'target' is not dependant on their shape. It is by the control of *"God Almighty"* (Revelation chapter 16 verses 2 & 14).

The seven 'Bowl Judgments' divide into a four and a three (we have seen this 4:3 ratio before), and the second group is even more narrowly targeted than the first. Proof, once again, to a world of 'God-deniers' and 'Dragon-worshippers' that it is God Himself who is in control, as men must acknowledge before the end of the final judgments. (cf. Revelation chapter 6 verses 15 to 16).

> **KEYNOTE: Bible Referrals.** It is good to have a Bible open, whichever version is referred to, and check the quotations in the text against your own Bible. Learn to cross-reference themes, events, persons, doctrines etc. for yourself. See **Appx. III** *'Subject Index'*.

Are the Bowl Judgments not parallel with the Trumpet Judgments?

That is a question that is often asked, because of the similarity of the activities, and targets, between the two sets of judgments. We have already indicated that they are not the same in their <u>time</u> period, we will now see that they are not the same in <u>intensity</u>. There is also one other very significant difference in the descriptions of the two sets of judgments.

We can compare them as follows:

The Trumpet Judgments	**The Bowl Judgments**
1. *"earth … trees … grass"*	*"earth … sores … men which had the mark"*
2. *"sea … sea life … shipping"*	*"sea … blood of dead things … all life died"*
3. *"rivers … fountains … waters … bitter"*	*"rivers … fountains … became blood"*
4. *"sun … moon … stars … shone not"*	*"sun … scorch men … great heat"*
5. *"pit of abyss open … scorpions… Apollyon"*	*"throne of the Beast … pain and sores"*
6. *"Euphrates angels … army 200,000,000"*	*"Euphrates … dried up … to Armageddon"*
7. *"Kingdoms of … His Christ … reign forever"*	*"It is done … a great earthquake … islands fled"*
(Rev. 8:7 – 9:20 & Rev. 11:15 – 19)	(Rev. 16:1- 21)

Similar but Different

We can see straight away where the two sets of judgments are similar, as indeed they are, and where they differ, as indeed they also do. In the 'Trumpet Set' the degree of the judgment is limited, *"one third of sea life died"* for example. In the 'Bowl Set' the intensity is ramped up, *"all sea life died"*. In the 'Trumpet Set' the sunlight is reduced by a third. In the 'Bowl Set' God turns the sunlight up so that it *"scorches men with fire ... and great heat"*. So, the *"bowl"* judgments are later in the judgment programme, they are more 'targeted', and they are also more 'intense'.

'What is the other significant difference?' you ask. Good question! The other key difference is this; The first group of four is targeted on *"the men which had the mark"* (Revelation chapter 16 verse 2 KJV), and the second group of three (*"bowls"* numbers 5 to 7) is targeted against the *"throne of the Beast and his kingdom"* (chapter 16 verse 10 NRB), and his capital city *"great Babylon"* (chapter 16 verse 19 KJV). That the gathering place of *"Armageddon"* is mentioned in connection with the sixth *"bowl"* judgment, and the fall of *"Babylon"*, the capital of the *"Beast"*, is mentioned in connection with the seventh *"bowl"* judgment are indications in themselves that these judgments are right at the very end of the seven year period.

> **KEYNOTE: Armageddon.** This 'gathering place' is mentioned here in Rev. 16:16, but much more detail can be gleaned about the 'last battle' in other scriptures. We will look at *"Armageddon"* as a separate topic in **Chp. 19**, and the *"Coming in Power"* of Messiah, in its various stages, in **Chp. 20**.
> See **Appx. III** 'Subject Index'.

Daniel tells us (in a connected passage in his prophecy) that at the end of his reign the *"King"* (that is the *"Beast"*) will be attacked by armies from the south, the north, and the east, and he will have to move his 'headquarters' to a position further west *"between the seas"*. Probably in the Sinai Peninsula, near where Moses received the Law on the mountain of Horeb. This will put him in a position to the south of Israel, below the Negev, where he will hope to make his 'last stand'. But Daniel prophesied (back in 530 BC), *"He shall come to his end, and none shall help him"* (Daniel chapter 11 verses 36 to 45 KJV). The *"Beast"* and the *"False Prophet"* will be captured by *"Messiah"* at His *"Coming in Power"* and all the armies both loyal and opposing to *"Antichrist"* – all of them 'Anti-God' – will be utterly destroyed (Revelation chapter 19 verses 11 – 21).

The Seven Bowls Poured Out

Let us look now at the detail of the *"Bowl"* judgments as we have them described for us by John, *"And one of the four living ones gave unto the seven angels seven golden bowls full of the wrath of God, who liveth for ever and ever. And the inner Temple was filled with smoke from the glory of God ... and no one was able to enter into the inner Temple, till the seven plagues of the seven angels were completed."* (Revelation chapter 15 verses 7 – 8 NRB).

Each angel agent is given a bowl, by one of the four Seraphim, filled with the *"wrath of God"* which will be poured out as *"plagues"* upon the earth, and upon mankind who have sided with the *"Beast"* and have taken his *"Mark"*. The pouring out of all *"seven golden bowls"* in order will bring us to the very end of the seven year judgment period.

Bowl One: Flesh-Eating Ulcers

When the first angel pours out his bowl upon the *"earth"* the immediate effect is a *"loathsome and malignant ulcer upon the men which had the mark of the Beast"* (Revelation chapter 16 verse 2 NASB). It is possible that the *"mark"* itself, whatever its nature whether 'cut into' the skin or not, becomes infected  from within. A God-sent targeted 'virus', it will eat the flesh of those who have received the mark. Now their association with the *"Beast"* will be turned against them by God Himself, because they *"worshipped the Image"* and turned their backs on *"the Lord's Christ"*. What seemed an attractive association a short time before now becomes a divine curse!

Bowl Two: Blood of Dead Things

John said, *"The sea became as the blood of dead (things); and every living soul died in the sea"* (chapter 16 verse 3 NRB). This is not *"a third"* of all life this time. This is the totality of all life in the sea. There is a phenomenon which occurs on the shores of the Pacific more than on the Atlantic. It is known as 'The Red Tide'. The technical term is 'dinoflagellate saxitoxin'.  Tiny organisms called 'dinoflagellates' swarm in billions to one area, and then die off. The fish that feed on them die too, and the fish become poisonous to animals and humans. That is just on a small scale, but God is in control of 'natural phenomena' – for He is the God of Creation – and He can 'scale up' any natural event He chooses, or use a different phenomenon if He prefers. There will be nothing edible from the sea, and probably an awful stench as well. The oceans will be as blood, and will stink too.

Bowl Three: Rivers of Blood

Not the 'blood-flow' from a great battle, which will come a little later, but *"rivers and fountains of water … became blood"* (chapter 16 verse 4 – 7 KJV). Note the order of the poisoning activity, the *"seas"*, then the *"rivers"* then the *"fountains"* of water. This is not natural order. Contamination of a water outlet, whether accidental or otherwise, flows from source to sea. Here God reverses the order He has placed in nature, to prove that the judgment is not of natural cause but from His direction. A manifestation of His *"wrath"*. 'Why such a judgment?' you might ask. Because it is a *"righteous"* repayment for the 'blood of the martyrs', whom we saw asking for vengeance at the mid-point of the seven year period, back at the time of the 5th Seal Judgment (Revelation chapter 6 verses 9 – 11).

Many martyrs, millions upon millions of them down through the ages, seem to have had their deaths unavenged by God. But not one has been unnoticed in heaven. Jehovah said to Cain (the first murderer), who killed his brother Abel (the first martyr to die for his faith), *"What have you done? The voice of your brother's blood is crying to Me from the ground."* (Genesis chapter 4 verse 10 ESV). God has taken note of every martyr since, through the 'Church Period' also, and will continue to do so through the terrible persecution of the *"Great Tribulation"* too. All will be avenged, and at the end, like the Nile in Egypt back in Moses' time, innocent blood shed will be returned as *"blood to drink"* (chapter 16 verse 6).

Bowl Four: Heat Turned Up

Much is made in our day of 'Global Warming' and Climate Change', where in reality the weather patterns of the globe have gone in long repeating cycles over hundreds of years. (It is interesting to hear a media announcer say, 'It was the warmest day for 60 years' or something similar. You might wonder, did they call it 'global warming' 60 years ago when records were broken back then?) At the same time, we must remember, the God of creation is in control of the weather and weather patterns. He can adjust sea temperature, current direction, prevailing winds, polar shift and anything else He chooses. And permit the surface temperature of earth (and sea) to rise, and to affect climate and harvest if He so wills. It will be happening for certain in the latter days of the *"Great Tribulation"*. We have seen and are still seeing in relation to 'last days' judgments, that God will use His control over the 'forces of nature' to hurt and torment those who have rejected Him, martyred His people, and murdered His Son.

"The fourth angel poured out his bowl upon the sun" (chapter 16 verse 8 NRB). The power of the sun – which has not been shining for a third of the normal day since the fourth trumpet judgment – will now not only be turned back to normal, but 'turned up'. God will adjust the sun's 'thermostat' so that mankind on earth will be scorched with *"fire"* and *"great heat"*. We cannot be totally sure what this means. It could be a huge increase in 'sunspots' and 'sun flares' (the very things which astronomers are saying are reducing). It might even be – as was suggested in relation to the trumpet judgments – that God

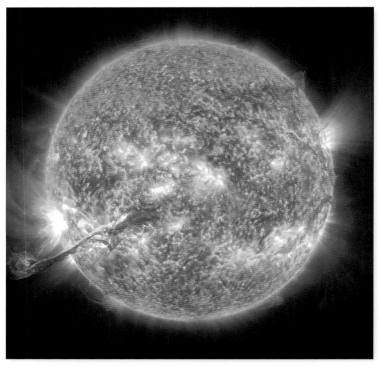

A solar-flare on the Sun's surface – August 2012

could shift the orbit path of our planet. Or even the 'tilt' of its axis?

By whatever means, whether by reducing the distance between us and the sun, removal of the ozone layer, increasing solar activity, whatever, we do not really know, nor as Christians do we really need to worry. Those of us who are *"born again"* will not be on earth in these terrible days, when God will make His power known and felt. Men will *"curse the name of God who had power over these plagues. They did not repent and give Him glory"* (chapter 16 verse 9 ESV).

> **KEYNOTE: 'Does God Believe in Athiests?'**[*]
> An amazing alteration of thinking through the 'Tribulation Period' seems to be – due to the direct and obvious intervention of God in the affairs of nature and humanity – the decline in 'atheistic' thinking. That is the 'belief system' that God does not exist, and consequently, matter 'generated' itself. And subsequently, there is no need for accountability to God at the end of life. Men will not *"repent"*, but they will acknowledge a.) the existence of God and b.) the reality of His intervention in world affairs. *John Blanchard, 'Does God Believe in Atheists?' (Evangelical Press, U.K. 2000).

Key Target Points

As we have already seen, the second group of *"Bowl"* judgments (Numbers 5 to 7) are even more 'targeted' than the first group (Numbers 1 to 4). If we take an overview quickly across the locations mentioned, we will note the following place names which are all connected in the *"Great Tribulation"* final stages:

1.) *"The Throne of the Beast"* – Is this a literal throne, in a Palace? In a new location?

2.) *"The great River Euphrates"* – The most significant river in the Bible.

3.) The city of *"Great Babylon"* – Again is this a literal place? A rebuilt city?

4.) *"The place called ... Armageddon"* – Is this a description of a 'gathering' or a literal place?

(Revelation chapter 16 verses 10, 12, 16 & 19)

The debate about the degree of 'symbolism' versus 'literality' in prophecy is very relevant here. Depending how the 'places' mentioned above are viewed will affect our thinking of how the 'last days' of the *"Great Tribulation"* play out. If we 'symbolise' all of these place names [As some have done. See **Appx. II**], we will have very little awareness of time or space, never mind location for these judgments; <u>where</u> and on <u>whom</u> they fall. If, however, we accept that these are all literal places, geographically located in the Middle East, a very clear picture emerges. God is narrowing the 'target area' of His final judgments right down, and controlling and 'manoeuvring' His arch-opponents into locations where He will carry out His final judgments on them; through the *"Coming in Power"* of His Son, the *"Messiah"*, *"Jesus Christ"*, the *"King of kings and Lord of lords"* (chapter 19 verses 11 to 16).

Bowl Five: Deep Divine Darkness

Let us look now at 'Bowl Judgment' number five, *"The fifth angel poured out his bowl upon the throne of the Beast; and his kingdom became full of darkness; and they gnawed their tongues for pain, and blasphemed the God of heaven, because of their pains and because of their sores ..."* (Revelation 16 verses 10 – 11 NRB). One judgment follows rapidly upon another. The *"sores"* from the first 'Bowl Judgment' are still present and now a deep unnatural darkness fills – not the whole world – but the 'Kingdom of the Beast'. Possibly a similar darkness to the second last plague in Egypt in Moses' time, *"darkness which may be felt"* (Exodus chapter 10 verse 21 KJV)? To those alive in that future day, and to all loyal to the 'First Beast', the 'Second Beast', and the *"Dragon"*, it will be obvious that these judgments are connected, and divinely controlled. Firstly, everyone who has the *"Mark"* gets extremely painful ulcerating sores. Then the sunlight comes back, stronger than normal, and men are scorched with heat. Now the geographical territory that the Bible calls the 'Kingdom of the Beast' has the light totally turned off, and all who are in it and loyal to him are helpless in painful darkness. What fearful conditions to be in, yet *"they repented not of their deeds ... to give Him (God) glory"* (Revelation chapter 16 verses 11 & 9 KJV).

The Throne of the Beast

The 'Old Roman Empire' – possibly – relating to the future Kingdom of Antichrist'.
Illustration from C. Larkin (1850 – 1924) 'Dispensational Truth' (Philadelphia PA: Larkin Est. 1920) Pg. 73.

'But is the *"throne"* literal, and is the *"kingdom"* a place?' Again, good questions and we must pause there for a moment. The *"Prince that shall come"* (of Daniel chapter nine) is not revealed as the *"Man of Sin"* (2 Thessalonians chapter 2 verse 3) until the <u>middle</u> of the seven year period, when he breaks the *"covenant"* he has brokered with Israel and introduces mandatory worship of himself, instead of worship of Jehovah or other gods: There is good reason to believe that this man, the *"King of Fierce Countenance"* (Daniel 8 verse 23 KJV), who will have put down other kings to rise to the top, will wish to have his own capital city from which to rule the territory he controls.

We are not actually told in prophecy how large his kingdom is. We know, from our previous studies, that it includes part of Europe, perhaps 'Latin Europe' around the Mediterranean Sea. Possibly Eastern Europe and parts of the old Byzantine Roman Empire as well? Many scholars have believed that it will be the 'Roman Empire Revived'. We cannot prove that from scripture, and – as far as northern Europe is concerned – his geographical boundaries may be much less. It will include the territory of Israel (possibly giving them more land than they occupy today), the territory south of Israel: down to the Red Sea and the Sinai Peninsula, possibly parts of Mediterranean north Africa. It will probably extend into most or all modern Iraq, and most likely have the Euphrates River as its eastern boundary. There is a possible prophetic 'picture' of this territory in the history of the kings of Israel, *"The King of Babylon had taken from the river of Egypt unto the river Euphrates all that pertained to the King of Egypt."* (2 Kings chapter 24 verse 7 KJV).

It is more than probable that he will wish to set his 'stamp' on a new desert-metropolis, a 'Dubai-by-the-Euphrates'. It is more than likely that though Jerusalem will still be permitted to be the 'Judeo-Christian' religious capital, he will build a new Babylon city, to rival that of Nebuchadnezzar, close to the old original site in the Babil province of modern Iraq, and close to the west bank of the Euphrates.

> **KEYNOTE: Babylon Rebuilt.** The possibility of an 'Anti-Christ Capital' is not merely speculative. When we look at the subject in more detail (Rev. chp. 18), we will find that certain key prophecies regarding the destruction of Babylon have never been fulfilled. So O.T. prophecy demands a new city; that it might meet the final doom as Jehovah decreed. Examined further in **Chp. 18**, *'The Fall of Babylon'.*

Bowl Six: The Euphrates Dried Up

This sixth 'Bowl Judgment' links directly with what has just gone before. If the Euphrates is the boundary of the 'Beast's Empire', it being *"dried up"* is hugely significant. Not only is this for military purposes *"that the way of the kings from the sun rising might be prepared"* (chapter 16 verse 12 NRB), enemies of the *"Beast"* who have never been under his full authority, but also, historically, the drying of the Euphrates led to the fall

of the kingdom of Babylon under Belshazzar (Daniel chapter 5), and its occupation by the Medo-Persian empire (modern Iran). As a man who will probably be a student of military history, the drying of this great river on his eastern border will probably generate great fear. He will probably be preparing to move his military 'HQ' eastwards when God strikes again.

The Time of the End

God is going – by the control of *"unclean ... spirits of demons"* from the mouths of *"the Dragon, the Beast and the False Prophet"* – to gather all the kings and their armies to surround the Land of Israel for the last great confrontation. Some armies will come as still loyal to the *"Prince"* who gave them power. Many others will gather to attempt an overthrow of a despot who now seems, after seven years of increasing trouble, to be increasingly vulnerable. Daniel says, *"At the time of the end shall the king of the south ... and the king of the north ... come against him ... (and) tidings out of the east and out of the north shall trouble him ..."* (Daniel chapter 11 verses 40 – 45 KJV). But it is God who is in control, and it is God who is drawing them *"to the battle of that great day of God Almighty ... and He gathered them together into a place called ... Armageddon."* (Revelation chapter 16 verses 14 – 15 KJV).

Bowl Seven: It is Done!

When the seventh angel pours out his *"Bowl"* there comes a great voice out of the Temple of heaven saying, *"It is done"*. The 'Tribulation Period' is now coming to a close, the city of Babylon is about to fall, *"Armageddon"* is about to take place, *"the sign of the Son of Man in heaven"* will be seen (Matthew 24 verse 30 KJV), and Jesus Christ will be just about to return ...

What about the Gap?

Good point. We did say there was a short gap between the descriptions of the sixth and seventh of each set of judgments. Here the 'parenthesis' is very small: Just one verse. God is not addressing the followers of the *"Beast"* whom He is judging. He is encouraging His 'tribulation saints' to keep alert, for the Coming of Jesus the Messiah is very close! *"Behold I am coming like a thief. Blessed is the one who stays awake and keeps his garments (on), lest he walk about naked and men see his shame."*

> **KEYNOTE:** *"Blessed is he ..."* There are 7 Blessings in the book of Revelation. All of them are addressed to the people of God here on earth, though not all within the same time period. Some of them – like this one – are not written to us directly, believers of the Church Age. But we can take an application to ourselves: We should be 'dressed' and 'watching', ready for the coming of our Saviour, Jesus Christ.

(Revelation chapter 16 verse 15 NASB). A number of versions put this verse inside brackets to emphasise that it is a parenthesis, spoken or written, to a different group of hearers.

Are there any other Judgments?

'Yes.' Right here in the context of Revelation chapter 16 there are. Before John is transported back in time to see greater detail of the destruction of the system and the city of Babylon [See **Chapters 17** & **18**], there comes a final earthquake, *"a great earthquake, such as* *came not since men came upon the earth"* (chapter 16 verse 18 NRB). This is most probably the same earthquake as at the 'Sixth Seal Judgment' (chapter 6 verses 12 – 17), bringing the end point of the three different sets of judgments together. This causes a total collapse of the remainder of the infrastructure of planet earth.

"The great city became divided into three parts, and the cities of the nations fell." (chapter 16 verse 19 NRB). The *"great city"* is most likely Jerusalem, as Babylon is referred to separately in the same context.

Is it not amazing that God can throw down all the remaining great cities of the world in a moment of time, and summarise it all in a phrase? Whatever cities that we know in our world that will still be standing will be demolished in an instant. How puny the skyscrapers of men! Islands and mountains are moved, and at the last comes a great hailstorm …

Just a Hailstorm?

Someone will say, 'Is a hailstorm such a terrible judgment?' God has used huge *"hailstones"* before as judgment (Exodus chapter 9 verses 18 – 19; Joshua chapter 10 verse 11). And He will again (Ezekiel 38 verse 22). Jehovah said to Job, *"Have you entered the storehouses of the snow, or have you seen the storehouses of the hail, which I have reserved … for the day of war and battle?"* (Job chapter 38 verses 22 – 23 NASB). When we consider the size of these hailstones, then we can understand. John says, *"Huge hailstones, about 100 pounds each (45kg), came down from heaven upon men"* (Revelation chapter 16 verse 21 NASB). God does not operate according to our scale of quantity, volume, or time. God will consume all who oppose Him in that final judgment day.

What about the Battle of Armageddon?

We haven't forgotten about that. The scene is set, the armies are being 'gathered'. The final battles will be fought on God's terms, territory, and time. [See a more detailed study in **Chapter 19**.] Before we arrive at the battle scene, we come to another parenthesis and another 'divided prophecy'. John is going to have his vantage position moved backwards to see *"Mystery Babylon the Great"* revealed, then he will move forward again in time to see the detail of prophecy fulfilled in the fall of *"the Great city Babylon"*.

Here we have 'Two Babylons': one a religious system and one a political centre. They will be our subjects for the next two Chapters.

Questions and Answers for Chapter Sixteen – 'The Bowl Judgments'

Chp. 16 – 'The Bowl Judgments'

Q1. How many Bowl Judgments are there?

Q2. What shape are the Bowls?

Q3. Who are they targeted against?

Q4. What happens to the sea? And the sea-life?

Q5. What happens to the water sources?

Q6. Why does God judge in this way?

Q7. Why is the great river Euphrates dried up?

Q8. What is in the 'parenthesis' in Chp. 16?

Q9. What is "Armageddon"?

Q10. Who controls the 'gathering' of the armies?

Chapter Seventeen

Mystery Babylon - The Scarlet Woman

We have arrived at what is one of the most difficult sections of the book of Revelation, possibly the most difficult chapter of all to interpret. When we get through this study, the second part of the 'Babylon visions' will be much easier to break down. Do try and persevere through this section. It is perhaps a comfort to know that no one who studies future events finds this an easy topic, author included.

Along with the continuity of the 'action visions' of the 'Seal Judgments, the 'Trumpet Judgments' and the 'Bowl Judgments' we have been introduced to various 'parentheses', which fit inside the 'timeline' of the seven years, where John is moved back in time – and forward again – to see additional detail that he was not shown in the overview of the three sets of seven judgments. Here (in Revelation chapters 17 and 18) is another 'parenthesis' which fits around the timeframe of the *"Bowls"* being poured out (Revelation chapter 16).

> **KEYNOTE: Time-shift.** As we get closer to the end of the 'Tribulation Period', and the end of John's visions, there are more of these backward 'time-shifts'. John gets his position moved back to see additional detail that the Spirit of God wishes to show him before his visions end. This is what is known as 'retrospection' or 'recapitulation'.

Some Hard Questions

Perhaps we should begin by setting down some of the hard questions which have been asked – and debated by scholars – about these two chapters, Revelation 17 and 18, for many years:

1. Are the contents of Revelation 17 and 18 all one vision?
2. If they are different, on what grounds do they differ?
3. If they are not one vision, where do they divide?
4. If the visions divide, what is the time difference?
5. Is there a real *"city"* in view? One city or two? Are both allegorical?
6. If there are two visions, what does the *"woman"* in the first vision represent?

In some respects, the last question is the easiest to answer, for it is explained in the text (within chapter 17). But let us address the others quickly ...

[From a 'literal-futurist' perspective, as set out in **Appx. II**.]

Two Chapters: One Vision?

'Are the two chapters one vision?' you might ask. The short answer is, 'No.' There are two separate visions here, both of which John is shown from a new 'vantage point', but separately. 'How do they differ?' That question will take all of this Chapter and all of the next to answer, but (in short) the first *"Babylon"* vision is of a 'religious system', the second *"Babylon"* vision is of a 'commercial and political system'.

Where do the Visions Divide?

That is a good question, for it is part of a key, not just of understanding these chapters, but of all of the book of Revelation. Remember John's 'time-shift' phrase, which indicates a 'chronological' move in his visions, *"after these things"*? [We examined it back in **Chapter 7**.] John heard it first from Jesus Himself as part of the three-fold division of the book *"the things which shall be after these things* ..." (Revelation chapter 1 verse 19 NRB). It was repeated twice in one sentence, at the point where John was called up into heaven (chapter 4 verses 1 – 2). This key phrase occurs nine times in Revelation, and it is right here in the centre of the 'Babylon visions', when John saw another angel *"come down out of heaven* ..." (chapter 18 verse 1 NRB).

Not every chapter division in the book of Revelation is ideal (chapter divisions and verses are not part of the inspiration of the scriptures), but here it is just right. One vision ends at chapter 17 verse 18, and the next vision begins, showing John a different activity at a different time in chapter 18 verse 1. The *"after these things"* at the start of chapter 18 refers to what has gone before, at a slightly earlier time period in chapter 17, where we now are in our study.

What is the Time Difference?

A good question also [which will be developed more fully in **Chapter 18**]. For now, let us suggest there is a time difference of 3.5 years between the two visions. Someone will say right away, 'That is significant, because 3.5 years is the dividing point in a great deal of the action of Revelation, and of the 7 year judgment period'. And rightly so. We will seek to confirm that these two chapters are fulfilled at the 'midpoint' and at the 'endpoint' of the 7 years of tribulation. In other words, at the commencement and the close of the *"Great Tribulation"* period.

A Vision of Two Cities?

Our next question was, 'Is there a real city in view?' and to get even more confusing, 'Might there be two different cities in view, both called *"Babylon"*?' The answer to that is actually, 'Yes.' It is possible that there are two cities in the two chapters, both real places, one called *"Babylon"* spiritually, and the other a different city called *"Babylon"* literally. At this point someone will say, 'I am confused!'

(Here we need to have a 'parenthesis' of our own: Let us look quickly at another example right inside our Revelation text to help us. When we were looking at the *"two witnesses"* [in **Chapter 10**] there was a detail we didn't examine. Look at two verses in that story, *"... the Beast ... shall kill them (the two witnesses). And their dead bodies shall lie in the street of the <u>great city</u>, which spiritually is called <u>Sodom</u> and <u>Egypt</u>, where also <u>our Lord was crucified</u>."* (Revelation chapter 11 verse 7 – 8 KJV).

If we did not have the last phrase of that verse, we would have no idea which 'literal' city was in view, for there are three 'symbolic' names given first. We have seen previously that *"the great city"* is used in Revelation as a descriptive name for Jerusalem. But, 'Why *"Sodom"*?' you might ask. And 'Egypt is a country, not a city.' Indeed so, but to a Jew reading this they would understand the analogy of *"Egypt"*, for it represented all the 'fleshly things' that the Children of Israel, in Moses' time, wanted to go back to. The name *"Sodom"* is a byword, not for materialism, but for gross immorality. The Spirit of God is letting us know the character of the city-dwellers in Jerusalem, who in a future day will rejoice over the death of the *"two witnesses"*. The confirmation that it really is Jerusalem which is in view is in the last description, *"where also our Lord was crucified"*, which cannot be mistaken.)

Here is another <u>key</u> point – which we will return to more than once – the cities being described in Revelation are seen as taking their 'character' from their <u>inhabitants</u>, not from the grandeur of their buildings! We are suggesting that the city of *"Babylon"* in the second vision must be real with an identifiable geographical location, and though a 'religious system' is the primary focus in the Revelation chapter 17 vision, there may be an actual central city in view also. Two different emphases, on two separate cities, in two slightly different time periods in one sector of John's visions.

That brings us to the last of the questions which we posed at the beginning; 'What does the woman represent?' Let us come to that now, for that is the main thrust of the first vision here:

More than One Woman?

We have seen previously [in **Chapter 12,** *'War in Heaven'*] that there are four key women depicted in the book of Revelation. John saw each one of them from a different 'vantage point' in different parts of his visions. We can review them as follows:

1. The rebellious *"Jezebel"* in the Church in Thyatira (Revelation chapter 2 verse 20), part of a vision that John saw while still on Patmos Island in his prison cell. Possibly an actual *"woman"*, leader of a false 'sect' within that professing church, or possibly a group or 'faction' within that professing church. Called *"Jezebel"* by the Lord Jesus Himself to indicate her character, and an historical parallel to one who led the people of God astray.

2. The *"woman clothed with the sun, and the moon under her feet, and upon her head a crown of twelve stars"* (chapter 12 verses 1 – 2 KJV), whom John saw in

the heavenly part of his visions, we deduced as being representative of the nation of Israel, from whom Messiah came.

3. The Scarlet Woman, *"the Great Prostitute … Mystery Babylon the Great"* (chapter 17 verses 1 – 6 ESV), whom John saw after he had been taken *"in Spirit into a wilderness",* a third change in his 'vantage points' and an appropriate location for what he was just about to see. We are working out who she is in this study.

4. Lastly *"the Bride, the Lamb's wife"**, whom John saw in Spirit on *"a great and high mountain"* (chapter 21 verses 9 – 10 KJV), after the kingdom part of his visions, another 'reprise', a looking back to see additional detail which John didn't see in his 'overview'.

[*Refer to **Chapter 23**, *'The New Jerusalem'*.]

We have also seen already that two of these *"women"* are representative of something <u>wicked</u>, and two of them something <u>good</u>. So, there are comparisons and contrasts between them, which John was meant to identify. The big question is, 'Are these actual individual women?' The first and third women represent systems of false religion, and at different stages of their development, although it is possible an actual woman may function as a figurehead in both cases. As in many false cults in our world, there may be a key woman who is at the source of the corruption of truth.

So it was, at the first Babil in the land of *"Shinar"* (Genesis chapters 10 – 11) where Semiramis the wife of Nimrod was instrumental in leading false worship. Where the city and the tower were built at *"Babel"*: Probably the first 'ziggurat' in history. She is referred to in Jeremiah's prophecy as the *"Queen of heaven"* (Jeremiah chapters 7 verse 18; 44 verses 17 – 18; 44 verse 25). So it was, with the original *"Jezebel"* leading the nation of Israel into *"Baal"*

A black & white illustration of Peter Breugel the Elder's (1525 – 1569) famous painting of 'The Tower of Babel'
(Upon which the 'European Parliament Building' in Strasbourg was designed)

' *So here ... we have another false system of worship, typified in a woman.'*

worship as the wife of Ahab (1 Kings chapter 16 verses 30 – 33). So it appears to have been with a group, or a woman, whom God calls *"Jezebel"* in the church in Thyatira (Revelation chapter 2 verses 20 – 23).

So here (in Revelation chapter 17) we have another false system of worship, typified in a woman, and possibly (we do not know) led by an actual 'Mother of False Religion' in the final days before God judges and destroys the system at the midpoint of the seven year period. After which, all worship of every kind having been stopped, the *"Dragon"* will introduce the *"Abomination of Desolation"* (Matthew chapter 24 verses 15 – 22): The last, the greatest, and the worst,

KEYNOTE: Worship. Is it not strange that mankind must worship 'something'? When people turn from God, they must worship something else, *"For although they knew God, they did not honour Him as God or give thanks to Him, but they became futile in their thinking, and their foolish hearts were darkened. Claiming to be wise, they became fools, and exchanged the glory of the immortal God for images resembling mortal man and birds and animals and creeping things."* (Romans 1:21–23 ESV). Into the 'spiritual vacuum' thus created will step Satan, *"The father of lies"* (John 8:44).
J. MacArthur *'Revelation 12-22'* (Chicago, IL: Moody Press, 2000), 156.

system of false anti-God religion ever. A system which God Himself will destroy at the end of a further three and a half years, at the *"Coming in Power"* of the Messiah, Jesus Christ.

A Woman, A System, A City ... Which?

The most cryptic, but probably the most correct, answer is: All of the above. We can begin where John's vision begins, with the introduction by the angel, *"Then one of the angels who had the seven bowls came and said to me, 'Come, I will show you the judgment of the great prostitute who is seated on many waters, with whom the kings of the earth have committed sexual immorality,* and with the wine of whose sexual immorality the dwellers on earth have become drunk."* (Revelation chapter 17 verses 1 – 2 ESV).

Let us recap quickly here: John (in Revelation chapter 16) saw the *"seven bowls"* being poured out. The 'bowl angel' is linked with the previous judgments. There is nothing to suggest it is the seventh 'bowl angel'. The timeframe of this vision may extend backwards, even before the bowls are poured out. We are suggesting, and will fill in more detail later, that what John is now seeing is the climax of all 'false religion', world over, unified and legitimised 'hand in hand' with global politics, until the very point in (a future) time when it is removed to make way for something worse, at the centre of the seven year period ... So here John is being taken 'backwards' to just before the midpoint of the seven years, just before the *"Great Tribulation"* commences.

KEYNOTE: 'Church & churches.' The 'living' part of the true Church cannot be found all in one place, nor in one 'denomination', nor any 'named' group today. All the local churches, world-over, which gather according to the *"apostles' doctrine"*, and New Testament church teaching, do not – combined together – equate to the true Church. Many believers meet in small companies in secret, with no visible presence. Many individual believers – for whatever reason – are still to be found within systems which are non-biblical. All of these individual Christians will be removed – from wherever – at the return of Jesus Christ for His Church. Everything visible and 'systemised' from then on will be false.

John is also moved in position. His 'vantage point' is again changed. This is the third vantage point that we are told of. The first was in his prison cell, the second was in heaven (chapters 4 – 16), here he is in the *"wilderness"* (chapters 17 – 18), and finally he will be on *"a great and high mountain"* (chapter 21 verse 10 KJV). Each 'viewpoint' gives 'perspective' to the things that John will be shown. He may have wondered, 'Why leave heaven to come to a wilderness?' But the sights in these visions are appropriate against a *"wilderness"* backdrop. Interestingly enough, when John is taken to his fourth 'vantage point' on the high mountain, after his 'kingdom vision', it will also be a 'bowl angel' who will take him there (chapter 21 verse 9) to see the *"Bride, the Lamb's Wife"* and her city, her place prepared as Jesus promised it would be. The two *"women"* in view in these two visions can be compared and contrasted, as well as their dwelling places.

[Examined more fully in **Chapter 23**, *'The New Jerusalem'*.]

The System Exposed

What we have here is one of the strangest sights, of all the sights, in John's apocalyptic visions, *"I saw a woman sit upon a scarlet coloured beast, full of names of blasphemy, having seven heads and ten horns ... and upon her forehead a name written, 'MYSTERY, BABYLON THE GREAT, THE MOTHER OF HARLOTS AND ABOMINATIONS OF THE EARTH', and I saw the woman drunken with the blood of the saints, and with the blood of the martyrs of Jesus."* (Revelation chapter 17 verses 3 – 6 NRB). This chapter, as we have said, is a very difficult one. P. Patterson

notes that 'the key to interpretation is identification' and suggests a list of features which can help to identify what the *"Mother of Prostitutes"* represents. We can list, and expand on, these features in order:

1.) The woman is a *"Great Prostitute"* (chapter 17 verse 1) – Representing spiritual fornication.

2.) The woman *"sits on many waters"* – Which are *"peoples ... and nations"* (verse 15).

3.) The *"Kings of the earth"* <u>have</u> debased themselves with her – Union of religion and state.

4.) The *"inhabitants of the earth <u>have been made</u> drunk ..."* – Stupefied, possibly deceived.

5.) The scene is viewed from a *"wilderness"* setting – Barren and nothing attractive.

6.) The woman is sitting on a *"scarlet coloured beast* (with) *seven heads and ten horns"* – A visual and a literal link to the *"Beast"* of Revelation chapter 13.

7.) The woman is *"arrayed in purple and scarlet, and adorned with gold and pearls"* – Royal attire, mock-priestly vestments, and evidence of great wealth.

8.) The woman has a *"golden cup"* – Ceremonial but terribly contaminated.

9.) The woman has a name which only God can reveal, a *"Mystery ..."* The last 'spiritual mystery' of the Bible.*

10.) Her name is *"Babylon the Great"* – A link back to the first organised false religion of the post-flood world (Genesis chapters 10 – 11).

11.) The woman is *"drunk with the blood of the saints ... and martyrs of Jesus"* – Are these two   distinct groups from different periods?

12.) John is greatly surprised, *"I wondered with great wonder"* (chapter 17 verse 6 NRB).
[P. Patterson, *'Revelation', NAC Series* (Nashville, TN: B&H Publishing, 2012), 217.]

Why Does John Wonder?

That is a very good question. The angel also asked John that. We might well wonder, but John should have got used to seeing strange sights and – once he has them noted down – to having them explained to him. So why such 'astonishment' here? Is it perhaps because he saw something which he himself recognised parts of in his own time? He would have a knowledge of the history of Genesis and the origins of Babylonish worship, and of *"Baal"* worship among his ancestors. He may even have known about the false cult springing up within the church at Thyatira. Perhaps his *"wonder"* is in being able to see the 'panorama' and to connect it all together? To see the full extent of the corruption that will come (after John's time) from the union of religious system with political system, seen even in the dealings of the Pharisees with the Romans in the time of Jesus. And finally, how the whole system is linked together in the last days, with the *"Beast"* who is the head of the last great political system, and the *"Great Prostitute"* the religious system that he carries.

> ***KEYNOTE: Mystery.** A *"mystery"* in the Bible does not mean something 'mysterious'. It refers to something which God kept 'hidden' until the time came for Him to reveal it. Jesus told His disciples of the *"mystery of the kingdom of God"* (Mk. 4:11), Paul wrote of the mystery of the *"blindness in part (which) is happened unto Israel"* (Rom. 11:25), the mystery of godliness, *"God manifest in the flesh"* (1 Tim. 3:16), the mystery of the gospel of Jesus Christ, *"kept secret since the world began"* (Rom. 16:25-26), the mystery of *"Christ and the Church"* (Eph. 5:32), the mystery of the change, *"we shall all be changed"* (1 Cor. 15:51) and the *"mystery of iniquity"* (2 Thess. 2:7). John wrote of the *"mystery of the seven stars"* (Rev. 1:20), the conclusion of the *"mystery of God"* (Rev. 10:7), and here we have the *"mystery of the woman and ... the beast"* (Rev. 17:5-7).

The *"woman* (is) *drunken with the blood of saints ... and martyrs of Jesus"* (chapter 17 verse 6). This confirms that the religious system the *"woman"* represents is false and has been 'anti-God' all the way down through the ages. It is possible the *"blood of saints"* refers to the martyrs of the Old Testament period (see Hebrews chapter 11 verses 32 – 38). The *"martyrs of Jesus"* refers to slain saints of the New Testament period, the millions of martyrs of the true Church, persecuted by the false religious systems of this world, linked with political bodies to give them legal authority to put to death whom they pleased. There were possibly 50 million martyred during the era of the 'Spanish Inquisition' alone (1478 – 1834). And the deaths of the 'Reformers' and 'Covenanters', the martyrdom of William Tyndale (1495 – 1536), who gave his life to give us the first English New Testament in an affordable print form, and the basis of the 'King James Bible' as we know it today. And thousands more ...

The System Explained

The bowl angel says, *"I will tell you the mystery of the woman and of the beast ... that carries her"* (Revelation chapter 17 verse 7). We have noted already, in relation to the 'features' of the woman, some aspects of the symbolism and explanations given here. In the second part of John's vision the angel will give him a full description of what he is seeing, along with additional detail about things that he has - and we have - already seen. The *"Beast"* we know is referring to Revelation chapter 13, the one *"coming out of the sea"*, the *"Prince"* of Daniel's vision, who will gain the support of ten other kings, broker a peace *"covenant"* with Israel and her neighbours for seven years, and present himself as a *"false Messiah"*, the rider on the *"white horse"* of Revelation chapter 6.

We have debated his 'assassination' [in **Chapter 13**], and questioned, 'Does he really die?' Now the angel reveals additional details of the *"Beast"* whom the woman is *"sitting on"*. If the *"woman"* represents 'formal false religion', we already know the *"Beast"* represents the King and his kingdom, controlled by the *"Dragon"*. Here the angel tells us that the Beast *"was, and is not, and is about to ascend out of the Abyss"* (chapter 17 verse 8 NRB). The Beast is the head of the seventh kingdom, but the passage also says, *"He is the eighth"* (chapter 17 verse 11). It is probable that there is a difference in character and type of the *"Beast"* in the days of his mandatory worship, after his resurrection at the midpoint of the 7 years.

The Ten Kings

The angel also tells John, and us, that the *"ten kings"*, who are linked with the *"woman"*, and have shared her lifestyle and luxury (nothing said of actual worship), and with the *"Beast"*, are kings *"which received no kingdom as yet; but receive authority as kings one hour with the Beast"* (chapter 17 verse 12 NRB). We have touched on this before. The possibility of monarchs, royal houses (with connected blood lines) but no official recognition nor political power. There are many in the 'Royal Houses of Europe' like that today, and in some Middle Eastern countries too. From them, perhaps, the *"Prince that shall come"* will get a power base, by the promise of power given to them. This will be fulfilled during the seven year period, but they will *"have one mind, and shall deliver up their own power and authority unto the Beast."* (chapter 17 verse 12 – 13 NRB). They will be controlled by the *"Beast"*, and by the *"Dragon"* his master, and so they will attempt to *"make war with the Lamb"* (chapter 17 verse 14). That united folly can have but one end, as we have seen, and we will see more of that in later Chapters.

Who is in Control?

A very good question. It is clearly not the *"ten kings"*, nor is it the woman, but is it the *"Beast"*? We saw back in Chapters 13 and 14 that both he and the *"False Prophet"* are controlled by the *"Dragon"*. 'But is that the ultimate authority?' No, the ultimate authority – this is one of the great themes of the book of Revelation – is the authority of God Himself, and His Christ. And so we see here, in the context of our final paragraph, the last part of this vision wherein John is being instructed by the 'bowl angel'.

The angel says, *"The ten horns … will hate the Prostitute. They will make her desolate and naked, and devour her flesh, and burn her up with fire."* (chapter 17 verse 16 ESV). 'What does this mean?' The angel is prophesying that – at the 'midpoint' of the seven years – when the *"Beast"* is assassinated, and returns from the Abyss, when the *"Dragon"* through his second *"Beast"*, the *"False Prophet"*, is about to stop all other worship and introduce 'compulsory Beast worship' … At that point Satan has no further use for a false religious system, so she and her possessions are expendable. The ten kings will see her weakness and loss of power, they will turn on her and (possibly literally) burn her Cathedrals, and steal all her great wealth for themselves.

'Why? Because the Dragon allows it?' No; Satan never has ultimate control. *"God put it in their hearts to fulfil His mind, and to agree, and give their kingdom unto the Beast, until* (all*) the sayings of God shall be fulfilled."* (chapter 17 verses 16 – 17 NRB). God has decreed the end of all false religious systems, and that they should also suffer the same end as they have given to the true martyrs down through the ages.

Is the City real, is it Rome?

That is one question which we did not answer, and it also provides a link with the next vision in the next Chapter. This angel's final words (for it will be other angels who will speak in John's next vision) are these: *"the woman that you saw is <u>the great city</u> that has dominion over the kings of the earth."* (chapter 17 verse 18 ESV).

'So is the city Rome?' you ask. 'We cannot say.' It is possible that (as far as the western world is concerned) the 'Papal System' of the Vatican City is the 'headquarters' of all that is false and 'anti-Christian' in the true sense of the word. Historically she has proved herself to fit with that description. And Rome today is greatly involved in the 'elevation' of Mary, far beyond where scripture has placed her as *"the mother of my Lord"* (Luke chapter 1 verse 43 KJV). 'Marianism' and "Mariolatry' are rife and hugely blasphemous in relation to true Christian doctrine.

'St Peter's Square' – from 'St Peter's Basilica' – in 'The Vatican City', Rome

But we must be very careful. We cannot be too 'Rome-centric' in our interpretation of prophecy (a common error of the Reformers, and probably excusable for them in their time). Though Rome has massive influence in the western world and in the 'Latin world' especially, there are a great many parts of the globe where Rome has little or no influence at all, nor has ever had. Today Roman Catholicism is not even the greatest 'religious system' numerically. That position belongs to Islam, the greatest (and parallel) false religious system of the east. As well as the myriads of 'polytheistic' religions of the eastern world; Hinduism, Buddhism, Sikhism, Shintoism, and perhaps the fastest growing religion of the west, 'Atheism' itself. 'Rome' cannot be seen to be the 'headquarters' of all of this historically. And yet …

'
In a day that may not be far in the future, all pseudo-Christian, Judeo-Christian, Chrislam and all other false worship must join together to form one religious system ...'

Rome And Islam

Strange and terrible days are coming. Stranger, and more troublesome than has ever been *"or ever shall be"* (Matthew chapter 24 verse 21). 'Papal Rome' as a system is changing on more than one front. The 'Anglican Church' and other branches are now in practical terms 'back in the fold'. Strange alliances are now being sought behind the scenes, not only with the Chief Rabbis of Judaism, but also certain more moderate branches of Islam. The present Pope has been to visit representatives of both these 'world religions at prime sites of each faith, in Jerusalem and Istanbul'.

From the far west of America, and parts of northern Africa, comes news of an unholy alliance stranger still; 'Chrislam'*, a seeking for common ground between Christian and Muslim. This new 'syncretism' may be well-intentioned in part, but it is highly combustible and doctrinally erroneous on all of the fundamental issues.

The 'Blue Mosque' in Istanbul – A meeting place of world religions? [cited Wall Street Journal Nov. 29th 2014].

In a day that may not be far in the future, all pseudo-Christian, Judeo-Christian, Chrislam and all other false worship must join together to form one religious system of spiritual *"fornication ... and blasphemy"* in order to fulfil the vision of John in this chapter of Revelation.

This city is more than likely real, and in an identifiable geographical place. It may be Rome – though the angel said, the *"seven mountains are ... seven kings"* (Revelation chapter 17 verses 9 – 10 NRB) not the 'seven hills of Rome'. It may even be Jerusalem, a less common theory, yet *"the great city"* (chapter 11 verse 8) is normally used within the book of Revelation as a name for the city of Jerusalem. Since the removal of this false system will leave space for what the *"False Prophet"* will introduce, might not that which will be destroyed and that which will come in its place be both based in the same global religious centre? Were not the sacred vessels of Temple worship used when they *"drank wine and praised the gods of gold, and of silver, of brass, of iron, of wood, and of stone."* in days gone past? (Daniel chapter 5 verses 1 – 4 KJV). Terrible days of idolatry are still to come, when mankind in general will have fully turned their backs on the one true God and His Son, who is now our Saviour, Jesus Christ.

Yet, even in those awful days, God – as He always has had in every age – will still have a remnant who have not 'bowed the knee' to any false god (1 Kings 19 verse 18).

*KEYNOTE: Christianity vs. Islam.** They are not compatible. The Bible and the Qur'an do not have a common source or message. This is 'syncretism' of the worst kind. Although the Qur'an does speak of 'Jesus', he is not the Jesus of the N.T. The truth of the Trinity is denied, as is the Fatherhood of God, the eternal Sonship of Christ, the deity of the Holy Spirit, the sacrificial death of Jesus on the cross and His bodily resurrection. The true gospel of Jesus Christ is the only good news for sinners, and He who died and rose again is sufficient alone for the forgiveness of our sins, and for eternal life.

Questions and Answers for Chapter Seventeen – 'Mystery Babylon- The Scarlet Woman'

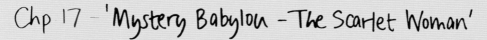

Chp 17 – 'Mystery Babylon –The Scarlet Woman'

Q1   There are four woman in the book of Revelation – Can you give their names? And the chapters where they are found?

Q2   Who does the "Scarlet Woman" we have studied in Chp. 17 represent?

Q3   Who is the "Beast" she is sitting on?

Q4   Who is in control, the Woman or the Beast?

Q5   Who is in supreme control?

Q6   Can you give a verse from Chp. 17 to confirm that?

Q7   Where does the "Mystery Babylon" false religion begin?

Q8   Can you give an O.T. Chp. reference to support that fact?

Q9   What is the end of the false religious system represented by the "Scarlet Woman"?

Q10   Why might Satan want the false religious system out of the way?

JOTTINGS

Chapter Eighteen

The Fall of Babylon

Following on quickly from where we were with John, in the previous part of his 'Babylon visions', we now come to the second phase; the fall of 'Babylon City'. In the previous chapter we looked at the fall of the 'Babylon System'; a coming together before the *"Great Tribulation"* period of all that is 'anti-God' as far as formal religion is concerned, and its God-ordained end. This makes way for something that is worse; the worship of the *"Beast"*, the *"Image"*, and the *"Dragon"* (Revelation chapter 13), before God Himself will also destroy all of that at the *"Coming in Power"* of Jesus Christ.

[See **Chapter 20**, *'Christ's Coming in Power'*.]

The Hard Questions Reviewed

We set out in the previous Chapter some 'difficult questions' which apply to both parts of the 'Babylon visions' that John sees introduced by various angels. Let us review and summarise the answers here, as they apply to this subject as well:

1.) <u>Are the contents of Revelation chapters 17 and 18 all one vision?</u> No; They are in two separate parts.

2.) <u>If they are different, on what grounds do they differ?</u> The first part is about a 'religious system', the second part is about a 'commercial city'. A political 'capital'.

3.) <u>If they are not one vision, where do they divide?</u> The visions divide at the beginning of chapter 18. The repetition of *"after these things"* (chapter 18 verse 1) is a key phrase in Revelation which marks a 'time-shift' in John's visions.

4.) <u>If the visions divide, what is the time difference?</u> The time difference here is three and a half years. The contents of the chapters make that clear, with reference also to the end of the 'Bowl Judgments' (Revelation chapter 16 verses 12 – 19).

5.) <u>Is there a real *"city"* in view? Or only an allegory?</u> The *"great city"* in the first vision may be symbolic, but it may also be a real place. Rome, Jerusalem, and the newly rebuilt Babylon are all possible candidates. The *"great city"* of the second part of the vision (chapter 18 verse 21) is a literal place, most likely the 'political capital' of the *"Beast"*, beside the Euphrates River, from where he will reign over his Empire, for possibly 7 years or more.

> *... the Babylon site is one of the few things not 'restored' in the Millennial Kingdom.'*

6.) <u>If there are two visions, what does the *"woman"* represent?</u> She represents the 'idolatrous religious system' in pictorial form. She is to be compared and contrasted with the other three *"women"* of the book of Revelation, as we have seen.

What the Angel Said

Following on from the phrase *"after these things"* John sees, *"another angel coming down out of heaven, having great authority; and the earth was lightened with his glory. And he cried mightily with a strong voice, saying, 'Babylon the great is fallen, is fallen, and is become the habitation of demons and a ward of every foul spirit, and a ward of every unclean and hateful bird."* (Revelation chapter 18 verses 1 – 2 NRB). This seems like symbolic and even 'hyperbolic' language, until we look at the Old

> ***KEYNOTE: O.T. References.** It has been said that the book of Revelation contains over 340 references to O.T. prophecies, some 95 of which are repeated (making close to 450 in all), an average of 20 per chapter, though no direct quotations at all. Therefore, the book of Revelation cannot be properly interpreted without studying the O.T. references, in context, both in relation to symbols and future events.

Testament prophecies concerning the 'Fall of Babylon' which have never been historically fulfilled*. We will also see – looking forward – that the Babylon site is one of the few things not 'restored' in the Millennial Kingdom. It is left as a testimony to gross and demonic rebellion against God for the whole of the 1,000 years. We will look at that in more detail later.

[See **Chapter 21**, *'The Millennial Kingdom'*.]

Babylon – Great City of the Future – Rebuilt to be Burned

Babylon Rebuilt?

Though it is true that, as has often been stated, there are no direct quotations from the Old Testament in the book of Revelation, yet in John's account of his vision of the 'Fall of Babylon' we come very close, more than once, to actual quotation from the prophecies of Isaiah and Jeremiah. This is highly significant and suggests right away that there are details relating to this event:

a.) Which were prophesied in the past, by the Old Testament prophets.

b.) Which have never been fulfilled before, in Old Testament or recent times.

c.) Which require a future literal *"great city"* to be built, for their final fulfilment.

All the more reason to expect that a new Babylon will be built (during the first part of the 7 years, or even before that), so that 'she' may suffer the fate God has long intended, for her past sins as well as future ones. Just as a 'Tribulation Temple' or *"Sanctuary"* must be erected – so that the sacrifices can commence and a *"Holy place"* be consecrated – before the *"Beast"* causes *"the sacrifice and the oblation to cease"* (Daniel chapter 9 verse 27 KJV) and a *"Holy place"* desecrated with his *"Image"* (Matthew chapter 24 verse 15). Though we are not told specifically of the building of such a *"Sanctuary"* it would appear, by the same method of spiritual deduction, that we cannot interpret a literal city as being finally destroyed, unless it is first rebuilt again and occupied.

What Isaiah said about Babylon

Isaiah prophesied about the fall of Babylon (city and kingdom) to the invading Medo-Persians, *"I will stir up the Medes against them ... and Babylon, the glory of kingdoms, the beauty of the Chaldees' excellency, shall be as when Elohim overthrew Sodom and Gomorrah."* (Isaiah chapter 13 verses 17 – 19 NRB). That prophecy sounds very like a destruction by fire, which historically has never happened, though Babylon did fall to the Medes (Daniel chapter 5). Here is another 'divided prophecy': The first part was fulfilled when Babylon fell in Daniel's time (538 BC), but the latter part has not been fulfilled, yet. The next part of Isaiah's prophecy is even more specific still: *"It shall never be inhabited, neither shall it be dwelt in from generation to generation ... But wild beasts of the desert shall lie there ..."* (Isaiah chapter 13 verses 20 – 22 NRB). The angel in John's vision expands on this prophecy, the *"wild beasts"* of the Old Testament prophecy (from 700 BC) are added to by *"demons and foul spirits"*. When we link the final iteration of Babylon with the kingdom of the *"Beast"* and the *"Dragon"*, the amplification here is very relevant, and refers forward to the Millennial Age.

In the second paragraph of Revelation chapter 18 we find another reference, and a partial quotation, which links back to Isaiah prophesying the end of Babylon, *"O daughter of the Chaldeans: for thou shalt no more be called 'The lady of kingdoms' ... thou hast said, 'I shall be a lady forever ... I, and none else beside me; I shall not sit as a widow, neither shall I know loss of children'."* The response of Jehovah through the lips of Isaiah is most final, *"But these two shall come to thee in a moment in one day, the loss of children, and widowhood ... For the multitude of thy sorceries, and for the great abundance of thine enchantments ... they shall be a stubble; the fire shall burn them ... thy merchants, from thy youth ... none shall save thee."* (Isaiah chapter 47 verses 5 – 15 NRB).

When we return again to our vision in Revelation, John hears another voice from heaven pronouncing the final doom of the city of Babylon in the last days, *"... How much she glorified herself, and lived luxuriously, so much torment and sorrow give her: for she saith in her heart, 'I sit a queen, and am not a widow, and shall see no sorrow'. Therefore shall her plagues come in one day ... she shall be utterly burned with fire: for strong is Jehovah Elohim who judgeth her."* (Revelation chapter 18 verses 7 – 8 NRB).

We see that the very words that Babylon the city – personified as a woman – speaks in Isaiah's time are repeated, some of them 'verbatim' (word for word), in John's vision. Babylon was overrun by the Medo-Persians (538 BC) and many years later the city fell into neglect through the ages. Saddam Hussein (President of Iraq from 1979 – 2003 AD), who saw himself as a modern successor of Nebuchadnezzar, was attempting a rebuild and had completed the reconstruction of the infamous 'Ishtar Gate' before his demise. The 'Babil' district today, where Babylon is sited, is home to over 2,000,000 Arab tribesmen living in villages around and within the city site. Never in history, nor in the record of scripture, has Babylon ever been completely destroyed. The 'burning with fire' and 'never to be dwelt in again' are still future judgments to be fulfilled at the end of the *"Great Tribulation"* period.

What Jeremiah said about Babylon

"The word that Jehovah spake against Babylon and against the land of the Chaldeans by the hand of Jeremiah the prophet ..." (Jeremiah chapter 50 verse 1 NRB). Here are some of the specifics that Jeremiah prophesied (about 100 years after Isaiah), *"Behold, the hindermost of nations shall be a wilderness, a dry land, and a desert. Because of the wrath of Jehovah it shall not be inhabited, but it shall be wholly desolate ... her foundations are fallen, her walls are thrown down: for it is the vengeance of Jehovah ... according to all that she hath done, do unto her"* (Jeremiah chapter 50 verses 1 – 29 NRB). *"The broad walls of Babylon shall be utterly broken, and her high gates shall be burned with fire"* (Jeremiah chapter 51 verse 58 NRB).

The ancient ruins of the walls of Nebuchadnezzar's Babylon – over 60 metres high – Excavated between 1899 and 1917 by a German team under Robert Koldewey.
Though buried under 100's of years of sand, Babylon was never "thrown down", as the prophets foretold.

Jeremiah expands on what Isaiah has already said and gives one of the most remarkable prophecies of the Old Testament, *"Therefore the wild beasts of the desert with the wild beasts of the islands shall dwell there … And it shall be no more inhabited <u>forever</u>; neither shall it be dwelt in from generation to generation. As God overthrew Sodom and Gomorrah … so shall no man abide there, neither shall any son of Adam dwell therein."* (Jeremiah chapter 50 verses 39 – 41 NRB).

As we have seen already, not only has Babylon never been destroyed by fire, but its walls have never been *"thrown down"*. Parts of the walls of Nebuchadnezzar are still a tourist attraction today, and some sections are more than 200 feet tall (see photo). Scripture is exceedingly precise, and what God says He will do, if it has not already been done, He most surely will. We have got a lovely picture in our minds of restoration and renewal in the 'Kingdom Age', which there will be. But there are exceptions: Satan and his angels have no opportunity of recovery; they are condemned forever. And the site of Babylon – for evil associations about which only God knows the full depths of wickedness – will have no restoration either in the Kingdom. There is also a third object which is not restored, but we will keep that until we study the *'Millennial Kingdom'* later. [See **Chapter 21**]

KEYNOTE: Jerusalem Attacked. In contrast to Babylon, Jerusalem *"the city of the Great King"* has been one of the most attacked and 'ransacked' cities in the world's history. It has been calculated that Jerusalem has been completely destroyed twice, besieged 23 times, attacked 52 times, and captured and recaptured 44 times. Some of these attacks have been due to her rejection of Jehovah, and His Messiah. Others are due to the hatred of Satan for what Jerusalem represents in the plans of God. As we have often noted, God will triumph in the end. We will study the *'New Jerusalem'* in **Chp. 23**.

Final Payback Time!

Another reason for the final destruction of the city of Babylon is because of what 'she' – as representative of 'Babylon the nation' – has done to Jerusalem and the nation of Judah in the past. Jeremiah again, as the spokesman for Jehovah, says, *"And I will render unto Babylon and to all the inhabitants of Chaldea all their evil that they have done in Zion in your sight, saith Jehovah … I will make thee a burnt mountain. And they shall not take of thee a stone for a corner, nor a stone for foundations; but thou shalt be desolate forever, saith Jehovah."* (Jeremiah chapter 51 verses 24 – 26 NRB).

These are strong words, but, as has often been said, 'God says what He means, and means what He says'. God will judge every evil action taken against His people. We have looked previously at divine retribution against those who martyred so many of the Church. Here we are looking at Jehovah's retribution against those who have attacked His earthly people the Jews, their earthly land Israel, and their capital city of Jerusalem.

Way back in our early Chapters we looked at the promises of Jehovah to Abraham, *"I will bless those who bless you, and the one who curses you I will curse"* (Genesis chapter 12 verse 1 – 3 NASB). Here we see the full and final working out of that 'covenant-promise'. More than 4,000 years later, that final *"curse"* will be worked out before the full 'Millennial Kingdom' blessing comes in.

When Babylon the city, personified as a woman, is heard as saying, *"I sit a queen, and am not a widow, and shall see no sorrow"* (Revelation chapter 18 verse 7 NRB), she is comparing herself against Jerusalem, whom she destroyed along with many others who attacked the city of Zion before that. Even though Babylon may be finally and fully rebuilt as the capital city of *"Anti-Christ"* (as we have suggested), even though she outlasts the other cities of the world which are destroyed during the final 'Bowl Judgments', yet because of her wickedness, at the very end of the 'Tribulation Period' God will bring her judgment to pass *"in one day"* (chapter 18 verse 8).

The Mourners at Her Burning

When we look at the description of all who *"mourn over her"* we can see a catalogue of those who have supported the *"Beast"* in his rise to power, and who in turn he had facilitated in trade permits and agreements connected with his *"mark"*. Do you remember, back in Chapter 15, we looked at the subject of the 'Mark of the Beast', where in order to *"buy or sell"*, the *"mark"* is needed? Many may take it gladly, even for commercial reasons, for personal power granted by their association with the *"Beast"*, and with the *"Dragon"*, as well as bowing to the authority of the *"Beast"*; for *"worship"* is not divorced from the commercial benefits. Just as the 'religious system' (Revelation chapter 17), which has the Devil at its core, is also interwoven with the 'commercial system', which, as we have seen in our study (in Revelation chapter 18), is also evil.

A summary of those who *"mourn"* at the demise of the commercial system, headed up in the new city Babylon, possibly a greater global trade alliance – for a short period – than anything ever seen before, looks like this:

1.) ***"The kings of the earth"*** (chapter 18 verse 9 KJV) The same group who had links with the *"Babylon the Great"* religious system will also have links with the commercial system. This is wider than the *"ten kings"* who originally supported the *"Great Prostitute"* and then turned against her. They did not mourn her passing, for they stole her wealth (chapter 17 verses 12, 16). As we have hinted before, the monarchical network of 'royal houses' are very literal (even if quite shadowy today in many lands) and may all come to the fore as 'sub-regents' with the *"King of Fierce Countenance"* (Daniel chapter 8 verse 23) at his rise to power. Now they will mourn the fall of the system that gave them prestige and wealth, but will also acknowledge that it is not accidental, but judgmental; *"Alas, alas, that great city Babylon, that mighty city! For in one hour is thy judgment come."* (Revelation chapter 18 verse 10 NRB).

2.) ***"The merchants of the earth"*** (chapter 18 verse 11 KJV) Here is a long descriptive paragraph (that runs to verse 17) that reads like the contents of an exotic eastern bazaar. We can almost see the sights, sense the perfumes, and hear the cries of the competing vendors! This merchant is trading *"gold, silver, precious stones"*, this one *"pearls, fine linen, purple, silk, and scarlet cloth"*. This one trading in articles of *"ivory, costly wood, bronze, iron, marble"*. Another one is importing *"cinnamon, spices, incense, myrrh, frankincense, wine, oil, fine flour and wheat"*. And another *"cattle, sheep, horses and chariots"*. And the last merchants listed, the most sinister of all, trading in *"slaves, that is human souls"*. Commodities that have been banned for years, even 'slave trading' will be back on the permitted list in those days. (Though 'human trafficking' is widespread now, in the western world, even in our time. Perhaps a 'sign of the times' in itself?)

3.) ***"All shipmasters, seafaring men and sailors"*** (chapter 18 verse 17b ESV) Interestingly, these words are not a repetition, they are describing three different groups of workers. The word *"shipmaster"* is not the owner or the captain of the vessel, it describes the 'steersman', the NRB has *"pilot"*, that is a specialist 'helmsman' for inshore or estuary navigation (we will come back to that point shortly). The *"seafaring"* word is descriptive of 'onboard sailors' generally, and the *"sailor"* word is 'mariners', we would perhaps put 'sea-farers' in there, men who go to far-off lands to bring home foreign goods to trade.

> **KEYNOTE: *"Merchants"*** This word is only used in two places in the N.T. Here in Rev. 18:11 & 15, and in Matt. 13:45. The word means a 'travelling trader' who buys rare and valuable commodities to re-sell to retailers. Here in the context of the 'Babylon-traders' this picture fits. But in the 'Parables of the Kingdom' passage the *"merchant"* sells everything he has already bought to buy a *"pearl of great price"* to keep! This is a picture – in context – of Jesus and His Church. But the comparison of the two kinds of merchants, their wares, and here, their loss of all is most significant.

All three of these groups (they are listed one by one, but their outcry is simultaneous) have a common response to one single event, *"when they shall see the smoke of her burning"* (chapter 18 verse 9 & 18 KJV). The sight must be fearful, a total modern metropolis all on fire at once. This is *"Sodom and Gomorrah"* on a much greater scale. The kings, traders, merchants, sea-crew (no inhabitants are mentioned which is a solemn thought), *"will stand far off, in fear of her torment"* (chapter 18 verses 10, 15 & 17 ESV). Each group also laments the suddenness of her destruction: *"For in a single hour your judgment has come"* (chapter 18 verses 10, 17 & 19 ESV).

Although an *"hour"* in prophecy can mean a short period of several literal hours, it is unlikely these three groups will know that. It may be terribly literal, *"Babylon"* the whole capital city of the *"Beast"*, the centre of his political, commercial, and possibly religious empire on the banks of the Euphrates River razed to the ground in one hour. Such is her wickedness, and such is her divine judgment, *"Pay her back as she herself has paid back others, and repay her double for her deeds; mix a double portion for her in the cup she mixed."* (chapter 18 verse 6 ESV).

Babylon by the Sea?

'Surely a mistake', you say, 'Babylon is not even on the Euphrates River today?' That may be so, and a good question, but topography changes over time, and looking forward

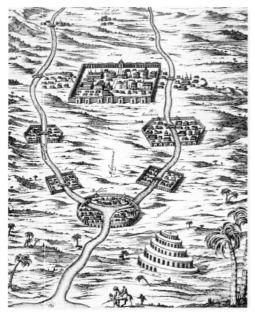

An illustration of the early site of the City of Babylon (c600 BC.) showing the channels of the Euphrates River on both sides.

prophetically it can change back to what and where it was before. Babylon in Nebuchadnezzar's time was on the east bank of the Euphrates, and had a man-made channel on right side, so that the city had a water barrier on both sides. Today the ancient city-site is further from the riverbanks than it was 2,500 years ago. But it is possible that *"the King"* will have his new city on the west bank in that future period. We may deduce that from *"tidings out of the east"* (Daniel chapter 11 verse 44), and the *"great River Euphrates"* being dried up, *"that the way of the kings from the sun-rising might be prepared."* (Revelation chapter 16 verse 12 NRB).

It would appear that the River Euphrates is his eastern boundary, possibly widened, excavated, and fortified. But it will be wiped out by God, in a moment, in the sixth bowl judgment.

What the Angel Said

As we have seen in our previous Chapter, John is introduced to the 'Babylon visions' by one of the bowl angels. He is shown these events after he has seen the 'bowl visions', but in chronological order the first vision comes in the middle of the seven-year period, before the 'Bowl Judgments' commence, and the second vision comes at the end of the seven years, coinciding with the last of the 'Seal Judgments'. That also coincides with the last of the 'Trumpet Judgments' and most pertinently, the last of the 'Bowl Judgments'. The first angel announces the *"judgment of the Great Prostitute"* (Revelation chapter 17 verse 1), and explains the mystery of *"Babylon the Great, mother of prostitutes and of earth's abominations"* (chapter 17 verses 7 – 18 ESV). The destruction controlled by God of the false religious system, the united global idolatry, before the rise of what is last and worst: the worship of the *"Beast"*, the *"Image"*, and the *"Dragon"* (Revelation chapter 13). The second angel announces the fall of *"Babylon the Great"*, the *"mighty city"* which is divinely judged and burned with fire.

We come now to the announcement of the third angel in the 'Babylon visions'. We have heard from a.) *"one of the angels which had the seven bowls"*, b.) an angel *"having great power"*, and now c.) *"a mighty angel"* (chapter 18 verse 21 – 24. This angel not only speaks, but he also acts out a demonstration of God's judgment, and the fulfilment of the last of our Old Testament prophecies still outstanding. We have looked back at prophecies from Isaiah, and from Jeremiah. We have examined them in order of their pronouncement, and brought them into the context of these 'Babylon visions'.

What Jeremiah Did

There is another outstanding prophecy of Jeremiah which has not been yet fulfilled, *"Jeremiah wrote in a book all the disaster that should come upon Babylon, all these words that are written concerning Babylon ... When you finish reading this book, tie a stone to it and cast it into the midst of the Euphrates, and say, 'Thus shall Babylon sink, to rise no more, because of the disaster that I am bringing upon her, and they shall become exhausted.'"* (Jeremiah chapter 51 verses 60 – 64 ESV). This is not only a prophecy but also a picture (we discussed that in the early Chapters). The *"book"* is the condemnation of Babylon, Jehovah's pronouncements against her, spoken aloud by the prophet and written down by his scribe. The binding of a stone to the book and the casting of it into the Euphrates River is a very graphic picture of Babylon's final end.

What the other Angel Did

When we come back to our chapter here, and John's second 'Babylon vision', what do we find? The 'third angel' in the narrative not only speaks, he also acts! *"And a mighty angel took up a stone like a great millstone, and cast it into the sea, saying, 'Thus with violence shall the great city Babylon be thrown down, and shall be found no more at all ...'"* (Revelation chapter 18 verse 21 NRB). The picture is the same, but the action is enhanced. The *"stone"* of Jeremiah's prophecy has now become a *"great millstone"*, to be thrown with violence from a great height!

An ancient pair of "upper and lower" millstones

'But', you ask, 'Has something else not changed? The quotation differs in relation to where the stone is cast'. Indeed, it does and a point worthy of note. Whereas in Jeremiah's demonstration the *"stone"* was thrown into the Euphrates River, now here, when her final judgment takes place, the angel throws the *"millstone"* into the sea. 'How can that be?' you ask, 'Babylon is not close to the sea!' Indeed, it is not. The site of today's ruins are more than 500 kilometres from the Persian Gulf. Was John mistaken? Is this a 'misquote' from Jeremiah? There must be a divine and prophetic reason for the alteration. All the other

> *Babylon, the city, is linked with persecution and martyrdom which will be worse than ever in the Tribulation Period.'*

references we have tracked from Isaiah and Jeremiah concerning *"Babylon"* have matched up, and confirmed that a literal city is required – in the future – for the specifics of these prophecies to be fulfilled. As the word of Jehovah always is. 'So why the change here?'

More Counterfeiting!

Remember we looked [in **Chapters 12** & **13**] at the extent of Satan's 'counterfeit' programme? And the number of items, persons, and events God will permit him to copy. There is a possibility that here is another, perhaps a final, counterfeit of something that will be future after the reign of *"Antichrist"* has ended. Jerusalem, when the city is restored and rebuilt at the beginning of the 'Kingdom Age', will become a seaport.

[See **Chapter 21**, *'The Millennial Kingdom'*.]

'How come?' you ask. The prophet Zechariah has the answer (he prophesied about 100 years after Jeremiah), *"On that day living waters shall flow out from Jerusalem, half of them to the eastern* (Dead) *sea, and half of them to the western* (Mediterranean) *sea. It shall continue in summer as in winter."* (Zechariah chapter 14 verse 8 ESV). This will be a permanent tree-lined waterway, joining the Mediterranean to the Dead Sea. The Land will become 'levelled up', *"turned into a plain"* (chapter 14 verse 10), so the Dead Sea will be raised in height, and its *"waters shall be healed"* (Ezekiel chapter 47 verses 8 – 9). The topography of Israel will be very different, and these two seas will be joined by the new river flowing through the city of Jerusalem.

Perhaps – for we cannot be dogmatic – Satan, who knows very well these prophecies of the Old Testament, will seek to counterfeit the same kind of 'alteration' to the Euphrates and the location of the new Babylon? Perhaps the River will be excavated, or perhaps the earthquakes will have altered its course and depth. Or perhaps both? One other detail worth recalling – from the earlier part of this study – was the *"helmsman"* (or *"pilot"* as the NRB has it). One of the tasks of a pilot is to navigate large ships up estuaries and rivers. Perhaps God is giving us a 'clue' in the use of that term here. We can imagine the great mass of shipping, that which remains of the ocean fleet after the 'Trumpet Judgments', many of them queued up in the Euphrates River estuary and having a 'grandstand' view of the burning of the very city that they were bringing their cargo to.

Babylon's Death Knell!

Babylon shall be found *"no more at all"*. This solemn phrase, like a tolling bell, is repeated seven times in the description of her destruction. Why so severe an end? And why such a severe conflagration? Not just because this Babylon has been a byword and centre-point for idolatrous worship down through the centuries. Not only because she will be rebuilt to become the political, commercial – and perhaps religious – capital of the *"Beast"*. But most of all because she is linked with persecution and martyrdom, which, perhaps, will be worse than ever in the 'Tribulation Period'. The angel tells John, *"In her was found the blood of prophets, and of saints, and of all that were slain upon the earth."* (Revelation chapter 18 verse 24 KJV). What she has done to others, as we have read, God will do to her. How solemn, and how fearful a warning to all who defy the God of heaven.

Q&A >

Questions and Answers for Chapter Eighteen – 'The Fall of Babylon'

Chp. 18 – 'The Fall of Babylon'

Q1. Do both "Babylon" visions happen at the same time?

Q2. How can we tell there is a time difference?

Q3. If the "Scarlet Woman" is a religious system, what is "Babylon the Great"?

Q4. What was similar about the city and tower back in Genesis Chp. 10 & 11?

Q5. What did the 'Tower of Babel' represent?

Q6. Which other cities in the O.T. that God destroyed, is this city also like?

Q7. What will happen to the future Babylon that never happened in the past?

Q8. Can you give a reference from the O.T. to support that?

Q9. Why does God judge the future Babylon in this way?

PART THREE

THE KINGDOM PERIOD ANTICIPATED

Chapter Nineteen

The Battle of Armageddon

After the 'hard stuff' of the Babylon visions, we come now to what is possibly one of the most interesting topics of the book of Revelation and another of the well-known titles from within the book. We have had the 'Four Horsemen of the Apocalypse' (within the Seal Judgments), the 'Mark of the Beast' and now the 'Battle of Armageddon'. We saw in a previous study [in **Chapter 9**] that the 'Four Horsemen ...' title is a misnomer (a wrong description). The '*apocalypse*' word is not connected with them, but with the *"unveiling of Jesus Christ"*. The word is translated *"Revelation"* and that is the only time it is used in the book (Revelation chapter 1 verse 1 KJV).

Likewise, when we come to *"Armageddon"*, we will find the familiar expression, '*The Battle of ...*' is also a misnomer. When we examine the Old Testament prophecies carefully, we find that there are more 'military marshalling plains' than Megiddo, but also there is no battle. We will see what happens instead, in this study and in the next ['*The Coming in Power*' **Chapter 20**]. We are doing a short reprise of our own, maybe even a 'parenthesis'. We have reached the end point of the seven years with the concluding 'Bowl Judgments'. We have been studying *"Babylon"* in detail, which is mentioned in connection with the seventh bowl, and now we are going back to look – before we move to the *"Coming in Power"* of *"Messiah"* Jesus Christ – at this other strange place, the *"gathering to ... Armageddon"* (Revelation chapter 16 verse 16) which relates to the sixth bowl.

Order of Events?

In strict chronological order the *"gathering"* by God, using the agents of the *"spirits of demons"*, to the battleground takes place just before Babylon falls. We noted that in an earlier study. When the *"Beast"* who is the *"King"* hears the *"tidings out of the east"* of a great army coming against him, as well as from other directions, he moves his 'campaign HQ' to a position in the Sinai Peninsula (Daniel chapter 11). It is probably at this point, either before he leaves, or just after, that God burns up his capital city. The 'Fall of Babylon' takes place as the armies are gathering, but the moment of climax at *"Armageddon"* is the last event of all, before the 'Kingdom of Messiah' will commence, which will last for 1,000 years.

> **KEYNOTE: Timing.** These events take place, not in the additional 75 days of Daniel chp. 12, but at the very end of the 1,260 days of the *"Great Tribulation"*.

We can break this study down into five key questions which any reader might ask:

The Land of Israel today – Showing the Valleys of Jezreel & Megiddo.

1.) Is *"Megiddo"* a real place?

2.) If so, where is *"Megiddo"*?

3.) Why is it called *"Armageddon"* in the book of Revelation?

4.) What happened there before?

5.) What will happen there in the future?

Is Megiddo a Place?

The answer is 'Yes!' In Bible history, in prophecy, and in secular history too, *"Megiddo"* is one of the most strategic sites of the Middle East, and connected with a great many famous battles down through the ages. There is a great deal of 'debate' between prophetic scholars as to whether the historic place *"Megiddo"* is exactly the same place as *"Armageddon"* in Revelation. We will have to make a decision on that, but not until later in the study …

Where is Megiddo?

Even that is not as easy a question as it seems, for, as we shall see, it depends which place called *"Megiddo"* we are talking about. Megiddo today is a small village, with a population of about 1,000 people, at the foothills of the mountains on the southside of the valley of the same name. If you asked there, 'Is this the original *"Megiddo"*?' you would be told, 'No, up in the hills are the ruins of an old hill fort, which the incoming Israelites captured back in 1,500 BC.' Way back in the days of Joshua, and through the times of the kings of Israel and Judah, the name *"Megiddo"* referred to different places, but all of them were strategically significant from a military point of view.

In the northern part of what became the Land of Israel there lies a great double valley which, down through the ages, became famous as a battle site (we will look at that in more detail in a moment).

KEYNOTE: '**Principles of Mention**'. These are very important and helpful aids in Bible study. Very often where a person, place, or subject is mentioned <u>first</u> in scripture it gives a lot of 'direction' as to the meaning attached to it. We have noted a 'first mention' in relation to the ‘number of rebellion’ (which connects with another study; Numbers in Scripture). ‘Principles of Mention’ include First Mention, Last Mention (“Har-Megiddo” also refers), Most Mention, Only Mention, and Omission (that is a book, or passage, in the Bible where an expected subject does not occur). A personal study of these lists is very much worthwhile.

“Megiddo” is mentioned by name 12 times in the Old Testament, which is probably significant in that the mention in Revelation – assuming that it is the same place – then becomes the 13th mention. And ‘thirteen’ in the Bible is a number connected with rebellion (Genesis chapter 14 verse 4). The ‘Battleground’ of Megiddo’s Valley is the site of the last great rebellion against God, by mankind and demons, of this age.

Why is it Called Armageddon?

That is the hard question. Once we get that out of the way, the rest of our study should be most interesting (especially for those who like war history). This is also where the division of opinion comes in, as to whether *“Megiddo”* and *“Armageddon”* are one and the same. One argument goes like this: John says, *“He* (God Almighty) *gathered them together into a place called in Hebrew tongue ‘Har-Megiddo’.”* (Revelation chapter 16 verse 16 NRB). Since John underlined that the name was in Hebrew, it should be taken as a translation of Hebrew, which means *“Har”* – ‘the mountains’ – and *“Megiddo”* which in Hebrew means ‘great multitude’ or possibly ‘slaughter place’. So *“Har-Megiddo”* could be read as, ‘The mountains where a great multitude has been gathered for slaughter’. Those who support this argument [J. N. Darby, T. Newberry, J. Allen and others] take the place to be the mountains of Judea around Jerusalem in the last days, as Jesus referred to in His ‘Temple Discourse’. *“When”*, He said, *“ye shall see Jerusalem compassed by armies, then know that the desolation thereof is nigh … for these be days of vengeance, that all things which are written may be fulfilled.”* (Luke chapter 21 verses 20 – 22 NRB).

‘So, the Megiddo place, in the north of Israel doesn’t figure in the last days?’ That depends on who you ask! There is another viewpoint, which goes like this: *“Megiddo”* in scripture can refer to the valley or plain, the river on the valley floor, the mountains around the plain, or the fortified ‘citadel’ which guarded a ‘path’ through the southern hills. So, we have the *“Megiddo”* citadel, guarding the entrance through the Megiddo hills, into the Megiddo Valley. The same name connects all of these with great military events of days gone by. The *“Armageddon”* of Revelation then refers to, ‘all of the above’. The Plain surrounded by hills which have guarded passes through them into the Valley. In the Hebrew here the *“Har-Megiddo”* refers, not to the ‘Mountains of Jerusalem’ – though they feature in connection with various ‘last battle’ armies – but to the ‘Mountains of Megiddo’ and the Megiddo Plain which they surround. [C. I. Scofield, J. F. Walvoord, D. G. Barnhouse, A. G. Fruchtenbaum, J. A. MacArthur, J. Phillips, S. Gordon, A. Tsarfati, and the author all take this viewpoint.]

One thing however is absolutely certain. Those living in these ‘last days’ will be able to recognise with absolute certainty that what is happening is the fulfilment of ‘End Time’ prophecy. They will be in no doubt as to the location, and the interpretation, of what John wrote here.

What Happened at Megiddo in the Bible?

East of Mount Carmel, which is the most westerly of the hills on the south side of the valley, there lies one of the mountain passes through the hills. Possibly the most accessible. This, from ancient times, formed a route from Egypt in the south through to Assyria and the north. The Romans called it '*Via Maris*', the 'way of the sea'. This became a significant 'waypoint' on the route for armies travelling north and south, into the territories they were invading, and so over time the Plain of Megiddo became a great 'battle-ground' where many campaigns were fought, famous victories were won, and famous defeats too.

The first mention of *"Megiddo"* in the Bible (for we need to focus primarily on scriptural history, and Bible prophecy) is in connection with Joshua's invasion of the land of Canaan, right at the beginning of his campaign. We are told of the *"kings ... which Joshua and the children of Israel smote on this side the Jordan on the west ... the king of Jericho ... the king of Jerusalem ... the king of Megiddo ... all kings thirty and one."* (Joshua chapter 12 verses 7 – 24 NRB). Many of these were strategic citadels. It seems Joshua travelled quickly through the land and *"smote"* the most significant of the fortified hill towns first. The tribe of Manasseh was allotted the Megiddo citadel as part of their possession (Joshua chapter 17 verse 11), but Manasseh did not fully *"drive out"* the occupants of these citadels, *"Beth-Shean"* on the Gilboan Hills to the east of the Valley, and *"Megiddo"* on the southwest side.

The ruins of the ancient citadel of 'Tel Megiddo' –
looking towards the Plain and the northern hills.

The next time we come across *"Megiddo"*, the name refers not to the citadel but the *"waters"*, linked with the *"River of Kishon"* on the west. Here *"Barak"* and *"Deborah"* defeated *"Sisera"* and the armies of the Canaanites (Judges chapter 4 – 5). There are faint pictures there of the 'last battle' for Jehovah said, *"I will draw thee to the River Kishon Sisera, ... with his chariots and his multitude; and I will deliver him into thine hand."* (Judges chapter 4 verse 7 NRB). So, God will *"draw"* the armies loyal to the *"Beast"* to *"Har-Megiddo"* for the last great victory on behalf of the remnant of Israel. The famous victory of *"Gideon"*, with his 300 men, over the Midianites also took place in the *"Valley of Jezreel"*, which is part of the 'Plain of Megiddo' (chapter 7 verses 1 – 25)*.

"Megiddo" is mentioned several times in the record of the Kings, directly and indirectly. Saul and his sons were slain *"on Mount Gilboa"*, on the hills at the eastern end of the valley, where the 'Golan Heights' are today (1 Samuel chapter 31). Solomon rebuilt it as a key 'fortified citadel' during his reign (1 Kings chapter 9 verse 15). Elijah, in the days of king Ahab and queen Jezebel, defeated the *"prophets of Baal"* on Mount Carmel, and had them slain at the foot of the mountain, at the *"brook Kishon"* (1 Kings chapter 18). When we come to the later record, in the last days of the 'Divided Kingdoms', we find another great battle took place there, *"Pharaoh-nechoh king of Egypt went up against the king of Assyria to the River Euphrates: and king Josiah* (of Judah) *went against him; and he slew him at Megiddo."* (2 Kings chapter 23 verses 29 – 30 KJV).

Zechariah, one of the last prophets (about 520 BC), makes the last Old Testament reference to *"Megiddo"*. He refers back to the mourning at the death of King Josiah, *"the mourning of* (at) *Hadad-Rimmon in the Valley of Megidd*o" and compares it, looking forward, to the *"great mourning in Jerusalem"* which will come when *"all nations gather against Jerusalem to battle"*. Jehovah will destroy *"all the nations that come against Jerusalem ... and they shall look upon Me whom they have pierced, and they shall mourn ..."* Even though only a third part of Israel will survive, the believing remnant will confess that the *"Messiah"* that they are hoping for to deliver them, was the one they rejected when He came the first time (as in Isaiah chapter 53). When they do confess, then the Lord will descend *"and His feet shall stand in that day upon the Mount of Olives, which is before Jerusalem on the east, ..."* (Zechariah chapter 12 verse 9 to chapter 14 verse 7 KJV). What a day for Israel, and for the surviving believers of the *"Tribulation"* that will be! The *"Megiddo"* of the Old Testament is linked to the final events of the defeat of the *"Beast"* and his armies when Jesus returns.

*KEYNOTE: Mapping Megiddo.** To plot the **'Plain of Megiddo'** for yourself, have a map of modern (or Bible Times) Israel to hand. Look for the following 'waypoints': **Mount Carmel** on the western side, almost beside the Mediterranean Sea. **Haifa** at the foot of Carmel. **Acre**, some 22km up the coast. **Nazareth** (the boyhood town of Jesus, where He read in the synagogue in Luke chapter 4). The present day **'Golan Heights'** on a modern map, or 'Mount Gilboa' on a Bible map. The town of 'Beit'Shan', or **'Beth-Shean'** on a Bible map, and the Jordan Valley. Now plot a line from Accra through Nazareth, approx. 60km, until you reach the Jordan. Draw another line, parallel to the first, from Haifa, through the old Megiddo citadel site, and down to the Jordan below Beth-Shean. What is contained within, with the strategic sites marked out, is the combined **'Valley of Jezreel'**, the **'Valley of Megiddo'**, and to use its modern name **'The Vale of Esdraelon'**. A double valley or plain which Napoléon Bonaparte (1769 - 1821) said was, 'The greatest natural battle-site in all the Middle East'.

What Happened at Megiddo in History?

*David's Tower & Museum – directly behind the Jaffa Gate –
through which General Edmund Allenby led his horse in victory
on the 11th of December 1917.
The plaque, with a painting of the event upon it, reads:*
'Allenby, a General and a Gentleman at the Gates of Jerusalem'.
Written in Hebrew, English and Arabic. (JHF)

That is a good question, for the military history of *"Megiddo"* does not end at 520 BC with the prophecy of Zechariah. It continues down through the ages, right up until recent times. At the end of the 'Crusades' the Moslem armies, under General Saladin, defeated the invading Crusader forces and over 80,000 English and French soldiers were slain, in the Valley of Megiddo (1187).

Allenby's Palestine Campaign: During the 'Palestine Campaign' of the First World War (from 1917 – 1918), General Edmund Allenby, who oversaw the Allied forces in the Middle East, defeated the enemy army in a series of battles beginning at 'Be'er Shevah' (the *"Beersheba"* of the Old Testament), and ending at the Valley of Megiddo in the north. The concluding battle was fought on the 19th to 25th September 1918 where 110,000 men met on opposing sides. In his despatches home General Allenby drew a map and marked on it in his own hand, 'The Vale of Esdraelon' (the modern name), 'The Valley of Jezreel' and the 'Plain of Megiddo'. There is no doubt, from many other known incidents, that Allenby had a good knowledge of prophecy, and understood the significance of the places where he had been victorious, Jerusalem included.

Megiddo also featured in the Israeli Wars of Independence, in 1948, in 1967, and in 1973 AD. In the *'Yom Kippur War'* and the *'Six Day War'* particularly, major skirmishes were fought on the Golan Heights on the eastern side of the Valley. The very place where Saul and Jonathan were slain, 3,000 years before.

What will Happen at Megiddo in the Future?

That depends, again, on who you ask. The excellent scholars who hold to the *"Jerusalem surrounded by armies"* prophecy (Luke chapter 21 verse 20) as being the 'mountains around Jerusalem' do not see the invading armies being as widespread as Megiddo to the north. They would contend that a.) Nothing happens at Megiddo, b.) The Plain is not large enough for all the competing armies to congregate to fight, and c.) If this were the case, how would Jerusalem be surrounded and attacked? Those are valid points, and must be addressed.

The alternative view, by just as excellent scholars (for these discussions are not on fundamental issues), hold that *"surrounded by armies"* can be taken from different perspectives. If the invading armies are spread over a 320 kilometre radius, north, east and south, Jerusalem will still be *"surrounded"*, and no doubt – to fulfil the prophecies of Zechariah and others including as far back as Moses – the city will again be besieged and ransacked. Also, it is not necessary to view the Valley of Megiddo as a 'battleground' in order that the prophecies may be literally fulfilled.

A Battle or Not?

Firstly: No battle will be fought in any case. Neither at Megiddo, Jerusalem, nor anywhere else! All of the combined enemies will be destroyed by the *"Word of God"*, that is the spoken word of Jesus the King, at His *"Coming in Power"*. [See **Chapter 20**]

Secondly: All the armies who *"gather against Jerusalem"* are not likely to manoeuvre toward Megiddo. On the contrary, certain key prophecies (which we shall examine) would indicate otherwise.

Thirdly: It is most probable that the army at Megiddo, contained within the surrounding mountains, the *"Har-Megiddo"* area, will be the forces of those who still remain loyal to the *"Antichrist-King"*.

Fourthly: The encroaching army from the east (whether a far-eastern army or a Mesopotamian one, or both combined), whose approach is facilitated by God in the drying up of the River Euphrates, will push the *"Beast"* and his *"False Prophet"* out of his capital Babylon into a temporary 'military HQ' in the Sinai Peninsula (Daniel chapter 11 verse 45).

> **KEYNOTE: Euphrates & Army.** Many have linked the *"Euphrates dried up"* and the *"kings from the sunrising"* (Rev. 16:12) with the army of the "200,000,000" (Rev. 9:16). This is not a sound comparison; the two are not connected. One is linked to the 6th Trumpet Judgment, the other to the 6th Bowl Judgment. The timing is different, as are the armies. The 'eastern army' are men, no number is given, Chinese or otherwise. The '200,000,000 army' are demonic, as the context makes quite clear.

Fifthly: He cannot remain there. The encroaching army from the south, as Daniel prophesied, *"at the time of the end shall the king of the south push at him"* (Daniel chapter 11 verse 40 KJV), will force him northwards to link up with his loyal western forces, and possibly win a minor victory over an 'opportunistic' invader from the north.*

[See **KEYNOTE** at end of **Chapter**.]

Armed Forces in Place

When all these opposing forces have settled into place – *"gathered"* and orchestrated by God Himself – then not only Jerusalem but all Israel will be surrounded. The eastern invaders will have encroached as far as the Plains of Moab and *"Edom"*, where the ruins of the old citadel of Petra still are. Some think this is the actual place where the escaped remnant from Jerusalem will be protected by God during the Tribulation: *"into the wilderness, into her place"* (Revelation chapter 12 verse 14 KJV).

The army from north Africa will be encamped in the Valley of Jehoshaphat, south of Jerusalem, *"Assemble yourselves, and come, all ye nations, And gather yourselves, together round about: … And come up to the Valley of Jehoshaphat … Put ye in the sickle, for the harvest is ripe … Jehovah also shall roar out of Zion, and utter His voice from Jerusalem …"* (Joel chapter 3 verses 11 – 16 NRB).

The western army will be 'marshalled' in the Valley of Megiddo. Not as a 'battle-ground' perhaps, but as a 'camp-ground' for the army of the *"Beast"* getting ready for his last stand against his two-pronged enemy assault. Just as the 'Home Counties' of England were a marshalling centre for a battle to be fought in France and Germany, preparing for 'D Day' and the 'Normandy Landings' (6th June 1944).

Thus, there will be three great armies encircling Israel. With the sea on her western boundary, all who are in the Land will be trapped. Each army will desire victory over the other two. Probably Satan will – at that point – not care who wins. His 'front-men' are expendable (as they have always been down through the ages). He will desire the extermination of Israel, and he may think – even if his destiny cannot be altered, even if Messiah cannot be conquered – that he can achieve this one long-standing goal. Such is his inveterate hatred of the tiny nation which gave birth to the 'seed of the woman', promised by *"Jehovah Elohim"* in Genesis chapter 3.

[Ref. **Chapter 2**, *'Does God have a Programme?'*]

Who Wins the Battle?

Here is a wonderful answer. (Are you expecting it?) None of the above! How often have we seen in our studies that Satan cannot win? Israel cannot be annihilated. The purposes of God must be worked out. Messiah must return. His kingdom must be established. God, and good, must triumph. We are coming soon to the *"Hallelujahs"* of Revelation. Right here in this context, and rightly so!

Joel and Zechariah, and a great many other prophecies besides, confirm that:

a.) When the Nation of Israel is closest to annihilation, God steps in.

b.) The *"Great Tribulation"* is partly to bring the Nation to repentance. It is the fulfilment of her *"Day of Atonement"*, the *"mourning in Jerusalem … every family apart … In that day there shall be a fountain opened … for sin and for uncleanness."* (Zechariah chapter 12 verses 10 – chapter 13 verse 1 KJV).

c.) The Nation of Israel will acknowledge, and repent, of her sin in the rejection of Messiah, as Peter accused them at Pentecost, *"Jesus of Nazareth … Him … ye have taken, through lawless hand have crucified and did slay."* (Acts chapter 2 verse 23 NRB).

d.) When they do so, when they acknowledge that the prophecy of Isaiah chapter 53 is for them to accept in that day, *"He was wounded … we are healed."* (Isaiah chapter 53 verse 5), and when they seek for Him to return, in that day their Messiah will come to their deliverance.

'"Armageddon" is not a battle, it is a campaign!'

The Order of Events

'Wait', you say, 'North, East, South are covered. The sea is on the west. What other direction remains from which deliverance might come?' There is always another direction to look for help. That direction is always UP ...

[See **Chapter 20**, *'The Coming in Power'*.]

Someone will ask, 'If there is no 'Battle of Armageddon', then what does happen?' That is an excellent question, and a good place to finish at. A. G. Fruchtenbaum says, 'Armageddon is not a battle, it is a campaign'. Though the Bible does not use those words, they do make sense. There is time and geographical movement involved. Every enemy will not be destroyed in one instant, but all will be captured and slain, to the last man and the last horse (for battles then may be as battles in Bible times).

'Is there an order of events?' you might ask. Very definitely, and discernibly, yes. It seems likely that the *"Sign of the Son of Man in the heaven"* (Matthew chapter 24 verse 30 NRB) may be a period of extended, and brighter, daylight after the twilight from the 'Trumpet Judgments'. Isaiah said, *"The light of the moon shall be as the light of the sun, and the light of the sun shall be sevenfold, as the light of seven days."* (Isaiah chapter 30 verse 26 KJV). The armies gathered to fight will gaze heavenward with superstitious awe. 'What new terror is this?' they may ask. And at some unknown hour within that seven day sign of intense brightness; out of the sun, with the armies of heaven following Him will come, *"The Word of God"* (Revelation chapter 19 verses 11 – 16).

'But is there an order to His Coming?' you ask. Yes, it will be measurable both in time and in direction, and the 'campaign' seems to be like this:

1.) **The Eastern army** will be destroyed first, on the Plains of Edom, at Bozrah, before Messiah arrives at Jerusalem. The 'watchman' on the south-eastern wall of the city will cry, *"Who is this that comes from Edom, in crimsoned garments from Bosrah?"* Is he a survivor from a conflict? Are the blood stains his own? The warrior will reply, *"It is I, speaking in righteousness, mighty to save."* The watcher will ask, *"Why is Your apparel red, and Your garments like his who treads in the winepress?"* The approaching figure will answer, *"I have trodden the winepress alone, and from the peoples no one was with Me. I trod them in My anger and trampled them in My wrath ... For the day of vengeance was in My heart, and the year of My redeemed is come."* (Isaiah chapter 63 verses 1 – 4 ESV). What stirring words! The *"Acceptable year of the Lord"* was concluded before the

"Day of Vengeance" began. Now that *"day"* is also concluding, and the *"Year of My redeemed"* is about to begin ...

2.) The Southern army in the Valley of Jehoshaphat will – probably – be destroyed next, then *"Messiah the King"* will set His feet upon the Mount of Olives. The mountain will divide east to west, forming a new valley in the mountain, a huge *"cleft in the rock"*. This will be a 'safe haven' for the rescued remnant of Jerusalem, *"Ye shall flee to the valley of My mountains"* (Zechariah chapter 14 verse 4 – 5 NRB), for the mountain will now be two. There they will be kept safe until the judgment is concluded.

> **KEYNOTE: Order of Armageddon.** We cannot be dogmatic as to the 'order of events'. Though some scholars go with the order as set out above, C. I. Scofield has the Megiddo destruction first, followed by the Moab destruction (Isa. chp. 63) second. We cannot be sure, but what A. G. Fruchtenbaum calls the 'Campaign of Armageddon', from south-east to north, seems to harmonise all of the scriptures together best. C. I. Scofield, *'Scofield Study Bible®'* (Oxford, UK: Oxford University Press, 1996) 1348-9.

3.) **The Northern army** will now be dealt with. They will have a few moments warning, maybe even a few hours? They will be *"gathered together to make war against Him that sat on the horse"* (Revelation chapter 19 verse 19 KJV), and to meet the attack from heaven. Some have suggested that ALL the armies will combine to fight a common foe, but that is not easily inferred from prophecy, and if the Isaiah 63 passage is literal, it does suggest an east to west, to northern movement of the returning *"King of kings"*. Some have also suggested that, through the earthquakes (Revelation chapter 6 verses 12 – 17 for example), God will close up the gaps in the hills around the Valley of Megiddo, and entrap the armies to await their doom. This could well be, but again, we cannot prove it from prophecy.

The 'Kidron Valley' (looking east) from the S E corner of Temple Mount with the Mount of Olives beyond   (JHF)
"And His feet shall stand in that day upon the Mount of Olives ... before Jerusalem on the east, and the Mount of Olives shall cleave in the midst thereof toward east and toward west, a very great valley ... ye shall flee to the valley of My mountains." (Zechariah 14:4-5 NRB)

4.) There will be no '**Battle of Armageddon**'. Even the armies of the *"Beast"* cannot protect him from the divine attack from out of heaven. The *"Beast was taken, and with him the False Prophet"*, seized first, and cast into a *"lake of fire"* John said (Revelation chapter 19 verse 20 KJV).

What About the Dragon?

We will have to keep the destiny of the *"Dragon"* for later studies. He does not have a good end, and he will ultimately join those who have served him, and have already come under his condemnation. Satan is a hard master, and a great deceiver. Pity any who think he is worthy of service, never mind voluntary worship.

[See **Chapter 20**, 'Coming in Power' & **Chapter 21**, 'The Millennial Kingdom'.]

---

*KEYNOTE: Northern Invader. One very difficult subject which we have not touched on is the *"Gog and Magog"* invasion prophecies in Ezekiel chps. 38-39. Again, the interpretations on these passages are diverse, both as to identity and to timing. Space does not permit a full explanation or analysis in this volume. One of the big questions is, 'When does the Gog and Magog invasion occur?' 'Does it match up with the *"Gog and Magog"* references at the end of the '1,000 Year Kingdom' (Rev. 20:8)?' 'Are Ezekiel chps. 38-39 all one prophecy, about one event?' The position of the author (we cannot be totally certain) can be summarised as follows: 1.) Ezekiel chps. 38-39 may be 'divided prophecies', as Daniel 9 and Rev. 17-18 etc. are. 2.) Chp. 38 may describe an invasion, just after the signing of the *"covenant"*, by a northern alliance opposed to peace with Israel, and taking advantage of their 'disarmed' state. God destroys this army and defends Israel, by an earthquake in the northern hills. 3.) The second invasion takes place at the end of the seven year 'Tribulation Period', and ties in with the *"king of the north"* invading as in Daniel 11:40, at the *"time of the end"*. This invasion is defeated by God again, but using the weapons of the invaders against them, within the borders of Israel. 4.) Neither passage in Ezekiel refers to the rebellion under Satan at the end of the '1,000 Year Kingdom'. There it is 'Gog like' in character (like *"Sodom"*), not *"Gog"* ethnically or geographically.

Q&A >

Questions and Answers for Chapter Nineteen – 'The Battle of Armageddon'

Chp. 19 – 'The Battle of Armageddon'

Q1. Is "Megiddo" a real place?

Q2. Is it found in the O.T.?
(Give an O.T. reference to prove that it is.)

Q3. Where was "Megiddo"?

Q4. Was it just a 'walled town' or 'citadel'?

Q5. What is "Megiddo" most often connected with?

Q6. "Megiddo" is also the name for a valley.
What are its approximate dimensions?

Q7. Can you name any of the O.T. characters who
had famous victories connected with "Megiddo"?

Q8. Were there any famous defeats also connected
with "Megiddo"?

Q9. What will happen at "Armageddon" in the
future?

Q10. When will this take place?

Chapter Twenty

Christ's Coming in Power

We have reached a major climax in John's visions and in the book which is the *"Revelation of Jesus Christ"*. Though the whole book, from beginning to end, is one 'unveiling' of Christ and His might, yet there is a sense in which the whole drama has been building to this point, His *"Coming in Power"*. The true manifestation, the unveiling of the one who is the fulfilment of all the purposes of God, the one whom future prophecy is centred around, for *"the testimony of Jesus is the spirit of prophecy"* (Revelation chapter 19 verse 10). This is His moment, every enemy will be put down, every imposter will be exposed, all His glory will be displayed. An old age – the longest in Bible history – will conclude, and a new age will dawn. Not the 'New Age' the world speaks of today (and cannot ever achieve), but an age which Christ in Isaiah called, *"The year of My redeemed"*. That which we call the 'Kingdom Age' is now about to commence ...

Why is Jesus Coming Back?

That is a great question, and there must be more than one answer. There is no doubt whatsoever that He must return. Whichever viewpoint prophecy is studied from, whether believing in a literal 'Kingdom Age' or not, whether looking for a 'pre-tribulation rapture' or otherwise, on this point we all must agree. The Jesus who came the first time (and was rejected) must come, visibly, the second time with *"great power and glory"* to reign, or else His own prophecies and promises to His disciples were false (Mark chapter 13 verses 24 – 26).*

Reasons why Jesus Must Return:

1.) To fulfil Old Testament prophecies not fulfilled at His first coming, for the manner and purpose of His first coming were very different to those of His second coming.

2.) To close up the 'gaps' in prophecies. We have seen in our studies that several key prophecies 'divide' in two.

3.) To fulfil the Old Testament (unconditional) covenant promises given to Abraham, to David, and to Jeremiah, which we have looked at in detail in previous studies.

[See **Chapters 1 – 3**]

4.) To keep the promises that Jesus Himself gave to His disciples before He went back to heaven, *"If I go and prepare for you a place, I will come again and receive you unto Myself"* (John chapter 14 verse 3 NRB). Also, the promises given to the Church, through the inspiration of the Apostles, *"... looking for the blessed hope, and the appearing of the glory of the great God and our Saviour Jesus Christ; who gave Himself for us, that He might redeem us ..."* (Titus chapter 2 verses 11 – 14 NRB), and other promises which we have already studied.

> ***KEYNOTE: The 'isms' of prophecy.** *Dispensationalism, Amillennialism, Postmillennialism & Premillennialism* etc. These and other 'isms', on which many Christians and students of prophecy agree to differ, are explained – in summary form – in **Appx. II. Note:** On a scale from 'totally allegorical' to 'totally literal', the author is much closer in interpretation to the 'literal' end of the spectrum than to the 'symbolic'. This is highly relevant in the closing chapters of the book of Revelation.

5.) To put down all rebellion and conquer all His enemies, *"This man, after He had offered one sacrifice for sins to perpetuity, sat down on the right hand of God; from henceforth expecting till His enemies be made a footstool of His feet."* (Hebrews chapter 10 verses 12 – 13 NRB). This was also prophesied by David in the Psalms, 1,000 years before His first coming, *"Jehovah said unto My Lord, 'Sit Thou at My right hand, until I make Thine enemies Thy footstool."* (Psalm 110 verse 1 NRB).

Jesus' First Coming & His Second Coming

Let us consider some of the key differences between the First Coming of the *"Messiah"* and His Second Coming:

His First Coming:	**His Second Coming:**
He came as a baby, *"wrapped in swaddling clothes, lying in a manger"* (Luke 2:12 KJV)	He will come as a <u>King</u>, *"behold a white horse: and He that sat upon him, called 'Faithful and True'"* (Rev. 19:11 NRB)
He came, *"<u>lowly</u>, riding upon a colt"* (Zech. 9:9), which was fulfilled at His entry to Jerusalem (Matt.21:1 – 11)	He will come in <u>power</u>, *"the Son of Man coming on the clouds of heaven with power and great glory."* (Matt. 24:30 NRB)
He was <u>rejected</u>, *"The Son of Man must suffer many things, and be rejected of the elders and chief priests and scribes, and be slain, and be raised the third day."* (Mk. 8:31, Luke 9:22 KJV)	He must <u>reign</u>, *"He shall reign over the house of Jacob forever, and of His kingdom there shall be no end."* (Luke 1:33). Not only a 'Millennial' kingdom, but an eternal kingdom without end, in a *"new heaven and a new earth"* (Rev. 21:1 KJV)

[See **Chapters 21** & **23**]

Prophecies Which Divide

Do you recall (many studies back) we used a phrase, 'The Mountain Peaks of Prophecy'? Probably 'coined' by a famous prophecy student called Clarence Larkin (1850 – 1924)*. We were reminded that many of the Old Testament prophets:

a.) Did not fully understand the meaning of their prophecies, at the time of their foretelling.

b.) Did not know the time of their future fulfilment, unless exact times were specified, as was the case in Daniel Chapter 9.

c.) Did not understand that some of the prophecies they gave by inspiration would have a 'divided fulfilment'. That is, a 'gap' would appear – which would be understood later – and that which seemed to be a single prophecy would become two linked events. Sometimes separated by a great deal of time. The 'classic' divided-prophecy of Daniel's *"70 weeks"* or '490 years' (Daniel chapter 9 verses 24 – 27) can be seen, looking back, to divide into three parts. The first part of 49 years, the second part of 434 years with no time-gap between these first two parts, and the third part of 7 years which is separated from the rest of the 483 years by a very long (and continuing) time-gap.

[Considered in some detail in **Appx. I** '*Daniel's 70 Weeks*'.]

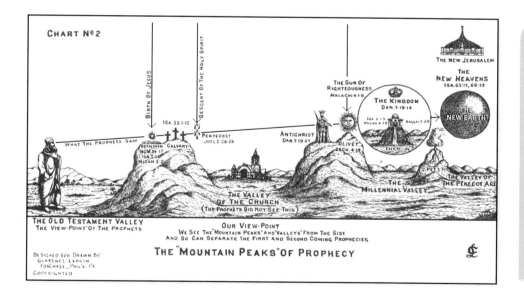

KEYNOTE: Perspective.

While we may not agree with every detail on Larkin's Chart (drawn over 100 years ago), it does give a clear diagrammatic presentation of how the perspective of the O.T. prophets differed from ours.

Another 'divided prophecy' which we have referred to often is found in Isaiah chapter 61 verses 1 – 2. Isaiah proclaimed both the *"Acceptable year of the Lord"* and the *"Day of vengeance of our God"* in the same verse. He could not have known that the first part, which Jesus confirmed at the beginning of His public ministry, the *"Acceptable year of the Lord"* began just then, when Jesus was on earth, and continues until now (almost 2,000 years later). The *"Day of vengeance ..."* on the other hand, which is found within the

'Tribulation Period', still has not commenced yet. And it will be followed immediately, as we saw in a previous study, by the *"Year of My Redeemed"* (Isaiah chapter 63 verse 4), the '1,000 year Kingdom' which is still to come.

After these things ...

As we saw earlier (Revelation chapter 18 verse 1) this recurring phrase indicates a 'time-shift' in John's visions. The previous two chapters of Revelation have been about the 'Two Babylons', with an *"after these things"* between the visions. Now John is looking forward again, not back, and is going to see the events that follow on from the end of the three sets of Judgments, from the fall of Babylon, and from the events surrounding *"Armageddon"*. On the previous occasion John saw the armies gathering as great military movements on earth, organised by the *"Dragon"*, controlled by God, and with the 'Antichrist-King' being pushed westwards as his empire crumbles and his city burns. Now John will be shown similar things from a heavenly standpoint ...

> **KEYNOTE: Heavenly Perspective.**
> Often in prophetic visions the *"Seer"*, or prophet, has his perspective changed. He is shown things from a 'manward' earthly point of view, then from a 'Godward' heavenly viewpoint. Daniel had this experience (Daniel chapters 2 & 7). Now John will be shown things on earth, from heaven's point of view. We do not have that capability unless God reveals it to us in His Word.

Heaven's Hallelujahs!

John hears another song in heaven, *"I heard a great voice of a great multitude in heaven, saying, 'Hallelujah; Salvation, and glory, and honour, and power, unto the Lord our God: for true and righteous are His judgments' ... And again they said, 'Hallelujah', and her smoke rose up for ever and ever."* (Revelation chapter 19 verses 1 – 3 NRB). We have said before, Revelation is not only a book of judgment, it is also a book of songs. The songs get longer, and since the numbers singing also grow, so probably does the volume as well! We often think of *"Hallelujah"* as being a 'praise word' connected with worship down here. It may have been in the Psalms (where *"Hallelujah"* occurs 24 times), but here in our passage are the only uses of the 'Praise to the Lord' phrase (literally *'Praise to Jah'* which is what *"Hallel-u-jah"* means) in the New Testament. It is interesting to meditate on the fact that all the *"Hallelujahs"* in the New Testament are in the book of Revelation, and are heavenly. And all the *"blessings"* in Revelation (7 of them) are for God's people here on earth.

These first three *"Hallelujah"* expressions connect us back to the fall of *"Babylon"* and God's vengeance on the system and city. This is not the language of our time. We – those who are saved – are believers of the 'Church Age', and we are not praying for vengeance on our persecutors, *"Our citizenship is in heaven, and from it we await a Saviour, the Lord Jesus Christ, who will transform our lowly body to be like His glorious body"* (Philippians chapter 3 verse 20 – 21 ESV). The context here shows that it is martyrs – probably mostly

> **'The Church is viewed in Scripture as, a "Building", a "Body", and a "Bride."'**

of the 'Tribulation Period' – who are crying, *"Hallelujah!"* at the destruction of their persecutors, and the enemies of God.

Who is to be Married?

Here is something that is new in John's visions. The fourth, and last *"Hallelujah"* is about a different subject altogether, *"Hallelujah: for the Lord God the Omnipotent, reigneth. Let us be glad and rejoice and give glory to Him: for the marriage of the Lamb has come, and His wife made herself ready ..."* (Revelation chapter 19 verses 6 – 8 NRB). 'To whom is the Lamb to be married?' you ask. That is a very good question. The *"Lamb"* is an important title of Jesus Christ, used more often in Revelation than in any other book in the Bible. 'But who is the *"Bride"*?' Paul gives us a clue in his letter to the church at Ephesus, *"Husbands, love your wives, even as Christ also loved the Church, and gave Himself for it ... that He might present it to Himself a glorious Church ... so ought men to love their wives ..."* (Ephesians chapter 5 verses 22 – 33 NRB). We saw in a previous study [in *'The Church Period'*, **Chapter 5**] that the Church is viewed as a *"Building"*, as a *"Body"* and as a *"Bride"*, and in that order. When we come to a later study [*'The New Jerusalem'*, **Chapter 23**] we will see the *"Bride, the Lamb's wife"* is connected with her dwelling place, which Jesus promised to go to prepare and then return to take her there (John chapter 14 verses 2 – 3). The *"Bride"* is the Church, and it is emphasised here that she will be dressed in *"fine linen, clean and bright: for the fine linen is the righteousness (acts) of the saints."* (Revelation chapter 19 verses 6 – 8 NRB).

When is the Wedding?

That is a hard question! It has been assumed [by numerous writers from a 'dispensational' viewpoint, see **Appx. II**] that the *"marriage of the Lamb"* occurs immediately after the *"Judgment Seat of Christ"*, which is the assessment point of our service for Jesus Christ for all the believers of the 'Church Age'. Paul says, *"We must all be made manifest before the Judgment Seat of Christ; that each one may receive the things done in the body, according to that he hath done, whether good or bad."* (2 Corinthians chapter 5 verse 10 – 11 NRB). We will see in a later study [*'Jesus Coming Quickly'*, **Chapter 24**] that the 'review and reward' assessment does occur immediately after we meet with Jesus in the air.

Whether the *"Marriage of the Lamb"* occurs immediately after that – or at any time during the 7 years of 'Tribulation' on earth while the Church is safe in heaven – is more of a conjecture, based on the traditions of a Jewish wedding from Old Testament times and the time of Jesus. In those days a 'marriage' would have taken place at the 'prepared place' the bridegroom had made ready, close to his father's home. The 'marriage supper' would then have been an extended event, sometimes over many days so that guests could be received who had travelled, and it could possibly even be in a different location from the 'wedding ceremony' itself.

So, the theory goes, the *"Marriage of the Lamb"* takes place in the *"Father's house"* (in heaven), just after the *"Judgment Seat"* assessment of our service – which is where we gain our *"fine linen"* composed of the garments of our 'righteousnesses' (Revelation chapter 19 verses 6 – 8 NRB) – and the *"Marriage Supper of the Lamb"* is for invited guests, back down here on earth, at the commencement of the 'Millennial Kingdom'.

Though we can deduce from the wording of the text in our passage that the *"Marriage"* and the *"Supper"* are two very distinct events, and that the 'invited guests' are *"called to the Marriage Supper of the Lamb"* only, there is also a tiny degree of spiritual speculation in our overall deductions. It is even possible that both events may take place in the 75 days 'gap period' between the end of the Great Tribulation and the beginning of the Kingdom Age itself. Daniel is told to add these 75 days on to the 1,260 days: *"Blessed is he who waits and arrives at the 1,335 days. But go your way till the end. And you shall rest and shall stand in your allotted place at the end of the days."* (Daniel chapter 12 verses 11 – 13 ESV).

Where is the Wedding Supper?

This passage from Daniel along with what we have here, and others such as the comments of John Baptist, *"The one who has the bride is the Bridegroom. The friend of the Bridegroom, who stands and hears Him, rejoices greatly at the Bridegroom's voice."* (John chapter 3 verse 29 ESV) would allow us to summarise these points as follows:

a.) The *"Marriage Supper"* – at least, if not the *"Marriage"* – is on this earth, after a 'cleaning up' and preparing period, either within the 75 day 'gap period' or early in the 'Kingdom Age' itself.

b.) The saints (followers of *"Jehovah"*) of the Old Testament period are the invited guests to the Marriage Supper.

c.) The Old Testament saints, up to and including John Baptist, are not part of the *"Bride"*.

d.) The *"Bride of the Lamb"* is the Church, not Israel. Israel is pictured in the Old Testament as the 'wife of Jehovah' who behaved adulterously with the false gods of the neighbouring nations.

e.) The *"Bridegroom"* is Jesus Christ as the *"Lamb"*, and He is also the *"King of kings"* over the earth.

f.) The *"Marriage Supper"* is one of the early joyful events which introduces the 'Millennial Kingdom'.

g.) The exact location of the *"Marriage Supper"* we are not told, it is probably in the Land of Israel.

h.) The *"Bride"* will live in her 'prepared place' afterwards, the *"Holy Jerusalem"* (Revelation chapter 21 verses 9 – 10), not only for the 1,000 years, but forever.

[See, *'The New Jerusalem'* **Chapter 23**.]

'
What John is now to see will confirm who the true "Lord of lords" is!'

John is so carried away with all that he has just seen that he almost worships the angel who has been explaining these things to him. The angel forbids him, *"'You must not do that! I am a fellow servant with you and your brothers who hold to the testimony of Jesus. Worship God.' For the testimony of Jesus is the spirit of prophecy."* (Revelation chapter 19 verse 10 ESV). What John is just about to see will confirm – if there was ever any doubt – who the true *"Lord of lords"* is, and who alone is worthy of worship, not only by John and the angels, but by us as well!

Heaven Open Again

John says, *"I saw heaven opened, and behold a white horse; and He that sat upon him was called 'Faithful and True', and in righteousness He doth judge and make war ..."* (chapter 19 verse 11 KJV).

Someone will say, 'We have seen these things before, have we not?' That is a good observation, we need to examine what we have here very closely. Firstly, was heaven *"open"* before? You might say 'Yes, when John was called up' (back in chapter 4 verses 1 – 2). But wait. When John was taken up in Spirit, he went through a door which he saw *"standing open in heaven"*. A small aperture, open to let him in (whether a picture of the 'rapture' or not). Here, at the *"Coming in Power"* it is not a door open in heaven, it is *"heaven opened"*: No greater sight has ever been seen before by human eyes, *"Behold, He is coming with the clouds, and every eye will see Him, even those who pierced Him, and all tribes of the earth will mourn on account of Him. Even so. Amen."* (chapter 1 verse 7 ESV). The remnant of Israel, now looking for Him, will see Him. Possibly even the Old Testament saints, for we are not truly certain at what point they are 'raised'. Certainly the *"Bride"*, who will be coming with Him. The angel *"armies in heaven"* will see His triumph, and join in His advance.

A White Horse Again?

Yes, but different. Different to the *"colt, the foal of an ass"*, as we have already seen. But different also to the *"white horse"* of the first Seal Judgment (Revelation chapter 6). The colt was for *"Messiah the Prince"* uncrowned, but this white war horse is the steed of the King. By contrast the white horse, which we saw as the first of the 'four horsemen', is the mount of the 'Imposter', the *"Prince that shall come"* (Daniel chapter 9 verse 26), Satan's counterfeit not only of the Messiah but even of His horse. He will be a false 'peace-maker'. A peace-breaker. Here we have the 'Prince of Peace' coming to make war on His enemies, that He might introduce true peace for 1,000 years. The *"Shiloh"* of Jacob's prophecy, the true 'peace-keeper', of whom Jacob said prophetically, *"and unto Him shall the gathering of the people be."* (Genesis chapter 49 verses 10 – 12 KJV).

One Rider – Four Names

Here is another lovely contrast! The 'four horsemen' had no names given, all shadowy figures of dark deeds. Here this singular rider on this white horse has four names. His identity can never be mistaken:

1.) *"Faithful and True"* (verse 11) – His <u>Honesty</u> – He will come, just as He said He would...

2.) *"A Name which no one knew"* (verse 12) – His <u>Mystery</u> – He knows, but we will be ever learning more of Him.

3.) *"Word of God"* (verse 13) – His <u>Eternality</u> – *"In the beginning was The Word"* (John 1:1).

4.) *"King of kings and Lord of lords"* (verse 16) – His <u>Authority</u> – over all (Col. 2:15).

> ***KEYNOTE: TYPES.** Titles iii – v (in the list) are used of Melchisedek, the earliest recorded King of Salem (Genesis chapter 14), the city which became Jerusalem. In the context of Hebrews chapter 7 they also apply to Jesus Christ, of whom Melchisedek is presented as a 'type' in the O.T. For this reason, he had no family record, and his birth or death was not recorded. 'Types' are people or objects in the O.T. portraying and pointing forward to Jesus, and usually referred back to in the N.T. as is the case with Melchisedek here, *"made like unto the Son of God"*. He was also both a priest and a king. 'Typology' – with care – is a fascinating study in the O.T. and helps us to find 'Christ in all the scriptures'.

One King – Seven Titles

Jesus Christ has seven 'Kingly titles' given to Him in the New Testament scriptures. They manifest His character, His rule, and His pre-eminence:

i.) *"King of Israel"* (John 1:49) – Nathaniel received a prophecy about His reign.

ii.) *"King of the Jews"* (John 19:19) – So called by Pilate, mocking but prophetic.

iii.) *"King of Salem"* *(Hebs. 7:1) – Old title for Jerusalem, *"City of the Great King"*.

iv.) *"King of Righteousness"* (Hebs. 7:2) – The righteousness of His rule (Isa. 32:1).

v.) *"King of Peace"* (Hebs. 7:2) – The *"Shiloh"* – 'Peace-keeper' for 1,000 years.

vi.) *"King of Nations"* (Rev. 15:3 ESV) – *"He shall speak peace unto the nations ..."*

vii.) *"King of kings ..."* (Rev. 19:16) – *"His dominion from sea to sea ..."* (Zech. 9:10 NRB).

One Person – Four Features

When John saw the glorified person of Jesus Christ in his prison cell on Patmos Island, he *"fell at His feet as dead"* (Revelation chapter 1 verse 17). Why? Because even though John was the disciple who walked and sat with Jesus (and stood by His cross) and was closest of all His male disciples, he had never seen Jesus in such a glorious form close up before, probably not even at His transfiguration. John describes seven physical features of Jesus which stood out in his mind after his visions. Most of those features are shared and emphasised to the seven churches which Jesus sends individual letters to (Revelation chapters 2 & 3), features which were appropriate for what He wanted to reveal to each church.

Here in the *"Coming in Power"* vision John emphasises four features of Jesus Christ:

1.) **His Eyes** – *"as a flame of fire"* – The Penetration of His vision. No hiding place.

2.) **His Head** – *"many diadems"* – The Perfection of His rule. The crowns are His own.

3.) **His Mouth** – *"a sharp sword"* – The Penalty on His enemies, *"slain with the sword"* (verse 21)

4.) **His Thigh** – *"a name written"* – The Power of His name – A symbol of His strength.

One Ruler – Four Symbols

1.) A Horse – *"a white horse"* – The mount of the King – *"The King of glory ..."* (Ps. 24:7-10).

2.) A Sword – to *"smite the nations"* (Rev. 19:15) – The weapon of the Conqueror.

3.) A Rod – to *"rule them with a rod of iron"* (Ps. 2:9) – The chastisement of His foes.

4.) The Winepress – *"He will tread the winepress ... of the wrath of God ..."* (Rev. 19:15 ESV) – The trampling of His enemies is again likened to the treading of grapes in a stone winepress.

Let us look at this symbolic picture of the winepress and the grape harvest in a little more detail, for we have met it before in our studies and now we have it here again:

Land of Israel – A Winepress

We have seen the symbolic picture of the *"winepress"* before, that in which the ripe grapes were placed, in the *'wine vat'*, to be trampled on by naked feet, so that the juice of the crushed grapes ran down into the lower wine vat. Messiah Himself uses this terrible language to describe His victory at Bosrah on the Plains of Edom to the watcher on the ramparts of the besieged city of Jerusalem, *"I <u>have trodden</u> the winepress alone"* (The first army, the eastern one, already destroyed). *"I <u>will tread</u> them in Mine anger* (The other armies will be destroyed in order), *and trample them in My fury; and their blood <u>shall be</u> sprinkled on My garments ..."* (Isaiah chapter 63 verses 1 – 6 KJV). Note tenses used.

Upper & Lower Wine Press

When we look back to the chapter of Revelation we have just referred to, the picture grows more fearful still. An angel cries, *"The harvest of the earth is ripe!"* (Revelation chapter 14 verse 15). The time of God's final vengeance has arrived. Israel will be trodden down no longer. God has *"gathered"* her enemies, not that she might be destroyed but that they, her historic and last-days enemies, might be trampled on. God describes the Land of Israel as one whole *"winepress"*. As if the mountains to the north, *"the Valley of Megiddo"* included,

Recent excavations in Judea, revealing an ancient 'wine press'. The unwanted outer skin etc. would sink to the lowest level. The 'good wine' would flow out through the channel in to the 'lower wine vat'. A very graphic illustration of the enemies of Jesus Christ being "trodden underfoot" (Isa. 63:1-4).

down to the *"Valley of Jehoshaphat"* in the south become one great stone receptacle for *"treading"* on His enemies: *"And the winepress was trodden without the city, and blood came out of the winepress, even unto the horse's bridles, by the space of a thousand and six hundred furlongs."* (Revelation chapter 14 verse 20 KJV).

'What can this mean?' you might ask, and 'Surely this must be some strange symbol, it cannot be literal?' Have we not seen already how prophecies that seem as though they must be symbolic, when viewed from far away, become so much more literal as they near their time of fulfilment? So many of the strange descriptions of the book of Revelation – that we have already studied – may possibly turn out to be very literal indeed, in a time not very far off. 'What of this prophecy here?' Remember that all the world's armies will be encamped in the Middle East around Israel and Jerusalem.

The seas, rivers and *"fountains"* will already have been turned into blood (in the Trumpet and Bowl Judgments). This won't be reversed until after *"Armageddon"* is complete, and the 'clean up' period for the kingdom has arrived. The '1,600 furlongs' measurement is 320 kilometres, exactly the length of Israel today. The height of a *"horse's bridle"* is close to 2 metres. Whether this means 'blood splashed up two metres high over a distance of 320 kilometres' or worse still, 'blood 2 metres deep for over 320 kilometres' the picture is terrifying, and possibly terribly literal. Not the outcome of a 'bloodbath' between entrenched armies (like the Flanders or the Somme battlefields of WW1), but every enemy of God, everyone who sided with the *"Dragon"* and the *"Beast"* trampled under the feet of one person: the *"Son of Man"*, the *"King of kings"*, in the day of His fierce anger.

The Last Supper?

We have been thinking about the beauty and grandeur of the *"Marriage Supper of the Lamb"*. In proper chronological order that *"supper"* is the last one in the Bible. (To describe the supper which is kept during the 'Church Age' as 'the Last Supper' is another misnomer.) The actual 'Last Supper' was the one Jesus kept with His disciples, the Passover Supper, the night before His death which was the fulfilment of all the Passover pictures. The *"Lord's supper"*, which Christians keep on the Lord's Day (Sunday) each week in New Testament order, is our 'commemoration' and is often called the *"Breaking of bread"*. It is a looking back to what Jesus has done for us in His death. But it is also an 'anticipation', *"ye do shew the Lord's death till He come"* (1 Corinthians chapter 11 verses 24 – 25 KJV). The remembrance aspect of the *"Lord's Supper"* will no longer be needed when we have an actual sight of Him. There will be no *"Breaking of Bread"* (Acts chapter 2 verse 42) in the 'Kingdom Age'. That symbolic act will be finished with when Jesus comes for His Church.

Here we have a supper of an altogether different sort, *"Come and gather yourselves together unto the Supper of the Great God; that ye may eat the flesh of kings ..."* (Revelation chapter 19 verses 17 – 19 KJV). The birds are called, not only the usual carrion birds, but the angel calls *"all the fowls that fly in mid-heaven"* (chapter 19 verse 17 NRB) to feast on the bodies of the slain. Part of the cleansing process, in preparation for the 'Kingdom Age', begins right here. God uses His own 'agents' *"the fowls"* to devour the flesh of the fallen armies who dared to fight against His Christ. The terrible 'last supper' of the Judgment Period.

The Last Battle?

John says, *"I saw the Beast, and the kings of the earth, and their armies, gathered together to make war against Him that sat on the horse ..."* (chapter 19 verse 19 KJV). Here is armed futility indeed! Such devilish arrogance, or perhaps deception. 'Do they think they can win?' you ask. Who knows what they will think at that point? Bravado, or desperation, or a lack of understanding of the true fierceness of the *"wrath of the Lamb"*. Not one iota of a possibility of success. Yet the deception – though coming from the Dragon – is God-controlled as we have already seen. Just as Pharaoh's heart was hardened in the days of the Exodus, for Jehovah said He would be *"honoured upon Pharoah, and upon all his host"* (Exodus chapter 14 verse 4 KJV), so here God will be honoured in the defeat of the enemies of His Son.

'Is there fighting?' someone will ask. 'No, none at all.' Just the spoken word of the King of kings on His horse, and every king and captain will be destroyed. The *"Beast"* and the *"False Prophet"* are reserved for a special condemnation. They have bowed before Satan; they have accepted his rule to receive his power. Now they will share his doom, and go there even before him. They are seized first, and *"The two of them were cast alive into a lake of fire burning with brimstone"* (Revelation chapter 19 verse 20 NRB).

So will the end be of all who refuse the *"gospel of the grace of God"* (Acts chapter 20 verse 24). Here ends all the rebellion of this age. The days of *"Great Tribulation"* are past for ever. The *"Year of My Redeemed"*, the 'Millennial Kingdom Age', the '1,000 Year Reign of Messiah, Jesus Christ' will be just about to commence. We, who will have already been in heaven – if we have accepted Jesus Christ as Lord and Saviour while the opportunity is available now – will be with Christ Jesus forever ...

> *'But forever I will be,*
> *With the one who died for me.*
> *What a day, glorious day, that will be.'*

(Jim Hill 1930 – 2018, Middletown OH.)

Q&A >

Questions and Answers for Chapter Twenty – 'Christ's Coming in Power'

Chp 20 – 'Christ's Coming in Power'

Q1. Can you give three main differences between Jesus' First and Second Comings?

Q2. Many of the O.T. prophecies – looking back – have a 'time gap'. Can you name one or more?

Q3. Something of each of these 'time-gap' prophecies was <u>not</u> fulfilled at Jesus' First Coming. Can you give an example?

Q4. How many "Hallelujahs" are there in Rev. Chp. 19? How many other "Hallelujahs" in the N.T.?

Q5. How many names does Jesus have at His "Coming in Power"?

Q6. Can you list some of them?

Q7. How many 'features' of Jesus are mentioned in Rev. Chp. 19?

Q8. Can you list them?

Q9. How many 'objects of rule' are mentioned?

Q10. Can you list them?

Q11. Who is seized first at "Armageddon"? Where are they put?

Chapter Twenty-One
The Millennial Kingdom

We are continuing with our 'climactic' scenes that began in the previous chapter of Revelation. There is no real division nor time-break between the end of Revelation chapter 19 and the start of chapter 20. It is all part of the one narrative. The next, and final, *"after these things"* occurs in verse 3, but it is referring forward to events at the very end of the 1,000 year period, which are expanded from verse 7 onwards. In our previous study we asked the question, 'Why is Jesus coming back?' and we saw that there are various reasons why He must, not least to keep the divine promises given in both the Old and New Testament prophecies, including His own.

There are some prophecy students who believe that Jesus is only coming back to: a.) Bring this earth as we know it to an end. b.) Meet with all the 'saints' – of all the ages – at the one time. c.) Judge all unbelievers – from all ages – and all the saints too at a 'General Judgment'. d.) Judge Satan and his demons at the same time. And, e.) Set up His eternal kingdom, which is called the 'Eternal State', on a *"new earth"*, without any literal kingdom on this earth first.

If you have heard these comments before, have read them, or have been taught them, you will also have recognised by now that the interpretation of prophecy followed within this book does not hold with any of the above. Since you have been patient enough to arrive at this point, I would ask you (as we said back at the beginning) to 'suspend your disbelief' and consider the weight of evidence in favour of the literal, futurist, and chronological programme which the remaining section of Revelation sets out.

> **KEYNOTE: 'Literal, Futurist etc.'** This major method of interpretation, a.) Takes all prophecy as being literally fulfilled at a point in the future, unless the prophecy itself states otherwise. b.) Accepts that all prophecy was given with a view to being fulfilled according to the chronology of God's programme, looking forward to the 'Kingdom Age' and the 'Eternal State' beyond. c.) Takes the literal fulfilment – in the N.T. – of many of the prophecies of the O.T. as an indicator that other prophecies, both O.T. and N.T., will also be literally fulfilled. This viewpoint is expanded further in **Appx. II** *'Amillennialism & Other 'Ism's'.*

We must make a clear distinction between the Church (a heavenly people) and Israel (God's earthly people). Between the 'Kingdom Age' and the 'Eternal State'. Between the earthly Jerusalem and the *"New Jerusalem"*. Between the judgments of saints, living nations, and resurrected unbelievers. Then what still lies in front, in the remainder of the book of

Revelation, becomes much easier to interpret. If we accept – as the author does - that the 'Kingdom Age' was promised in the Old Testament and that it will be here on this earth, that Jesus must reign as Messiah and *"King of kings"*, and do so for 1,000 years, in a newly rebuilt Jerusalem city, we will have no trouble with what we are about to examine.

Jesus is coming back to this earth to reign because, as well as the prophecies of Old and New Testament requiring fulfilment [examined in **Chapter 20**], Satan must be finally dealt with. The saints who are raised, from the Old Testament period, and from the Tribulation period, must have their destiny given to them as promised, *"What shall I say more? ... These all, having obtained witness through faith, received not the promise ..."* (Hebrews chapter 11 verses 32 & 39 NRB). Those who are still alive at the end of the Tribulation – whether good or bad – must be judged on the evidence of their works. Not only must the Land of Israel be cleansed, and almost all the earth as well (you may recall that the 'Babylon site' will not), but Jerusalem must also be restored, a 'Millennial Temple' and a palace built (Ezekiel chapters 40 – 47). The tribes of Israel must be regathered and identified, to possess the Land in a new tribal 'layout' not seen in the Old Testament, even in King Solomon's time (Ezekiel chapter 48).

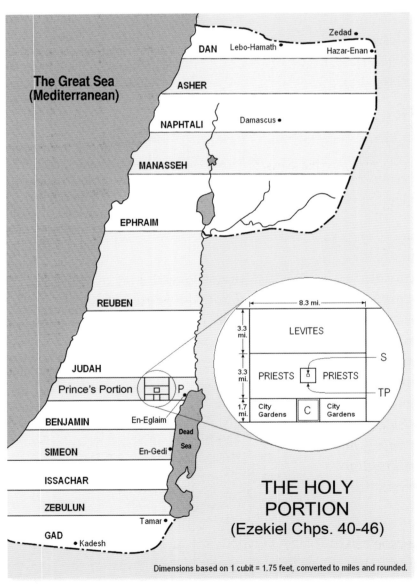

The New Territorial Possession of the Tribes of Israel in the Millennial Kingdom Age.

If these key events – and others – do not take place on this earth within the context of a literal kingdom as prophesied, then many of the promises of God, which were a spiritual incentive to a great number of martyrs of every age (as we saw in Hebrews chapter 11), were not meant to be 'interpreted' as they were received. Literally, <u>God did not mean what He said</u>. And that is a very serious accusation indeed.

226

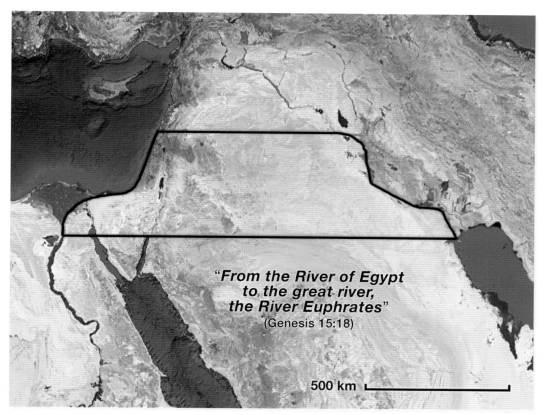

"From the River of Egypt to the great river, the River Euphrates" (Genesis 15:18)

500 km

The Kingdom under Solomon (c. 1000 BC) was the largest that it has been historically. Some scholars assume the future 'Millennial Kingdom' will be similar in size, with only the tribal boundaries differing. Consider the possibility of the Kingdom of Messiah, "a greater than Solomon", extending westward to the Nile, and eastward from Ezion-Geber to the mouth of the Euphrates.

Where does the '1,000 Years' Come From?

'But wait,' someone says, 'The 1,000 year kingdom is never mentioned in all the O.T. prophecies. Who says it will be that long?' That is a very good observation. And quite right too. Nowhere in all the Old Testament prophecies concerning the coming kingdom of Messiah does it mention a specific length. In fact, David probably thought that the future earthly kingdom God promised him was to be forever! Jehovah said to David, through Nathan the prophet, *"I will set up thy seed after thee, which shall proceed out of thy bowels, and I will establish His kingdom. He shall build an house for My name, and I will establish the throne of His kingdom forever."* (2 Samuel chapter 7 verses 12 – 16 KJV).

While we understand, from the perspective of a completed revelation (small 'r' – that is all revelation that God intends us to have – not just the book of Revelation), that our

> **KEYNOTE: Boundaries of Israel.** The Tribal positions are scriptural, the outer boundaries are suggestive. The breadth of the Land will be determined by how much of the eastern boundary extends along the River Euphrates, and if the S. W. boundary goes to the River Nile, as it was promised to Abram long ago, *"from the River of Egypt unto the ... River Euphrates."* (Genesis 15:18 KJV). If the eastern boundary extends down the Euphrates (as it may) then the lower portion of the Land may be 1,500 kilometres in breadth.

earth time and God's 'forever' time are not the same, the O.T. saints and even the Hebrew language itself didn't convey such a thought. The Hebrew word translated *"forever"* comes from 'Ôlâm' which means 'continuous' or 'concealed from sight'. What we have referred to here is another 'divided prophecy'. Part of it relates to Solomon, *"He shall build a House for My name"*, and part of it refers to Messiah, *"I will establish the throne of His kingdom forever."* (2 Samuel chapter 7 verses 13).

David may even have thought that God was promising him a long line of kings, following on from Solomon his son. We know that the *"forever"* is fulfilled in one unique 'greater Son', Jesus Christ Himself. Even then, David, and others in the Old Testament, may have not seen the difference between the future earthly kingdom and the eternal kingdom. We know that Jesus will reign forever, in the ultimate sense of the word. But His kingdom – on this earth – we also know will be of a fixed duration, measurable in 'earth time'.

The '1,000 Years' is Where?

Here, on this planet earth! But perhaps you are not asking, 'Where is the 1,000 year Kingdom?' But, 'How do we know from scripture that it is 1,000 years long?' The answer is right here, in our passage. John says, *"I saw thrones, and they sat upon them … the souls of them that were beheaded on account of the witness of Jesus … those which had not worshipped the Beast, neither his image, neither received the mark … and they lived and reigned with Christ the thousand years. But the rest of the dead lived not again until the thousand years were finished."* (Revelation chapter 20 verses 4 – 5 NRB).

We have here two resurrections in view. The *"resurrection of life"* and – after the 1,000 years are finished – the *"resurrection of judgment"* (John chapter 5 verses 25 – 29 NRB). The Spirit says, *"Blessed and holy he that hath part in the first resurrection: over these the second death hath not authority"* (Revelation chapter 20 verse 6 NRB), one of the latter of the '7 blessings' in Revelation. So, the *"first resurrection"* and the *"second death"* are spiritually mutually exclusive. No one – from any age – can have part in both. That is a very comforting thought indeed.

The Kingdom Commences

We saw in our previous study some of the detail of the *"Coming in Power"* of the *"King of kings"* to set up His global theocracy. It is interesting that a fully documented 'order of events' of how the kingdom commences is not given to us. We can draw together from many different prophecies details concerning the kingdom, and its inception. But the order of activities at the commencement are set down with some degree of spiritual conjecture.

As we said previously, we do not know when the *"Marriage Supper"* will commence, where exactly it will be held, and for how long it will last. We will know when we get there … Likewise we don't know how long it will take to 'clean up' the Land of Israel, and the whole of the inhabited world. We don't know how long it will take to rebuild Jerusalem, cleanse the Temple Mount, and erect the Millennial Temple. But we do know it will be done literally as Ezekiel described. It is probable that most of these activities will begin in the additional *"75 days"* which Daniel refers to between the end of the Tribulation and the start of the 'Kingdom Age' (Daniel chapter 12 verse 12).

When we do come back again to John's vision, we see something very interesting: None of the above prophetic events are described as the 'starter' event of the Kingdom Age. John says, *"I saw an angel come down out of heaven, having the key of the Abyss and a great chain in his hand. And he laid hold on the Dragon, the old Serpent, which is the Devil, and Satan, and bound him a thousand years, and cast him into the Abyss, and shut him up, and set a seal over him, that he should deceive the nations no more, till the thousand years should be fulfilled."* (Revelation chapter 20 verses 1 – 3 NRB). For all of the above <u>blessed</u> events to take place, one singular and strategic <u>negative</u> event must happen: Not only will Satan be judged for his long history of rebellion, but he must also be confined for the total duration of the Kingdom Age, so that *"he should deceive the nations no longer"* (chapter 20 verse 3).

Why is Satan Bound?

'Why does the Devil not go straight to the Lake of Fire, why bind him temporarily in the Abyss?' That is another good question, and not an easy one to answer. God will demonstrate His power over *"the Dragon"*. It is possible that this 'binding' and 'locking up' is visible and public. Whereas the *"Beast"* and the *"False Prophet"* were 'removed' to the *"lake of fire"* instantly, at the close of the 'Armageddon Campaign' (chapter 19 verse 20), here the defeat of Satan is seen at the commencing of the 'Kingdom Age'. Just as in Old Testament times, where victorious kings paraded the defeated king before slaying them, so here the *"King of kings"* will show not only who the ultimate enemy is – not the *"Beast"* but the *"Dragon"* – but also His power over him. With the full authority of Jesus Christ, it is an unnamed angel – not even a high ranking one – who will be able to chain up the *"Dragon"*.

The Kingdom Conditions

Firstly: In the confining of Satan, all who are alive – including possibly his followers who have not yet been judged (Matthew chapter 25 verses 31 – 33), and who will share his final fate – will see the supremacy of *"The Lamb"* [We will look at that more closely in a few moments].

Secondly: God will show – in the Kingdom Age – that confinement is not corrective. The heart must change, give up its rebellion, and agree with God. The 'correctional services' of our world, in many cases, have the opposite effect from that which is hoped for. Inmates come out unchanged, to go back to what they did before ... So it will be with Satan, after a confinement of 1,000 years.

Thirdly: God will show that the 'sin nature' is inherent in each individual person. And inherited from our fore-parents, Adam and Eve. The removal of the influence of the Devil (which even in our world is blamed for things which belong in mankind's own heart) will not bring the loss of a desire to rebel.

Fourthly: God will also demonstrate that sinning or wrongdoing is not a product of our environment. The conditions of this world in the Kingdom Age will be almost 'Edenic'. That is, like the conditions in the *"garden of Eden"* before the 'Fall'. Not quite the same mind you! For though the environment will be very similar, the individuals who are born during the 1,000 year kingdom will be different to Adam and Eve. They did not have a 'fallen nature' at creation. They chose to rebel against God's instruction [As we saw earlier in **Chapters 2** & **3**] and so became sinful.

[We will say a little more about the 'conditions of the kingdom' later.]

Fifthly: Something that has been demonstrated during the 'Tribulation Period', but which will become even more obvious at the end of the Kingdom Age: Those who do not want to follow God will still follow 'some god' and will follow any false god, even Satan again. At the last.

For all these reasons Satan is *"bound ... till the thousand years should be fulfilled: and after that (literally, "after these things") he must be loosed a little season"* (Revelation chapter 20 verse 3 NRB). Here we have the very last of the 'time-shift' phrases in the book of Revelation. The 'age' that follows the 'Kingdom Period' will have no end, it cannot be calculated (though the Bible does not say 'time will end'), here is the last chronological movement in John's visions. The '1,000 year Kingdom' will culminate in the release, final rebellion, and eternal judgment of the ultimate rebel, *"Lucifer"* the high angel, who became *"Satan"* at his fall. Downwards we see him continue. Always down, until his final end.

What will the Environment be Like?

> **KEYNOTE: Earth's axis tilt.** Many students of both 'early days' as well as 'last days' believe that the 'tilt' of the axis of the earth (22.1 – 24.5 degrees) was altered by God during or after the Flood, and contributed to the Ice Age. If so, a tilt backward could very well contribute to 'pre-flood' (ante-diluvian) weather conditions being restored.

That is a good question. We have already compared it to the *"Garden of Eden"*. It is probable that climatic conditions – though we cannot be sure of every detail – will be similar to Eden as well, and so will the 'flora and fauna' environment too. Strange things will have happened to the surface of our world during the Tribulation Period. The *"earthquakes"* and floods will possibly be generated by what we call 'tectonic shift', possibly even 'polar shift' (which scientists are able to measure the beginning of even today), all under a divine hand. We know that great topographical

'
God will then do things with a 'restoring' purpose, not a 'judgmental' one.'

upheaval is possible, and in the 'record of the rocks' it did happen in the past, no doubt in some way connected with the 'Genesis Flood'. God prepared instruments of judgment in His creation and, as we have seen already, used them in His timing and for His purpose.

When it comes to the changes of earth's surface to prepare for the Kingdom environment, God will do things with a 'restoring' purpose, not a 'judgmental' one. Isaiah said, *"The voice of him that crieth in the wilderness, 'Prepare ye the way of Jehovah … Every valley shall be exalted, and every mountain and hill shall be made low: And the crooked shall be made straight, and the rough places plain: And the glory of Jehovah shall be revealed …'"* (Isaiah chapter 40 verses 3 – 5 NRB). Here is another 'divided prophecy', for the <u>first part</u> of this paragraph is confirmed in the New Testament as speaking of John Baptist, the *"forerunner"* of Messiah at His first coming (John chapter 1 verses 21 – 23). The <u>second part</u> is 'Millennial', and has clearly not been fulfilled yet. It will be fully fulfilled at Christ's second advent.

The 'Dead Sea' from the Judean Hills looking towards the Edom – the lowest place on earth. (JHF)
"The waters shall be healed. And it shall come to pass … fishers shall stand upon it from En-Gedi even unto En-Eglaim; they shall be a place to spread forth nets; … their fish shall be … exceeding many." (Ezekiel 47:8-10 KJV).

The prophecy concerning the valleys and the mountains is almost certainly literal, and in its fulfilment will have a great impact on the climate of our world, as well as movement of people across its surface. The Hebrew word for *"exalted"* is 'nâśâ' (interestingly enough) and means to 'lift up or cause to be borne up'. The deepest valleys on earth are in the oceans – deeper than Mount Everest is high – the lowering of mountains will increase the 'fertility line', *"… upon the top of the mountains; the fruit thereof shall shake like Lebanon"* (Psalm 72 verse 16 KJV). The *"valleys lifted up"*, especially if ocean valleys are in view, will lower the depth of the seas, which in turn will raise their temperature, which will cause a temperate climate to spread, probably over the whole world.

Amos, speaking of the days when the captivity of Israel would be over forever, said *"'Behold the days are coming', declares the Lord, 'When the ploughman shall overtake the reaper and the treader of grapes him who sows the seed; the mountains shall drip sweet wine, and all the hills shall flow with it.'"* (Amos chapter 9 verses 13 – 15 ESV). No want, no rationing, and no famine. No greed and no shortage of supply. All perfectly controlled by one of whom Joseph – in his premiership in Egypt – is a lovely 'type'.

A 'wadi' (dry river bed) in the hills beyond 'En-Gedi' and the 'Dead Sea'. (JHF)
"The wilderness and the solitary place … and the desert shall rejoice, and blossom as the rose." (Isa. 35:1 KJV).

What about the Animals?

They do get a mention as well. And 'back to Eden' is still the recurring theme. Isaiah prophesied, in a very 'Messianic' passage speaking of the time when the *"Branch from (Jesse's) roots" will be Judge, "The wolf shall dwell with the lamb, and the leopard shall lie down with the young goat, and the calf and the lion … together; and a little child shall lead them. The cow and the bear shall graze; … and the lion shall eat straw like the ox."* (Isaiah chapter 11 verses 6 – 9 ESV). Why should such a description not be literal? If it was so before the Fall, why should it not be so again? All of this is just the removal of the influence of the 'Fall of Man' on what became, back then, a cursed creation.

What about the Serpent?

That is an outstanding question, and connects directly into our theme. For did not the original *"serpent"* – the reptile not the Devil – allow itself to be used by Satan? If Eve was not surprised by an upright, talking, snake (which she doesn't appear to have been), she should have been by the suggestion of the Serpent to disbelieve God! Some time back, in a previous Chapter, we noted

'
Will God turn the 'human age clock' back as well? Yes, indeed He will.'

but did not elaborate on, one other thing that would not be changed in the Millennial Kingdom. Here we have it; the form and propulsion of the serpent. God will not permit it to go back to its former stance or glory, even though so much else has been restored. Note the prophesy of Isaiah again *"The wolf and the lamb shall graze together; the lion shall eat straw like the ox, and* <u>*dust shall be the serpent's food*</u>*."* (Isaiah chapter 65 verse 25 ESV).

What about People?

'Well, if living conditions will be changed, if climate will be changed, if food quality will be changed, then should people not live longer? Like they did before the flood?' Great observations. The average age of men before the flood was 900+ years, many of them living between 900 and 969 years (the age of Methuselah who was the oldest recorded male).

Will God turn the 'human age clock' back as well? 'Yes, He will.' Those born during the Kingdom Age [We will talk about the original inhabitants in a moment] will live – if they are obedient to the King – for all the remainder of the 1,000 years. Sin will be judged by Jesus Christ before it has the opportunity to hurt or affect others: *"They shall not hurt or destroy in all My holy mountain" (Isaiah chapter 65 verse 25), "for the young man shall die a hundred years old, and the sinner a hundred years old shall be accursed … for like the days of a tree shall the days of My people be … They shall not labour in vain or bear children for calamity* (on the breast)*, for they shall be the offspring of the blessed of the Lord."* (Isaiah chapter 65 verses 20 – 23 ESV).

Many will see the glory of the *"King of kings"* when they come to Jerusalem to keep the *"Feast of Tabernacles"*. As D. Baron writes: 'The spiritual truths set forth by this particular type shall then be realised, for Jerusalem shall then be the metropolis of God's Kingdom on earth, and the joy … will not only be the portion of saved Israel, but shall pervade all the nations of the earth.' *Many more will hear of it who have not visited Jerusalem, or made the annual pilgrimage there (Zechariah chapter 14 verses 16 – 21). Many will acknowledge His 'Kingship' in their heart. Sadly many – despite the perfection of their environment and the perfection of His government – will not. Many will rebel, both inwardly and outwardly. Grace will be shown, though chastisement will follow. Where evil is intended, death will come. And open revolt will be judged in a judgment of fire, as we have seen.

Why this should be so is hard for us to understand. Why should any heart rebel? What an amazing group of prophecies are given at the conclusion of the book of Isaiah, and what a prospect to look forward to: Children who never grow old, grandparents who stay young as well. And a perfect environment in which to raise little ones. How different from the sad, degenerating (and worrisome) environment we find ourselves in today. How wonderful that a day of perfect rule is coming soon.

[*D. Baron '*Zechariah*' (Grand Rapids, MI: Kregel Publications, 2001), 521.]

Who will have Children?

'Not the Christians from the Church? Nor the Old Testament saints?' Good questions. 'Do we not have glorified bodies, as Jesus has?' 'Yes, that is so.' Resurrected saints – from any age – including the 'caught away' saints at the end of the Church Age will not have bodies suitable for marrying or for bearing children. We will have 'glorified bodies', *"we look for the Saviour, Lord Jesus Christ: who shall transform the body of our humiliation, that it may become like unto the <u>body of His glory</u> …"* (Philippians chapter 3 verse 20 NRB).

'So, who will be the children that were spoken of in Isaiah's prophecy?' They will be the children born during the 1,000 years of the Kingdom. But we need to consider to whom. The initial population of the Kingdom will probably comprise three parts:

Firstly: The *"144,000"* [whom we looked at in **Chp. 10**]. They will live through the Tribulation Period and go <u>alive</u> into the Kingdom to be seen, with the *"Lamb"* on *"Mount Zion"* right at the commencement of the *"Year of My Redeemed"* (Revelation chapter 14 verse 1).

Secondly: The *"remnant"* of Israel. Not only those who will be hidden *"in the wilderness"* (chapter 12 verse 14), but also those who will be gathered from the surviving nations. *Jehovah says, "I will send survivors* (the remnant Jews) *to the nations … that have not heard My fame or seen My glory. And they shall declare My glory among the nations. And they shall bring <u>all your brothers</u> from <u>all the nations</u> … to the Lord … to My holy mountain Jerusalem … And some of them also I will take for Priests and for Levites"* (Isaiah chapter 66 verses 18 – 21 ESV).

Thirdly: Those whom Jesus called *"the sheep"* in His 'Olivet Discourse'. At the judging of the surviving nations which will come after *"Armageddon"* is over, and probably after Satan is bound. *"When the Son of Man … shall … sit upon the throne of His glory: and before Him shall be gathered all the nations: and He shall separate them from one another, as the shepherd divides the sheep from the goats: and He shall set the sheep on His right hand, but the goats on the left."* (Matthew chapter 25 verses 31 – 46 NRB). The *"sheep"*, those of the nations who gave comfort and refuge to persecuted Jews during the Tribulation, will be allowed *"to inherit the Kingdom"*.

Not all who refused the *"mark"* or refused to *"worship the Dragon"* will be arrested and put to death. There will probably be many who have believed the message preached initially by the *"144,000"* and who are (in their heart) looking for a true Messiah to come. The *"goats"*, on the other hand, will be those who persecuted the Jews, and those who followed the *"Beast"* but were not involved in the 'Armageddon Campaign'. Every heart will be exposed for its true allegiance. And for those whom Jesus will separate to His left hand, they *"shall go away into everlasting punishment: but the righteous into life eternal."* (Matthew chapter 25 verse 46 KJV).

So, here we have three main groups, as set out above. All of these will be <u>distinct</u> from Old Testament saints, or Church saints, in this respect. They will <u>not</u> have *"spiritual bodies"*, they will have *"natural bodies"*. They will <u>not</u> have died, <u>nor</u> will they be resurrected. They will go into the Kingdom as the early population who will be able to have *"infants"* as we have looked at earlier.

What about Resurrected Saints?

They are very different. And they can be divided into three groups as well:

Firstly: The resurrected saints from the Old Testament period (we have mentioned Daniel and John Baptist already), and the Church saints from this age (which commenced at Pentecost). The Old Testament saints will be resurrected at the end of the Tribulation, possibly to join the *"Coming in Power"*, or possibly during the 75 days of Kingdom preparation. We are not specifically told, certainly they will be raised before the *"Marriage Supper"* commences.

Secondly: The Church saints, who will have been 'raptured' earlier, they will be part of the *"Coming in Power"* from heaven. Both of these vast companies will have 'resurrection bodies' for *"there is a natural body, and there is a spiritual body."* (1 Corinthians chapter 15 verses 42 – 47 KJV).

Thirdly: The resurrected martyrs of the Tribulation Period, they will be raised also, and have a very significant role in the Kingdom. There is still one other important difference within these groups; the Old Testament Hebrew saints, and Tribulation Jewish martyrs, will inherit the Land of Israel along with the surviving *"remnant"* Jews. The 'Church saints' however have a different dwelling place altogether.

[We will look at that in **Chapter 23**, *'The New Jerusalem'*.]

Is there a Government in the Kingdom?

That is a great question. It would be very strange if there was not! We can put the 'tiers' of government together relatively easily, from different parts of scripture:

Firstly: We have confirmed already in our minds that Jesus will return, as *"King of kings"* to reign for 1,000 years. We are told six times over as to the length of His reign in the earthly kingdom, in our passage here in Revelation chapter 20.

Secondly: We are told that the 'Church saints' will reign with Him, as the *"Bride, the Lamb's wife"*. Paul encourages Timothy with these words: *"Faithful is the word, for if we died with Him, we shall also live with Him: if we endure, we shall also reign: if we deny, He also will deny us: if we believe not, He abideth faithful: He cannot deny Himself."* (2 Timothy chapter 2 verses 11 – 13 NRB). Even if we doubt His promises – for some Christians do doubt the very promises about His return – yet He must be faithful to Himself. He has promised to return. He has promised us a 'prepared place' and He has promised us a share in His kingdom reign.

Thirdly: This is most interesting – though not all scholars agree – it is most probable there will be a 'Vice-Regent'. That is a *"Prince"*, who will sit upon the throne in Jerusalem if the King is elsewhere. 'But', you say, 'Is Jesus not present everywhere at once. Is He not 'omni-present'?' 'Yes, that is true, in Spirit.' But just as in His public life and in His resurrection appearances, He will not be seen in more than one place at one time. 'So, who is the Prince?' you ask. Again, that is not difficult. If we accept that a 'Vice-Regent' will be appointed there is only one candidate in prophecy: *"And I Jehovah will be their Elohim, and <u>My servant David a Prince</u> among them; I Jehovah have spoken it."* (Ezekiel chapter 34 verses 23 – 24; chapter 37 verse 25 NRB).

There are those who disagree, and they will say, '*"David"* is being used as prophetic title for Jesus, who is David's descendant'. That might be possible, but it does not fit with every prophecy that was given, which it must. Ezekiel also said, speaking of the offerings (or sacrifices) and *"Feasts"* to be kept, *"The Prince shall bring near unto Jehovah in the Sabbath day six lambs without blemish, and a ram without blemish ..."* (Ezekiel chapter 46 verses 4 – 5 NRB). It is impossible that the *"Prince"* in this passage is speaking of *"Messiah"*. Jesus Christ – who is the *"Prince"* in Daniel's prophecy, in relation to His first coming, but the *"King of kings"* in relation to His second coming – cannot be the one to offer sacrifices to Jehovah. He did that once. *"But when Christ had offered for all time a single sacrifice for sins, He sat down at the right hand of God."* (Hebrews chapter 10 verses 11 – 14 ESV). So, linking it with the other passages, we must assume that it is David who will be Prince in the 'Millennial Kingdom Age'.

What about the Apostles?

KEYNOTE: 12 Apostles; But Who?
There has been much debate about a.) *"Matthias"* who was the replacement for Judas (Acts 1:15-26), and b.) *"Paul"* who said, *"the gospel of the uncircumcision* (that is non-Jews) *was committed unto me."* (Gal. 2:7-9), as to which is the 12th Apostle in the Kingdom context. Paul was the *"Apostle to the Gentiles"*, and as such the 'replacement position' seems to be filled by Matthias. Again, we cannot be dogmatic on the point.

Fourthly: And a good question too: Jesus told His disciples who in the Kingdom are the *"Twelve Apostles of the Lamb"* (Revelation chapter 21 verse 14) that, *"in the regeneration when the Son of Man shall sit on the throne of His glory, ye also shall sit upon twelve thrones, judging the twelve tribes of Israel."* (Matthew chapter 19 verses 27 – 30 KJV). Israel will be in tribal order in the Land; a different 'map' from Old Testament times, and a different tribal order, with a very special layout around Jerusalem in the centre (The tribal layout is set out in the last chapter of Ezekiel, chapter 48, as we saw in our map earlier). The *"Apostles"* in an undisclosed order, will be responsible as a kind of 'Jewish Cabinet' for one tribe each*.

‘
There is NO 'general resurrection' taught in any of the prophetic scriptures.'

When we come back to our passage here, we see that 'Tribulation Martyrs' will also have a place in the government of the Kingdom. John said, *"I saw thrones ... and those which had not worshipped the Beast ... neither received his mark ... they lived and reigned with Christ the thousand years."* (Revelation chapter 20 verses 4 – 6 NRB).

Will there be Sacrifices in the Kingdom?

We have already suggested that there will be. Linking the Old Testament prophecies together which deal with this subject we find varied references to *"ascending offerings, sin offerings, trespass offerings and gift offerings"*. Sacrifices of 'commemoration' and sacrifices of 'cleansing'. M. Sweetnam says that the 'sacrifices (are) for cleansing from ritual defilement'. Five different 'End Times' prophets speak of them (Isaiah chapter 56 verse 7; Jeremiah chapter 33 verse 18; Ezekiel chapter 42 verse 13; Zechariah chapter 14 verses 16 -21 & Malachi chapter 3 verses 3 – 4). There are also two annual 'Feasts' to be kept, *"The Passover"* and *"The Feast of Tabernacles"*, both on their original dates (Ezekiel chapter 45 verses 21 – 25).

[M. Sweetnam, *'To the Day of Eternity'* (Cookstown, NI: Scripture Teaching Library, 2014), 113.]

Perhaps the simplest way to understand it is this: In our time, we have a *"supper"* which contains 'symbols', *"bread and the cup"* (1 Corinthians chapter 11 verses 23 – 26). These help us, who were not present at the time, to remember the Lord's death on the cross. This supper of *"remembrance"* will end when Jesus returns for His Church, as we have seen. But likewise, millions will be born during the 'Kingdom Age' who have known nothing else but peace. They also will have 'visual symbols' to cause them to ask about the past, and the reason for what we believe will be the still visible wounds in the hands of Messiah. And so, to appreciate that the King on the throne was the *"Son of Man"* who was rejected, by His own people the Jews, at His first coming.

> **KEYNOTE: Kingdom Age vs. Eternal State.** More will be said about the distinction between the 'Millennial Kingdom Age', the *"Holy City"*, and the 'Eternal State' as we go forward. All are different, yet with characteristics that are similar. From Rev. 20:1 through to 22:6 the visions and record moves between all three. A breakdown between the 3 topics will be examined when we come to study *'The New Jerusalem'* in **Chp. 23**.

The Millennial Kingdom Ends?

Yes, it does. Most definitely. The 'Eternal State' will follow, but with the 'Final Judgment' between. Up to this point only those who share in the *"resurrection of life"* have been raised. Those who will experience the *"resurrection of judgment"* will still not have been raised (John chapter 5 verses 25 – 29 NRB). This is another of our 'divided prophecies'. There is NO 'general resurrection' taught in any of the prophetic scriptures.

The 'thousand years', measured in earth time (though possibly still in the 'prophetic year' of 360 days) will count down. Satan himself will know that the time for him to be *"loosed a little season"* (Revelation chapter 20 verse 3) is getting close. But nothing about him has changed. His depraved mind is still totally rebellious. And still full of hatred against his Creator. That does not surprise us. Nor does it surprise us that he *"shall go out to deceive …"* (chapter 20 verse 8 KJV). What is most shocking is that he gets a response! Yet should we be totally shocked? Were not our 'first-parents', in their 'Edenic' environment, at least as well cared for and blessed as any kingdom dweller will be? Yet they listened, Eve was deceived, and they both rebelled against God. So too it will be at the end of the Millennial Kingdom …

Rebels after 1,000 Years of Peace?

'Yes!' Those who have been born in the Kingdom who do not love the King. Who do not wish to sit *"down under His shadow …"* (Song of Songs chapter 2 verse 3 KJV). Who have no desire to live near Jerusalem, nor to go on pilgrimage to visit once a year, *"to worship the King, Jehovah of hosts, and to keep the Feast of Booths"* as will be commanded (Zechariah chapter 14 verses 16 – 20 NRB). Who have moved rather to *"the four corners of the earth"* (Revelation chapter 20 verse 8 NRB), where they will be as far from the Land of Israel as they can get. 'What happens then?' you ask.

It seems that Satan will gather a huge army from all over the world. We are not sure if they openly march on Jerusalem. How could this be permitted? It is possible that they actually do come up as 'pretend pilgrims', on the seventh month, to arrive at Jerusalem on the fifteenth day. To build their *"booths"* to *"camp"* with the saints around the *"beloved city"*, the restored Jerusalem, the *"city of the Great King"*. Hoping – possibly under cover of darkness – to attack the true pilgrims, to attack the city and to defeat the King … 'How foolish', you say, 'Does Satan never learn?' We have asked that question before, and sadly, the answer is, 'No.' In fact, his rebellion seems to grow worse, and there will be men too – even in the beauty of the Kingdom Age – who want to side with the Devil.

Still Born Sinful?

'Yes. Why would this not be so?' Even a perfect environment will not produce a reformed heart. Only the work of God's Spirit can regenerate that which is born 'dead'. Paul said, *"But God, who is rich in mercy on account of His great love wherewith He loved us, even when we were dead in sins, quickened us (made us alive spiritually) together with Christ, by grace ye are saved."* (Ephesians chapter 2 verse 4 NRB). Jeremiah said, *"The heart is crooked above all, and it is incurable: who can know it? I Jehovah search the heart."* (Jeremiah chapter 17 verse 9 NRB).

'How will they tell the rebels from the true pilgrims?' someone asks. The answer to that is simple, yet profound. *"For the Lord sees not as man sees: Man looks on the outward appearance, but the Lord looks on the heart."* (1 Samuel chapter 16 verse 7 ESV). John says, *"Fire came down from God out of heaven, and devoured them."* (Revelation chapter 20 verse 9 KJV). As it was 1,000 years previously, at the end of the 'Tribulation', when God smote the armies around Jerusalem (Zechariah chapter 14 verses 12 – 15), so it will be again at the last rebellion. God will know every false heart, and He shall *"devour them"* in His wrath.

What about the Devil?

Yes, he is the arch-deceiver. From Genesis chapter 3 through to Revelation chapter 20, the record of the Word of God concerning *"the Dragon, the Serpent of old, the Devil and Satan"* does not change. And neither does he. To his eternal doom he must go, *"cast into the lake of fire"*. Where after 1,000 years have passed *"the Beast and the False Prophet are, and shall be tormented day and night for ever and forever."* (Revelation chapter 20 verse 10 NRB). The last rebellion is over. The 'Kingdom Age' is closed. The 'Last Judgment' is about to happen. But all the *"saved"* of all the ages will be secure for all eternity, in a *"new heaven and a new earth"* (chapter 21 verse 1), with their Saviour, Jesus Christ, forever ...

Oh what glory awaits me in Heaven's bright city
When I get there, such sights to behold.
A million scenes of rare beauty
Will demand that I view them;
Still Jesus will outshine them all!

The sparkling river is flowing, happy faces all glowing
Land of splendour where night never falls.
The golden glass gives reflection
To that city's perfection,
Still Jesus will outshine them all.

Mansions will glisten on the hills of Glory
Happy reunions on streets of gold;
Angel choirs singing glad praises forever,
But Jesus will outshine them all.
Jesus will outshine them all ...

[*Gordon Jensen (1951 -) Gallatin, TN.*]

Q&A >

> **KEYNOTE: Kingdom Prophecies.** Numerous of the 'latter day' and 'exile' prophets have been quoted, those who told of the fall of Jerusalem and the captivity. Those who saw it happen, and those who lived during the exile in Babylon and Medo-Persia. Many of them encouraged the 'true remnant' among the Nation of Israel by pointing them forward to a day of future Kingdom glory, when Messiah their Prince would reign. It is a worthwhile study to examine the closing chapters of ALL the O.T. prophets, and see how they finished on a 'Kingdom' view. There are two prophets who did not, as you will discover. Perhaps you will be able to work out why not.

Questions and Answers for Chapter Twenty-One – 'The Millennial Kingdom'

Chp. 21 – 'The Millennial Kingdom'

Q1 What reasons can you give for Jesus coming the second time?

Q2 Can you name any OT "covenants" which must be finally fulfilled?

Q3 We examined a list of things which must be done before the Kingdom is set up. How many can you list?

Q4 At the start of the '1,000 year Kingdom', where is Satan put? For how long?

Q5 What detail of the Kingdom is <u>not</u> told in O.T. prophecy?

Q6 Who is included in the government of the Kingdom?

Q7 What will be the main characteristics of the Kingdom?

Q8 What happens at the end of the Kingdom?

Chapter Twenty-Two
The Final Judgment

We have now come to the end of the 1,000 year 'Kingdom Age'. Satan has been released – for his final act – and has found an echo in the hearts of mankind to answer to his rebellious spirit against God and His Christ who has been on the throne for all the 'Millennial Reign'. This last rebellion has been put down – once again no war is fought – and Satan has been sent to his final doom, which was made ready for him when he rebelled in heaven in the early days of the universe, a place of *"everlasting fire, prepared for the Devil and his angels"* (Matthew chapter 25 verse 41 KJV). Where he will join the *"Beast"* and the *"False Prophet"* who have been there for 1,000 years. The human rebels are all slain by *"fire (that) came down from God out of heaven, and devoured them."* (Revelation chapter 20 verse 9 KJV).

The End of the Rebels?

Someone may ask, 'Is that the end of the rebels?' 'No! It is not.' No more so than any other person who has died, down through the ages of time, in a state of rebellion against God. How foolish are the hearts of people today who believe in 'annihilation', the idea that for humans there is nothing remaining after death: That there is no *"spirit"* within man which will live forever. Or perhaps, even more confusing in the thoughts of some; that by 'cremation' or 'immolation' or some other manner of destroying the body, <u>accountability to God</u> can be avoided.

Jesus said, *"Fear not them which kill the body, but are not able to kill the soul: But rather fear Him (God) who is able to destroy both soul and body in Gehenna (the fire)."* (Matthew chapter 10 verse 28 NRB).

Where is the Judgment?

That is the question which we will now deal with:

It is called the '**Judgment of the Great White Throne**' (Revelation chapter 20 verses 11 – 15). It has been said before, but it is worth repeating: The throne is *"Great"* because of the <u>Majesty</u> of the one who sits on it. The same one, Jesus Christ, who judged the living in the Kingdom. Now He will judge the *"dead"*. It is *"White"* because of the <u>Purity</u> of the judgment that will be handed down. No taint of corruption, no 'lobbying' in the corridors, no 'deals' of any sort. Every sinner, from every age, will stand exposed and alone before the throne. It is a *"Throne"* because of the Authority of the Judge and the judgment. There is no 'plea bargaining', no 'appeal'. Everyone who is there is *"judged … according to their works"* (chapter 20 verse 12 KJV). Their sentence will be final. And eternal. There is no reprieve. What a solemn 'last judgment' that will be.

John says, *"I saw a great white throne, and Him that sat on it, from whose face the earth and the heaven fled; and there was found no place for them."* (Revelation chapter 20 verse 11 NRB). There will be no hiding place. This earth will be finished with once the dead have been delivered up. The *"… heavens shall pass away with a rushing noise, and the elements shall be dissolved with fervent heat, earth also and the works that are therein shall be burned up."* (2 Peter chapter 3 verses 10 – 12 NRB). The contamination of our world, by the lifestyle of mankind, will all be consumed. God will create a new heaven and a new earth*. But the *"works"* of wickedness, all that has not been repented of and forgiven, will be finally exposed at the Great White Throne Judgment.

[*See introduction to **Chapter 23**, *'The New Jerusalem'*.]

Who will be There?

KEYNOTE: 'Pre-eminence'. *"He (Jesus Christ) is the Head of the body the Church: who is the beginning, firstborn from among the dead; that in all He might become pre-eminent (superior above all)"* (Col. 1:18 NRB). Will there be more in heaven than will be lost? We do not know, but it is possible – if we count the souls of the 'unborn', the stillborn, the infant mortality figures, and the like – that in that too, in number as well as in majesty, Jesus will be supreme. What an amazing thought!

The answer is succinct and solemn: 'The dead.' Not all who have died, for those who died believing in Messiah, those who died looking for Jesus to return, those who died in martyrdom for Him, will ALL already have been raised, in various stages, which we have considered already. *"The rest of the dead lived not again until the thousand years were finished."* (Revelation chapter 20 verses 5 NRB). Only the 'unbelieving dead' will be at this judgment in space; *"The sea gave up the dead in it; and death and Hades delivered up the dead in them: and they were judged every man according to their works"* (chapter 20 verse 13 NRB).

'How many?' We have no idea. Millions of dead people raised, John says, *"I saw the dead, small and great, stand before God …"* (chapter 20 verse 12 KJV). One of the most astonishing and terrifying phrases in all the Word of God.

Why 'Second Death' not 'Second Resurrection'?

A good question, and worth considering. The words John records here are not his own commentary, nor even those of an angel, they are the words of Jesus Christ Himself, *"Blessed and holy is he that hath part in the first resurrection: over these the second death hath not authority ...*" (chapter 20 verse 6 NRB). This is the <u>fifth</u> of seven *"blessings"* in the book of Revelation, all given by Jesus to His people who are still on earth. This one is pronounced on all those who have been '<u>raised</u>' at the beginning of the Kingdom Age. They died once. A human – and at times a violent and unnatural – death. But not a spiritual death, and they are promised never to die again. What we are looking at here, by comparison, is very much in the negative.

The '<u>raising</u>' of sinners for the last judgment is not called the 'second resurrection'. It is called – by Jesus Himself – *"the second death"*. These two terms are totally mutually exclusive (That is, no one can be in both groups). Our salvation is eternally secure, having part in the *"first resurrection"* (for all who have died *"in Christ"*). The remainder awaiting the judgment of the *"second death"*.

How Are the Dead Judged?

Out of the *"books"*. We can identify four books at least, possibly even five, at the Great White Throne Judgment scene. In order of mention, they are:

1.) The '***Book of the Living***' – This appears to be a record of all who have lived, from Adam onwards to the end of the Kingdom Age. In the Old Testament the judgment of Jehovah was spoken of as a 'blotting out' of this book. Moses, in intercession for the whole nation of Israel, asked Jehovah to spare them, and *"Blot me, I pray Thee, out of Thy book which Thou hast written."* (Exodus chapter 32 verse 32 KJV). God refused, and told Moses that the 'blotting out' judgment would be individual, upon *"Whosoever sinned against Me"* (chapter 32 verse 33 KJV).

2.) The '***Book of Life***' – Also called the *"Lamb's Book of Life"* (in Revelation chapter 21 verse 27). Paul speaks of *"my fellow labourers, whose names are in the book of life"* (Philippians chapter 4 verse 3 KJV). John was told – in stark contrast – that those *"whose names are not written in the book of life of the Lamb ..."* (Revelation chapter 13 verse 8 KJV) will worship the "Beast" during the Great Tribulation period.

3.) The '***Book of Works***' – All unforgiven sin will be exposed, and will determine degrees of punishment in the eternal judgment. Jesus said, speaking of Capernaum where He did many miracles, *"It shall be more tolerable for the land of Sodom in the day of judgment, than for thee."* (Matthew chapter 11 verses 23 – 24 KJV).

4.) The '***Word of God***' – Though not mentioned by name, we can count four books (at least) being opened. The scriptures which could have made *"wise unto salvation"* (2 Timothy chapter 3 verse 15 KJV) will in that day condemn all who refused the call of God, whether from a knowledge of the Bible, or from the witness of creation, or from conscience.

5.) The *'**Seven Sealed Scroll**'* (from Revelation chapters 4 – 6). We are not told that it will be, but if the scroll is the 'Title Deed of Creation', with penalties contained within for rebellion against the government of God (as was suggested previously), then it is possible that it could an 'open testimony' at the last judgment alongside the other books listed.

What is the Outcome?

The *"dead, small and great"* who are at the 'Great White Throne Judgment' are there for one reason only. They were guilty – in their lifetime – of a rejection of God. The evidence of God is not only found in the Bible, but also in the 'voice' of creation, which does not have language barriers to overcome: *"The heavens declare the glory of God; and the expanse sheweth* (shows) *His handiwork ... There is no speech nor words, without their voice being heard."* (Psalm 19 verses 1 – 3 NRB). The creation witness, which is so denied today by the 'religion' of evolution – which is a 'pseudo-science' of man's own invention – is the evidence of God's 'fingerprints' which He has put upon His own universe. Proving not only where everything, humanity included, came from but where we will go; the final destiny of all, who will someday be judged by Jesus Christ, whom God raised from the dead.

> **KEYNOTE: Creation Witness.** God is proven, not just in the existence of our Universe, but in its order and maintenance. God – as His *"Ye-Hov-Jah"* title indicates – is a God of the future, the present, and the past. The maintaining of constant 'order' in the stars and planets, in consistent gravity, in the regularity of seasons etc.: All point to the existence of an 'Originator' and a 'Maintainer' outside of the 'system' itself. Paul told the pagan Athenian debaters on Mars Hill, *"The God who made the world and everything in it ...* (so) *that they should seek God ... He commands all people everywhere to repent, because He has fixed a day on which He will judge the world ... by a man whom He has appointed ... by raising Him from the dead."* (Acts chapter 17 verses 22 – 31 ESV). All of creation points to the one who is *"The Word"*.

Is there More than One Judgment?

God has decreed that Jesus, whom He raised from the dead, will judge the dead. Paul says, *"But now hath Christ been raised from the dead, becoming the firstfruits of them that slept ... For as in Adam all die, even so in Christ shall all be made alive."* (1 Corinthians chapter 15 verses 20 – 22 NRB). The idea of *"firstfruits"* would have been very clear to a Jew of Paul's time. The *"firstfruit"* was a 'type' of Christ. The first ripe sheaf of the harvest was taken in by the priest before Jehovah: Promise, and proof, that the full harvest would follow. Such was the resurrection of Jesus – that which fulfilled the Old Testament 'type'* – and so every person who has died will live again, through the power of the risen Christ. If Jesus did not rise again from the dead, then not only is all resurrection suspect, but the very foundation of the gospel is void.

Paul argues, *"How say some among you that there is no resurrection of the dead? But if there be no resurrection of the dead, then hath Christ not been raised; and if Christ hath not been raised, then our preaching is vain* (of no substance), *and your faith is also vain ...*" (1 Corinthians chapter 15 verses 12 – 22 NRB). All will not be raised at the same time, however, and all will not be judged at the same time either, or have the same kind of judgment. There is more than one resurrection, and there is also more than one judgment scene.

> *KEYNOTE: 'Type & Anti-type'.* It has been explained already what a 'type' is in scripture: A personality, an item, or an event in the O.T. which points forward to the person and character of Jesus Christ. Scholars use the expression 'anti-type' to pinpoint exactly where an O.T. 'type' is fulfilled. A good example is the *"serpent ... upon a pole"* (Num. 21). Its *"lifting up"*, Jesus said, was a 'picture' of Himself, and His death. *"And as Moses lifted up the serpent in the wilderness, so must the Son of Man be lifted up, that whoever believes in Him may have eternal life."* (John 3:14-15 ESV). King Melchisedek – whom we looked at earlier as a 'type' – is shown to point, in more ways than one, to Jesus who is the perfect 'anti-type' (Hebs. chp. 7).

There is no 'General Judgment'?

'No! There absolutely is not.' That expression or phrase is not found anywhere in the Bible. Even if – like some scholars – you do not believe in a 'rapture' of the Church, nor even accept the evidence of a literal 1,000 year Kingdom on earth, even so, one judgment of all, good or bad, cannot be interpreted from any passage of scripture. 'So, there is more than one judgment?' you might ask. 'Yes. Definitely so.' Just as there have been numerous judgments by God in the past, so there are still a number of different judgments that are future (from the here and now).

Let us set them out in the order in which they will take place:

1.) The "***Judgment Seat of Christ***" – We have mentioned this judgment before. It takes place immediately after the removal of the Church [See **Chapter 24** '*Jesus Coming Quickly*']. It is a judgment for Church believers only, from *"Pentecost"* to the '*rapture*'. Those who have died will be raised, with heavenly bodies, and the living will be changed. We will go immediately to the assessment of our service for Jesus Christ, the first event of all, after leaving earth. Paul speaks of this *"Judgment"* in three passages, each with a different emphasis: **Firstly**, 'Loving our brothers' (Romans chapter 14 verses 10 – 13). **Secondly**, 'Labouring in building' in a local church testimony (1 Corinthians chapter 3 verses 12 – 17). **Thirdly**, 'Living in my body', my personal behaviour (2 Corinthians chapter 5 verses 10 -11).

2.) The '***Judgments of the Tribulation***' – These can be broken down into several parts. The list is not exhaustive, and depends how one views the *"Seals, Trumpets and Bowls"* as being individual judgments, or as groups. There are, at least, the following:

a.) The 'Judgment of the False Religious System' (Revelation 17)
b.) The 'Judgment of the Commercial System' (Revelation 18)
c.) The 'Judgment of the Persecutors of the Saints' (Revelation 16:7)
d.) The 'Judgment of the *"Beast"*, the *"False Prophet"* and their armies' (Revelation 19:17 – 21)

3.) The **'Judgment of the Living Nations'** – The *"sheep"* and the *"goats"* (Matthew 25:32)

4.) The **'Judgment of Satan'**: a.) Bound for 1,000 years (Revelation 20:1 – 6)
b.) In the *"Lake of fire"* forever (Revelation 20:10)

5.) The **'Judgment of the Great White Throne'** – The Last Judgment (Revelation 20:11 – 15)

This is the judgment we are examining here. It is a judgment only for sinners. No saved person, from any period of time, will be judged at the Great White Throne.

Will Christians Be There?

'If saints are not being judged, are they there as spectators?' That is a very difficult question, and one that is often asked: 'Will we be observers at the Great White Throne?' An honest answer to these questions is: 'We don't know, because we are not told.' We could 'infer' from the silence of scripture that we are not, but it is not always safe to build a doctrine on silence. God has not told us, one way or the other. Many Christians would say, 'Personally I would prefer not to be there. I would see people I know, even loved ones, being consigned to eternal punishment'. That is a valid comment, but it is grounded on our thinking 'down here'. We should balance that with the first three *"Hallelujahs"* of Revelation chapter 19. They are expressed by saints in heaven around the throne, about the judgment of God on sinful people here on earth.

'If there is no heaven, and no earth, then where else could we, those who are *"saved"*, be? Must we not be where Jesus is?' Again, good questions. And the short answer to that may be found in the promise, *"so we will always be with the Lord. Therefore encourage one another with these words."* (1 Thessalonians chapter 4 verses 17 – 18 ESV). We are not specifically told but there is one other possibility, an alternative location, which we will examine later in our next Chapter.

[See **Chapter 23**, *'The New Jerusalem'.*]

A Perfect Balance

We have one great divine recourse when we approach these kind of difficulties (of which there are quite a few in relation to future events), and that is the great rhetorical questions asked between Jehovah and Abraham long ago in relation to Lot and his family and the judgment of Sodom (to which we have already referred):

- *"Is anything too hard for Jehovah?"* – **No** (Genesis chapter 18 verse 14 NRB).

- *"Shall not the Judge of all the earth do what is just?"* – **Yes** (chapter 18 verse 25 ESV).

Between those two great pillars of God's righteousness and His 'omniscience' (His all-knowing) hang all the divine decisions of both His judgment and His mercy.

The Final Fall

Sin and rebellion against God do not pay. From 'original sin' (which was that of Lucifer the angel), through the sin of our fore-parents Adam and Eve in the Garden of Eden, through the murder of Abel by his brother Cain, the murder of Hebrew baby boys in the Nile, the genocide campaigns of all the ages, the 'Holocaust' murder of millions of Jews ... And all *"unbelieving"* today included.

A catalogue of increasing evil and defiance against God. Culminating in the two great rebellions we have been studying in the 'End Times'; the rebellion of the global armies against Christ at the end of the Tribulation, and the rebellion of those from the *"four corners of the earth"* against the saints at Jerusalem ... All rebellion against God will be put down, and put down forever.

Sin degrades, and destroys. And – if unforgiven – sin condemns. The path is ever downward, never upward. And unforgiven sin, for every sinner, from every age, will bring them to the last judgment. There to be condemned to eternal judgment, *"And death and Hades were cast into the lake of fire. This is the second death. And if anyone was not found written in the book of life, he was cast into the lake of fire."* (Revelation chapter 20 verse 15 NRB). Banished from the presence of God and Christ forever.

'Why? For great and terrible sins, like some of those mentioned above?' Murderers, yes. But they do not head the list. *"The fearful and unbelieving"* are first and second on the list of those who will go to the *"lake of fire"* (Revelation chapter 21 verse 8). How sad, to miss the way to heaven, forever, because of being fearful in this life. Too frightened to trust in Jesus? Perhaps, but not frightened enough of being lost ...

Are any Precondemned?

In other words, 'Does God pick people in advance to go to the lake of fire?' Absolutely not. That is not part of the gospel of the grace of God, a God who, *"so loved the world* that He gave His only begotten Son, that whoever believes in Him should not perish, but have eternal life."* (John chapter 3 verse 16 NASB). If we can limit the *"world"* in that message of the gospel from Jesus to the Pharisee, then we can limit those who can receive it!

Paul wrote, *"I urge that entreaties, prayers, petitions, thanksgivings, be made <u>on behalf of all men</u>, for kings and <u>all</u> who are in authority (in order that we may lead a tranquil and quiet life in all godliness and dignity). This is good and acceptable in the sight of God our Saviour, <u>who desires all men to be saved</u> and to come to the knowledge of the truth. For there is one God and one Mediator also, between God and men, the man Christ Jesus, who gave <u>Himself as a ransom for all</u>."* (1 Timothy chapter 2 verses 1 – 4 NASB).

[*Underlining by the author]

All Must Mean All

If Jesus did not die for *"<u>all</u>"* then God does not desire the salvation of *"<u>all</u>"*, and we have no mandate to pray for *"<u>all</u>"*, nor to preach a message for *"<u>all</u>"*. It should be obvious that the *"<u>world</u>"* (in John chapter 3 verse 16) is the world of 'mankind'. Not our planet, but *"all"* those who live on it. And the 'world of mankind' is the *"all"* that Paul is speaking of to Timothy. Those who arrive at the judgment of the *"Great White Throne"* do so; not because they were 'unloved' by God, nor excluded from the offer of salvation provided by Jesus in His death and resurrection: All who will be there will have refused that which is freely available, from the heart of a God who Himself is *"Love"*.

Questions and Answers for Chapter Twenty-Two – 'The Final Judgment'

Chp. 22 – 'The Final Judgment'

Q1. What does <u>not</u> happen at the start of the '1000 year Kingdom'?

Q2. The "first resurrection" concludes at the beginning of the Kingdom. Where does it begin?

Q3. What would be the greatest problem if there was no resurrection?

Q4. What is the "second death"?

Q5. Why is it contrasted with the "first resurrection"?

Q6. Why is the judgment throne described as a "Great White Throne"?

Q7. How many books, at least, can we tell are opened?

Q8. Can you name them?

Q9. What happens after the Last Judgment?

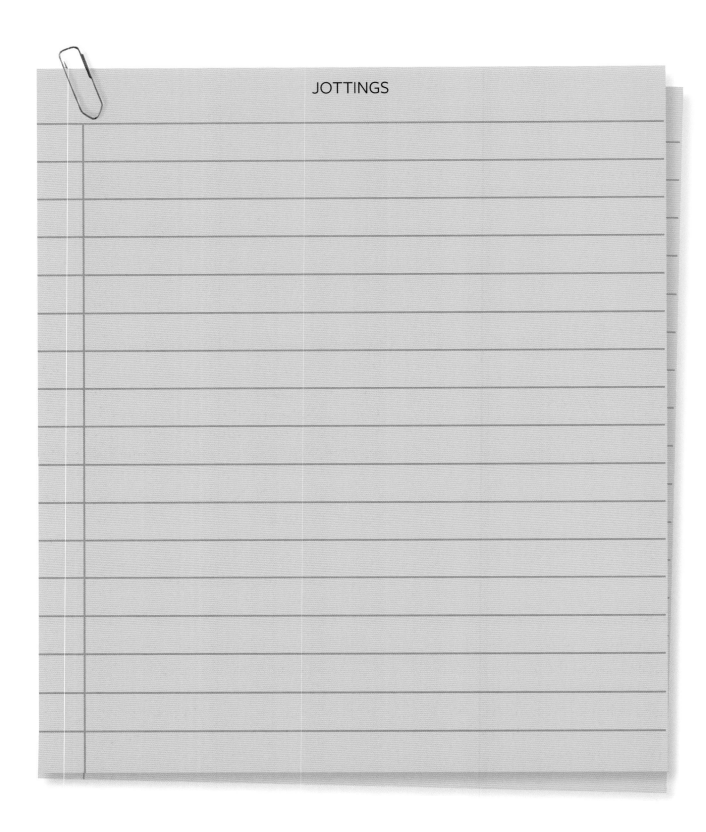

JOTTINGS

Chapter Twenty-Three

The New Jerusalem

We have arrived at what is possibly one of the most intriguing – and most debated – topics in the whole of the book of Revelation. Possibly even in all of 'eschatology' (prophecy still to be fulfilled). The *"Holy City, New Jerusalem"* as John calls it (Revelation chapter 21 verse 1 – 2). Where each scholar or student positions themselves on the 'allegorical to literal spectrum' in relation to prophecy* will determine their approach to this subject.

> ***KEYNOTE: 'Allegorical'.** The Cambridge Dictionary definition is, *'a story, play, poem, picture ... in which the characters and events represent particular qualities or ideas that relate to morals, religion or politics. Augustine's 'City of God' (book) is an allegory of the triumph of Good over Evil',* which is most apt, as it was Augustine who spearheaded the doctrine that John's 'revelation' was an 'allegory' and that the *"New Jerusalem"* was not 'actual'. **See Appx. II** for further discussion.

Some say, 'It is only a descriptive picture of the Church in heaven'. Others, like W. Scott say, 'It is a description of the Church, not a city at all'. Others say, 'It is symbolic of the dwelling place of the saints in the eternal state, but the description is not literal'. Still others, like H. M. Morris say, 'It is a literal city but only in an eternal setting'. And a fourth group will say, like H. A. Ironside, 'It is a literal city, and has a definite role both in the 'Kingdom Age', and in the 'Eternal State''. Since we have argued mostly for a <u>literal</u> interpretation, and against a totally allegorical one throughout (unless where it is clearly indicated in a biblical context), we are going to take up this last view and see how much support can be found for it in scripture.

The Final Breakdown ...

Something which we mentioned previously, and we now need to look at in detail, is the breakdown of the final sections of the book of Revelation, from chapter 20 verse 1 through to the end. The chapter divisions – as is often the case – are not the most helpful, and we need to be clear which of the end subjects John is talking about, in which section of his final visions. W. A. Criswell says, 'Revelation 22:1-5 are the concluding verses of chapter 21.'

[W. A. Criswell *'Expository Sermons on Revelation'* (Dallas TX: Criswell Publishing, 1995), 124.]

> **'**
>
> *... the Eternal City ... is divine in its <u>origin</u> and will be eternal in its <u>duration</u>.'*

We can break the final 3 chapters of Revelation down, by subject, as follows.

Subject:	Reference:
1.) **'The Millennial Kingdom'**	(Rev. 20:1 - 10)
2.) **'The Great White Throne Judgment'**	(Rev. 20:11 – 15) & (Rev. 21:8)
3.) **'The New Heaven & New Earth'**	(Rev. 21:1 - 7)
4.) **'The New Jerusalem'**	(Rev. 21:9 – 22:5)
5.) **'The Last Sayings of Jesus'**	(Rev. 22:6 – 21)

Section One is future, and is of exactly 1,000 years duration.

Section Two we are not given a time frame for. It will be after the Kingdom Age is concluded, it will be conducted in space, but as to duration, we are – as with the *"Judgment Seat of Christ"* – given no detail as to how, or for how long, the judgments will be conducted. The additional comment (chapter 21 verse 8) is connected. The intentional contrast is between the place of eternal bliss and the place of eternal torment. The 'overcomer' will inherit a place in the eternal kingdom, with Christ, a wonderful spiritual incentive to be faithful to Him and for Him down here.

Section Three commences after the 'Kingdom Age' and the 'Great White Throne Judgment' concludes, and will last forever. There are no time limits, but scripture does <u>not</u> say that *'time will be no more'*. That concept comes from 'hymnology', and is a misinterpretation of one verse, *"the angel … sware … that there should be <u>time</u> no longer."* (Revelation chapter 10 verse 6 KJV). Although the original word is *'chrónos'* (the usual word for time), in the context it cannot mean 'end of time' and is quite often translated (as ESV) *"no more delay"*. We do not know if we will be able to measure 'endless days' forever. But it will be an endless or *"eternal"* state.

Section Four is about the *"New Jerusalem"*. The interpretation of the descriptions and dimensions in this passage – as well as the 'literality' of it – is where much confusion lies. There is a very good reason why one verse, which is about the *"lake of fire"* (chapter 21 verse 8), splits the heavenly narrative [We will come back to that later]. The *"New Jerusalem"* section begins at chapter 21 verse 9 and continues across the chapter division, as far as chapter 22 verse 5. What is contained in this passage is not the conditions of the 'Eternal State', but the conditions within the 'Eternal City'. Because – regardless of when we see the city coming into use first – it is divine in its <u>origin</u> and eternal in its <u>duration</u>. We must be totally clear on that.

Section Five also causes some confusion, as some scholars see it as a continuation of the future aspect of John's visions. It is not. Just as John was taken 'outside of time' (back in Revelation chapter 4), and moved forwards and backwards on the 'time continuum', so, at the end of the book, he is seen as being back in his 'earthly' condition. He is again, as he was at the beginning, identifying himself with Church believers everywhere and appealing, as the Holy Spirit also does, to those who have not yet received Jesus as Saviour.

Why is the Eternal State not Put Last?

That is a great question, and of course – chronologically – it is last. But we have been emphasising more and more as we have progressed that the sections of the book of Revelation, and John's visions, are not all in chronological order. The end of the '1,000 year Kingdom' joins directly to the beginning of the 'Eternal State', which is why John is given an overview first (chapter 21 verses 1 – 7).

John is also emphasising – by the Spirit's guidance – the terrible contrast between the destiny of the <u>unsaved dead</u> and the destiny of the <u>saved of all the ages</u>. He moves in vision, and in record, from the awfulness of being *"cast into the lake of fire"* to the eternal bliss of a forever with God. John heard a voice saying, *"Behold the tabernacle of God with men, and He will dwell with them, and they shall be His people, and God Himself shall be with them, their God."* (chapter 21 verse 3 NRB). As has been said often, 'Heaven is heaven because Jesus is there.' The same is true in a wider sense of the 'Eternal State'. Heaven and earth will become one perfect united 'universe of bliss' because we, the saved of all ages, will be in the presence of Jesus Christ forever:

> **KEYNOTE: Separation from God.** The *"second death"* is awful in its separation from God forever. The presence of God is not there. Though many today are rejecting God, He is still – in grace – 'showering' blessings of all kinds on mankind. At the final scene of judgment, God's grace will be removed. And all who are condemned will be removed from His presence. Forever.

> *'Throughout the universe of bliss*
> *The centre Thou and Sun,*
> *The eternal theme of praise is this,*
> *To heaven's beloved One.*
>
> *Worthy, Oh Lamb of God, art Thou,*
> *That every knee to Thee should bow.*

[*Josiah Condor (1789–1855) Hampstead, London*]

What is the New Earth Like?

That is a hard question, because we don't know. And we do not know because God chose not to tell us, most likely because we would not comprehend it if He did. Paul said, *"I will come to visions and revelations ... I knew a man in Christ ... (whether in the body ... or whether out of the body, I cannot tell ...) caught up even to the third heaven ... caught up into paradise and heard unspeakable sayings, which it is not lawful for a man to utter."* (2 Corinthians chapter 12 verses 1 – 4 KJV).

Again, it is an amazing thought that much of what John writes of the 'Eternal State' he did not *"see"*; he *"heard"*. It was a *"great voice out of heaven"* which said, *"God shall wipe*

> **KEYNOTE: 'No More …'** Some of the things John listed, in the negative, he saw and heard in relation to the *"Holy City"*, but the city, from its first appearing, has <u>eternal character</u> and cannot ever be contaminated. So, what is in the city environmentally is also true of the *"new earth"* eternally. Discussed in more detail later in this **Chapter**.

away every tear from their eyes; and there shall be no longer death, neither sorrow, nor crying, neither shall there be any longer pain: for the former things are passed away." (Revelation chapter 21 verses 3 - 4 NRB). Much of what John describes of the *"new heaven and new earth"* is told to us in the <u>negative</u>.

We get comfort in the 'here and now' from what will be absent in the 'by and by'!

Missing But Not Missed!

Let us list some of the things John describes that will not be found in the *"new earth"*, nor in the *"New Jerusalem"* either. We should remember that whether it is the *"new earth"* which is being referred to (first), or the *"Holy Jerusalem"* (later), the <u>conditions</u> and <u>character</u> are the same:

"There shall be no longer any more …"

• **No Sea**	**(chapter 21:1)**	
• **No Tears**	**(chapter 21:4)***	[See ***KEYNOTE** on opposite page]
• **No Death**	**(chapter 21:4)***	
• **No Sorrow**	**(chapter 21:4)***	No 'grieving' – connects with *"death"*.
• **No Crying**	**(chapter 21:4)***	No 'crying out' – not necessarily 'weeping'.
• **No Pain**	**(chapter 21:4)***	Includes 'intense longing'.
• **No Temple**	**(chapter 21:22)**	For *"God and the Lamb are the Temple"*.
• **No Sun**	**(chapter 21:23)**	For *"the Lamb is the light …"*.
• **No Moon**	**(chapter 21:23)**	
• **No Night**	**(chapter 21:25)**	Permanent Light of glory.
• **No Sickness**	**(chapter 22:2)**	Healing, *'therapeía'* and health available for all.
• **No Curse**	**(chapter 22:3)**	The 'Fall of man' reversed in every detail.
• **No Lamps**	**(chapter 22:5)**	No artificial light ever needed.

A 'day' which will never end, and a *"Son"* which will never set, *"Jehovah God giveth them light"* (Revelation chapter 22 verse 5 NRB).

The Alpha & The Omega Again

Two of the wonderful 'theme words' of the book of Revelation, and the theme of our Chart and Book as well. Angels have spoken often, elders have spoken, *"living creatures"* have spoken, choirs have sung. Even John has spoken too. But as we move towards the close of the book, God Himself and *"Jesus"*, who is the *"Lamb"*, will speak more often and directly to John, and to us as well!

> *'He that sat upon the throne said*
> *Behold, I make all things new*
> *He said unto me, Write these words*
> *For they are faithful and true,*
> *And it is done …*
> *He is the Alpha and Omega*
> *The Beginning and the End*
> *The Son of God, King of King*
> *Lord of Lords, He's Everything …'*

[*W. J. Gaither (1936 -) Alexandria, IN.*]

Here is an interesting statement, *"I will give unto him that is athirst of the fountain of the water of life gratuitously."* (Revelation chapter 21 verse 6 NRB). Perhaps someone is saying, 'This sounds very like a gospel invitation'?' 'Yes, because it is.' The visions are nearing an end. We cannot NOT be affected if we have read the book of Revelation, thoughtfully, as far as this point. There is but one chapter – two scenes – remaining. And, if we are not certain about the context of the *"free gift"* offer here, there is no doubt at the very end of the book, when the *"I Am the Alpha and the Omega"* statement will be repeated by Jesus Himself for the last time. And the offer of the *"water of life as*

> *****KEYNOTE: 'No tears etc.'** Are the *"tears, sorrow, crying and pain"* not done away with in the Kingdom Age? 'No.' Many dear believers have gotten confused between the conditions of the 'Millennial Kingdom' and the conditions of the 'Eternal State'. Though Jesus Christ will reign forever, the conditions of the 1,000 year Kingdom are not the same as the eternal conditions. Sin, rebellion, and capital punishment will be present in the Kingdom Age, as we have seen. It is probable that the 'mourning' and 'grieving' relate to 'death' for there will be no sickness. But sin cannot be present in the Eternal Kingdom, and so mourning and tears are gone forever. The word for *"tear"* (Rev. 21:4) is not a plural. How tender. God Himself wipes away *'each last tear'*.

a free gift" can only be a final call from Jesus Himself in the gospel. God alone knows the time of opportunity that remains. It is good to be sure of sins forgiven, and 'heaven as home'. For the two destinies are forever, and there is no alteration of status nor position on the other side!

Why the 'Second Death' Insertion?

Another good question. And one which we need to answer carefully. For it seems to 'jar' on the senses, after the beautiful description of all that will be absent on the *"new earth"*. We have enjoyed the thought of: *"no death, no tears, no mourning, no pain ..."* Now this: *"But as for the cowardly, the faithless, the detestable, as for murderers, the sexually immoral, sorcerers, idolaters, and all liars, their portion will be in the lake that burns with fire ... which is the second death."* (Revelation chapter 21 verse 8 ESV). The 'juxta-positioning' of this statement against all that has gone before shakes our comfort zone. And well it might. For God is telling us here that first on the list of those who miss heaven – and the new earth – forever, are *"the fearful"* (KJV).

The other possible reason for the *"second death"* verse being introduced into the narrative may be to make a clear distinction between the two parts of the chapter on either side: We have suggested in our breakdown of the final sections that one paragraph closes at the end of chapter 21 verse 7. And a new paragraph commences at chapter 21 verse 9. Thus, making chapter 21 and verse 8 a marker between the two sections. S. W. Jennings says, 'If the suggested division is correct, then only these verses (chapter 21 verses 1-8) speak of the eternal state in the book of Revelation. Seven as touching the saved, and one (verse 8) as concerning the unsaved ... Why so little information about the endless condition of the saved? ... It would seem as if God were to say, "Wait and see".'

[S. W. Jennings, *'Alpha and Omega'* (Belfast, NI: Ambassador Productions Ltd., 1996), 308.]

Too Fearful of What?

Friends, peers, associates, partners? Fearful of rejection on the corridors of society? Fearful of refusing to take the *"mark"* or bow before the *"Image"*? Not fearful enough of rejection by Jesus to the caverns of the lost? We can only appeal, by the Spirit of grace, to all our readers. Jesus says today, *"Come unto Me!"* (Matthew chapter 11 verse 28). In that day, He will say, to the *"fearful and unbelieving, 'Depart from Me!'"* It is of eternal importance to be sure of salvation.

Is the New Jerusalem the Old Jerusalem Restored?

This is quite a strange question, but it has been asked before so is deserving of an answer. Which is, 'No. It is not.' Whether you view the subject 'allegorically' or totally 'literally', it cannot be the Jerusalem of today. That famous (and so often fought over) city in Judea in Israel has a long history. Almost as long as that of Babylon. First referred to as

"*Salem*", the 'city of peace' (Genesis chapter 14 verse 18) in the story of Abram and his meeting with King Melchisedek. Then called, for the first time, "*Jerusalem*", 'founded on peace', in the early days of the Canaan conquest under Joshua (Joshua chapter 10 verse 1). Later referred to as "*Jebus*" during the days of the judges (Judges chapter 19 verse 10). During the early days of the reign of David (when he was king in Hebron), he captured the "*stronghold of Zion: the same is the city of David.*" (2 Samuel chapter 5 verse 7 KJV).

The city was extended later through the purchase by David of the "*threshing floor of Araunah the Jebusite*" (2 Samuel chapter 24 verses 15 – 25), after the "*pestilence*" was stopped there. Which area in turn was donated to his son Solomon to be the site for the first Temple. The early 'citadel' site developed in a north easterly direction, following the escarpment of the Kidron Valley in the time of the latter Kings of Judah (c. 975 BC – 606 BC), before being ransacked and burned by the Babylonian troops (as we saw previously). Restoration to a degree took place under Zerubbabel, Ezra, and Nehemiah (536 BC – 435 BC) of the Temple, and the city walls and gates, which continued until the days of Malachi. The biblical record is then silent, as far as God speaking, during the 'Intertestamental Period' (397 BC – c. 2 AD) until the announcement of the birth of "*John Baptist*", and what is termed the 'annunciation'; the announcement by Gabriel to Mary about the birth of Jesus.

Plan of Modern Jerusalem in the 21ˢᵗ Century

Key to Sectors:

Armenian Quarter = *'City of David'*

Jewish Quarter = *Extensions in the time of Solomon & the Kings.*

Muslim Quarter *(lower)* = *Growth in time of the Herods.*

Temple Mount = *Site of 'Herod's Temple' (c.15 BC – 70 AD)*

Christian Quarter = *Outside of walls of 1ˢᵗ Century City. Possible site of 'Skull Hill' and the 'Garden tomb'.*

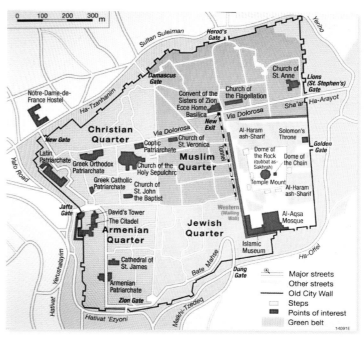

'City of Jerusalem Map', close to 'David's Tower' in the oldest sector (JHF)

Golden Gate = *Jesus' 'Triumphal entry' on a 'colt'. The traditional 'Eastern Gate' through which He will return at His 'Second Coming'.*

Note: *Site of 'Solomon's Temple is uncertain. Possibly close to 'Al-Aqsa' Mosque. Most likely NOT under 'As-Sakhrah' Mosque ('Dome of the Rock').*

> ' *All the cities of Jerusalem in the Bible are literal, including the future "New Jerusalem".'*

But is the Millennial City Different?

Good observation, 'It is very different!' The topography of Mount Moriah, Mount Olivet, the Jordan Valley, the Dead Sea (the lowest water surface on earth, 422 metres or 1,385 feet below sea level) and Jerusalem city itself will all change. The Jordan valley will be <u>elevated</u> and a new 'water course' will flow between Jerusalem, the newly living *"Dead Sea"*, and the Mediterranean. The man in Ezekiel's vision said, *"The waters shall be healed … and everything shall live whither the river cometh … fishers shall stand upon it from En-Gedi … to En-Eglaim."* (Ezekiel chapter 47 verses 1 – 12).

The <u>demography</u> of the Land will be different (as we saw in a previous map of the 'tribal possessions'). And the national <u>territory</u> will be different, and greater, too. But all this answers to the prophesied restoration of earthly Jerusalem. Not a description of the 'heavenly Jerusalem' which must come down *"from God out of heaven"* (Revelation chapter 21 verse 2). The <u>architecture</u> will be different as well, for the reconstructed earthly city will be built according to the 'drawing plans' revealed to Ezekiel (chapters 40 – 47), which fit within the redrawn tribal territories.

'But' someone will ask, 'Is the city of Ezekiel's vision literal?' 'Yes, it is.' All the cities of Jerusalem are literal. Each one as much as the other. Just as 'David's Citadel' was very different to Solomon's City and Temple, and just as the grandiose Palace and Temple of Herod the Great (which he extended the mountain to accommodate) were all different. The Jerusalem of today will become very different when she is constructed to a glory that has not been seen before, not even under Solomon.

'Well then,' you say, 'Is the *"Holy City"* of John's vision the same as the 'new city' of Ezekiel's vision?' That might be logical thinking, but it is not sound interpretation. They are of different origin and with different occupants. One is a rebuilt earthly city for the <u>Nation of Israel</u> to dwell in during the 'Millennial Kingdom'. The other is a brand-new construction, for the '<u>*Bride of the Lamb*</u>' initially. Its origin is heavenly, from whence it comes. And it is not connected to this earth at all.

The Heavenly City is a Different City?

'Which city was Abraham looking for then, the earthly one or the heavenly one if they are different?' That sounds like a hard question, but it isn't really. Abraham – along with all the listed faithful in Hebrews chapter 11 – was looking for a 'forever-city'. Not another temporary one. For even the Jerusalem of Ezekiel's vision is only to be occupied for 1,000 years. 'How do we know that they were not looking for a city on earth?' We are told that in the 'By Faith Catalogue' in Hebrews chapter 11:

a.) They were looking for a permanent city, *"He* (Abraham) *looked for a city which hath foundations, whose artificer* (designer) *and constructor is* God." (Hebrews chapter 11 verse 10 NRB).

b.) They were looking for a *"better country ... an heavenly."* (chapter 11 verse 16 KJV).

c.) They were looking forward to *"a good report through faith"* (chapter 11 verse 39 KJV), which they have already received.

d.) They were looking for the fulfilment of the promise, which they have <u>not</u> received. Not yet (chapter 11 verse 39).

But the 'Holy Jerusalem' is for the 'Bride'?

'Yes. Does that create a problem?' There are two parts to the answer, and they connect to the two 'phases' or 'locations' that the *"New Jerusalem"* will occupy: Firstly, as a dwelling in the '<u>Millennial Kingdom</u>' and, secondly, in the '<u>Eternal State</u>'.

'But the *"Holy City"* isn't a literal city!' someone will say. 'Well, a lot of people have been saying that about a whole lot of John's visions, for a long time, never mind those of Ezekiel, Daniel, and Zechariah as well!' If we have carried the 'literality' of interpretation thus far (and you have all been patient), let's go a little further still. As has often been said, 'Consistency is key'. And that is never truer than in relation to interpreting future events.

The eleven disciples (the early apostles) in the *"upper room"* were promised four specific things:

1.) If Jesus went away, He would prepare a place for them.

2.) He would come back and take them there.

3.) While He was gone, He would send *"the Spirit of truth"* to be His replacement here, *"for He dwells with you and will be in you."* (John chapter 14 verse 17 ESV).

4.) He would be gone for a *"little while"*, they would not see Him, then for a little while they would see Him, *"Ye shall weep ... but the world shall rejoice: and ye shall be sorrowful, but your sorrow shall be turned into joy."* (John chapter 16 verses 16 – 23 KJV).

Therefore, just as we know that Jesus died and rose again, and ascended back to heaven, so, we are also sure that He must come again, and take His *"Bride"* to a place which He has already prepared for her. We would expect both Christ and His Bride to be there forever (once they arrive together). Would we not expect to have something of the beauty of that 'prepared place' to be revealed to us before the end of the Bible record? We would think so!

The 'New Jerusalem' has Two Locations?

'Yes, that is more than possibly correct.' And that answers some of the difficulties raised above. We are going to suggest now – even if all do not agree – that the *"Holy City"* has a role both in the 'Millennial Kingdom' and in the 'Eternal State'. This is a point where many students and commentators agree to differ, even among those who remain convinced that the *"Holy City"* (including its descriptions and dimensions) is totally literal. Quite a few will argue that the city is a part of the *"new earth"* only, and that John saw it in relation only to the *"new heaven and new earth"* part of his visions.

An interesting point (which W. A. Criswell expands on) is that, according to the wording of the text, the *"Holy City"* exists prior to John seeing it. The city comes down, *"from God out of heaven, prepared ..."* (Revelation chapter 21 verse 2). John, though describing the detail later, from top to bottom including the foundations, does not see any construction. It is the 'finished article' when it is being revealed to John. W. A. Criswell, again, has a (minority) view that the city has not only long since existed in heaven, but that it is the dwelling place of the *"Bride"* up there, the saved already in heaven. It is the possible location for the *"marriage of the Lamb"*, then coming down to earth to be the Bride's continued eternal dwelling, in the 'Millennial Kingdom' and in the 'Eternal State'. Though this cannot be proven, it is an interesting thought and perhaps scripture does not argue against it?

[W. A. Criswell, *'Expository Sermons on Revelation'* (Dallas, TX: Criswell Publishing, 1995) 128.]

The City Can Only Come Down On the New Earth!

KEYNOTE: Differ Agreeably ... There are many of the less-fundamental parts of prophecy (even among those who take a literal view) that are disagreed on. No opinion can be dogmatic, in some cases we do not really know, and scriptural evidence (both O.T. and N.T.) is scant. Such is the 'dual location' of the *"Holy City"*. Those who see it as literal but only eternal include; W. Hoste, J. F. Walvoord, R. L. Thomas, J. Allen, and J. MacArthur. Those who see the city as having a 'Millennial function' as well as 'eternal' include; J. N. Darby, W. Kelly, W. Scott, F. A. Tatford, S. W. Jennings, W. A. Criswell, J. Phillips – and the author.

There are those who will counter that the *"Holy City"* only comes down onto the *"new earth"*. Again, neither position can be proven with complete confidence – not until we arrive there – but don't forget, John saw the *"Holy City"* <u>coming down twice</u>. He says so, *"descending out of heaven from God"* twice over (chapter 21 verses 2 & 10). 'But' you might say, 'John writes of the *"new earth"* location first, how would that make sense?'

We should remember something that has appeared often in our studies: John is not 'time-bound' as we are. He has been taken *"in Spirit"* (as is emphasised again here, chapter 21 verse 10) outside of time, and has been already moved both forwards and backwards. Remember also that it was a 'bowl angel' who shewed him the visions of the 'Two Babylons' (chapter 17 verse 1). Here (in verse 9) it is also a 'bowl angel' who shows him *"the Bride"* and *"the Holy Jerusalem"*. S. W. Jennings says, 'It would seem that from chapter 21 verse 9 the angel takes John back to former Millennial scenes. Proof of that can be seen in some of the subjects that appear ...' If we can accept that the second viewing (connecting back to the beginning of the 'Millennial Kingdom', after the end of the 'Bowl Judgments') is <u>first in time</u>, it may make the picture clearer to our thinking.

[S. W. Jennings, *'Alpha and Omega'* (Belfast NI: Ambassador Productions Ltd., 1996), 315.]

The Description is only an Allegory?

That is a common argument, and often heard even today. The simplest rejoinder, on the grounds of faith in an infinite architect (which God undoubtedly is), is: Why cannot everything as described be literal? Coming from the hand of a God who made the universe (which is still astronomically unmeasured). A God who made *"man, dust of the ground"*, to live forever. A God who provided an infinite salvation at incalculable cost: Why can that God not make this city just as John described it? Remember we were told (in Hebrews chapter 11 verse 10 NRB) that Abraham was looking for a city, *"whose artificer and constructor is God"*, and that city cannot be the earthly Jerusalem.

If John saw the city descend twice, assuming (for the moment) that the second 'coming down vision' takes place first in time, chronologically. And assuming that the *"Holy City"* initially is for the *"Bride"*, but that residency may alter, and widen, in the 'Eternal State'. And assuming that the description and dimensions are truly literal; let us work through the 'specification list' that John saw, and that the angel with the 'golden measuring staff' marked off:

The Specification List

1.) Her *"radiance"* (verse 11 NRB). The word is *'phostēr'*, from which comes our English words, 'phosphor' and 'phosphorus'. The 'radiant' light is reflected, as from a *"clear crystal"*, another Greek word *'krustallizō'* which we also recognise in English. The city has a reflected radiance, but the 'light source' is not revealed, just yet …

2.) A *"wall"* with *"twelve gates"*, three on each side (verses 12-13). The gates are *"one pearl"* each (verse 21). Perhaps a link to the single *"pearl of great price"* in the parables of the Kingdom (Matthew chapter 13 verses 45 – 46), a Church symbol. Yet the tribal names of Israel are written, one on each pearl (verse 12). A lovely picture of two groups of believers combined.

3.) There are *"twelve foundations"* beneath the wall, which are probably one *"precious stone"* each (verse 19 NRB). The text appears to convey the meaning of 'one precious stone per foundation', not the idea of stones 'attached' to each 'pillar'. The names of the *"twelve apostles of the Lamb"* are inscribed in the foundation stones. Very fitting, for are not the apostles in the foundation of the Church? (Ephesians chapter 2 verse 20).

4.) The city is square, *"the length is as large as the breadth"* (verse 16), and the *"length and the breadth and the height are equal"* (We will come back to that in a moment). The angel had a *"golden reed"* to measure the city, the gates, and the walls. Interestingly enough, the person who showed Ezekiel the plans for the Millennial City and the Temple also measured with a *"reed"* (Ezekiel chapter 40 verse 5). Perhaps a 'Millennial' link in more ways than one?

5.) The wall is *"144 cubits"* in size. Quite a few scholars who interpret point (4.) as meaning 'cubic' in shape, take this measurement as the <u>thickness</u> of the wall. We are not told here which 'cubit' the angel had marked off on his reed. If we take the 'Ezekiel cubit' (the longer one)** then the wall has a height of 252 feet (77 metres). Neither 'length' or 'height' are mentioned, we should not rule either out. The walls are of *"jasper … clear as crystal"*, but the meaning of *'krustallizō'* has more to do with 'cleanness' rather than 'clearness': Pure walls.

6.) The city is *"pure gold, like unto clear glass"* (verse 18 KJV). Some students have a problem with this description, they say 'gold cannot be as clear as glass'. John is describing what he saw, in first century terms. The word *'hualos'* actually means, 'pure as a translucent stone'. It doesn't mean 'see through' in 21st Century terms. Historically some of the ancient civilizations, who had high quality refining abilities, could make gold exceedingly thin and of a 'mirror like' finish. However, this is a divinely constructed dwelling, so again, we should not limit God's capability.

7.) The city had *"<u>no Temple therein</u>: for the Lord God Almighty and the Lamb are the Temple of it."* (verse 22 KJV). Those who equate the 'earthly Jerusalem' (including Ezekiel's vision) with the *"New Jerusalem"* see a conflict here. But if we agree that this is a city of heavenly origin, and construction, and that there are two future 'Millennial' cities called Jerusalem then the problem disappears.

8.) The city has no *"<u>need of the sun</u>, neither of the moon"* (verse 23 KJV). The glory of God and the Lamb are the light source, and there is *"no night"*, the light is permanent. There is no need to 'shut the gates' for there is no darkness associated with the city internally. The 'city' referred to cannot be the earthly 'Millennial Jerusalem' either. The *"sun"* and *"moon"* have a normal role in the '1,000 year Kingdom'.

9.) Nothing *"<u>unclean will ever enter it</u>, nor anyone who does what is detestable or false, but only those who are written in the Lamb's book of life."* (verse 27 ESV). Again, those who see the *"Holy City"* as being on the *"new earth"* only, have an interpretative problem with this comment. It is often taken to mean, 'everyone that is defiled has gone to the lake of fire, so only pure people are in the city, in eternity.' That, however, is turning a scriptural negative into a positive, and it is not what the verse says. If 'nobody defiled can get in', past the twelve angels guarding the twelve gates (verse 12), then that suggests that there could be those who <u>are</u> unclean, on the <u>outside</u>. A millennial role (prior to an eternal one) answers that problem as well.

10.) The *"<u>nations</u> …*… <u>shall walk by its light</u>, and the kings of the earth shall bring their glory into it … and they shall bring the glory and honour of the nations into it."* (verses 24 & 26 NASB).

Herein lies another problem text. It is possible to divide the inhabitants of the 'Eternal State' up into a.) The Old Testament Jewish saints, the tribulation Jews, and the 12 tribes of the Millennium, making one group of the *"sons of Israel"* (verse 12 NRB). b.) The Church, the *"Bride, the Lamb's wife"*, assuming that they are distinct forever. And, c.) The *"Gentiles"* (which, as J. F. Walvoord points out is how the word '*ethnos*' is often translated rather than 'nations'), who are in reality 'everybody else'. That is both the 'Gentiles' of the Old Testament era, and the saved born during the '1,000 year kingdom'. Though this answers some problems it generates others, and it does not answer the question as to, 'Who are *"the kings"*?' (A word that can be translated as '*Prince*', '*Lord*' or '*King*'.)

Regarding the 'Millennial Kingdom' this is not a difficulty. Jesus Christ must, *"put down all* (singular) *rule, and* (all) *authority and power. For He must reign, till He hath* (conclusively) *put all enemies under His feet. The last enemy that shall be abolished is death."* (1 Corinthians chapter 15 verses 25 – 26 NRB). So, in context, all rule except His own is *"put down"* at the same time as the last enemy also is. Not Satan, but *"death"* itself. This happens at the end of the 1,000 years. This would suggest that even if we allow for 'Gentile nations' in the 'Eternal State', we still have a problem with *"kings"*, if the *"Holy City"* is only in the 'Eternal State'. Again, if we allow the *"Holy Jerusalem"* to have a role in the 'Millennial Kingdom Age', this problem becomes redundant.

> ***KEYNOTE: "them that are saved"**
> JND, RV, NASB, & ESV texts omit this phrase. J. Allen says, 'having very weak manuscript evidence'. Some believe this points to the 'Eternal State' where there are no unsaved. Although national movements to and from Jerusalem in the 'Millennium' cannot be excluded.

What About the Size?

Here is another common argument against the *"Holy Jerusalem"* having a place in the 'Millennium'. The dimensions of the *"new earth"* are unknown, and we can assume it could be on a grander scale than this earth, if God so desires. But a traditional argument has been, 'The city – if the dimensions are actual – won't fit on our planet earth'. In a kind of circular argument, many assume that the dimensions can't be 'real' because they don't 'fit' our own current earth from our point of view. Again, if God is the designer and constructor, no dimensions are a problem to Him, any more than the building materials we have examined.

Let us look at what seem to be problematic dimensions, before we finally decide where we might – on a scriptural basis – put the *"Holy City"* in the 'Millennial Kingdom':

a.) The *"length and the breadth and the height of it are equal"* (verse 16 KJV). Most scholars take this to mean that the city will be a 'cube', and reinforce that argument by referencing the 'Holy of Holies' in the Tabernacle, which was assumed to be cubic in dimension. (There is a technical issue there, as the outside Tabernacle building dimensions tends to have us assume that the *"most holy place"* was equal in length, breadth, and height, by a process of subtraction.) The internal area was never specified by Jehovah. In a sense the 'Holy of Holies' was dimensionless, and continued in a smaller shape while travelling, still internally inaccessible (see Exodus chapter 36 verses 20 – 33).

b.) There is no reason why, as H. A. Ironside suggests, the *"Holy City"* cannot be 'pyramidal' in shape, a square base with the height the same. Those who object say, as H. M. Morris does, 'The pyramidal shape ... seems always to have been associated with paganism, with the pyramid's apex being dedicated to the worship of ... the host of heaven.'* There is a sense in which that is a 'reverse argument'. We do not know the origin of the pyramid shape. It does not have to have begun with a 'ziggurat' at Babel. The Devil – the arch-counterfeiter – may have once again copied a shape that he knew God would ultimately use. A 'sloping city' will simplify some of the detail at the beginning of Revelation chapter 22, the *"throne of the Lamb"* could be at the apex, the *"river of life"* flowing down from the throne, with the *"tree of life"* on each side of the four branches of the river. The original 'River of Eden' also had four branches (Genesis chapter 2 verses 10 – 14). The dimensions are *"12,000 furlongs"* which is equal to a base of 1,380 miles / 2,220 kilometres each side**.

c.) This appears to create a proportion problem with the wall height (252 feet / 77metres) if the city is cubic, which some get round by making it the 'thickness'. But if the city is a sloping pyramid of graduated storeys, then a 250 foot high wall, with 12 access gates is still proportionate.

[*H. M. Morris, 'The Revelation Record' (Tyndale House Publishers, 1983), 450.]

Where Would it Go?

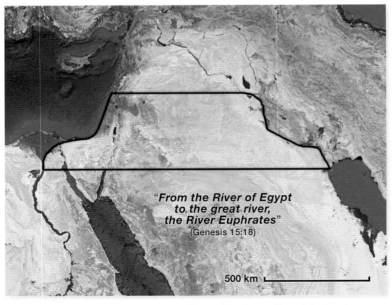

"From the River of Egypt to the great river, the River Euphrates"
(Genesis 15:18)

500 km

Possible national boundaries of Israel in the Millennial Kingdom.

'This city, be it pyramid or cube, won't fit on this earth!' That is an old, and often rehearsed, argument. We are not saying that the *"city"* <u>must</u> fit on earth, but in actual fact it could. The base is equal to 4.9 million square kilometres. A quick calculation (easily done nowadays) tells us that; Russia, China, the U.S.A., Canada, Brazil, and Australia could all accommodate the city inside their present national boundaries. 'But' you say, 'Israel is very tiny by comparison, the *"Holy Jerusalem"* wouldn't come near fitting there!' An accurate observation, even allowing for the possibility of the larger dimensions we looked at earlier, with the Euphrates being the full eastern boundary. If we allow for the Nile Delta across to the Euphrates Delta to be the southern boundary of the 'Kingdom of Messiah', this would be 1,500 kilometres, and Israel's internal territory becomes 450,000 square kilometres. But still nowhere near sufficient to accommodate the *"Holy City"*.

Connected To but Not On …

We said, further back in our study, that there was another option in relation to the city having Millennial connections, but not on this earth. It is possible – and scripture may support the idea – that the city is 'suspended' for the 1,000 years. It is formed as an eternal dwelling, it is heavenly in character, it cannot be contaminated, it 'comes down out of heaven', and the 'saved' of the 'Millennial Kingdom' are blessed by its presence. You might say, 'I agree with the commentators who say this is fanciful. Surely it cannot be a satellite?' Just be patient a little longer (and we don't need to have a mental image of a 'space station' 100 kilometres up). There are highly respected scholars such as H. A. Ironside and C. C. Ryrie who do see a 'floating city' linked with the earthly Jerusalem. There is a relevant picture in the Old Testament, and a prophecy too, and we need to examine them both.

Let's look at the prophecy first: Isaiah said, *"For upon all the glory shall be a covering. And there shall be a tabernacle for a shadow in the daytime from the heat, and for a place of refuge …"* (Isaiah chapter 4 verse 6 NRB). This strange comment is set in the context of a Millennial passage. Much further back, in the time of the Patriarchs, we have the story of Jacob's dream, or 'Jacob's ladder' as it is known (another misnomer), *"And he dreamed, and behold a <u>way cast up</u> on earth, and the top of it reached to the heavens: and behold the angels of God ascending and descending on it."* (Genesis chapter 28 verse 12 NRB). Jesus referenced this scene, angels *"ascending …"* (going up first) in His conversation with Nathaniel, *"Ye shall see heaven open, and the angels of God ascending and descending upon the Son of Man"* (John chapter 1 verses 47 – 51 KJV).

We see here a prophecy of a *"way"* between earth and heaven which angels go up and down on. And the possibility – no more than that – of the *"Holy Jerusalem"* being present over the earth in the 'Millennial Kingdom'. As a 'canopy' or shade over the extended, and elevated, land of Israel. The verses we have already looked at, *"the nations shall walk in the light of it: and the kings of the earth do bring their glory and honour into it … they shall bring the glory and honour of the nations into it. And there shall in no wise enter into it anything that defileth …"* (Revelation chapter 21 verses 23 – 27), in light of this interpretation, do make literal sense. Isaiah in the same context (chapter 4 verse 5) also speaks of, *"A cloud and smoke by day, and the shining of a flaming fire by night"*. If this is literal, and millennial in fulfilment, it would be associated with the "Holy Jerusalem", and visible continually. Possibly answering – in 'anti-type' – to the pillar of fire and cloud linked with the wilderness journeyings of Israel, and the *"Shekinah"* presence.

‘
John saw the "Holy City", "New Jerusalem" descend twice out of heaven.'

The City is Not Eternal After All?

'But that is just the point!' The *"Holy City"* is eternal in its <u>existence</u>! Once it has been prepared in heaven (and it already has), it will be <u>unchanged</u> and <u>unaltered</u> forever. If it is present – as the continued dwelling place of the *"Bride, the Lamb's wife"* – through the 'Millennial Kingdom' and into the 'Eternal State', it cannot be contaminated in any way. No sin can enter. No sun is needed, for the *"Lamb is the light"*. No darkness will ever come. Perfect continuity. Perfect companionship. The heavenly city is a <u>foretaste</u> of our eternity, bearing eternal character. Even while visible to other 'earth-dwellers' in the 'Millennial Kingdom'.

Do you recall, many studies ago, we asked a question about the whereabouts of the saints during the 'Great White Throne Judgment'? (Which is referred to here between the two accounts of the *"New Jerusalem"* coming down.) Here is another wonderful possibility; the city may be the 'dwelling place' for the saints, which will carry them from the conclusion of the earthly kingdom (before this earth is dissolved), and land them safely on the *"new earth"*, to be there forever.

Can You See the Foundations?

One last comment before we close the topic. John saw, as we have said, the *"Holy City"* descend twice. We would contend that he did because it <u>does</u> descend twice. Once over the earth, and once on the new earth, in order of time. There are several differences in the two descriptive passages. S. W. Jennings lists at least eight. You may decide which viewpoint you prefer, and study them up for yourself.

[S. W. Jennings, *'Alpha and Omega'* (Belfast, NI: Ambassador Productions Ltd., 1996), 316.]

Consider this point last of all, as we leave this wondrous double vision: When John saw the *"New Jerusalem"* coming down on the *"new heaven and new earth"* (Revelation chapter 21 verses 1 – 2), no mention is made of foundations. The 'eternal city' is grounded and founded forever. But when John sees the *"Holy Jerusalem"* coming down – in the context of the Millennial Kingdom – the foundations are on view, visible and describable. How could that be? They are not the kind of 'cement and reinforcing' that go into foundations in our world, never to be viewed once the building is erected, but they are *"every precious stone"*. Perhaps the description here is very literal indeed? The *"foundations"* are intended to be on display as a thing of beauty, from an earthly perspective, for all of the 1,000 years. Made by a Divine *"constructor"*, even the foundations visible to be viewed and admired, along with the majesty of the walled city itself, until she – both *"City"* and *"Bride"* – reach their eternal destination. Forever.

Literal, the city MUST be. 'Allegorical' only, it CANNOT be. Prepared already, it HAS TO BE. Contaminated, it can NEVER BE. Eternal, it WILL BE. Praise God for That!

Perhaps the only question truly unanswered is, 'Where and when will we see it first?' It will not be long until we know for sure …

Q&A >

**KEYNOTE: Biblical Dimensions: Some of the biblical measurements are quite obscure, but they are also most interesting. What is known as 'Imperial Measurement', an early form of which is found in the Bible, is based on the human body:

No other '*ruler*' was needed. The 'rule of thumb' was literally that; the breadth of a male thumb pressed down, equal to 1 inch. A 'foot' was the length of a foot, likewise. A 'cubit' was 18 inches, the distance from elbow to the fingertip. The 'long cubit' (as referenced in Ezek. 40:5) was elbow to fingertip + a 'handbreadth' (not splayed, just across the knuckles), reckoned as 21 inches, but able to be measured off rapidly by alternating left arm with right hand. (Try that out!) A 'span' was the hand splayed, top of thumb to small finger, and reckoned at 9 inches (which was ½ of a 'short cubit').

The "*furlong*" (in Rev 21:16 KJV) and in some other versions is a mistranslation (and also the wrong measure, 660 feet). The word is, '*stádion*' in singular, and '*stádia*' in plural (where our English word 'stadium' comes from). The length referred to is 600 feet / 182.8 metres, the length of the straight running track in the Greek stadium, from one end to the other end.

Holy City Dimensions:

The "*length*" (of the city) = 12,000 '*stádion*' x 600 feet = 7.2 million feet ÷ 5,280 (feet in 1 mile) = 1,364 miles / 2,220 kilometres.

The "*height*" (of the walls) = 144 cubits x 21 inches (assuming the 'Ezekiel long cubit') = 3,024 inches ÷ 12 = 252 feet / 76.8 metres.

Questions and Answers for Chapter Twenty-Three – 'The New Jerusalem'

Chp. 23 – 'The New Jerusalem'

Q1. How many 'new things' are mentioned at the start of Rev. Chp. 21 ?

Q2. Can you name them in order ?

Q3. Is the "New Jerusalem" a real City ?

Q4. Is it the same place as Jerusalem today ?

Q5. Are the dimensions symbolic, or literal ?

Q6. What shape is the "Holy City" ?

Q7. What size is the City ?

Q8. Would it fit on our world ?

Q9. Does it have to 'sit' on our world ?

Q10. Where will it rest finally ?

PART FOUR

THE NEARNESS OF COMING EVENTS

Chapter Twenty-Four
Jesus Coming Quickly

There is no longer anything new left to be shown. John has been given a glimpse into eternity, both for the saved and the lost. Not that there is nothing new left to see, or hear, or know. But all that God desires us to know down here about the 'hereafter' has been drawn to a climax and shown in vision form to the last surviving Apostle in what is the closing book of the 'canon', the complete written Word of God. John is now moving into the very last scene of all the *"Revelation"* visions of *"Jesus Christ"*.

We left John in our last study – as far as the chronology of the book of Revelation is concerned – at the beginning of the 'Kingdom Age'. It is possible that John has not only been moved back to see the *"Holy Jerusalem"* come down for the first time, but that he is also being moved back through the whole of the 'time spectrum' that he has travelled across in his visions. He does not appear to move forward again in these last paragraphs of the book. If anything, he is moving backward further still, to the position where he was at the very beginning (in Revelation chapters 1 – 3): On Patmos Island, in isolation, but anticipating the coming of the Lord Jesus ...

We concluded our previous study at Revelation chapter 22 verse 5. The following verse is a 'link sentence', spoken by the angel, referring back to what has gone before, and linking forward to what is still to be told, *"These words are faithful and true: Jehovah God of the holy prophets sent His angel to shew unto His servants things which must shortly be done."* (chapter 22 verse 6 NRB). It is also – and this is significant – a link sentence back to the very beginning of the book, *"The revelation of Jesus Christ, which God gave unto Him, to shew unto His servants things which must shortly come to pass; and He sent and made it known by signs, through His angel unto His servant* John ..." (chapter 1 verse 1 NRB).

Back to the Future

The very wording of the introductory sentence to the final paragraph indicates a 'time-shift' movement for John back to where he started chronologically. John is overwhelmed by this the latest of his visions. *"I, John, am the one who heard and saw these things. And when I heard and saw them, I fell down to worship at the feet of the angel who showed them to me, but he said to me, 'You must not do that! I am a fellowservant with you ... worship* God.'" (Revelation chapter 22 verse 8 – 9 ESV). Here again, in John's error in falling in homage to an angel, we have an echo – not of his prostration at the beginning, for there he was aware of the identity of the glorified Jesus Christ – but of his same mistake in worshipping the angel who shewed him the events surrounding the *"marriage supper of the Lamb"* (chapter 19 verse 10). This is, perhaps, a further link back to the pre-millennial part of his visions as well.

If all these 'pointers' indicate that John's 'vision clock' is unwinding, and he is being transported back to where he commenced (in Revelation chapter 1), then it seems obvious that these closing verses are set, not in the 'Tribulation Period', not in the 'Kingdom Age', not in the 'Eternal State', but in the 'here and now'. At the end of the first century (for John), but also the beginning of the twenty first century (for us)! We are in the same divine time-period as John was. We, the readers, and hearers, of his writings are in the 'Church Age', also anticipating the coming of Jesus Christ as we shall discover as we progress in this study. Just over 1,900 years have come and gone since the last of the Apostles went back to heaven – for the second time – but we are also waiting for the promise of Jesus to be fulfilled, *"If I go … I will come again, and receive you unto Myself"* (John chapter 14 verse 3 KJV). As the early Christians are reputed to have said when taking leave of one another, 'Perhaps today!'

Seven Last Sayings of Jesus

In these last 15 closing verses, John is no longer focused on what he sees. He is attuned to the voice of Jesus, and he is recording what he hears. The narrator may be an angel, but the key statements – all identifiable as to their source – come from the lips of Jesus Christ Himself. And include the last two of the 'seven blessings' which are spread throughout the book (from chapter 1 verse 3 to chapter 22 verse 14).

Let us look, in turn, at each of the occasions when Jesus speaks to John – and to us – in these closing few verses. Though it is difficult, at first glance, to distinguish between the words of the narrator-angel, the commentary of John, and the sayings of Jesus, we will see on closer examination that each time the Lord Jesus speaks, He refers to Himself by a 'first person pronoun'. This is never inappropriate, for it is a Divine person who is speaking, and there is no higher plane to direct our eye or ear to than to Him.

It should not surprise us that, just as there are 'seven blessings' (as well as '7 years', '7 seals', '7 trumpets', '7 bowls'

> **KEYNOTE: Read It!** There are seven blessings to be found in the book of Revelation, all for God's people while still on earth (in different ages). The first blessing is for reading (aloud) and for hearing *"the words of prophecy"* (Rev. 1:3). The last two are for those who *"keep"* and *"do His commandments"* (Rev. 22:7 & 14). Here is progression! Reading – hearing – keeping – doing. How needful to have a 'reality check' on our practical Christianity today.

> **KEYNOTE: Seven and Counting …** A great exercise is to mark, and follow, every 7 that is found in the book of Revelation. No scholar has a definitive number, for every time you read, another 7 will be found. Walter Scott said that he had found more than 250 sevens, but that was not exhaustive.

and so on …) here there are the last, the 'seven sayings of Jesus'. The number seven is probably the most significant KEY number in the whole book of Revelation. Some 'sevens' are clustered together, and some are spread across a number of paragraphs, and some – like the blessings – are spread throughout the book.

The First Saying: *'I Come Swiftly … Keep the Words of prophecy.'*

"Behold I come quickly: blessed is he that keepeth the Words of the prophecy of this book." (Revelation chapter 22 verse 7 NRB). A great deal of confusion, even date setting, and then subsequent disappointment has come from a misconception, and by times a mistranslation, of the word *'tachu'* which means 'without delay'. It does not really mean *"soon"* (as translated by the ESV and NIV), and perhaps an even better translation than *"quickly"* is *"swiftly"* (J. B. Phillips and Wycliffe Modern English). We might sing, *'Jesus is coming soon …'* but once again, we should be careful not to base our eschatology on our hymnology!

We should be very clear that the coming of Jesus – for His Church – is locked into the 'timetable of heaven', under the control of His Father, only fractions of which have been revealed to us. Jesus said, *"It is not for you to know times or seasons, which the Father put in His own authority."* (Acts chapter 1 verse 7 NRB). As we will see in our following (and concluding) Chapters, the 'Second Coming of Jesus' is one prolonged event, with a number of key connected stages. Even if, for the Church, the 'rapture' is the next 'waypoint' on God's programme after the Church was born (in Acts chapter 2) over 1,900 years ago, we should remember the 'rapture' is tied into other key events in God's programme which must follow through, without interruption, such as the 'Judgment Seat of Christ', the 'Marriage of the Lamb' and others. But the 'rapture' event – as we have seen – is not set out in scripture as the 'trigger-point' for the 'Judgment Programme'.

The 'rapture', however, cannot be disconnected from the rest of God's final programme, nor – as we have stated previously – considered as a separate 'Second Coming' preceding a 'Third Coming'. This is not a correct way of looking at the doctrine of 'End Time Events'.

At Any Moment …

'But', you say, 'we have been taught that Jesus could come at any moment. Is that wrong?' 'No. It is not wrong.' He could, and He might come today. But we must proceed with caution. Let us illustrate from the perspective of John himself: The early disciples understood very well the meaning of living in the 'expectation' of Jesus coming back. They knew He must return – however short or long the 'Church Age' was – before the *"wrath"* commenced. Before the *"day of the Lord"* began. Before the *"Man of Sin"* was revealed, before the *"Lawless one"* became active …

They did not know, however, how many of the 'signs' of the 'Olivet Discourse' (Matthew chapters 24 & 25) would begin to be fulfilled while the Church was still on earth, the *"wars and rumours …*", the *"famines, and pestilences, and earthquakes …"*. The affliction, hatred, betraying and killing. They did not know how long, and to what degree, the Church must suffer before Jesus would return to keep His promise. We should not really attempt to 'fit' the rapture of the Church into prophetic statements that largely concern the future of Israel and the nations.

His Coming is 'Imminent'

This is not a scriptural term, but it used often by those who believe in a 'pretribulation' rapture of the Church as the next event on God's calendar. The reason why the word *'imminence'* ('something that could be just about to happen') is used in relation to the removal of the Church is that the 'rapture' is a 'sign-less' event. (Not necessarily a silent event. We have no scripture to prove that. Nor an invisible event either.) No Old Testament or New Testament *"signs"* or prophecies need to be fulfilled, or connected directly, with the sending of Jesus Christ to the air to remove His Bride from earth. In that sense it could – the removal of the Church – happen 'at any moment', and without any warning.

KEYNOTE: Persecution. We should not be *"soon shaken"* in our faith (2 Thess. 2:2), even if loss of liberty, or even outright persecution for identification with Jesus Christ were to come our way before He calls us home. What is very real – a daily way of life for many believers in many other lands – could come the way of 'western Christianity' all too soon. Before the 'rapture' event takes all the saved away.

We have become so comfortable in so many parts of our world that we have almost forgotten the bloody history of the Church. Tertullian (160 – 225 AD) said, *'The blood of the martyrs is the seed of the Church'*. Perhaps we should consider that, except for the divinely granted spur of persecution, – in whatever form – the true Church which is the Body of Christ may grow larger numerically, but weaker spiritually. And more *'Laodicean'* in character, the church of which Jesus said was, *"neither cold nor hot … So then because thou art … neither cold nor hot, I am about to spew thee out of My mouth."* (Revelation chapter 3 verses 15 – 16 NRB). Our church testimony should be that of the *"open door"* of Philadelphia, not the 'closed door' of Laodicea, as we look for His return …

Don't Seal the Words of Prophecy

Here we see an interesting contrast, which underlines the points made above. Daniel, when receiving his prophecies, was told: *"Shut up the words, and seal the book, to the time of the end …"* (Daniel chapter 12 verse 4 NRB). 'Why the difference?' you might ask. Because the 'period' Daniel was living in had to end, and the 'Church Period' (which he knew nothing of) must also begin and conclude, before the *"time of the end"* would commence. Not so for John. He is – as we have already seen – within the 'Church Age' and no prophecy given needs to be *"sealed up"* before the events anticipated in these verses will happen. They could commence at any moment …

The angel relays to John four key 'imperatives' (commands associated with immediate action) from heaven, and the reason why the commands are being issued (which is also an imperative): *"Seal not* (an imperative) *the words of the prophecy of this book: for the time* ('*kairos*' the season) *is nigh."* (chapter 22 verse 10 NRB). J. Allen says, 'This is the season when God will bring all things to completion, and it is described as 'near' ... the prophecies given to him (John) were imminent in the sense that no major event had to take place before they could be fulfilled. From the prophetic standpoint the towering peaks of 'End Time' events cast their shadows (back) across the ages.'
[J. Allen, '*Revelation*', *What the Bible Teaches* (Kilmarnock, Scotland: John Ritchie Ltd., 1997), 535.]

The four 'imperatives' conveyed to John, and to us, indicate that so *"swift"* will be the coming of Jesus Christ to remove all true believers that no time will be available for anyone to make a change. The strange thought (held onto by some) that, 'there will be time to be saved at the rapture', is totally denied by the wording, and grammar, of this group of statements (chapter 22 verse 11):

He that is:	**Let him be:** (continue as found ...)
1.) *"He that is unjust* (in actions before God)"	*"Let him be, unjust still."*
2.) *"He which is filthy* (unclean before God)"	*"Let him be, filthy still."*
3.) *"He that is righteous* (in actions before God)"	*"Let him be, righteous still."*
4.) *"He that is holy* ('sanctified' before God)"	*"Let him be, holy still."*

Unclean or sanctified. Saved or not. Truly *"born again"* or only an outward pretence? No one will be able to alter the spiritual condition they are found in, at that moment of Jesus' return for His Church (which is what is in view here). S. Gordon says, 'This verse is best understood in the context of the entire chapter where the emphasis is on the (second) advent of Jesus Christ ... men will not have time to change their character or adopt a different lifestyle. John is advocating the 'status quo' for the believer and the non-believer.'
[S. Gordon, '*All Hail the Lamb*' (England UK: Christian Year Publications, 2014), 430.]

The Second Saying: '*I Come Swiftly ... My Reward is With Me.*'

Jesus is coming swiftly, and He will reward His own for their service for Him, immediately after His coming. We have referred already to the three aspects of service examined at the *"Judgment Seat of Christ"* (2 Corinthians chapter 5 verse 10), where we will receive reward for the things *"done in* (our) *body ..."*. Though we are not told exactly when and where the judgment for our service will take place, the passage here would indicate that it will happen immediately after we *"meet the Lord in the air"* (1 Thessalonians chapter 4 verse 17 KJV), for John is told to tell us, that Jesus is bringing *"My hire* (fruit for our toil) *with Me"* (Revelation chapter 22 verse 12 NRB).

'Does everybody get a reward?' someone will ask. The answer is, 'No, some will not.' None who are truly *"born again"* can ever be lost, but wrong motive, wrong activity, wrong teaching ... many things can result in 'fruitlessness' in the lives of Christians. Paul warns us, *"If any's work abide ... he shall receive a reward. If any's work shall be burned* (by the assessing of fire), *he shall suffer loss* (of reward): *but he himself shall be saved; yet so as through* fire." (1 Corinthians chapter 3 verses 12 – 15 NRB). The prospect of a *"well done"* from the lips of our Saviour should be sufficient to spur us to live, not only as He would wish us to, but as we would hope for Him to find us, at the moment of His return. An 'any moment' whose timing we do not know ...

The Third Saying: *'I am Alpha and Omega ...'*

Jesus Himself – not the angel nor John, both of whom also speak alternately in the passage – speaks again: *"I *Am the Alpha and the Omega, beginning and end, the first and the last."* (Revelation chapter 22 verse 13 NRB). The first *"Alpha and Omega"* (chapter 1 verse 8) of the book is linked with the *"Coming in Power"* of Jesus Christ to this earth: *"every eye shall see Him ..."* (chapter 1 verse 7). This last *"Alpha and Omega"* is linked with His coming for those of us who have trusted Him, the future inhabitants of the *"Holy Jerusalem"*, referred to here and which we have been studying in our previous Chapter.

[*Our normal English language does not convey the majesty contained in this title: He is *"The I AM"* – where the *"I"* is emphatic (as we will find it again twice in verse 16) – *"I Am"* is a Divine title and means the one who is 'self-existing': Not only, *"Alpha"* to *"Omega"*, but one who was ever-existing, self-existing, trinity in harmony, manifested creatorially, revealed personally; the *"Jehovah the Saviour"* come in flesh. That through Him we might have the hope of living eternally.]

The last (of the seven) 'benedictions' or *"blessings"* is here too. And the 'thread' of those blessings pronounced by Jesus, by an angel, and sometimes by John, run also from the first chapter to the last. Again, we are reminded of the importance – in light of the swiftness of His return – to listen, to hear, to keep, and to do, the commands of Jesus Christ.

The Fourth Saying: *'I Jesus ... sent Mine angel to testify ...'*

What beauty is in the simplicity, yet divine profundity, of the name by which Joseph, Mary, John, and the other early Galilean disciples knew Him first: *"... call His name Jesus* (meaning 'Jehovah the Saviour'): *for He shall save His people from their sins."* (Matthew chapter 1 verse 21). It is the risen, exalted, soon coming Jesus who is speaking directly to us, *"I Jesus (have) sent Mine angel to testify unto you these*

KEYNOTE: "The Churches". The first time *"churches"* have been mentioned since the end of the first section of the book (Rev. 3:22). This is highly suggestive. Even if we take the *'wife of the Lamb'* (Rev. 19:7) to refer to the Church, it means there is no mention of the Church on earth all the way through the judgment section of the book, until now. Where we are now seen, with John, as being still in the present 'Church Age'. Those scholars who view the '24 elders' as symbolic of the Church in heaven (even if it is not specified), point out that the last mention of the *"elders"* is Rev. 19:4, just before the Church – in her Millennial condition – is seen. Though not a 'proof text', it is also suggestive.

things in the churches." (Revelation chapter 22 verse 16a KJV). The *'have'* is an insertion, to indicate that the commissioning of angels is concluded, in the past. 'But' you will say, 'The angel activity of the Tribulation is still future, is it not?' Good comment, and the answer is, 'Yes, it is.' But what has still to happen – in the Divine programme – has now been revealed to us through John's visions. Not necessarily the *"times"*, but the *"seasons"* as we have seen, and the order and connection of the events and judgments. The 'order of events' in relation to the sending of angels – like all else – has been established from 'Alpha to Omega', and has now been revealed.

Though the primary meaning of the phrase here, *"testify ... in the churches"*, probably refers back to the seven letters to the *"seven churches which are in Asia"* (Revelation chapters 2 – 3), there is little doubt that it can be applied to every local New Testament church today. Jesus is speaking directly to us, and we would do well to examine in detail what He has told us. It is His programme, and it is our future!

Have Sent My Angel

It is worth listing – without much comment – for our meditation, the number and order of angelic messengers who came connected directly with Jesus' first coming. (Not counting Old Testament prophets, some of whom, like Daniel, received information by angels about Messiah's first and second comings.) The New Testament record of angelic revelation reads like this:

Angel Sent To:	Reason For:	Reference:
• Gabriel to Mary – birth of Jesus (at Nazareth)		(Luke 1:26-38)
• Angel to Joseph – marriage to Mary / birth of Jesus		(Matt. 1:20-23)
• Angel to shepherds – birth of Jesus – in Bethlehem		(Luke 2:8-14)
• Angel to Joseph – flee to Egypt – preservation of child		(Matt. 2:13-14)
• Angel to Joseph – return to Israel		(Matt. 2:19-23)
• Angels at the temptation of Jesus – comforting Him		(Matt. 4:11)
• Angel in Gethsemane – strengthening Him		(Luke 22:43-44)
• Angels at the tomb – *"He is not here!"*		(Luke 24:3-7)
• Angels at His ascension. – *"This same Jesus ... shall so come"*		(Acts 1:10-11)

The Fifth Saying: *'I Am ... the Root of David ... the Morning Star.'*

This *"I AM"* is also an emphatic, as we have noted, *"I Am the root and offspring of David, the bright and Morning Star."* (Revelation chapter 22 verse 16b NRB). There are a cluster of divine titles here, all of them linked to the hope of Israel, and one of them also linked to the hope of the Church. And all of them fulfilled in one person, Jesus Christ, the coming one. (Here is another place in Revelation where we come very close to an exact 'quotation' from the Old Testament, much more than an 'allusion'.)

This reference, in what to our eyes is a strange mix of titles, goes back to the prophecy of Isaiah (chapter 11 verses 1 – 2 NRB) and is taken from another Millennial passage, *"And there shall come forth a Rod out of the stem of Jesse, and a Branch shall grow out of His Roots: And the Spirit of Jehovah shall rest upon Him ..."* These titles in Isaiah are also referred to by the *"elder"* who introduces the *"Lion of Judah"* to John, in his throne room vision just after he was taken up to heaven (Revelation chapter 5 verse 5).

We have here a group of at least six connected titles:

1.) The Lion of Judah.

(Which comes originally from Jacob's prophecy in Genesis chapter 49 verses 8 – 12.)

2.) The Rod out of Jesse's Stem.

3.) The Root of David.

4.) The Offspring of David.

5.) The Branch.

6.) The Morning Star.

Rod out of Jesse' Plaque at 'Garden Tomb' 'Jerusalem (JHF)

J. Allen suggests that the *"Root of David"* does not refer to Jesse's family line (back to Abraham), but spiritually, 'the one from whom David sprang', so that as the 'Root of David' He is David's ancestor and then, as the 'Offspring of David' He was David's descendent according to the flesh (Romans chapter 1 verse 3). This paradox could be fulfilled only in one who voluntarily stepped into manhood (Matthew chapter 22 verses 41 – 45).'
[J. Allen, *'Revelation'*, What the Bible Teaches (Kilmarnock, Scotland: John Ritchie Ltd., 1997), 539.]

The *"Morning Star"* (despite what some suggest) is not exclusively a title of Jesus for the Church. It is referenced from the prophecy of Balaam (Numbers chapter 24 verse 17) as part of the hope of Israel, but it is applied by Jesus Himself as a gift to the church in Thyatira (in Revelation chapter 2). It has often been said that the *"Morning Star"* is significant not only for its brightness – as underlined here – but also because it appears, out of the darkness, just before the breaking dawn.

It should be no surprise that the response from us, the saved of the 'Church Age', *"the Spirit and the* Bride" (Revelation chapter 22 verse 17a) is, *"Come"*. We cannot alter the moment, but we should be longing for the return of our Saviour, Jesus Christ. There is a gospel appeal here also – before the window of opportunity closes – *"And let the one who is thirsty come; let the one who wishes take the water of life without cost."* (chapter 22 verse 17b NASB). A 'free offer' to the receiver, but we should never forget the cost to the giver. He who said, while here on earth, *"If any thirst, let him come unto Me, and drink."* (John chapter 7 verse 37 NRB).

The Sixth Saying: *'I testify …'* Don't Alter!

We might call this a 'Prohibition of Alteration'. It was given also to the first biblical writer, in his last and fifth book. Moses was to convey the same warning, *"You shall not add to the Word that I command you, nor take from it"* (Deuteronomy chapter 4 verse 2). The content and the completeness of the Word of God cannot be added to, nor taken away from, and the *"plagues that are written in this book"* are promised as a judgment on those who do. How solemn is that?

> **KEYNOTE: Accuracy of Translation.** Though we do not have any of the 'autographs' (the original writings, which were inspired), and though accidental copy error (of addition and omission) may have crept in over the centuries, yet we should seek out in our studies to get as close to the origins of the biblical text as possible. Note: 'Hard copy' Bibles are still a valuable resource, we know which version and which edition we hold. On electronic media 'alterations' can occur without our knowledge. Many 'latest editions' of 'modern versions' are quite different to the 'first editions' of 30 or 40 years ago.

The Seventh Saying: *'Surely I come quickly.'*

Our English word 'surely' does not really convey the weight of what is coming in these last few lines of text! The small word *'nai'* is defined in Strong's Lexicon as 'a primary particle of strong affirmation'. Some translations have, *"Yes, I am coming …"* but that is weak. We might put, *"Assuredly, truly, undeniably …"*. What is it that carries so much weight? We are back to where we commenced in our Chapter, the 'swiftness' of the coming of Jesus Christ: It is He Himself who repeats for the third time in one paragraph, *"I come quickly"*.

The Right Response

What do we say in return? Those of us who are saved, and living in the expectation of Jesus' return? We might read this small group of short sentences too hurriedly and mistakenly think that the *"Amen"* comes at the close of the statement of Jesus. It does not. His affirmation is the *"Surely"* which comes at the beginning. Here it is our 'expectation' even more than our 'affirmation' that is expressed in one single, *"Amen."*

How often do we use it and miss its weight? When Jesus spoke His 'Amen' at the beginning of His statements, *"Verily, verily …"* (for it is the same word in John's gospel), it means 'It must be so …' When we utter it silently, or verbally after the prayers of others – as we ought – we mean, 'Let it be so'. May what has been prayed be God's will. And whatever is God's will, 'So be it ...'.

The word '*amēn*' was carried from Hebrew, to Greek, and over to English unchanged. Here we have it – unusually so – at the beginning of our closing response to the closing words of *"the prophecy of this book"*. In response to all that WE have seen and heard, through the eyes, ears, and pen of the apostle John, we say, *"Amen. Even so* (most surely), *come, Lord Jesus."* How could our heart response be anything less?

John closes his writings – and whether he knew it then or not – the whole canon of scripture, with this lovely short benediction, *"The grace of our Lord Jesus Christ be with you all. Amen."* Or, as J. N. Darby puts it in his translation, *"The grace of our Lord Jesus Christ be with all the saints. Amen"*. We should make full application to ourselves, as the saints of the 'Church Period' to whom these closing verses are directly addressed.

And yet ... We should not forget that 'Tribulation saints' – who must live through the worst period of persecution this world has ever known – will turn here for comfort too. If they have no Bibles (which may all be removed and banned by law), passages like these will be burned into their souls, watching – not with us but like us – for His *"Coming in Power"* to the air. Not to 'receive' but to 'relieve' His own.

We too can only repeat, as a lovely refrain, *"Amen. Even so. Come, Lord Jesus."*

> *He is coming, coming for us;*
> *Soon we'll see His light afar,*
> *On the dark horizon rising,*
> *As the Bright and Morning Star.*
> *Cheering many a weary watcher,*
> *As the Star whose kindly ray*
> *Heralds the approaching morning*
> *Just before the break of day.*
> *Oh! What joy as night hangs round us,*
> *'Tis to think of morning's ray;*
> *Sweet to know He's coming for us,*
> *Just before the break of day ...*

[*Anon. Public Domain. Pub. 1944*]

Questions and Answers for Chapter Twenty-Four – 'Jesus Coming Quickly'

Chp. 24 – 'Jesus Coming Quickly...'

Q1. Is the last part of Chp. 22
   a) After the 'Kingdom Age'?
   b) After the "new heaven"?
   c) Or during 'the Church Age'?

Q2. Who is Jesus speaking to
   in the last paragraph of Rev. Chp. 22?

Q3. How many times does Jesus speak
   in the last part of Chp. 22?

Q4. What does "Alpha" and "Omega" mean?

Q5. How many times were angels seen,
   and heard, at Jesus' first coming?

Q6. Can you list some of them?

Q7. Who is speaking right at the end
   of the book of Revelation?

Q8. Who is replying?

Q9. Who speaks last of all?

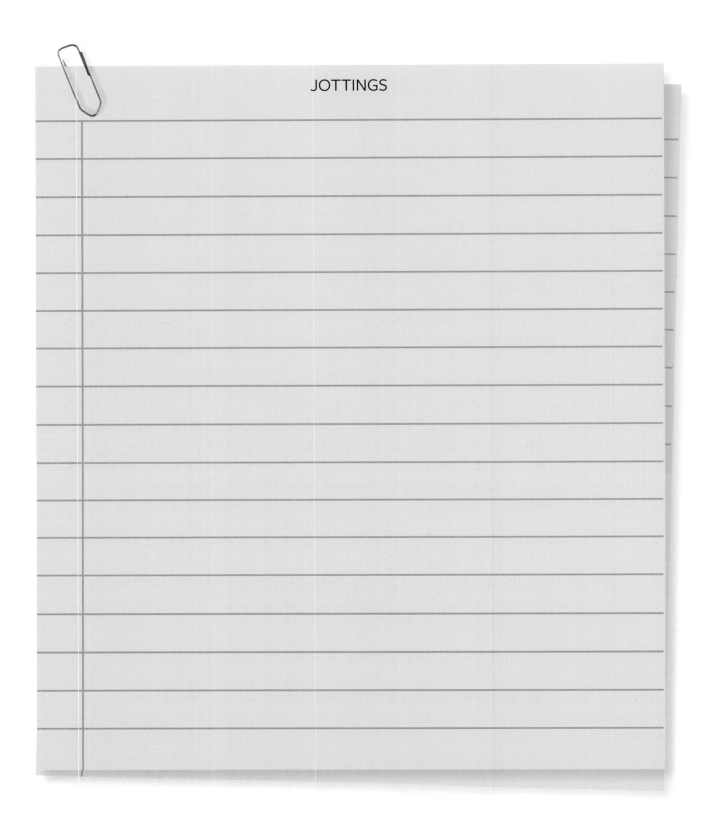

JOTTINGS

Chapter Twenty-Five
Events that Could Happen Soon

'**What's going to happen next?**' An age-old question, quite often asked by someone almost overwhelmed with unexpected events and crises of one kind and another. Or to put it another way, '**What in the world is happening?**' Within the realms of 'eschatology' (the branch of theology dealing with final events and the afterlife), these two questions – even though they appear similar – may have very different answers:

What will Happen Next?

For the Christian, the *"born again"* believer in Jesus Christ, the most significant event that they are expecting is the return of Jesus to the air for His Church (1 Thessalonians chapter 4 verses 13 – 18). As far as the 'End Times' programme is concerned there is no other event that <u>must</u> happen on God's 'timeline' before Jesus is sent from heaven to bring home His *"Bride"* [See **Chapter 6**, '*The Church Removed*']. That is not to say that some very significant events could not take place on earth before the Church is removed. As has been said already, the programme of God for, a.) the Nation of Israel and their Land, and b.) the rest of the nations of this world, *"Gentiles"* as they are sometimes called in the Bible and by Jews, does not directly interlock in prophecies given to us, with what Jesus Christ has planned for His Bride, the Church, at least not until the 'Kingdom Age'.

Attempts to combine both 'programmes' and both subjects of prophecy by means of turning literal prophecy into 'allegory', by reading the Church into the Old Testament prophetically, or by regarding the Old Testament prophecies, promises, and covenants as all having their fulfilment in the 'Church Age', only serves to create a great deal of confusion in scripture, and worse still confusion in the minds of Christians today.

The 'hope' of Israel – not only political but Messianic – is literal and <u>earthly</u>. The 'hope' of the Church is literal and <u>heavenly</u>. Both will be 'coterminous' in the 'Millennial Kingdom' when the *"Jesus"* of the Christian faith will be revealed as the *"Jehovah the Saviour"* of Israel, both one and the same (we, the Church, will only be in heaven initially for a very short time). However, that does not argue for a conflation of the two separate parts of God's programme in the immediate future. One is <u>heavenly</u>, and will become 'earth connected' because Jesus Himself will reign in His '1,000 year Kingdom' with His *"Bride"*. The other is <u>earthly</u>, and will remain so, for they have a land to be restored, tribal possessions to be marked out, a Temple to be built, and a priesthood with *"sacrifices"* and *"feasts"* to be established in the '1,000 year Kingdom' here on this earth.

When we move into the subject of the 'future earthly kingdom' (never mind the 'eternal kingdom') it all seems so far off for so many. Even for some who have an interest in such things. But it is not as far off as it seems. And events on this earth leading up to the 'return of the King' could develop very quickly indeed ...

> **KEYNOTE: Time Frame.** The Church could be gone in a moment. Or not. The *"time"* in God's plan is not revealed to us as to when the Church is removed. When the 'judgment programme' begins, when the *"Lamb"* opens the 'Sealed Scroll' there will be 7 years remaining until the '1,000 year Kingdom' begins. We could be 7 years maximum away from Jesus *"Coming in Power"* and then 1,000 years until the beginning of the 'Eternal State'.

'What in the world is happening?' is a different question altogether, with a focus on the 'here and now' and on events on this earth. Events that could – and may – happen even before Jesus comes for His Church.

[In the final **Chapter**, *'Things that Must Happen'* we will have an overview of all of God's programme, which will include things that CANNOT happen, on earth, until the Church has been removed.]

The 'Clock of Prophecy' has Stopped!

'But', someone is saying, 'I have heard that the 'Clock of Prophecy has stopped'. Is that wrong?' That's a great question and the correct answer is, 'No. Not really.' Which doesn't sound very helpful! The expression *'The Clock of Prophecy has stopped'* has often been quoted, yet it is very difficult to pin down a source for the phrase, and the accuracy of the comment relates to the context in which it is placed. It is most often, and specifically, applied to the '490 year' time-line prophecy of Daniel (in Daniel chapter 9), of which 483 years have been fulfilled – up to 32 AD – and 7 years have still to be fulfilled, linked to the beginning of God's 'judgment programme'. The period between *"Messiah ... cut off"* and the signing of a seven year *"covenant"* between Israel and her allies and enemies (brokered by the 'Coming Prince') is often referred to as the period in which the 'Clock of Prophecy' is stopped.

In a wider context, however, this phrase cannot be applied to ALL prophecy, from Daniel's time to the beginning of the 'seven year covenant' period. Here again we see the difference in what Jesus referred to as *"times"* and *"seasons"*. He told His disciples, just before He went back to heaven, before the Spirit descended (and the Church was born), *"It is not for you to know times ('chronos') or seasons ('kairos'), which the Father put in His own authority."* (Acts chapter 1 verse 7 NRB). There are a.) 'times' and 'seasons' which God has revealed, sometimes very specific times, and b.) 'times' and 'seasons' for which God has not revealed their beginning and ending or duration, and c.) 'seasons' which God has given us a clear time frame for, but not the starting 'time' or date. Even in Daniel's 'timeline', Jehovah set a very clear starting event, which could be counted accurately from, but did not tell – in advance – when that date would be, nor did Daniel himself know.

Messiah Cut Off ...

The 490 year 'time-line' of Daniel did stop, when *"Messiah (was) cut off"*. Though even that is not strictly accurate, as we shall see. And the final 'seven years' of the 490 have still to be fulfilled, the broader 'Tribulation Period' which includes the 42 months of the *"Great Tribulation"*. But did ALL prophecy stop when the 'timeline' of Daniel stopped? That is the big question.

The answer to that is, 'No, prophecy did not stop.' We should clarify the point regarding the 'timeline' stopping at the death of Messiah, because that is not what Daniel prophesied. He said, *"And <u>after</u> the threescore and two weeks* (62 added to the previous 7 = 69 weeks of years*) *shall Messiah be cut off"* (Daniel chapter 9 verse 26 NRB). The end of the 69 weeks has been calculated as the Sunday of the 'Triumphal Entry' by Jesus into Jerusalem riding on the colt (Matthew chapter 21 verses 1 – 10)*. But the actual rejection of Messiah, and His death was *"after ..."* The fact that only 4 days transpired between the 'timeline' stopping, and Messiah's death does not alter the fact – and this is very important – that the death of Messiah is NOT inside the 483 year section of the 'timeline'. It is in the 'gap' between the '69th week' ending, and the '70th week' commencing.

We are going to look now at other prophetic events which have occurred, and could yet occur, inside that 'gap period' which lies within the 'timeline' of Daniel's *"seventy weeks"*.

[*See **Appendix I** *'The Seventy Weeks of Daniel'*.]

The 'Eastern Gate' in the north-east sector of the Temple Court outer wall – Historically accepted by Jews, Christians, and Muslims alike as the Gate through which Jesus entered on what is known as 'Palm Sunday'.

Rebuilt on top of the ruins of the original gate around 500 AD. First walled up by Saladin in 1187 AD, then reopened, walled up again by Sultan Suleiman in 1541 AD. The Muslim cemetery immediately in front was commenced at the same time – believed to be an attempt to stop the re-entry of the prophesied Jewish 'Messiah' across 'polluted' ground – How small are the minds of men in relation to the Coming King. (JHF)

What in the World Has Happened?

Our other question at the opening of the discussion was, 'What in the world is happening?' We noted that the answer to this question could – potentially – be different to, 'What's going to happen next?' which we have looked at. Let us reverse back a little in time and list the prophetic events which <u>have</u> already occurred, since Daniel's 'timeline' stopped:

Prophesied Events – Already fulfilled	**(Listed in order of fulfilment)***
• The death of Messiah -	Foretold by David, Isaiah, Daniel, Simeon, and by Jesus Himself in His public and private ministry.
• The resurrection of Jesus -	Foretold by Himself – in public and private.
• The ascension of Jesus to heaven -	Foretold by Jesus – to His disciples.
• The descent of the Spirit to earth -	Foretold by Jesus – to His disciples.
• The baptism in the Spirit at Pentecost -	Foretold by John Baptist, and Jesus.
• The gospel going to the Gentiles -	Foretold by numerous Old Testament prophets, by Simeon at Jesus' birth, and by Jesus Himself.
• The destruction of the Temple -	Foretold by the latter Old Testament prophets (Solomon's Temple), and of Herod's Temple by Jesus.
• The curse on the Nation -	Foretold by Moses, and Jesus, in the *"fig tree"* picture.
• The final scattering of the Nation -	Foretold by Old Testament prophets, from Moses.
• The re-birth of the Nation -	Foretold by Isaiah, Jeremiah, Ezekiel, and Jesus
• The *"signs"* of Jesus coming -	Connected to the *"end of the age ..."*.

Israel, The Nation Reborn

Let us pause there for a moment, for not all will be in agreement with the last two points: 'Has the *"parable of the fig tree"* been fulfilled?' And some will ask, 'Is the regrowth of the fig tree linked to the 'practical' parable of the fig tree being cursed?' Those are excellent questions, and we need to go over the ground one time more.

> **KEYNOTE: References.** The Bible references for the list of prophecies, and their fulfilment have not been given. All have been referenced more than once in our studies so far. It would be a good exercise to see how many can be listed from memory. Also refer to the *'Subject Index'* **Appx. III**.

Some modern scholars do believe that the 'regathering in unbelief' of Israel (as it is termed), a movement which began in the late 19th Century, and led to the recreation of the State of

Israel in May 1948, is the fulfilling of the 'leaves on the fig tree', illustrating national development, but not spiritual rebirth. Amir Tsarfati (a Christian Israeli Jew) says, 'The fig tree that Jesus spoke of is Israel ... In the Bible, the nation of Israel is likened to three different plants; the vine, the olive tree, and the fig tree. The vine is the symbol of Israel's spiritual privileges (Psalm 80:8) ... The same is true with the olive tree (Hosea 14:5-6) ... a symbol of Israel's religious privileges.'

> **KEYNOTE: Israel Today.** One of the earliest events in the modern history of Israel's national restoration was the 'Balfour Declaration' (of 2nd November 1917). The British Foreign Secretary wrote to Sir James Rothschild stating that 'His Majesty's Government' would support a national home for the Jews. Only five weeks later (9th December 1917) General Edmund Allenby captured Jerusalem from the Turks, without a shot being fired. On 14th March 1948 at 4pm., the State of Israel was declared established, with David Ben Gurion as the first Prime Minister. After 1,870 years of nothingness, the first regathering of Israel had begun. The modern history of Israel reads like O.T. history. There is no doubt that, though mostly in unbelief, the Nation is being preserved by Jehovah.

[A. Tsarfati *'The Day Approaching'* (Eugene, ON: Harvest House Publishers, 2020), 33-37.]

The present growth of Israel as a Nation is 'physical' – the dry bones of the valley have been brought together (Ezekiel chapter 37 verses 7 – 9) – but the *"second time"* of regathering (Isaiah chapter 11 verses 11 – 12) will be spiritual, when the breath of the Spirit of God must regenerate them again. That is still future, at the end of the *"Great Tribulation"* as we have already seen. David Dunlap says, 'Israel is first restored physically ... the (second) spiritual regeneration will not take place until Messiah returns. The process of physical re-gathering to the land has already begun ... The only reasonable conclusion is that the first international re-gathering must be ... in preparation for the tribulation (Isaiah chapter 11 verses 11 – 12).'

[D. Dunlap *'The Glory of the Ages'* (Port Colborne, ON: Gospel Folio Press, 2008), 190-191.]

Foreign Office,
November 2nd, 1917.

Dear Lord Rothschild,

I have much pleasure in conveying to you, on behalf of His Majesty's Government, the following declaration of sympathy with Jewish Zionist aspirations which has been submitted to, and approved by, the Cabinet

"His Majesty's Government view with favour the establishment in Palestine of a national home for the Jewish people, and will use their best endeavours to facilitate the achievement of this object, it being clearly understood that nothing shall be done which may prejudice the civil and religious rights of existing non-Jewish communities in Palestine, or the rights and political status enjoyed by Jews in any other country".

I should be grateful if you would bring this declaration to the knowledge of the Zionist Federation.

The 'Balfour Declaration' of 2nd November 1917.

After four wars, and the ongoing *'intifada'* with *'Hamas'* and *'Hezbollah'*, Israel is still there, and progressing beyond expectation. Yet her worst days of trial are still future ... Nevertheless, there are some who do believe that the events of 1948 were part of the *"fig tree"* coming back to life. If that is so, Jesus said, *"This generation shall not pass, till all these things be fulfilled."* (Matthew chapter 24 verse 34). Not the '70 AD' generation, but the generation that sees the fig tree come back to life …

The Signs of His Coming

The 'Signs of His coming' was the concluding point in the list of 'Prophesied Events Already Fulfilled' above. Some consider that the 'Olivet Discourse' (Matthew Chapters 24 – 25) may possibly be a separate, private, teaching session from the 'Temple Discourse' (Mark chapter 13 & Luke chapter 21), though given in the same time period, and with many points in common. If this be the case then the Mark and Luke accounts are warnings to the Nation, whereas the Matthew account is a warning to the 'believing remnant'. We might suggest, for the sake of discussion, that:

a.) The 'signs' of the 'Olivet Discourse' etc., are not the same, in event or time, as the 'Seal Judgments' (of Revelation chapter 6).

b.) The 'rapture of the Church' is not referred to by Jesus in the 'Olivet Discourse' and should not be 'read in' to any of the parable illustrations.

c.) The *"birth pangs"* of Israel may possibly begin before the Church is removed.

d.) Therefore, some of the 'early signs' listed may be seen, and by the Church also, as a warning that the 'End Times' are approaching.

None of the above conflict with scripture – even if not all 'Dispensationalists' agree – and none of them suggest that either, a.) A date can be set for the 'rapture', or b.) That the Church will go through *"The Tribulation"*. Very definitely not, as we have discussed in previous Chapters.

[See **Chapter 6**, *'The Church Removed'* & **Chapter 15**, *'The Mark of the Beast'*.]

KEYNOTE: Context Again. There should be no confusion as to the 'identity' of each group being addressed, even if it is the same 'physical' group of persons in both cases. The context, setting, and language used is very different indeed. Check the 'Jewish' terminology used in the 'Olivet Discourse'. Church saints are not dwellers "in Judea", nor would be concerned with fleeing "on the Sabbath". These are warnings for Jews, and Judean Jews in particular.

When Shall These Things Be?

That was the question of the disciples, a small private group, sitting on the slopes of Olivet, in full view of the Temple and its court which Jesus, just a few moments before, had declared would be pulled down, *"There shall not be left here one stone upon another …"* (Matthew chapter 24 verse 2 KJV). This group of disciples are being addressed – not as the nation – but as representative of the *"remnant"*, whom we read of in Revelation chapter 12.

[See **Chapter 12**, *'The War in Heaven'*.]

Later the same group - partly in the *"upper room"* and partly on the way to *"Gethsemane"* - will be given another discourse, what is known as the 'Upper Room Ministry' (John chapters 13 – 17). There they are not representative of the Jewish believing *"remnant"*, but of the Church, pre-empting its birth by just over 50 days.

What In the World is Happening?

Let us now examine the list of *"signs"* Jesus set out in His 'Olivet Discourse':

1.) False Christs: *"I am the Christ"* (Matthew chapter 24 verse 5 NRB) – Interesting that Jesus said *"many"*, so this does not – initially – refer to *"The Anti-Christ"*. In Mark's account (chapter 13 verse 6 NRB) the quotation is only *"I Am"*, an expression which is used often by charismatic 'healers' today.

2.) Hear of Wars and Rumours: *"... but the end is not yet."* (Matthew chapter 24 verse 6) – The first part of this 'sign' is seldom emphasised, *"hearing of ..."* coupled with *"rumours"* is very 21st Century! The 'world wide web (www)' only came into existence in 1989, 'Google®' in 1998, and 'Facebook®' in 2004. News – whether substantiated or not – goes around the world in an instant. Daniel said, *"Many shall run to and fro, and knowledge shall increase."* Daniel chapter 12 verse 4 ESV).

3.) Nation against Nation: *"kingdom against kingdom"* (Matthew chapter 24 verse 7). The history of national conflict – since 70 AD – is long and varied, but the standout conflicts that were – for the first time – global in scope were the 'First World War' (1914 – 1918), and the 'Second World War' (1939 – 45). It may be true enough to say that 'globalization' as a concept probably began following the end of WW1. *"Kingdom against kingdom"* is a different, 'intra-national' conflict, often termed 'Balkanization' after the repeated Balkan conflicts and minor wars in that area up to 2008.

4.) Famines: (Matthew chapter 24 verse 7) After a period of decrease, *"famine"* has been on the rise globally since 2010. Presently it is estimated 10% of the population of the world are in famine conditions; more than 700 million souls. Famine is exacerbated by 'displacement'. It is also calculated that there are more 'displaced persons' in the world than ever in history, 82.4 million in 2020, just under one in ten of the world population.

5.) Pestilences: (chapter 24 verse 7) The word includes 'plagues', 'pests', and 'disease'. The recent (late 2021) 'world count' for 'SARS-CoV-2' infections (so labelled by W.H.O. 11th Feb. 2020) is above 240 million. The 'Spanish Flu' (H1N1) of 1918-1920 infected 500 million, close to 33% of the population of the world at that date. The increase in 'globalization' has in turn impacted on the spread of disease in the last 120 years. Pest and 'bug' resistance – to methods of eradication – is now becoming common. 'Superbugs' (like M.R.S.A.) are a recent, and – for now – uncontrolled phenomena: 'Signs of the times' indeed.

6.) Earthquakes: *"in divers places"* (chapter 24 verse 7). It is possible that *"earthquakes"* are more widespread, though only records of very large ones exist historically. However, the death toll from earthquakes is increasing, due to urbanisation and overall population growth. The Haiti earthquake of 1770 is recorded as killing 300 persons, the 2010 earthquake, in the same place, killed approximately 250,000.

Jesus said, *"All these are but the beginning of the birth pains."* (chapter 24 verse 8 ESV). The 'birth pains' are usually connected with Israel (Isaiah chapter 66 verse 8; Revelation chapter 12 verse 2). 'She', the Nation, brought forth Messiah the 'promised seed' but her 'labour pains' will follow later. *"Who hath heard such a thing?"* Isaiah said. This keeps the above signs in a Jewish context, yet they will be obvious to the whole world.

7.) False Prophets: *"And many false prophets shall rise, and shall deceive many."* (Matthew chapter 24 verse 11 KJV). How true! We have never seen – nor heard, thanks to multimedia – so many 'prophets', who have also proved to be *"false"*. Recent events have made that very clear. Wrong predictions abound, yet many still would rather listen to a *"false prophet"* than study the scriptures for themselves!

8.) The Abomination of Desolation: *"... stand in the Holy Place."* (chapter 24 verses 15 KJV). We have been here before in our studies, this is the *"midst of the week"*, when he – the *"Prince that shall come"* – shall *"cause sacrifice and oblation to cease."* (Daniel chapter 9 verse 27 NRB). The *"Great Tribulation"* will commence, and the Judean Jews are commanded to *"flee into the mountains"*, again linking with what we saw in Revelation chapter 12.

[See **Chapter 12**, *'The War in Heaven'*.]

9.) False Christs and False Prophets: *"and shall shew great signs and wonders"* (Matthew chapter 24 verses 23 – 26 KJV). Interesting that these are in the plural, yet we know there is <u>the</u> *"False Christ"* and <u>the</u> *"False Prophet"*, who head up the deception on the *"Dragon's"* behalf.

10.) The Sun Darkened: *"the moon shall not give her light ..."* (chapter 24 verse 29 KJV). Spoken of by Jesus as *"after the tribulation ..."*, at its conclusion, setting the background for:

11.) The Sign of the Son of Man: *"in the heaven"* (Matthew chapter 24 verse 30 NRB). We have dealt with this before, and connected it to light returning (after the 'Trumpet Judgments'), also to no darkness at night. It is also linked to the miracle that took place in the days of Joshua, and possibly lasted for seven days ...

12.) The Son of Man Coming: *"on the clouds of heaven with power and great glory."* (chapter 24 verse 30 NRB). This takes us to the scene in Revelation 19, and the defeat of the *"Beast"* and the *"False Prophet"* and *"Satan"*. The visible-to-all, *"Coming in Power"* of the *"Messiah"*, Jesus Christ, the *"King of kings"*.

'
The "signs" ... are progressive and run ... up to the "Second Coming" of Jesus Christ.'

We can see clearly that this list of twelve *"signs"* is progressive and runs into and through the 'Tribulation Period' right up to the manifestation of Jesus Christ at His 'Second Coming'.

Nothing Can Happen Until the Church is Gone!

'But', some will say, 'None of the above signs can apply to Church believers, for nothing can happen until the Church is gone!' We might ask in return, 'But where did you hear that?' Can we find scripture to back that up? We have seen that some – clearly not all – of the above signs are possibly being fulfilled even now. While the Church is still here on earth. And the possibility – underlined often – that the part of the Church that has not known persecution for almost 400 years may be greatly tested before she is 'raptured' home.

There are also other impending events, outside the list of Jesus' signs, but connected with biblical activity that could, and possibly will, also happen before the Church is *"caught up"*.

Let us list and examine a select few of these here:

Things That Could Happen ...

1.) Israel in Their Land: (15th May 1948) – We have noted this already, but prior to 1947 and the U.N. Resolution, certain prophetic scholars believed that the return of the Nation State could only be facilitated by Anti-Christ. The 'End Times' Charts dating from the early 1900s reflected that clearly.

2.) Jerusalem Controlled by the Jews: The 'Six Day War' (from 5th June 1967) saw Israel defeat 5 armies on 3 fronts and more than double the size of the territory they occupied, including East Jerusalem and Temple Mount. Part of this territory was handed back, and is under Jordanian 'WAQF' Islamic supervision at present. This is voluntary, and changing.

3.) Jews Ascending Temple Mount: This huge square (150,000 m² or 37 acres), holding the three Mosques and the four minarets has 11 gates, 10 of which are for Muslims, and 1 for 'other faiths'. For many years it was exceedingly difficult for a Jew to even gain a 'permit' to access the Mount. Now, Jews are being given increasing freedom to 'ascend' and are being encouraged by the 'Temple Institute' to do so. A new daily record was set on *'Tisha B'Av'* (18th July 2021), the anniversary of the 'Day of Destruction' of both the First and Second Temples, when 1,679 Jews ascended Temple Mount. This would have been viewed as impossible a very short time ago.

[cited, *'Israel Hayom'* 07-18-21.]

The 3 Mosques on 'Al Aqsa Compound' as it is known to Muslims – The 'al-Aqsa' Mosque, the 'Dome of the Rock', and the 'Dome of the Chain' – yet with much of the 37 acres still open space. (JHF)

4.) Jewish Worship on Temple Mount: Part of the agreements following the cessation of hostilities after the 1967 War was that the Jewish police would enforce a 'zero policy' on public prayer by 'non-Muslims' including banning the wearing of prayer shawls and 'phylacteries' by Jews. The external foundation wall, or 'Wailing Wall' as it became known, was the only permitted, and controlled, prayer site for Jews until now. Since July 2021 this has also changed, and (as of October 2021) ratified in law. Jews are now being permitted to hold morning prayers, in groups, on Temple Mount. This is a major shift, and was an arrestable offence up until mid 2021. Events are moving very rapidly indeed!

Following a prolonged civil court battle, the Jewish National Anthem, *'HaTikavah'*, can now be sung on Temple Mount. This was also done formally by a group of singers on 'Tisha B'Av', in a position close to the inside of the 'Golden Gate'.

['Israel Hayom' 07-18-21.]

The Western 'Wailing Wall', 'HaKotel HaMa'aravi' to the Jews. Part of the artificial ramparts commissioned by Herod the Great to increase the size of the 'Temple Courtyard' above it. (JHF)

5.) A 'Kosher' Red Heifer: The 'Raise a Red Heifer in Israel Project' has been one of the great objectives of the Temple Institute since 2015, based on the requirements of Numbers chapter 19 for a *"red heifer without spot, wherein is no blemish"* to be *"burned without the camp"* and the ashes to be mingled with flowing *"water of separation"* to create a purifying liquid for washing and sprinkling with *"hyssop"*. Rabbinical tradition has it that from the time when Moses consecrated the Aaronic Priesthood, until the destruction of the 'Second Temple', in 70 AD, only nine heifers have been slain and their ashes preserved.

'Raise a Red Heifer Project' (pic. The Temple Institute)

They are actively seeking now for the 'Tenth Red Heifer'. The breeding programme is well advanced, bull calves are slaughtered, red heifer 'candidate' calves are kept until 36 months, and must have 'not one white hair'. Thus far only two heifers are in the 'qualification process', all others having been discarded. The Rabbis involved firmly believe that *"Jehovah"* (or 'G_d' as they write it), will grant them a 'pure animal' when the time for Messiah is near.

We have considered before the *"blindness in part ..."* of Israel as a nation, yet it is only in *"part"*. Perhaps some of these devout souls, who long for true liberation under a coming *"Messiah"*, will one day soon acknowledge that He has already come, the first time, and that they rejected Him!

6.) A Priesthood Established: *'Kohanim'*, the descendants of the sons of Aaron, are being encouraged to have their ancestral history confirmed, and to present for training as a *'kohen'* for the purposes, not only of synagogue duty, but as fully fledged 'sacrificing' priests. This despite the 'water of purification' (5.) not being ready, but 're-enactments' of certain Jewish Feasts are being carried out (as tourist tableaux) at the Wailing Wall. This conforms to current restrictions, but the sight of a 'Passover Lamb' sacrifice – even as a re-enactment – was, until 2019, an unprecedented sight in Jerusalem.

7.) Sacrifices Re-Commenced: Strange events are taking place in Jerusalem, and very rapidly. It would not be surprising – if consecrated priests were prepared and trained – to see the senior Rabbis give permission for 'token sacrifices' even without a 'Third Temple' or Jewish Court.

8.) A Sanctuary – Holy Place: 'What will this be?' And 'When will it be constructed?' some will ask. Others will confidently affirm, 'The Third Temple can only be built by Anti-Christ!'

Only After the Rapture?

Let us pause here for a moment and regroup in our thoughts. Some will already be reading down the list and thinking, 'Surely most of the above can only happen after the true *"Church"* has gone?'

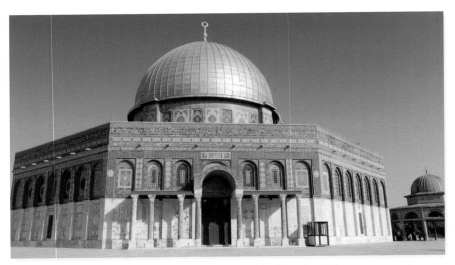

The 'Dome of the Rock' – 'Qubbat As-Sakhrah' – the oldest monument of Islam & The 'Dome of the Chain', the 3rd Mosque. There is more than sufficient room for a 4th 'Shrine'. (JHF)

We would like to be gentle, yet true to conviction, and it is why we began with: (1.) 'Israel in the Land'. Just as prophecy does not specify which *"covenant"* will be the 'Daniel covenant', just as the *"Man of Sin"* will not be identified as such – by the Jews or anyone else – until he 'breaks' the *"covenant"* halfway through its set period.

Just as we are not told specifically when the *"Day of the Lord"* will commence (*"as a thief ..."*), nor whether the opening of the *"First Seal"* marks the beginning of the *"Day of the Lord"*. So, there are events which have often, and for years past, been assumed as 'post-rapture' and 'facilitated by the Anti-Christ' which may indeed not be so ...

If we arrive at '**Point 7**' in the list above, '**Sacrifices Re-Commenced**' – and we are on the verge of '**Points 5** and **6**' being completed – then should we be surprised if a 'Shared Worship Agreement' is soon extended to a token 'Sanctuary' being erected? Prophecy does not require a 'Third Temple' (there is good argument to support the position that 'Ezekiel's Temple' in the 'Millennial Kingdom' will be the 3rd Temple), but only a *"Holy place"*. This could be a secular building which will be 'sanctified' by the 'water of purification' to allow it to function as a 'Holy Sanctuary'. There is no requirement for the *"Shekinah"* presence either, just as there is no record of the divine presence ever being in Herod's Temple, nor the *"Ark of the Covenant"* being there.

KEYNOTE: Sanhedrin Chamber. The plans for a modern 'Hall of Hewn Stone' to house the 71 member Sanhedrin Council (which was re-established in October 2006) were passed in 2012. No site has been agreed, but the historic site (on the S.E. corner of Temple Mount) is vacant. It is possible this structure could be erected, and subsequently 'purified' as a working 'Sanctuary' in a 'shared access agreement' at a time not very far off.

Will The Church go Through the Tribulation?

At this point some will be asking, 'Does all this mean that the Church does go through the *"Tribulation"*?' The answer is, 'No! Absolutely not.' We have discussed the reasons in detail in previous Chapters.

[See **Chapter 6**, '*The Church Removed*' and **Chapter 7**, '*The Symbols Explained*'.]

The *"Church"*, of which the 'upper room' group of disciples were representative, to whom Jesus promised that He would come and *"receive you unto Myself"* (John chapter 14 verse 3 KJV), will

> '*The one coming event that will have the greatest impact on our world, and remove the full restraint on all wickedness ... is the removal of all truly "born again" people ... the "Church", both living and in the grave.*'

be *"delivered"* from *"the wrath which is coming here."* (1 Thessalonians chapter 1 verse 10 NRB). The true *"Church"* will be *"snatched away"* ('raptured'), out of harm's way (1 Thessalonians chapter 4 verse 17), and will be kept from *"the hour of trial which is coming on the whole world, to try those who dwell on the earth."* (Revelation chapter 3 verse 10 ESV).

We have also seen – though not proof texts in themselves – that the references to *"churches"* and *"church"* in the *"things which are"* section of Revelation (chapter 1 verse 19 KJV), across to the references to the *"Bride"* and *"churches"* in the 'Millennial' and closing sections (chapters 19 – 22), do generate a significance – by the 'principle of omission' – of the *"Church"* having zero mention in the chapters between: from Revelation chapter 4 verse 1 through to chapter 19 verse 7.

[See **Chapter 24**, *'Jesus Coming Quickly'*.]

What we have been considering are, 'Events that could happen, while the Church is still here'. It is salutary that – unnoticed by many except 'Israel watchers' – quite a few of these events are falling into place, without being facilitated by the 'Coming Prince', or by a 'seven year covenant' being drawn up between Israel and her neighbours. What will come next, we do not know. Events in our world today, and in the theatre of the 'Middle East', can change exceedingly rapidly, as we have already seen.

The one coming event that will have the greatest impact on our world, and remove the full restraint on all wickedness (so that things will get infinitely worse), is the removal of all truly *"born again"* people – the *"Church"* – that has not taken place. Not yet ...

A man and wife asleep in bed,
She hears a noise and turns her head,
He's gone.
I wish we'd all been ready.

Two men walking up a hill,
One disappears and one's left standing still,
I wish we'd all been ready.

There's no time to change your mind,
How could you have been so blind?
The Son has come and you've been left behind ...

[L. Norman (1947-2008) Salem, ON.]

Q&A >

Questions and Answers for Chapter Twenty-Five – 'Events that Could Happen Soon'

Chp. 25 - 'Events that Could Happen Soon'

Q1. What does the expression mean,
'The clock of prophecy has stopped'?

Q2. What is the difference in "times" and "seasons"?

Q3. Which prophecies can you list, that have been
fulfilled <u>since</u> Jesus' death?

Q4. Are there "signs" of Jesus' 'Second Coming'
being fulfilled now?

Q5. Can you list any?

Q6. What might happen in Israel, while the
Church is still here?

Q7. Can the "Church" go through the
"Great Tribulation"?

Q8. Can you give any scriptural reasons why not?

Chapter Twenty-Six

Events that Must Happen ... Review

We do owe a sincere 'Thank you!' to everyone who has made the journey to this point. It may not have been easy, for if the 'Mountain peaks of prophecy' were difficult even for the Old Testament prophets themselves, it is no disgrace that some of us have struggled in the foothills! Yet there is no more rewarding discipline in the study of the Word of God than to search out Jehovah's revealed purposes and the exaltation of His Son therein, *"For the testimony of Jesus is the spirit of prophecy."* (Revelation chapter 19 verse 10 KJV).

Back to the Beginning

At the very commencement of our studies, we posed three <u>KEY</u> questions:

    1.)   **Why 'End Times for Beginners'?**
    2.)   **Does God have a Programme?**
    3.)   **What is Prophecy?***

We have seen – as suggested often – that in the study of 'eschatology', many of us are 'beginners', we are in God's 'kindergarten' relative to the volume of Old and New Testament material to be studied. We have satisfied our minds that God does have a programme, and the 'working out' of this programme is based on the declared purposes of a God who is 'proactive', rather than 'reactive' to the calamitous failures of His human creation.

Our third question, 'What is Prophecy?' took us back to the Garden of Eden (Genesis chapter 3), the 'Fall of Mankind', the curse pronounced, and the promise given. Then forwards to the first and second comings of Jesus Christ. We have in a very real (though quite superficial) sense, gone from, 'A to Z', from *"Alpha"* to *"Omega"*, and from the book of Genesis through to Revelation, as all who study biblical prophecy must eventually do.

[*See **Chapters 1 – 3**.]

There are those, however, who will have read one or two other 'key' chapters in this 'End Times' Book, and will have arrived here via a 'short cut'. They will be saying, like a famous king in Jerusalem long ago, *"Let us hear the conclusion of the whole matter ..."* (Ecclesiastes

> **KEYNOTE: Summary Sections.** Do read the concluding Section, **Chps. 24** through **Chps. 26**, and, possibly, **Appx. I** *'The Seventy Weeks'* & **Appx. II** *'Amillennialism and other 'isms'.* This gives a better overview of the basis for interpretation, as well as the concluding statements.

chapter 12 verse 13). As we said before in a previous Chapter, 'You are most welcome here!' Perhaps, after you have discovered the 'End Point', you will go back and pick up on some of the 'way points' along the journey?

We have reached the conclusion of the matter, as far as this volume is concerned. But this is no work of 'fiction' even if the musings of 'mere men' are here. What has been written – we trust – is founded on *'sola scriptura'*, the Word of God alone. Therefore, we have not reached 'The End' at all, we have not even reached the 'beginning of the end', for the great majority of the events discussed in this volume [primarily from **Chapter 6** onward] are still future. How wonderful to put a book down, even 'The Book', the Word of God, and say, 'It is not finished yet. The next stage is just about to begin.'

What John Anticipated …

So too it must have been for the Apostle John. Was he disappointed when the light of glory faded? When he found himself descending from his *"great and high mountain"* vista (Revelation chapter 21 verse 10 KJV), back 'in the body' in the discomfort of his continued isolation in his cell in Patmos prison? We do have reason to believe that he was eventually released from confinement (probably about 96 AD) and returned to the fellowship of the assembly in Ephesus, remaining there until he died at over 100 years old. (Other stories of his end are 'apocryphal' and cannot be confirmed.) He must have lived out his last years in an anticipation of the coming of his Lord Jesus like no believer before or since, for no member of the *"Body of Christ"* had a greater grasp of what lies before us than John himself.

On the same occasion that Peter was told he would die for his Lord, *"'When you are old, you will stretch out your hands, and another will dress you and carry you where you do not want to go'. (This He said to show by what kind of death he was to glorify God)."* (John chapter 21 verses 18 – 19 ESV), the Lord Jesus also made a very different prediction concerning John. Jesus said, *"If it is My will that he remain until I come, what is that to you?"* (John chapter 21 verse 22 ESV). Of course, John did not live to see the 'rapture' happen – the first stage of the 'Second Coming of Jesus Christ' – but he did live to see it in vision, with the 'Judgment Period', the 'Kingdom Age', and the 'Eternal State' that would follow.

Perhaps we should consider, as the time of His coming gets closer, that just as John was representative of those who will live to see Jesus return (lifting his spirit above personal hardship), so Peter was representative of those who will willingly lay down their lives in martyrdom for Jesus Christ. We do not really know how well our resolve would be tested, nor how much grace we would receive until we, in God's sovereign will, arrive at either point …

Which Period Are We In?

Before we look at a summary of events that will soon – *"surely"* – happen in God's programme, let us establish clearly where we are right here and now. We need to get back to biblical terminology to find our base. We have previously found that <u>present</u> and <u>future</u> *"times"* on this earth – not counting the 'Eternal State' or the *"Day of God"* as Peter termed it (2 Peter chapter 3 verse 12) – divide into three main '*epochs*' or periods:

1.) The Acceptable <u>Year</u> of the Lord   (Isaiah chapter 61 verse 2; Luke chapter 4 verse 19)

2.) The <u>Day</u> of Vengeance of our God   (Isaiah chapter 61 verse 2; Isaiah chapter 63 verse 4)

3.) The <u>Year</u> of My Redeemed   (Isaiah chapter 63 verse 4)

We have determined that a kind of 'biblical shorthand' lies within the above statements, God is telling us about *"seasons"* or periods of *"time"* but not – at the point of giving the prophecy – specifying exact dates for, or the extent of, the period referred to. Let us set these periods out as well:

a.) A ***"year"*** in prophecy (with no quantity attached) is a <u>lengthy period</u>, but undefined.

b.) A ***"day"*** in prophecy (with no quantity attached) is a <u>shorter period</u>, by comparison.

c.) An ***"hour"*** in prophecy (with no quantity attached) may be longer than '60 minutes', but it is by comparison a <u>relatively shorter</u> prophetic period than the others.

At times – in subsequent prophecy or narrative – we are then allowed to learn the 'time periods' that God had in view when some of the 'undefined' periods were first 'told forth'. The *"hour"* spoken of so often in the Gospels by Jesus looked forward to His trials as is indicated relative to its fulfilment, *"This is your hour, and the authority of darkness."* (Luke chapter 22 verse 53 NRB). So, the *"hour"* of that prophecy becomes a period of slightly more than 12 literal hours; 9pm (when Jesus was arrested) to possibly midday (before the darkness at the cross).

The *"day"* spoken of in the Isaiah prophecies (Isaiah chapters 61 & 63), is shown to fall between the two *"year"* periods mentioned, without any of the three being defined as to, a.) start point, or b.) duration, when foretold by Isaiah (in approximately 700 BC). However, we can define the *"day"* and the second *"year"* periods from later prophecies. And because the *"day of vengeance"* is referred to in <u>both</u> Isaiah passages, we can connect all three (undefined) periods together, right from the start.

The Acceptable Year of the Lord

When Jesus came back to Nazareth, at the commencement of His 'public ministry', He went into the synagogue on the Sabbath, and He *"stood up for to read."* (Watch this narrative unfold carefully.) The gospel record says, *"He ... stood up ..."* This – on a human level – is only an indication that Jesus, Mary's son, was willing to read the portion chosen by the rabbi for the occasion. *"And there was delivered unto Him the book of the prophet Isaiah. And when He had unrolled the book, He found the place where it was written* (and He read) *'... to preach the acceptable year of the Lord.' And He rolled up the book, He gave it again to the attendant, and sat down."* (Luke chapter 4 verses 16 – 21 NRB).

When we go back to Isaiah chapter 61 (where Jesus was reading from) we can see He stopped 'mid-verse'. Not only that, but He did not appear to choose which prophet to read from. The attendant rabbi or Levite did. Yet, at that very point, Jesus went on to say, *"This day is this scripture fulfilled in your ears."* Not only was the *"acceptable year of the Lord"* now 'underway', but the *"day of vengeance ..."* clearly was <u>not</u>. And an undefined period was introduced between the two; a 'divided prophecy' again. When we cross over to Isaiah's other prophecy (in chapter 63) we see that the *"day of vengeance"* is picked up again and elaborated on, after the long prophetic 'gap'. This is now the end of the 'Tribulation Period' and in this prophecy Jesus is trampling on His enemies even as He speaks, yet He also says, *"And the year of My redeemed is come"*.

Dead Sea Scroll – recovered from the Qumran Caves.

When we join all that we have studied together we discover that; a.) We still have not determined a duration for the *"acceptable year of the Lord ..."*. b.) The *"day of vengeance"* will commence after the first *"year"* period closes, and stop immediately before the other *"year"* period starts. Therefore the *"day of vengeance"* can be found in the 'Tribulation Period', during the 'last week' (of the *"70 weeks"* of Daniel chapter 9). The *"year of My redeemed"*, however, does not get defined until we reach Revelation chapter 20, where we are told (six times over) that it is the *"one thousand years"* of the 'Millennial Kingdom'.

'But', someone will ask, 'what about the first period, *"The acceptable year of the Lord"*, how long is that?' That is another good question. We have got a starting

> **KEYNOTE: Dead Sea Scrolls.** The discovery of 981 'fragments' of O.T. manuscripts in sealed jars in caves at 'Qumram' near the Dead Sea (1946-1956) greatly enhanced the knowledge, and translation accuracy of many of the ancient scriptures. A few are lengthy and almost intact, among which are Psalms and Isaiah. The Isaiah scroll, when fully unrolled, is 22 metres long. Yet Jesus opened the Nazareth synagogue scroll, put His finger on one verse, and divided it, prophetically, in two.

point, a *'terminus a quo'* (as scholars might say) for the period in question. It began at the commencement of Jesus' public ministry (dated c. 28 AD). The big question is: 'Do we have an end point, a *'terminus ad quem'*? And if so, 'Does that tie into the *"day of vengeance of our God"*?' Let us hold that question for just a moment ...

What About the 'Church Age'?

Another question which will arise in connection with the above is: 'When did the 'Church Age' commence? Is it the same period as the *"acceptable year of the Lord"*?' The answer to the second question is, 'Strictly speaking, No.' The 'Church Age' and the *"acceptable year of the Lord"* (though they <u>may</u> be coterminous) did <u>not</u> commence at the same time. Jesus introduced *"The acceptable year of the Lord"* at the beginning of His public ministry when He spoke in Nazareth. The period following, when He called His disciples and commissioned them to preach to the *"lost sheep of the house of Israel"* the message that *"The kingdom of heaven hath drawn nigh."* (Matthew chapter 10 verse 7 NRB), was a period of the *"gospel of the kingdom"* being declared (as it still is though with a different emphasis). In the 'Tribulation Period' the gospel of the kingdom will also be told *"in all the habitable world for a witness unto all the nations; and then shall the end come."* (Matthew chapter 24 verse 14 NRB).

'But, what about the beginning of the 'Church Age'?' someone will ask, 'Did it not start at the same time?' The answer to that question is, 'No. It did not.' As we have seen in our studies [**Chapter 5**, *'The Church Period'*], the Church was 'born' at *"Pentecost"*, on the *"Feast of weeks"*, just as Jesus had promised. The *"Holy Spirit"* descended and became *"in"* and *"with"* the early disciples, and they were *"baptised into one body"*, a corporate activity not an individual one (1 Corinthians chapter 12 verse 13). So, the 'Church Period' fits within the *"acceptable year of the Lord"*, but commences some three and half years later.

The 'Church Age' and the *"acceptable year of the Lord"* may – possibly – conclude together, though scripture does not say so. That would depend, to a degree, on whether the *"day of vengeance of our God"* covers the <u>whole</u> of the seven year 'Tribulation Period', or only the second three and a half year *"Great Tribulation"* period (or a period greater than 3.5 years but less than 7 years). If the *"day of vengeance ..."* commences at the *"42 month"* point, then the *"acceptable year of the Lord"* may not conclude until then. This would 'bracket' the 'Church Age' within the longer period, at both ends. We cannot be totally sure either way.

Like the *"day of the Lord"* [which we will come to now], we know exactly when the *"day of vengeance ..."* concludes, but we are not told specifically of its commencement time. It may be that both of these periods – *the "day of the Lord"* and the *"day of vengeance ..."* commence at exactly the same time. They are most definitely <u>not</u> coterminous.

[We will also examine that later.]

When are the 'Last Days'?

Someone will say, 'Are we not in the *"last days"*?' Another good question. Others will say, 'But we have been told we are already in the *"last days"* for generations. How do we know what 'last' really means?' That is also a good question. Let us ask again, 'What does the scripture say?' Some think that the *"last days"* are the <u>end</u> of the 'Church Age'. They will look at events in the world around and say, 'Oh! We are in the last days!' Others will ask, 'How should the Church respond to 'last days' conditions?' The answer to that may surprise some: 'Just as the Church did at the beginning!'

The birth of the Church, at *"Pentecost"*, and the *"signs"* that accompanied it, indicated that the *"last days"* – as far as God's reckoning was concerned – had <u>begun</u>. The prophet Joel (c. 800 BC), who spoke of 'End Times' and the 'Messianic Kingdom', described future conditions as revealed to him: *"And in the last days it shall be, God declares, I will pour out (of*) My Spirit on all flesh, and your sons and daughters shall prophesy, and your young men shall see visions, and your old men shall dream dreams; even on My male servants and My female servants in those days will I pour out (of) My Spirit, and they shall prophesy. And I will show wonders in the heavens above ... blood and fire ... Before the great day of the Lord comes ... everyone who calls upon the name of the Lord shall be saved."* (Acts chapter 2 verses 17 – 21; Joel chapter 2 verses 28 – 32 ESV).

[*NRB adds, *"of"*.]

At first reading – and in context – we might put this passage at the end of the 'Tribulation Period', but again, it is a 'divided prophecy' as we have seen in other places. Peter – by the Holy Spirit – reveals that in his *"Pentecost"* message to the Jews of the dispersion who had come to Jerusalem for the Feast: *"And it shall come to pass in the <u>last days</u>* (here is a Divine New Testament addition), *saith God, I will pour out of My Spirit upon all flesh* (change of order from the Joel prophecy): *and your sons and your daughters shall prophesy ..."* (Acts Chapter 2 verses 17 – 21 NRB). The 'birth of the Church' is thus indicated by God to mark the commencement of the *"last days"*.

'But', someone will ask, 'How can the *"last days"* continue for 2,000 years?' There are two answers to that question: 1.) God doesn't measure time as we do. Peter says, *"With the Lord one day is as a thousand years, and a thousand years as one day."* (2 Peter chapter 3 verse 8 NASB). And, 2.) God is longsuffering. Peter again says, *"The Lord is ... not slow about His promise, as some count slowness, but* (He) *is patient toward you, not wishing for any to perish but for all to come to repentance."* (2 Peter chapter 3 verse 9 NASB).

What Happens Next?

The 'Church Age' cannot continue forever, even with God's patience or *"longsuffering"* as the KJV has it. There will come a moment when He will bring this period to a conclusion. The two-fold promise of Jesus must be fulfilled: 1.) As He went away, so He must return for

His Church, *"If I go … I will come again, and receive* you …" (John chapter 14 verse 3), and 2.) He must *"deliver"* the Church, 'catch up' His *"Bride"* from the *"wrath"* which is coming here, the *"hour of testing, that which is about to come upon the whole world."* (Revelation chapter 3 verse 10 NASB).

We have looked previously [in **Chapter 25**, '*Events that Could Happen …*'] at things which God <u>could</u> permit to happen before the Church has been removed. But there are KEY events, and the bringing onto the 'stage of the world' of KEY personalities which God <u>cannot</u> allow to happen while the Church is still on earth, and her 'restraining influence' is present. [We will look at that point shortly.] We have said before that some of the final stages of God's programme do not have the '*terminus a quo*' – the starting point – revealed to us. We do not know exactly when (even if we now know the approximate length of the period) the following events will take place:

The Times We Are Not Told …

1.) The moment when the Church is *"caught up"* – The 'rapture' – An event that is 'sign-less' (no indicators in advance) and *"swift"*, but perhaps not as 'secret' as has been imagined?

2.) The beginning of the *"day of the Lord"*. Peter – who mentions it more than once – says it will *"come as a thief in the night"* though it will conclude with a *"great noise"* (2 Peter chapter 3 verse 10). This is NOT the same as the *"day of vengeance of our God"* which we considered earlier. Though <u>both</u> events may commence at the same time, the latter lasts <u>only</u> until the end of the *"Tribulation"*: The *"day of the Lord"* however, includes events at the end of the 'Millennial Kingdom'; the defeat of the last rebellion, the final judgment of Satan, and possibly the 'Great White Throne Judgment' as well. The *"day of the Lord"* MAY commence immediately after the 'rapture'. There is no scripture to say otherwise (nor should we postulate a long 'gap' before Daniel's '70ᵗʰ week' begins …), but neither does scripture record that the 'rapture' WILL 'trigger' the *"day of the Lord"*. As we have said often, the 'rapture' is an event connected solely with the Church and the conclusion of the 'Church Age'. We have no scriptural mandate to put it in 'lock-step' with events related to Israel, even less to make it the governing event for the *"day of the Lord"* to commence, or the *"covenant"* to be signed.

3.) The timing when *"a covenant"* is *"confirmed"* between Israel, her enemy neighbours, and other western nations who support the 'accord'. Though it is not likely – for reasons we will come to now – that this will happen before the 'rapture', scripture again does not specify. It is possible that a variety of 'accords' will be signed, and the significant – and prophetic – one may only be identified retrospectively, when it is broken. (We have seen this principle of 'retrospective revelation' play out in other prophetic events as well.)

4.) The opening by *"the Lamb"*, in the throne room of heaven, of the 'Seven Sealed Scroll'.

We can – with a little bit of 'prophetic conjecture' – align together:

a.) The Opening of the *"first seal"*, and its resultant Judgment.

b.) The Commencement of the *"day of the Lord"*.

c.) The Commencement of the *"day of vengeance of our God"* (Assuming this period runs the full 7 years, not just the 2nd half).

d.) The Commencement of the '70th Week' of Daniel's 'timeline'. The final 7 of the 490 years, which 'paused' at Year 483 (in 32 AD).

e.) The Signing of the 'Seven Year Peace Covenant', brokered by the *"Prince"*.

f.) The Emergence of the *"Prince that shall come"*, the rider on the *"White horse"* who comes *"conquering"* without warfare, as a 'world leader.

> **KEYNOTE: Silence in Scripture.** We can – in some cases – build teaching on the 'silence of scripture' (which was referred to previously as the 'Principle of Omission') but we should be careful not to set *"times"* and pre-determined order, against events which we know are related, but for which God Himself has not fully revealed the order, nor the full relationship in the 'timing'.

All of the above events may – very likely – be preceded by the 'rapture' of the *"Church"*. It is <u>not</u> a linked event in the way that those listed above are, but there is a strong possibility that it will take place before these listed events – all coinciding – begin to happen, both in heaven and on earth.

[Cp. Comments in **Chapter 25**, *'Things that Could Happen ...'*]

We Won't See the 'Day of the Lord'?

'Why use the word 'conjecture'?' some will ask. 'Are we not sure of the judgment programme?' And 'Does the *"day of the Lord"* concern the Church?' Good questions again. Let us answer them carefully. One of the most difficult passages of prophecy to interpret – in relation to its link with the 'rapture of the Church' event – is 2 Thessalonians chapter 2. Let us look at a summary of this passage now.

An additional question (after the 'rapture' question) which the church at Thessaloniki addressed to Paul was this: 'How do we answer those that say – because persecution has commenced – that the *"day of the Lord"* has begun?' (2 Thessalonians chapter 2 verse 2). Many of the problems with this passage rest on the translation of key words or phrases. Firstly, *"day of Christ"* as some translations have it (2 Thessalonians chapter 2 verse 2, W. Tyndale, Geneva, KJV) is not considered accurate, and *"day of the Lord"* is preferred (J. N. Darby, J. Wycliffe, NASB, ESV). So let us read the query – in context – as relating to the *"day of the Lord."*

We do not know who told the believers in Thessaloniki that the *"day of the Lord"* had begun, but we do know their motive was suspect. Why? Because they backed up their claim with a forged letter, seemingly from Paul. We know – from our studies – that the *"day of the Lord"* is not connected with the period of the Church being on earth. So that is problem number one resolved without too much difficulty. (We should, by now, surely know more of the 'End Times' than a 'infant' church, only a few months old.)

The second problem is more difficult, Paul continues *"Let no man (fully) deceive you by any means: for (that day shall not come) except there be a falling away first, and the Man of Sin be revealed …"* (2 Thessalonians chapter 2 verse 3 NRB). There is a slight problem with the word translated *"falling away"*. It comes from a word in the original language, '*apostasía*', which means 'to depart' in a neutral sense. But it also can be used to mean 'desert from one's post' in a military sense. It has been transliterated into English as 'apostasy' (and taken to mean 'departing from truth previously held'). Some translations have *"apostasy"* (NASB), or *"rebellion"* (ESV, NIV), and some leave the word as *"departing"* (W. Tyndale, Geneva, J. Wycliffe). Even if we assume that it does <u>not</u> translate as 'departing' (and therefore cannot apply to the 'rapture of the Church' in context), it still <u>cannot</u> mean, 'a falling away from salvation' (as some consider 'apostasy' to mean). W. Hendriksen says, 'There is no such 'falling away'. The Good Shepherd knows His own sheep, and no man shall ever snatch them out of His hands. It does mean the 'faith of the fathers' … will be abandoned by many of the children … by and large, the (apparent) 'visible' Church will forsake the true faith.'
[W. Hendriksen, '*1&2 Thessalonians, New Testament Commentary*' (Carlisle, PA: Banner of Truth, 1972), 169-170.]

The third problem in the passage is to identify:

a.) the *"<u>what</u> restrains"* (verse 6 NASB)

b.) the *"<u>who</u> now restrains"* (verse 7 NASB).

Whole chapters of books by learned scholars have been written on this subject, and, in some cases, on these two terms. Suffice to say this: The *"what"* is restraining a *"him"*, and *"the He"* is restraining the *"mystery of lawlessness"* (verse 7 NRB). Who and what are these entities? An honest answer is, we cannot be totally certain, but the 'infant' church in Thessaloniki knew, and Paul did not feel the need to elaborate to them. That must be significant.

Therefore the *"who"* and the *"what"* were a '<u>person</u>' and a '<u>thing</u>' that the first century church, in context (on receipt of the epistle) could understand, and so should we likewise. The 'restrainer' cannot be the 'law and order' of the Roman Empire regime. Though that might have made sense to a church in the capital of a Roman Province then, it does not make sense now. The interpretation must fit, a.) the understanding of the <u>original</u> recipients, and b.) believers, worldwide, today. It is possible that the 'restrainer' is the *"Church"*, and therefore the *"Man of Sin"* and the *"Lawless One"* (to convey the sense of two persons) cannot be *"revealed"* – have their 'unveiling', their *'apocalypse'* – while the Church is presently 'restraining' on earth.

The *"Who"*, the restraining person, is more difficult. It may have been that Paul was referring to the *"Holy Spirit"*, who indwells each believer in the 'Church Age'. This interpretation would fit both then (the first century churches) and now. But it does <u>not</u> imply that the Holy Spirit will not function during the 'Tribulation Period'. He may *"come upon"* people as He did in Old Testament times.

So *"The Lawless One"* being revealed (verse 8), indicates the final phase of the *"mystery of iniquity"* being fully effectual – the deception of Satan which we have studied previously – and whom the Lord will destroy with *"the manifestation of His coming"* (verse 8 NRB), at His *"Coming in Power"*.

The final problem in the passage is in identifying the <u>timing</u> of *"the strong delusion"* and *"the lie"* (verse 11). We are not told exactly what (or when) each is. Suffice to know, they are in the control of God. It is He who has been rejected, by those *"who did not believe the truth"* (verse 12 NASB), who in His own sovereign purpose will control the *"lie"*, and those who believe it. We might link this passage to the vision of John in relation to the *"three unclean spirits ... out of the mouth of the Dragon ... the Beast ... and the False Prophet."* (Revelation chapter 16 verse 13). Because many have refused to believe revealed and understood truth, they will – post rapture – believe *"the lie"*.

D. M. Martin says, 'God is ultimately in control of the 'End Times'. If this is true, then God is also in control of the events themselves. For the people of God, then, peace and assurance come not from a full knowledge of the *"times and seasons"*, but from a personal knowledge of the God who rules the times and seasons.'
    [D. M. Martin, '*1,2 Thessalonians*', NAC Series (Nashville, TN: B&H Publishing, 1995), 242.]

The Church is Not Linked to a Time of Judgment Here?

'Absolutely not.' We have covered this in our studies numerous times [See **Chapter 22**, '*The Final Judgment*']. We should recall that *"judgment"* for the Church is not 'punitive'. We, who are saved, <u>will</u> be judged for *"faithfulness"* for our service, and for motive, at the *"Judgment Seat of Christ"* (2 Corinthians chapter 5 verse 10). The Judgments of God on sinners, and the *"wrath of the Lamb"* (Revelation chapter 6 verse 16), are poured out on this earth, <u>after</u> the Church has been taken home. We will be observers – as John was – of the 'Seal Judgments', the 'Trumpet Judgments' and the 'Bowl Judgments', from our place of safety in heaven.

At the end of the 'Tribulation Period' – seven years at the most – with the second half of 42 months being the *"Great Tribulation"*, will come the final *'dénouement'* of all the rebellions of this age. The 'Campaign of Armageddon' [examined in **Chapter 19**] will result in the destruction of all who oppose Jesus Christ, and all those who have sided with the Devil and his forces of evil. The *"Coming in Power"* of the *"King of kings"* will see His Kingdom set up on earth, which will last for 1,000 years.

The Kingdom is Literal?

Again, very definitely, 'Yes.' [See the *'Coming in Power'* in **Chapter 20**, and the *'Millennial Kingdom'* in **Chapter 21**.] Jesus will reign, with His *"Bride, the Lamb's wife"*, the *"Church"* of this age, not only *"over the House of David"*, the re-gathered Nation of Israel, but over the whole world. *"And He shall speak peace unto the nations: And His dominion from sea to sea, and from the river to the ends of the earth."* (Zechariah chapter 9 verse 10 NRB).

The Kingdom is Forever?

'No. Not this Kingdom which we are speaking of here.' There <u>will</u> be an 'Eternal Kingdom', but the two are not the same [We studied that in some detail in **Chapter 23**, *'The New Jerusalem'*]. The first kingdom – the earthly one, the 'Millennial Kingdom' – will last for 1,000 years (John confirms this in Revelation chapter 20 verses 1 – 10). It will be brought to an end by the release of Satan from his prison, where he will have been *"bound for 1,000 years"*. He will find rebellion in the hearts of many, and he will attempt to raise a last attack against the King, the *"Word of God"*, who was his Creator. His effort is doomed to failure, and his destiny will be realised at last, the *"lake of fire"* forever.

What About the Unbelieving Dead?

Someone will ask, 'What about those who rejected God, in every age?' And 'When are they raised? When are they judged?' Again, excellent questions. [The detail is in **Chapter 22**, *'The Final Judgment'*.] The last judgment will be that of the *"Great White Throne"*. It will be in space, for this world and the heaven above us *"shall be dissolved"* and be *"burned up"* (2 Peter chapter 3 verse 10). All sinners who are there will be condemned to the *"lake of fire"*, where the Devil, the *"Beast"* and the *"False Prophet"* will already be. And where they will be forever.

Is that the End?

There is no end. There is *"everlasting destruction"* (2 Thessalonians chapter 1 verse 9) for all the unbelieving of all ages, from the beginning of creation to the end of the 'Kingdom Age'.

For those who are saved, from all 'ages' of human history, there will be *"The everlasting kingdom of our Lord and Saviour Jesus Christ."* (2 Peter chapter 1 verse 11). This kingdom is what we call, 'The Eternal State'. It will be forever. The Psalmist said, *"Thy kingdom is an everlasting kingdom, and Thy dominion throughout all generations."* (Psalm 145 verse

13 NRB). In one sense, the 'Kingdom Age' or the 'Millennium Period' is but a precursor to, and a prelude of, a continuous kingdom of divine rule which will last forever …

What a hope to gladden the heart of every believer – of whatever 'Age' – the expectation, and the glorious contrast, of a kingdom of eternal peace and purity, with Jesus Christ as King forever.

> *Jesus shall reign where'er the sun*
> *Doth its successive journeys run,*
> *His kingdom stretch from shore to shore,*
> *Till moon shall wax and wane no more.*
>
> *To Him shall endless prayer be made,*
> *And praises throng to crown His head,*
> *His name like sweet perfume shall rise,*
> *With every morning sacrifice.*
>
> *Let every creature rise and bring*
> *The highest honours to our King,*
> *Angels descend with songs again,*
> *And earth repeat the loud, 'Amen.'*
>
> [*Isaac Watts 1674-1748, Southampton UK.*]

Questions and Answers for Chapter Twenty-Six – 'Events that Must Happen ... Review'

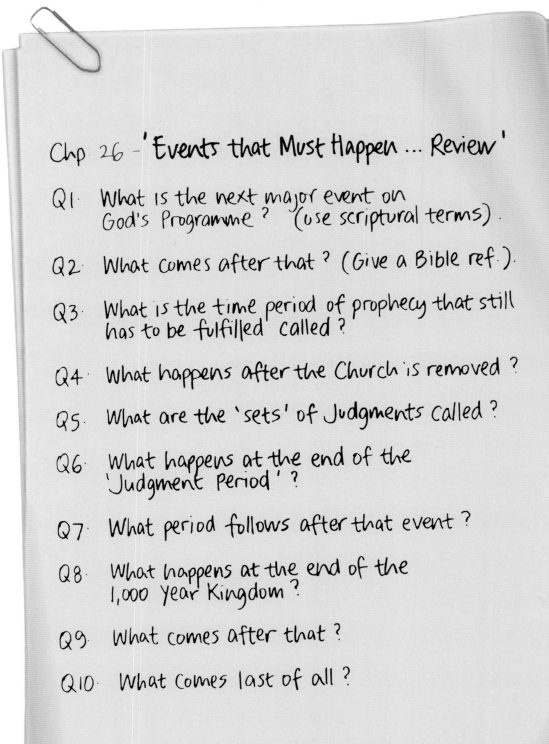

Chp 26 – 'Events that Must Happen ... Review'

Q1. What is the next major event on God's Programme? (use scriptural terms).

Q2. What comes after that? (Give a Bible ref.).

Q3. What is the time period of prophecy that still has to be fulfilled called?

Q4. What happens after the Church is removed?

Q5. What are the 'sets' of Judgments called?

Q6. What happens at the end of the 'Judgment Period'?

Q7. What period follows after that event?

Q8. What happens at the end of the 1,000 Year Kingdom?

Q9. What comes after that?

Q10. What comes last of all?

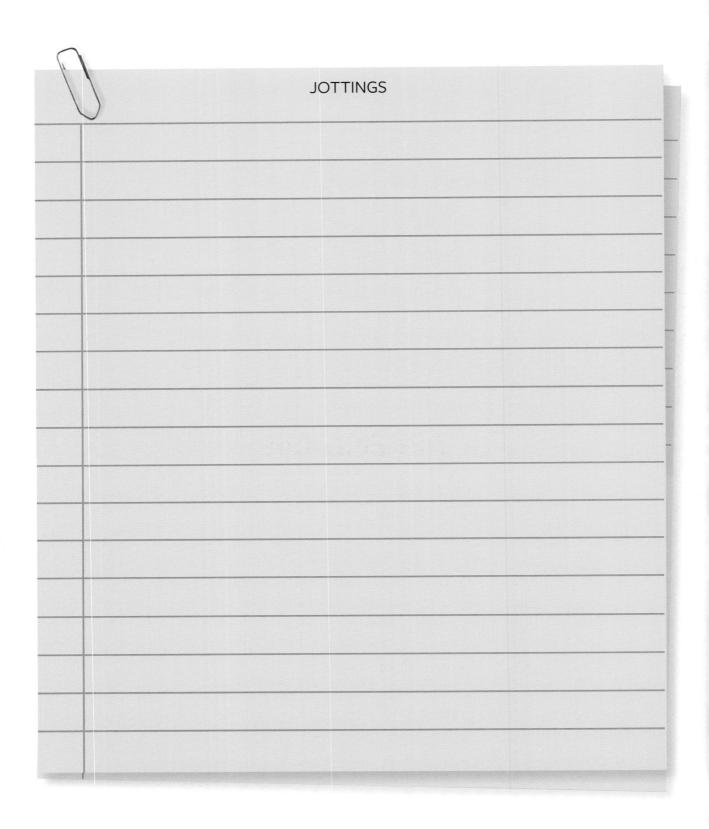

JOTTINGS

PART FIVE

APPENDICES

Appendix I:

The "Seventy Weeks" of the Prophecy of Daniel

Daniel's *"seventy weeks"* (Dan. 9:24) have been referred to numerous times throughout the book. At no point have we given a full explanation of either the context or meaning of this term, except to interpret it as representing '490 years of prophecy' with a division into '483 years already fulfilled' and '7 years still to be fulfilled in the end times'. This is another example, as has been already stated, of a 'divided prophecy'. It is needful now to address the wider context of Daniel himself, the era of his life and the context of his prophetic book, as well as the specifics of the *"seventy weeks"* timeline, as it has often been referred to.

Daniel the Prince

Daniel, most probably a prince of the house of Judah, was taken captive by the Babylonians in the reign of Jehoiakim, King of Judah, when the armies of Nebuchadnezzar besieged Jerusalem and destroyed the city and the Temple. This happened – as Jeremiah the prophet said it would (Jer. 25:11-12; 29:10) – in 606 BC, but Jeremiah also prophesied a return, commencing 70 years later, in 536 BC. Daniel was chosen, along with other Judean princes, for his *"wisdom ... knowledge ... and understanding science"* (Dan. 1:3-4 KJV) and was put into a 3 year training programme in the court of King Nebuchadnezzar in Babylon.

Assuming that Daniel was 15-16 years old at the time of his captivity, so that he was 'officially' an adult when he stood before the King, the timeline of his life and his prophetic, 'apocalyptic', book would be as follows:

Timeline of Daniel

Chapter:	Date BC:	Daniel's Age:	
1	606	15 – 18	[At his captivity]
2	603	20	[King Nebuchadnezzar's 1st vision]
3	601	23	
4	571	53	[King Nebuchadnezzar's 2nd vision]
5	539	84	[Belshazzar's Feast]
6	537	86	[The Den of Lions]
7	553	70	[Vision during Belshazzar's reign]
8	551	72	[Vision during Belshazzar's reign]
9	538	85	[Prayer & vision in 68th year of captivity]
10-12	536	88	[Last visions – to 'End Times']

[J. Allen, *'Daniel Reconsidered'* Pg. 41]

Divisions of Daniel

You will see from the Table above that the book does not run in strict chronological order. If we put the chapters into their chronological order, they would go something like this:

Chapters: 1 – 2 – 3 – 4 – 7 – 8 – 5 – 9 – 6 – 10 – 11 – 12

[S. Gordon, '*Great God of Heaven*' Pg. 26]

The traditional division of the book of Daniel is into two sections: Chapters 1-6 and 7-12, and is based on the fact that the first six chapters are historical, and the latter six are prophetical. Chapter 1 is seen as Introductory. However, an alternative division appears when we look at the original languages in which the book was written by Daniel:

1. Introduction (Dan. 1:1-2:3) – written in **Hebrew**.
2. 'The Times of the Gentiles' (Dan. 2:4-7:28) – written in **Chaldee**, or "*Syriack*" (Dan. 2:4).
3. 'The Future of Israel, in relation to the Gentiles' (Dan. 8-12) – written in **Hebrew**.

'This may not be the majority view, but it does highlight God's differing programmes for the Gentile and the Jew, up to the Kingdom Age (Dan. 12:13).'

[J. F. Walvoord, '*Daniel*' Pg. 18-19]

Visions in Daniel

Daniel is a book of "*visions*", and as we can see from the structure, the visions are not all Daniel's, nor are they all in the 'prophetic' section of the book:

Vision 1: Nebuchadnezzar's 1st Dream – The Image of 5 Metals / Kingdoms (Dan. 2:1-45)

Vision 2: Nebuchadnezzar's 2nd Dream – the Tree cut down / 7 years deposed (Dan. 4:1-37)

Vision 3: Daniel's 1st Vision – The Four Great Beasts / Kings (Dan. 7:1-28)

Vision 4: Daniel's 2nd Vision – The Ram and the He-Goat / 2 Kings (Dan. 8:1-27)

Vision 5: Daniel's 3rd Vision – The Seventy Weeks / 490 years (Dan. 9:20-27)

Vision 6: Daniel's 4th Vision – Invaders of Israel / Time of the End (Dan. 10:1-12:13)

Daniel's Third Vision – The "Seventy Weeks"

Having set out something of the background of Daniel, an amazing courtier and prophet, who lived to be almost 90, through the reign of five kings: Jehoiakim the last proper king of Judah, Nebuchadnezzar King of Babylon, Belshazzar vice-regent of Babylon, Darius the Mede, and Cyrus the Persian (Dan. 1:21). And also, something of the structure and timeframe of the book, we need to look at our main point of concern: the third vision of Daniel and the breakdown of Chapter 9, as well as the breakdown of the 'timeline' itself.

Daniel Chapter 9 divides into two main sections:

Daniel's Prayer (vs. 1-19)	490 years looking backwards.
Gabriel's Prophecy (vs. 20-27)	490 years looking forwards.

Why do we say that Daniel was 'looking backward' in his prayer? Because, as an 'intercessor' like Abraham, Moses, Jeremiah and others before him, Daniel was confessing the sins of the Nation, (Dan. 9:8-17 ESV). *"We have sinned against You ... and have not obeyed the voice of the Lord our God ... and the curse and oath that are written in the Law of Moses ... have been poured out upon us, because we have sinned against Him ... O our God, listen to the prayer of Your servant, and to his pleas for mercy, and for Your own sake, O Lord."*

He knew that 70 years of captivity was Jehovah's punishment for their rebellion (Jer. 25:11-12; 29:10), and, to give the land *"her sabbaths ... to fulfil threescore and ten years"* (2 Chron. 36:21 KJV). The Land was meant to have a year's *"rest"* from sowing and harvesting every seven years. Which means calculating back, this had not been done for 490 years if the land was in 'debit' 70 fallow years. If we reckon backwards 490 years from 606 BC, the year of the captivity of Judah, this takes us back to 1096 BC, which is the very beginning of the monarchy under Saul (1 Sam. 8:22). The extra expense of supporting a monarchy had overburdened the nation, and the land. And the *"sabbath"* for the land had not been kept. Thus, there were two reasons why Jehovah put the people of Judah out of the land for 70 years:

1.) Their chastisement for rebelling against the Law and the worship of *"Jehovah"*, the one true God.

2.) The need for the Land to have her 70 years of 'backdated' rest.

Daniel knew this: he also knew that the time of *"captivity"* was nearing an end (Daniel Chp. 9 is set in 538 BC approx.), and the people in captivity in Babylon did not seem burdened about either repenting or returning. The old prophet gets again before Jehovah in prayer, mourning and confessing the spiritual departure, not just of 70 years but of 490 ... But Gabriel, the messenger angel who appeared to Daniel in a previous vision, interrupts his prayer: *"O Daniel, I have now come out to give you insight and understanding. At the beginning of your pleas for mercy a word went out, and I have come to tell it to you, for you are greatly loved. Therefore consider the word and understand the vision."* (Dan. 9:22-23 ESV).

Daniel tells us that Gabriel arrived with him at the *"time of the evening oblation"* (3 pm.) indicating that the old prophet was still spiritually in tune with a Temple 'timetable' which had long since ceased, but still significant to him in his exiled condition.

What are the "seventy weeks" – How do we know what length of time is being measured?

The first word in this oft repeated phrase, *"seventy"*, gives us no trouble. We know that it is 7 x 10. But many people (even scholars in the past) have become confused as to the meaning of the second word: *"weeks"*. Does this mean – as it looks at face value – 1 year and 18 weeks or about 16 months? Or does the word *"weeks"* mean something else numerically? A *"week"* is a *"seven"*, and has been since creation (Gen. 1). Quite a number of Bible translations, from the 'Authorised Version' (KJV) onwards have the phrase as *"seventy weeks"*. The ESV and the NASB in their footnotes have *"seventy sevens"*, and Newberry (NRB) has in his margin *"weeks of years"*. Does this help us? Only a little!

The Greek word (from the 'Septuagint' Greek O.T.) is 'heptad', which we can guess at in English. Like 'polygon' and 'octagon', a 'heptagon' is a shape, but with 7 sides. So, we can translate our phrase as 'seventy sevens'. This calculates as 490. But is this still a year and a bit? Was Gabriel speaking of '490 days', or '490 months' or '490 years'? And what would Daniel <u>himself</u>* have made of the period referred to when he heard it first?

[*This is one of the KEY 'Principles of Interpretation'. **See Appx. II**]

We should remember that 7, 49, and 490 were ALL very significant numbers in the history of Israel. We have already mentioned 7 as the "*week*" of creation. Seven years was the farming cycle which the Nation of Israel ignored, and Jehovah gave the land 70 years backdated rest! 49 years was the cycle of 'ownership' and land and servants reverted to their original owners after 49 years, the "*year of jubilee*" (Lev. 25).

'From the call of Abraham to the Exodus from Egypt was approximately 490 years (as best as we can reckon). From the Exodus to the building of the Temple was also 490 years. From the beginning of the Monarchy to the Captivity in Babylon was another 490 years. From the Dedication of the Temple to the end of the Captivity (536 BC) was 490 years as well. And we should remember, as we have stated, that Daniel was reviewing at least one of those '490 year' periods in his prayer, when he was interrupted by Gabriel.'

[S. Gordon, '*Great God of Heaven*' Pg. 278]

If we assume – for the moment – that the prophetic period Gabriel was announcing was another 490 years, can we prove that from within the passage itself? We shall see that that is not a difficulty. But we will leave that for now.

What were the "seventy weeks", or 490 years, intended to accomplish?

Six things were to be accomplished, in the timeframe set out, or "*cut out*" as a literal reading (NRB) suggests, regarding Israel and Jerusalem:

1. "*to finish the transgression*" (Dan. 9:24 KJV). This refers to the 'rebellion' of Israel, and the word "*finish*" means to "*shut it up*" (NRB). The rebellion of Israel would be brought to a full conclusion, when the 490 years were complete.

2. "*to make an end of sins*" (Dan. 9:24 KJV). J. Allen says, 'The sins of daily life would be brought to an end. Israel would not sin again'.

[J. Allen '*Daniel Reconsidered*' Pgs. 396-8]

3. "*to make atonement for iniquity*" (Dan. 9:24 NRB). Jesus atoned for sins on the Cross, but that will not be applied to Israel as a nation, until they accept Jesus as their Messiah.

[R. Showers '*The Most High God*' Pgs. 118-119]

4. "*to bring in everlasting righteousness*" (Dan. 9:24 KJV). Righteousness for ever, the phrase literally translates as, '*righteousness of the ages*'.

5. "*to seal up vision and prophet*" (Dan. 9:24 NRB). No further prophecy regarding Israel is needed. Their "*sins*" will be ended, and so will be all the prophecy concerning their chastening.

[R. Showers]

6. "*to anoint a Holy of holies*" (Dan. 9:24 NRB). This refers to the Holy of holies in the New Temple in Jerusalem, in the Millennium Period. (Ezek. 43:1-5).

[J. F. Walvoord *'Daniel'* Pg. 273]We have (for now) assumed the time frame as being 490 years. And considered the purpose or accomplishments: All relative to Israel, and their spiritual chastening and recovery (not fully accomplished, even by their *"captivity"*), as Daniel's prayer has shown. But what of the start of the timeline, and the end? Which will confirm its length, years or otherwise. Those are the BIG questions …

The 490 Years – Beginning and End:

Let us look at an 'overview' of the timeline first: The period divides into two parts, and the first part also divides into two as well. There are two *"Princes"* in the prophecy: *"Messiah the Prince"* and one we will call the *"Coming Prince"*. (Dan 9:25-26). The *"city"* and the *"sanctuary"* are rebuilt, and also destroyed. And rebuilt again. There will be a 'seven year covenant' with a specified number of 'signatories', including the *"Coming Prince"* and Israel. This *"covenant"* will be broken halfway through, but God will still be in control, and will bring judgment on the *"Desolater"*, another title, in context, for the 'Coming Prince' (Dan 9:27 NRB).

So, we have two parts to the period, two Princes in the prophecy, two reconstructions of the City of Jerusalem (and the Sanctuary), one *"covenant"*, which also divides into two parts. All of this will make much more sense once we determine when the period commences, and when it concludes. The 'commencement' date needs to be identified with care. If the prophetic 'timeline' leads to the date of the death of *"Messiah"*, then only 'years' can be reckoned in, not 'months' or 'days'. We must find a start date that fits the end date of the 69 *"weeks"* which are indicated in the passage, *"Messiah … cut off"* (Dan. 9:26) In fact both start date and end date are clearly defined, and confirm that the *"weeks"* are 360 day prophetic years.

The commencing point of the 'timeline' of 490 years is not really so difficult to determine, even from within the Bible record. Yet many have stumbled over it, forgetting to distinguish, historically, between *"decrees"* to restore the Temple, and a *"commandment to restore and to build Jerusalem"* (Dan. 9:25 KJV). There were four decrees in total, but only one fits our starting point, and also the 'end point' of Messiah's death:

> **KEYNOTE: Start Date.** There has been some debate over whether 445 or 444 BC. should be regarded as the date of the *"month Nisan in the twentieth year"* of Artaxerxes (Neh. 2:1). Artaxerxes, historically, reigned from July 465 BC, so the Jewish month *"Nisan"* – approximately our March – still fell inside his 20th year. Some have suggested that the first 'part year' of his reign doesn't 'count', i.e. July to December, as this was the convention for Jewish Kings (ref. King David, six months is not counted in Hebron, 40 years in total 2 Sam. 5:3-6). Nehemiah was born in exile, not like Daniel, and grew up under the Persian regime. There is a sound case to take March 445 BC as the starting point of the 490 year timeline, as numerous modern scholars do.

1. A decree of **Cyrus the Persian** (2 Chron. 36:22-23; Ezra 1:3) *"to build the House of Jehovah"*. This was not a decree to rebuild Jerusalem, and this was also still in Daniel's lifetime.

2. A decree of **Darius Hystaspes** (Ezra 6:6-12) reaffirming the decree of Cyrus. This was connected with the ministry of Haggai and Zechariah, and dated 520 BC, but again concerning the Temple.

3. A decree of **Artaxerxes Longimanus** (Ezra 7:12-26), issued to Ezra who led the second return.

4. A second decree of **Artaxerxes** (in the 20th year of his reign, 445 BC) issued to Nehemiah, who led the third return, this time to rebuild the <u>city</u> and the <u>walls</u>.

The first three decrees, when examined closely, are all to do with the rebuilding of the "House of Jehovah". There is NO mention of the rebuilding of Jerusalem until the fourth decree given to Nehemiah, in relation to the *"city ... of my fathers' ... and the gates ..."* (Neh. 2:3). Thus, the second decree of Artaxerxes (Decree No. 4) is the only one – almost 90 years after Daniel's death – which fits the starting point of the 490 year timeline.

[J. Allen '*Daniel Reconsidered*' Pgs. 404-409]

Why are the 490 years divided up?

This is slightly simpler ground, and brings in details which have been referred to throughout the text. If we accept that the *"weeks"* are 'heptads' of 'sevens of years', then calculating the rest of the timeline falls into place relatively easily.

The 490 Years Part One:

"... from the going forth of the commandment to restore and to build Jerusalem unto Messiah Prince, seven weeks, and threescore and two weeks: the street shall be built again, and wall, even in troublous times." (Dan 9:25 NRB).

The *"seven weeks"* = 49 years, and the *"sixty two weeks"* = 434 years, so giving a total of 483 years, and thus leaving 7 years of the full total remaining. The reason for the first period being divided in two is given in the text; the conclusion of the rebuilding of the *"wall"*, hindered by trouble and difficulty, as the story of Nehemiah tells. When we subtract 49 years from 445 BC we come to 397 BC, which is also end of the prophetic days of Malachi, and the end of the O.T. recorded period.

This 434 year period then bridges across the period between the O.T. and the N.T. and goes forward into the Gospel record. We should remember that – as we have already discussed – Revelation proves by comparative periods that a 'prophetic year' is 360 days (as were the years before the Flood), not 365.25 days. Also, there is no 'Year 0', when counting down the BC era; 1 BC goes directly to 1 AD. The calculations to convert these dates from 360 day years, and accounting for known 'leap years' etc., was done by Sir Robert Anderson with the assistance of the British Astronomer Royal. Their calculations came to 173,880 days, which Anderson held began on the 14th March (1st Nisan) 445 BC, and comes forward to April 6th 32 AD. Anderson concluded that this date was the day of Jesus' entry to Jerusalem on *"a colt the foal of an ass"* (Matt 21:1-16; Zech. 9:9). After which, *"Messiah shall be cut off"* (Dan 9:26).

[Sir R. Anderson '*The Coming Prince*' Pgs. 95-105.]

Taking all of this together, we can see that the 7 *"weeks"* plus the *"62 weeks"* total 69 of the *"70 weeks"* of Daniel's prophetic timeline, and take us from the decree for the rebuilding of the City of Jerusalem to the arrival of *"Messiah the Prince"* into Jerusalem, 483 years afterwards. And only 4 days before He was rejected by the rulers and crucified by the Romans; after the end of the 483 years *"shall Messiah be cut off"*.

The 490 Years Part Two:

We have now covered 483 years of our 490 year 'timeline' given in Gabriel's vision to Daniel. 'But what of the remaining *"week"* of 7 years? Do they get added on immediately after the death of Messiah, at His first coming?' 'No.' We now come to another of our (by now familiar) prophetic 'gaps' or 'divisions within a prophecy'. Historically we know that Messiah was crucified (as we have calculated from scripture) in 32 AD. During the final days of His public ministry, He prophesied events which would take place shortly – but not immediately – after His death, and His resurrection.

This included the destruction of Jerusalem (again), and the Temple as well: *"Do you see these great buildings? There will not be left here one stone upon another that will not be thrown down."* (Mark 13:2 ESV).

This was fulfilled in 70 AD by General Titus and his regiments: *"the people of the Prince that shall come shall destroy the city and the Sanctuary"* (Dan. 9:26). The prophecy of Jesus confirmed that the LAST part, the remaining *"week"* or 7 years, was NOT directly 'attached' to the 483 years. There came in a gap of 38 years after the death of Messiah, before the destruction of the Temple (70 AD – 32 AD = 38 years between). The *"people of the Prince"* come into the picture, but not the *"Prince"* directly. The 'Coming Prince' and the 'confirmed covenant' have not appeared yet. The breaking of the *"covenant"*, and the stopping of ceremonial sacrifices, takes place in the middle of the 'week' of 7 years. Therefore, the first part of the 7 years (and the rebuilding of a Sanctuary and the restoration of Jewish sacrifices) are implied. We can clearly see that the last 7 years have been separated from the continuous timeline of the 490 years, and given the clear prophetic specifics connected with that final 7 years (just as with the start of the timeline), we can confirm that the last *"week"* of 7 years has NOT commenced yet …

We come now to the last 'gap': This unidentified *"Prince"*, who is ethnically linked to the people who destroyed Jerusalem (in 70 AD), will *"make a firm covenant with the many for one week"* (Dan 9:27 NASB, NRB). This *"Prince"* will also be the same person whom prophetic scripture calls the *"Man of Sin"* (2 Thess. 2:3) and the *"Antichrist"* (1 John 2:18). He will appear on the 'world stage' as a 'peace maker' and a 'peace broker' in the troubled Middle East. He will not be recognised for who he really is. At the first.

But as his *"peace"* begins to break down, and when he deliberately breaks the *"covenant"* with Israel in the middle of the seven years (42 months and 1,260 days), and *"causes sacrifice and oblation to cease"* (Dan 9:27 NRB), then, the discerning, who understand the *"times"*, will identify the *"Prince"* for who he really is: The *"Beast"* who will introduce the period called *"Great Tribulation"* (Matt 24:21). And they will know that the final *"week"* of 7 years is already half-way through.

[Refer to **Chps. 9** & **13-15**]

The last 'gap' in Daniel's 'timeline' will have then closed. As has been said by others, 'The clock of prophecy will have restarted', and the last seven years of the 490 years will be completed when the believing remnant of Israel will acknowledge their national *"sin"*, and look for their coming *"Messiah"*. He will then come, as surely as He did the first time, when the full time period of Daniel's vision has ended, and all the 'gaps' have been closed up. This will be His *"Coming in Power"* [which we dealt with in **Chp. 20**]. We are presently in the long 'gap' period; the 'Day of Grace', the *"Acceptable year of the Lord"*, when individual Jews and Gentiles can come into the blessing through the death of Messiah Jesus Christ, which took place at His first coming, and His *"cutting off"*.

> **KEYNOTE: Identity.** The identity of the *"Prince that shall come"* may NOT be made known by the ceremonial signing of *"a covenant"*. The text does not say *"THE covenant"*, though it does say *"THE many"*. This would indicate that there may be many covenants signed with Israel in the last days, but the PERIOD – 7 years – and the PEOPLE – with whom it is signed – may be the significant features which will reveal the fulfilment of this prophecy. The full and final confirmation will not be the 'signing' of the *"covenant"*, but the 'breaking' of it, which will take place at exactly the mid-point of the 7 year period; 1,260 days forward from the commencement.

JOTTINGS

Appendix II:

'Amillennialism' vs. 'Premillennialism' & other 'isms'

The Past, the Present and the Future in Relation to Unfulfilled Prophecy:

> **KEYNOTE: Summarising.** The topics being dealt with in this Appendix have had whole books written, in some cases on one topic or one single approach. Some of these, for the benefit of a more in-depth examination by those interested, will be found in the Bibliography including all books cited or quoted. Of necessity what we have here is a short summary of each position for the purposes of biblical comparisons.

We have taken the interpretative position in this volume of what is called the 'historical, grammatical, literal and futurist hermeneutic'. That is:

a.) To discover, if possible, the biblical author's intended meaning, and what his 'verbal' prophecy might have meant to the initial audience in his time.

b.) To take the text as being literal wherever possible unless it is clearly indicated as being 'allegorical' or 'symbolic' within the context of the relevant passage.

c.) To examine the grammar, the syntax, and the context of the writing, in whatever language we are able to study, to help in understanding the 'literality' of the passage.

d.) To understand that the meaning of the text and the 'application' may differ. Where an 'application' may be used, out of context, it does not impact on the original meaning of the text.

e.) That a significant percentage of both O.T. and N.T. prophecy has still to be fulfilled, and literally so.

What has become known as the 'Golden Rule of Interpretation' summarises this position. It is often referred to within 'futurist' prophetic writings, though not always as a complete quotation. The author Cooper wrote,

> *'When the plain sense of Scripture makes common sense, seek no other sense; therefore take every word at its primary, ordinary, usual, literal meaning unless the facts of the immediate text studied in the light of related passages and axiomatic* (self-evident) *and fundamental truths indicate clearly otherwise.'*
>
> [Dr. D. L. Cooper (1886-1965), *Bible Research Society*, Los Angeles, CA.]

Having said that, it must be admitted that unfulfilled prophecy (both O.T. and N.T.) can be very difficult to interpret, and to maintain a right balance between what is – more than likely – literal at the point of fulfilment, and what are – more than likely – 'symbolic' figures of speech. The demarcation is not always clear, and the farther that the prophet, and his hearers, had to look into the future the more difficult it was, and is, to distinguish between 'allegorical' and 'literal'. For unfulfilled prophecy, even in our day, some of this still holds true, especially in relation to the book of Revelation; the summation and terminus of all biblical prophecy. MacArthur writes 'Revelation's picturesque images, mysterious symbols, and apocalyptic language make it one of the most challenging books in Scripture to interpret'.

[J. MacArthur *'Revelation Chps. 1-11'* Pg. 9]

The interpretative approaches to prophecy may be summarised into four main groups:

1.   The Preterist Approach:

The 'preterist' description comes from another Latin word, '*praeter*' meaning 'in the past', or 'beyond'. Those who hold to this view of prophecy, and of the book of Revelation in particular, are known as 'Preterists'. That is, they see everything in Revelation up to Chp. 20 as having already been fulfilled at the time of John's writing, towards the end of the first century (95 AD approx.). The book represents history – told in symbolic language – not prophecy at all. The 'second advent' of Christ is linked with the fall of Jerusalem, in 70 AD. The *"Beasts"* of Rev. Chp. 13 are represented as Imperial Rome and the Caesars.

The obvious problems with this school of interpretation are twofold: 1.) Although there was fierce persecution of the Church from around 50 AD onwards, there was no obvious judgments of God on her enemies. And 2.) If the contents of the book are historic, and long since fulfilled, where in history is the Second Coming of Messiah to earth? Or the return of Jesus Christ for His Church? As Jim Allen states, 'This kind of interpretation carries its own refutation, and all who acknowledge the claim of the book to be a genuine prophecy (Rev. 1:1-2) find little substance in it.

[J. Allen '*Revelation*' Pg. 10]

2.   The Historicist Approach:

The 'historical' approach, held by those who are called 'Historicists', also hold the events of the book of Revelation to be real, but they believe it to be an unfolding of Church history from the Apostolic period to the Second Coming of Christ. Most who take this approach hold *"Babylon"* to be both pagan and papal Rome. Though this viewpoint is not a 'majority' opinion today, it is perhaps not so hard to see how the early 'Reformers' kept to it. In coming out of the system of Rome, and in their persecution by Rome, they must have felt that the *"Tribulation"* period was not only literal, but present. Luther, Calvin, and many of the early reformers held to this view. Accordingly, much of the book is 'allegorised' so that the rise of Papal Rome, the advent of Islam, and the French Revolution are all to be found in picture form within John's visions.

MacArthur writes, 'Like the preterist approach, the historicist view ignores Revelation's internal claims to be prophecy. It also robs the book of any meaning for first century believers to whom it was addressed. And it removes the interpretation of Revelation from the realm of literal, historical hermeneutics, leaving it at the mercy of the allegorical and spiritualised meanings invented by each would-be interpreter.'

[J. MacArthur '*Revelation 1-11*' Pg. 10]

3.   The Idealist Approach:

The 'idealist' takes a 'topical' approach to prophecy and the book of Revelation. 'Timeless truths' in the battle between good and evil throughout every age are presented as 'allegories' or 'spiritual myths'. Like the 'historicist' approach, this method denies the internal claims of Revelation to be prophetic truth and reduces the Book to a 'collection of myths designed to convey spiritual truth'. Jim Allen summarises, 'While appealing to a certain type of mystical mind and while emphasising certain spiritual truths, there is no scriptural foundation for interpretation of this kind'.

[J. Allen '*Revelation*' Pg. 11]

4. The Futurist Approach:

This is the approach held to by the author, and many other contemporary writers, often classified as 'Dispensational' (although that title has a wide variety of subsections, which we have not gone into in this volume), which, as has been stated earlier, takes a 'literal' and 'future fulfilment' view of many O.T. and N.T. prophecies, including all of the book of Revelation from the end of Chp. 3 forwards into Chp. 22.

This approach holds that the primary interpretative key to the book of Revelation is in the divisions given directly by Jesus Christ Himself to John the Apostle on the Isle of Patmos during his imprisonment:

1.) The *"things which thou hast seen"*, John's vision of Christ (Chp. 1).

2.) The *"things which are"*, the 'Church Period' and the letters to the Seven Churches (Chps. 2-3).

3.) The *"things which shall be after these things"*, that is, the prophetic and still future sections of the Book (from Chp. 4:1 to Chp. 22:6). This KEY phrase *'meta tauta'* in the original language, where it is repeated in the plural, forms 'time-shifts' or chronological phases within John's visions. Thus Chps. 6-19 describe the seven years of tribulation which, within the book, divide evenly at the centre point; 1,260 days and 42 months in each half.

The 'futurist' view offers us 'the only scheme of interpretation where the grammatical-historical-theological golden rule of interpretation, given above, can be employed without 'special pleading'. Scripture is allowed to mean exactly what it states without spiritualisation or allegorisation ... It is the only feasible explanation that incorporates the O.T. and N.T. prophecies in perfect harmony and confirms the basic truth of the consummation character of the last book of the Bible'.

[J. Allen *'Revelation'* Pg.12]

MacArthur summarises the position thus, 'Anything other than the futurist approach leaves the meaning of the book to human ingenuity and opinion. The futurist approach takes the book's meaning as God gave it'.

[J. Mac Arthur *'Revelation 1-11'* Pg. 11]

Among those who hold to the 'futurist' position, however, there are three distinct groups of scholars. The differences of opinion are in relation to the 'Millennial Reign of Christ' and the relationship of the 'Rapture of the Church' to that reigning period. They are known as, 1.) Amillennialism, 2.) Postmillennialism, and 3.) Premillennialism. We shall look at each of the three positions in summary form, and in that order:

Amillennialism:

One of the key exponents of the 'Amillennial' doctrine in the early Church period was <u>Augustine of Hippo</u> (354 - 430 AD). In his major published work *'The City of God'* he rejected the 'premillennial' position which he had once held, and which had been the doctrinal position of the apostles and the early 'church fathers' for 300 years. He taught that there would be no literal reign of Christ on earth for 1,000 years. The 'Millennium', so called, was the present Church age. The Second Coming of Christ would introduce a general judgment and the immediate movement into the 'Eternal State'. Satan had been 'bound' at the cross, not literally in the future, and the blessings of the Church are to be found in this present age.

This body of doctrine became the core teaching of the Church of Rome on future events, and while most of the 'reformers' were clear on foundational doctrines, such as '*sola fide*', justification by faith alone, they did not separate themselves from the position of Rome on 'eschatology', which in the main became the position of Reformed Doctrine also, and became enshrined in the '*Westminster Confession of Faith*' (1646 AD).

One of the major flaws in the arguments for 'Amillennialism' is found in the way that N.T. authors evaluate O.T. prophecy. Patterson notes, 'The symbolic nature of Revelation is apparent to all, but such symbolism does not negate actual events and persons that lie in the bosoms of the symbols. That Satan is imaged as a *"Great red dragon"* (in Chp. 12) does not mask his real identity, nor does it prevent the reality of his assault on heaven, nor his loss of status there. In the end 'amillennialism' defaults to 'premillennialism' because of the natural reading of Scripture employed by the latter.'

[P. Patterson '*Revelation*' Pg. 38]

Pentecost wrote, 'Inasmuch as God gave the Word of God as a revelation to men, it would be expected that His revelation would be given in such exact and specific terms that His thoughts would be accurately conveyed and understood when interpreted according to the laws of grammar and speech'.

[J. D. Pentecost '*Things to Come: A Study in Bible Eschatology*' Pg. 10]

Postmillennialism:

This approach to futurist prophecy was popularised in the seventeenth century by Daniel Whitby (1638-1726). As one of its later exponents, Loraine Boettner (1901-1990), stated, 'Post-millennialism is the view of last things which holds that the Kingdom of God is now being extended in the world through the preaching of the gospel ... and that the world will eventually be christianised, and that the return of Christ will occur at the end of a long period of righteousness and peace, commonly called the millennium ... followed immediately by a general resurrection'.

[cited by, J. Allen '*Revelation*' Pg. 13]

As Patterson comments, 'The insurmountable flaw of the 'postmillennial' approach is that it differs diametrically with Revelation Chps. 19-20 where the obvious sense is that sequentially Christ returns to earth inaugurating His reign over the earth. There is no evidence of an agency (i.e. the Church) through which this is accomplished'.

[P. Patterson '*Revelation*' Pg. 37]

The other even more elementary flaw in this doctrine is that, since the wars and conflicts of the twentieth century, and since the advent of a 'post-modern' and 'post-Christian' liberal society in the west, the concept of the world being 'christianised' in preparation for the return of Jesus to a kingdom – which has been made ready by us for Him – carries no credence whatsoever.

Premillennialism:

We come now to the last of our differing 'futurist' approaches, one which the reader will identify as having been presented, with increasing emphasis, throughout the Chapters of this volume. The critics of 'premillennialism' have two main objections (both of which we will address):

Firstly, a suggestion that this doctrine was not held by the early Church and was only formulated by men like J. N. Darby (1800-1882) in the nineteenth century and popularised by C. I. Scofield (1843-1921) in his '*Scofield Reference Bible*' (1905).

Secondly, and more insidiously, many critics claim that the teaching of a 'premillennial' and 'pretribulational' rapture for the Church equates to a 'fly away from tribulation theory … to fool God's people so that they will not be on the firing line for God'.

[R. Cameron '*Scripture Truth about the Lord's Return*']

However, even some of the critics of this approach do accept, strangely enough, that the known teaching of the post-apostolic Church reflected a premillennial, pretribulational perspective. G. E. Ladd (1911-1982), though not in favour of a 'pretribulational' eschatology, demonstrated at some length that the faith of the early Church was premillennial. Citing the writings of Justin Martyr, Irenaeus, Hippolytus, the epistle of Barnabas and others, he confirmed that those closest to the time of the Apostle John held to this perspective up until the time of Augustine.

[G. E. Ladd '*The Blessed Hope*' Pgs. 20-31]

J. D. Pentecost stated that the 'overwhelming testimony from the early church rightly leads one to realise that a premillennial belief was the universal belief of the church, immediately following the death of Christ and (the time of) the teaching of the Apostles.'

[J. D. Pentecost '*Things to Come*' Pg. 374]

Working backwards (from Rev. 22:6 back to Rev. 4:1-2) we may quite clearly determine the following:

Coming Events – in Reverse Order:

1. There will be an 'Eternal Kingdom' which will be pure, holy and without end.
2. There will be the final judgment at the Great White Throne – of the unsaved dead of all ages.
3. There will be a final judgment of Satan, and his banishment to the *"Lake of fire"*.
4. There will be a literal 1,000 year 'Millennial Kingdom' of peace, Christ as *"King of kings"* reigning here on this earth, from Jerusalem (after a short 75 day period of renewal and restoration).
5. Israel will be the head of the nations and the centre of world government.
6. There will be a final end to the rebellion of this age. Messiah will appear at His *"Coming in Power"*.
7. There will be a period of tribulation for 7 years, the second half Jesus called the *"Great Tribulation"*.
8. There will be peace *"covenant"* with Israel and her neighbours for 7 years, brokered by the ruler who will be revealed as the *"Man of Sin"*, halfway through the period, when he breaks the covenant.
9. The Church saints – after being *"raptured"* – will be judged for their service at the *"Judgment seat of Christ"*.
10. The Church will be removed, *"raptured"*, delivered, from the *"wrath"* which is coming here.

All of these key points of a 'literal-futurist-hermeneutic' have been expanded in this book [from **Chp. 6** on]. They are summarised here in very few words. Associated argument and scriptural support will be found in the relevant Chapters. Not all exponents of a 'futurist' and 'premillennial' position agree on <u>all</u> of the points set out above. Those who do (including the author) are usually referred to as 'premillennial' also 'pretribulational' or, to use a common shorthand, 'Pre-Trib & Pre-Mill'.

Those who differ divide into three main 'camps', apart from the 'pre-trib' group, thus 4 'pre-millennial futurist' groups in all. Working backwards (again) from where they see the <u>point of removal of the</u>

Church (which is the key differential), the positions would be as follows: Post-Tribulational, Pre-Wrath, Mid-Tribulational, and Pre-Tribulational. We will summarise each of these in turn:

Post-Tribulational:

Those who hold to this approach believe that the Church will endure the entire 'Tribulation Period', the full 7 years. The *"rapture"* will take place just prior to the *"Coming in Power"* of Jesus Christ. It therefore cannot be a going to a *"prepared place"* (John 14:3), nor a going up to heaven at all. It is the reuniting of the souls, spirits, and bodies of dead saints, a meeting with living saints, a going up to meet a returning Jesus, and an immediate return to witness the scenes of *"Armageddon"* and the setting up of the *"Kingdom"*.

> **KEYNOTE: Courtesy & Humility.** It is worth noting that these differing opinions within a 'pre-millennial' position, and indeed within all prophetic interpretation, should be held with courtesy and respect on every side. None of us have a 'monopoly of exactitude' when it comes to interpreting 'future events'. Many who have held to the positions summarised above have still been true believers in the Lord Jesus and are a part of the Church which is His Body. All of us – the present author included – will be corrected on some points when we get to heaven, when the Lord Himself will be our Bible study leader.

Apart from a negation of what seem to be clear promises – which we will come to in the last section – there appears also in this school of thought to be no place for the *"Judgment Seat of Christ"* (2 Cor. 5:10), nor for the *"Marriage of the Lamb"* (Rev. 19:7) until after the earthly Kingdom has been established. Nor does there appear to be a clear distinction between the *"hope"* of the Church, and the *"covenant"* promises to Israel. The tribulation period should be seen as primarily the *"time of Jacob's trouble"* (Jer. 30:7), her final chastisement, to bring her to faith in her true Messiah, whom she rejected at His first coming.

It also, as Cameron states, moves the concept and timing of the *"blessed hope"* (Tit. 2:13), 'to a point only when the *"Great Tribulation"* is drawing to a close … The espoused *"Bride"* has to view earth's bloodiest battlefield, before she gets to see the place her Bridegroom has prepared for her. Think about that!'

[D. C. B. Cameron 'The Blessed Hope' Pg. 61]

If the *"rapture"* is only an event leading to a 'U-turn' in the sky, there is then a question-mark as to what kind of bodies we require? (1 Cor. 15:35-58). Do we need 'heavenly' bodies for the Kingdom? And what of the *"sheep"* (Matt. 25:31 – 33), are they judged at the same time as the Church is going to meet Christ? Do they get 'heavenly bodies' also, to enter the Kingdom? Are the Church saints then to be viewed within the 'Olivet Discourse'? There are a great many problems with this interpretative position on the timing of the *"rapture"* of the Church.

Mid-Tribulationism:

We should understand that the term 'Tribulation Period' is a title of convenience. The second half of the *"seventieth week"* of Daniel's prophecy is properly called the *"Great Tribulation"* (Matt. 24:21). The most clearly defined future event – apart from the *"Sign of the Son of Man in heaven"* (Matt. 24:30) – is the mid-point of that 7 year period. We have noted many significant prophetic events which align there, and from which the 'count-down' to *"Armageddon"* and the *"Coming in power"* of Messiah will be known.

Cameron quotes a writer in the 1940s, Norman B. Harrison, as possibly the originator of the 'mid-tribulation' title. Though some who hold to the timing of the *"rapture"* at that point do not strictly see themselves as 'mid-trib', as they do not regard the first 3.5 years of Daniel's final *"week"* as part of the tribulation, yet those who hold to this timing have also doctrinal problems to face.

[D. C. B. Cameron *'The Blessed Hope'* Pgs. 75-76]

A major difficulty with this timing for the *"rapture"*, as also with the previous 'post-trib' timing, is that they set a discernible time for the removal of the Church to take place. Not only does this alert Satan as to when Christ intends to take His Bride home, but it also removes the *"hope"* of Christ's return from every generation of the Church until a date still future: after the first part of the *"covenant"* period, and after the *"war in heaven"*, after Satan is cast down, and the revelation of the *"Man of Sin"* have all taken place. Paul commended the young church in Thessaloniki (who had a tremendous zeal for 'End Times' truth), that they *"turned to God from idols … to wait for His Son from the heavens … Jesus, our deliverer from the wrath coming* (here)*."* (1 Thess. 1:10 NRB). Though the Devil may plan for such events in every generation, and though certain individual saints (like Peter and Paul) knew they would be martyred before Jesus returned, yet the 'hope of the Church' has been – and was intended to be – alive in every generation and century since Pentecost, including our generation today.

Pre-Wrath Tribulationism:

This is a relatively recent (though growing rapidly in the USA and other places) position in relation to the timing of the *"rapture"* of the Church. This doctrine is largely the work of one man, Marvin J. Rosenthal, who was formerly 'pre-trib' in his eschatology (and a contemporary of Renald Showers, who has critiqued the 'pre-wrath' approach). This position has gained followers from a 'post-trib' position, but also some who have moved away from what was a more traditional 'pre-trib' background. When we consider where – within the 7 year period – this 'rapture position' is placed, we should ask ourselves, 'Why should this position be gaining ground?' And, 'Why should Rosenthal predict that it would?'

Rosenthal himself argues that, 'Some believe Jesus could rapture the Church at any moment, others say He won't until the middle of the tribulation; still others place the rapture at the end of the Tribulation. Are any of them right, or does the Bible teach something else?' M. Kober says of Rosenthal's teaching, 'The 'Pre-Wrath Rapture of the Church (is) a new understanding of the Rapture … [His] none-too-subtle criticisms … focus on the pretribulational rapture position, the Scofield Reference Bible, and the men of Dallas Theological Seminary, who have written widely on the Rapture; Walvoord, Ryrie, and Pentecost are especially singled out'.

[Manfred Kober *'Is Rosenthal Right About the Rapture?'* Faith Pulpit, Ankeny, Iowa.]

Rosenthal divides the *"70th week"* of Daniel into two halves of 42 months each, but also divides the 'second half' into two equal parts as well, 21 months each (with no apparent Biblical support). The first part he calls the *"Great Tribulation"*, and the second part he contests is the *"Day of the Lord"*. He argues that the *"rapture"* will be before the 7th Seal judgment, which is the day of *"God's wrath"*. Hence a 'pre-wrath rapture' doctrine.

[M. J. Rosenthal *'The Pre-wrath Rapture of the Church'* Pg. 60-61]

Once again, the truth of the *"blessed hope"* of the Church through the ages is lost. According to this new doctrine the final generation of Church-saints will see the covenant signed, *"Anti-Christ"* revealed, the *"False Prophet"* manifest, the *"mark"* introduced, the *"trumpet"* judgments endured, and at least some of the *"bowls"* poured out. And the return of Christ for His Church can apparently be dated exactly 630 days after the centre point of the 7 year period! In terms of error (and timing) there is very little between this 'pre-wrath' position and the historically longer established 'post-tribulational' position.

So, What Remains?

Of the four 'pre-millennial' positions mentioned, the last (but by no means least) that we now come to is that of a 'Premillennial' and also a 'Pre-Tribulational' *"rapture"* of the Church. That is the position which has been adopted throughout this book, and which is the considered personal position of the author.

Pre-Tribulationism:

Pretribulational teaching is often associated with 'Dispensationalism'. The term is taken from the phrase, *"the dispensation of the grace of God which is given me ..."* (Eph. 3:2 KJV). Paul, in context, may have been referring to a personal 'stewardship' or 'laws of the house' which is how the word *'oikonomia'* would have been normally understood. Patterson writes, 'The term has become associated with what is known as 'dispensational theory', usually (but not exclusively) seven periods in which God varies His methods of dealing with the human family ... Not all 'pretribulationists' are 'dispensationalists'. My own position is that the dispensations ... constitute an imposed grid that has no specific support from scripture.'

[P. Patterson *'Revelation'* Pgs. 40-41]

While the author would be 'broadly dispensational' in viewpoint, one would be agreed that it is only a 'useful framework' through which to look back at the ages past, and God's changing dealings with mankind. At times the boundaries are not as precise as we might wish to define them, and we should bear in mind that our God is not constrained by any frameworks or boundaries which are, at best, of human thinking. To quote Patterson again, 'Salvation itself was always mediated by grace through faith (Gen. 15:6), and that always on the basis of the work of Christ on the cross (Rev. 13:8)'. We should not confine the work of redemption to persons or periods from a human perspective.

As we have considered at some length in previous Chapters in the Book [**Chps. 5-7**], the expectation of the disciples, even before the Church was born at *"Pentecost"*, was that Jesus – who was going away – would come again and *"receive* (them) *unto Myself"* (John 14:3 KJV). Since they subsequently saw Him go visibly *"toward heaven"* (Acts 1:9-11), their expectation would have been for Jesus to return – <u>from</u> heaven – and take them <u>to</u> heaven, to the *"Father's house"* (John 14:2). Where it is most likely that the *"Marriage of the Lamb"* will take place (Rev. 19:7). Whereas the *"Marriage Supper of the Lamb"* is most probably a Millennial event on earth, with O.T. saints in attendance. Any 'premillennial' position which does not allow for a set period <u>in</u> heaven, before returning with Christ at His *"Coming in power"* (Rev. 19:11), falls short of what the first century Church believers would have anticipated, and taught.

The Lord Jesus also confirmed that at His coming for His saints He would bring *"My hire with Me, to give to each one ..."* (Rev. 22:12 NRB). This fits with Paul's exhortation in relation to believers having to *"be made manifest before the Judgment Seat of Christ."* (2 Cor. 5:10 NRB), and would suggest that immediately after the Church, intact and entire, both *"alive and remaining"* and *"sleeping in Jesus"* (1 Thess. 4:13-18), is 'snatched up', we will be assessed for our service for Jesus

Christ in our lifetime. This – coupled with the unexpectedness of when that might happen – is a tremendous spiritual 'spur' to our motive and activity today.

Again, the one who is coming to 'snatch away' the Church, so that we will *"be caught up"* ('raptured' as in the Latin Vulgate N.T.) to *"meet the Lord in the air"* is the same *"Jesus"* as was promised in Acts 1:10-11. To the same local church in Thessalonica, Paul affirmed that their testimony was, they *"turned to God from idols to serve the living and true God; and to wait for His Son from the heavens, whom He raised from the dead, even Jesus, our deliverer* (other saints included) *from the wrath coming* (here)." (1 Thess. 1:9-10 NRB).

To the local church in Philadelphia, the church of the *"open door"* which no man could shut, to them Jesus promised, *"I also will keep thee from the hour of temptation, which is about to come upon all the inhabited world, to try them which dwell upon the earth. Behold I come quickly ..."* (Rev. 3:10-11 NRB). Fruchtenbaum says, 'In this passage the Church is promised to be kept from the period of trial that is about to fall upon the whole earth. In the context of Revelation ... this is the Tribulation found in chapters 6-19 ... If Revelation 3:10 only means that the Church will be kept safe <u>during</u> the trial, then something goes terribly wrong. Throughout the Tribulation saints are being killed on a massive scale (Rev. 14:13). If these saints are Church saints, they are not being kept safe and Revelation 3:10 is meaningless.' [<u>underlining</u> by author]

[A. P. Fruchtenbaum *'Footsteps of Messiah'* Pgs. 152-153]

We have seen that a 'pretribulational' approach confirms the promises made from before the birth of the Church, through to the end of the first century, and the conclusion of the Biblical record. We have also seen that the promise of Jesus to *"come again"* could have been fulfilled in any generation, as God might determine, our generation included. This is usually referred to as the doctrine of 'imminence'. Cameron states, 'There was in the early Church a very deep sense of the potential imminency of the Lord's return. Few indeed had all the Scriptures available ... but the two epistles to the Thessalonians tell us that the Lord's Second Coming had been expounded to them at the outset; it was evidently considered standard rather than advanced or obscure doctrine ... The present day lack of persecution in the west is no doubt a major cause of the apathy towards the *"signs of the times"*.'

[D. C. B. Cameron *'The Blessed Hope'* Pgs. 34-35]

Final Note of Caution:

As has often been said, 'Studying prophecy does not make us prophets'. There are certain events in God's prophetic *"End Times"* programme, which although they <u>appear</u> to be 'coincidental' we cannot be certain – nor dogmatic – that they are fully aligned:

We have no scriptural proof that the *"Day of the Lord"*, though it *"will come as a thief in the night"* (2 Pet. 3:10) is precipitated by the *"rapture"*. Nor can we prove likewise, that the *"Day of the Lord"* commences with the signing of the *"covenant"*. Though we <u>are</u> certain that the *"confirming of a covenant"* will commence the counting down of the last *"week"* of Daniel's '70 week timeline' of 490 years [See **Appx. I**]. Nor can we prove that all of the above are consequent upon the opening of the *"First Seal"* (Rev. 6:1-2), though that is very probable.

Likewise, we cannot prove that the Church must be 'raptured' before the *"covenant"* is signed. Many respected and highly regarded expositors hold this position – which may be correct – but it cannot be corroborated by 'chapter and verse'. The *"revelation"* of the *"Man of Sin"* (2 Thess. 2:3-

11) refers to the breaking of the *"covenant"*, not its signing. Only when he takes the place of God will he confirm his true, and infernal, identity.

'So', you may ask, 'When will the *"rapture"* take place?' The honest answer is, we do not know. We should not 'read it in' to Matt. chps. 24-25, though we can identify events that the rapture of the Church must precede. 'Will we see Anti-Christ?' 'No, not identifiably so.' But who knows if both the *"Beast"* and the *"False Prophet"* are now alive, and waiting their moment already behind the scenes? 'Will we see the Israeli Peace Covenant signed?' Who knows – in advance – which 'covenant' will be the fulfilment of Daniel's prophecy? There may be many 'peace accords' with Israel and her neighbours, or great turmoil and war in the Middle East first, or both!

Will the Church See Persecution?

Much of the Church today, in many parts of the world, already does. It is possible (as has already been suggested) that persecution may come to the Church in the west, and that a great many conveniences and liberties may be taken away – by the will of the Lord – before the Church is *"snatched up"* to heaven. A 'pretribulational' position should NOT be confused with a 'wish list' of ease and protection until we all get safely home.

Not one true *"sheep"* of the Body of Christ, not one *"born again"* saint of the 'Church Period', can either be *"lost"* or 'left behind'. But we should not be stumbled in our faith in a risen, swiftly coming, Lord Jesus by a belief that our witness and testimony (both personal and corporate) may not be tested, before we are taken home, at the conclusion of the 'Church Age', at the end of *"the Acceptable Year of the Lord"* (Isa. 61:2).

> **KEYNOTE: 'Pre-Tribulationism'** - as some critics have alleged – is not a 'doctrine of cowardice', but rather a position of being on the 'tiptoe of expectancy', being fearless and outgoing in our testimony, lest at His 'any moment' return, we might be found at ease or in comfort and not in a state of 'watchfulness', working, waiting, and warning others of His Coming, as was the early Church.

Appendix III:
Subject Index

> **KEYNOTE: Omissions.** Certain key words have been omitted from the Subject Index due to their frequency of use. Examples include: Daniel, Devil, End Times, Genesis, God, Jesus, Lamb, Luke, Jehovah, Jerusalem, John, Matthew, Mark (including the references cited in the 4 Gospels), Messiah, Prophecy, Revelation, Scroll, Saviour, Temple, 7 years.
>
> **NOTE:** Though a full **Scripture Index** has not been included, Bible books cited have been referenced separately from references to the authors.

Appendix IV:

Answers to Questions

(As they Appear at the End of each Chapter)

The Answers to the Questions are given in abbreviated form. This is the minimum information readers/students should have gleaned at first reading. It may be necessary to read some of the Chapters again, especially if you are unfamiliar with the content. Comprehension and recall will increase as reading and study progress. There is some overlap in the studies, so material already studied will be kept in focus throughout.

Study Q&A Notes are available in pdf form, for Bible study groups etc. (Questions separated from answers) Email a request to: endtimesforbeginners@gmail.com)

Questions & Answers for Chapter One – 'Introduction to Prophecy':

Question 1: How much of the Bible is prophecy? (A fraction or percentage). If you don't remember, look back and note it, because a great part of the Bible was given as prophecy!

One Quarter, or 25%.

Question 2: Where does prophecy start? Look for the first promise and the first prophecy in the word of God. Note down the Bible reference and remember it:

The promise to the first woman, "Eve"; her seed would triumph over the Serpent's seed (Gen. 3:15).

Question 3: How much of the Bible is already history? How long a period, approximately, does the Bible cover? If you draw a 'timeline', where are we on it just now?

The Bible 'Time-line' concerning humanity is approximately 7,000 years long. 4,000 years were "BC", before Christ. 2,000 years AD (Anno Domini – the Year of our Lord) have passed, and the present period is almost ending (as our studies have shown). 7 years of "tribulation" are still to come, and then 1,000 years of Kingdom Rule. Approximately 7,000 years overall. So, 6/7 of the period has passed.

Question 4: We come to the period in which we live, what is it most often called?

 (There are three or four answers, write down as many as you can): *The 'Day of Grace', the 'Church Age', the 'Year of our Lord'. There is a proper biblical title which isn't mentioned in Chp.1, "the Acceptable Year of the Lord (Isa. 62:1).*

Question 5: Why should we study 'End Times'? There is more than one answer to that question:

We should know that God is in control. That Satan cannot win. That God's programme must be fulfilled. That the end for all believers is eternally good. That there is much encouragement in prophecy for all who face persecution, in any age.

Questions & Answers for Chapter Two – 'Does God have a Programme?':

Question 1: We looked at periods in God's Programme, in which mankind behaved in different ways – quite often in rebellion – and God brought different judgments. Yet He also worked in grace. Can you list at least SIX of those periods?

Creation – Mankind in Eden (Gen. 1-3). From the 'Fall' to Noah and the Flood (Gen. chps. 6-9). The flood to Babel and the Scattering (Gen. 10-11). Abraham and the Patriarchs (Genesis 12-50). Moses and the Law (Exodus-Deuteronomy), to the Land and the Kingdom (1 Samuel-2 Chronicles), the period between the O.T. and N.T.: The birth of Jesus, His life, death, resurrection, and the Church Period. Christ's Coming in Power and the 1,000 Year Kingdom. The Eternal State; the New Heaven and New Earth.

Question 2: Can you list some of the judgments God brought on those who rebelled?

Adam – driven out of the Garden of Eden. Noah's generation drowned in the Flood. The people of Babel scattered. The Israelites in bondage in Egypt. The Nation of Israel and their captivity in Babylon. The destruction of Jerusalem in 70 AD. The future 'tribulation judgment'. The 'Great White Throne judgment', at the end of the 'Millennium'.

Question 3: Can you find at least one promise of God that He must keep? A promise that cannot be removed because it had no "conditions" attached to it?

God promised Abraham a blessing, a nation, and a land (Gen. chps. 12,15,17). This "covenant" is unconditional.

Question 4: What is meant by an "unconditional promise"?

God 'binds' Himself to the promise, but the other party (like Abraham) was not bound, nor are we. There are no 'conditions' on our side, in order for God to keep His covenant promise.

Questions & Answers for Chapter Three – 'What is Prophecy?':

Question 1: What is prophecy? Can you give a definition of the term?

'A divine ability to say what God will do in the future'. Also a 'forth-telling of the mind of God'.

Question 2: What is the first prophecy in the Bible? (There might be more than one answer.)
(Don't forget, prophecies can be positive OR negative):

"You shall surely die" (Gen. 2:17) was a negative promise. "He (seed of the woman) shall bruise your head" (Gen 3:15) was a positive promise, for the benefit of mankind.

Question 3: Can you give the detail of a short prophecy – fulfilled within a short time period?

There are many. One example is, God told Moses the Egyptians would give the Israelites jewels and clothes at the time of their "Exodus" (Ex. Chps. 3,12).

Question 4: Prophecies are often also promises. And pictures or symbols as well. Can you give an example of where a prophecy is also a promise and a picture?

Again there are many, A lamb for a sacrifice (Abel in Gen. 4). The lamb was a picture of the sacrifice of Jesus, the "Lamb of God". A rainbow for Noah (Gen 9), a promise to never destroy the world by a flood again. And a rainbow still seen in the storm clouds. Both clear examples of 'promises' and 'prophecies'.

Question 5: Can you draw out a 'timeline', beginning from Creation (Gen. chp. 1), to the lifetime of Jesus, including the 'Church Age' and the 'Kingdom Age' still to come?

> **KEYNOTE:** The O.T. is 4,000 years long. So far, 'The Church Age' is almost 2,000 years long. The 'Tribulation Period will be 7 years long. After that 'The Kingdom Age' will be 1,000 years.

Questions & Answers for Chapter Four – 'The First Coming of Jesus':

Question 1: Who were the two old people at the start of the chapter who came to the Temple, to see the baby that God had promised they would?

Simeon and Anna.

Question 2: Why were they looking in the Temple and not in Bethlehem?

Because all baby boys must be brought to the Temple at 40 days old.

Question 3: What were they looking for?

They were looking for "Jehovah's anointed", the "Lord's Christ", the promised Messiah.

Question 4: Why did Joseph and Mary have to go to Bethlehem? (You might want to write out a sentence or two to answer that question):

Caesar Augustus in Rome ordered a census. Everyone had to go to their birth-town. Joseph and Mary were both from Bethlehem, so they had to go there, even though Mary was expecting her promised child.

Question 5: Why did Jesus come? (There are various answers to that question):

To bring the "Acceptable year of the Lord". To be rejected – according to God's purposes – to die as Saviour, to rise from the dead. To provide a message of "good news" for all people.

Question 6: What happened to Jesus, at the end of His period of teaching?

He was rejected by the rulers. He died, but He rose again the third day. He ascended back to heaven 40 days later.

Question 7: Remember the 'Timeline' that you have previously started; are there any new dates or details that can now be added to it?

The date of Jesus' death, His ascension back to heaven.

Questions & Answers for Chapter Five – 'The Birth of the Church':

Question 1: Is the Church to be found in the Old Testament?

No. The "Tabernacle" is not a picture of the Church.

Question 2: Is the Church foretold in prophecy?

Yes, but not until Matthew Chapter 16, in the New Testament.

Question 3: Can you give one reason why the Church is different to Israel?

The Church has no Temple, no Headquarters on earth. No Feast days, and no animal sacrifices.

Question 4: Which Jewish Feast was Jesus' death a fulfilment of?

The "Passover Feast" (Ex. chp. 12).

Question 5: Why do we know this?

Jesus told His disciples – in the Upper Room – it was the last Passover, before He suffered. There are other passages in the Epistles which confirm this (e.g. 1 Cor. 5:7), but we haven't studied any of them at this point.

Question 6: Which Jewish Feast was Jesus' resurrection a fulfilment of?

The "Feast of Firstfruits".

Question 7: How many days after the resurrection was the Church born?

The Church came into existence 49 days from the Sunday on which Jesus rose from the dead. Or, 50 days from the "Sabbath" after the Passover (the Saturday), as the Jews counted. Which is where the "Pentecost" name comes from.

Question 8: What did the "Holy Spirit" do on the day of Pentecost?

He descended, as Jesus promised (John 14), and indwelt the Christians.

Question 9: If you have been drafting out a 'timeline', you should have some more new events and dates to add on to it:

The Birth of the Church, at Pentecost. The beginning of the 'Church Period' or the "Acceptable year of the Lord", which still continues today.

Questions & Answers for Chapter Six – 'The Church Removed':

Question 1: Why is Jesus coming back?

He promised His disciples He would (John chp. 14). He promised David that his son would reign forever (2 Sam. 7).

Question 2: Who is He coming for first of all?

The Church. The "saved" of this age, living and dead.

Question 3: Why is Jesus coming for the Church?

He promised His disciples He would. He promised to "deliver from wrath" (1 Thess. 1:10).

Question 4: What happens after Jesus takes the Church away?

The "Man of Sin" will be revealed, in his true character, during the 'seven year period' (when he breaks the covenant). The "great tribulation" will commence. The "day of the wrath of the Lamb" will come (Rev chp. 6).

Question 5: What names did we use for the world ruler who is coming?
"The Antichrist", the "Man of Sin", the "Lawless One", the "Beast".

Question 6: Who is he linked to?
His master, the Dragon. Satan who is the Serpent.

Question 7: Have you any more dates to add to your 'timeline'? (e.g. The first English Bible):
The destruction of Jerusalem 70 AD, the first English Bible 1520 AD, the rebirth of Israel 1948 AD, etc.

Questions & Answers for Chapter Seven – 'The Symbols Explained':

Question 1: What do the two symbols which come at the beginning and end of the Chart mean?
"Alpha" means beginning, first, source.
"Omega" means ending, conclusion, all of God's purposes fulfilled in Jesus Christ.

Question 2: What is the phrase (in Isaiah 61), which describes the time we are in now?
"The Acceptable Year of the Lord".

Question 3: What is the phrase, in the same verse, which describes the judgment period?
"The Day of Vengeance of our God".

Question 4: What is the next event on God's programme?
The 'rapture' of the Church (1 Thess. Chp. 4). The Christians will be "caught up".

Question 5: How long is the whole of the Judgment Period?
Seven years in total, divided into two halves. 3.5years each.

Question 6: What are the three sets of judgments pictured as?
The 7 Seals, 7 Trumpets, and 7 Bowls.

Question 7: Can you suggest any difference in time between the Seals and the Bowls?
The Bowl Judgments are last of all, right at the end of the judgment period. The Seal Judgments go from the beginning of the 7 years to the end.

Question 8: How long is the Kingdom Age?
It will be 1,000 years. A "Millennium".

Question 9: What do we call the last period, after the Kingdom on this earth has finished?
The 'Eternal State'.

Questions & Answers for Chapter Eight – 'The Sealed Scroll':

Question 1: Where was John when we are introduced to him first?
On Patmos Island, a prisoner for Jesus.

Question 2: Why was he there?
For the "testimony of Jesus", part of God's plan. To receive the "End Times" visions.

Question 3: What did John see first in Chapter 4?
A door open in heaven.

Question 4: What did John see round the throne?
A rainbow.

Question 5: Who do you think are the "Four living ones"?
The "Seraphim" (Ezek. chp. 1; Isa. chp. 6).

Question 6: What was the challenge of the strong angel?
"Who is worthy to take the scroll?"

Question 7: Why did the challenge go out in heaven, earth, and under the earth?
To see if any angel, man, or even Satan could come near God's presence, or imagine they might have any claim to the Scroll.

Question 8: Who took the Scroll? (More than one name was mentioned):
The "Lion of the tribe of Judah", the "Overcomer", the "Slain Lamb standing", the "Lord Jesus".

Question 9: Why is the Lamb worthy?
"He has redeemed us to God by His blood."

Questions & Answers for Chapter Nine – 'The Four Horsemen':

Question 1: Can you note down the colour of the horses, and in the right order?
White, red, black, green or pale.

Question 2: How many Seals are opened in total?
Seven.

Question 3: Why is the first horse white?
The rider comes as a 'peacemaker', a false Messiah.

Question 4: Why are the 2nd, 3rd and 4th horses different in colour from the first?
The peace is soon broken, red means war, black means famine or scarcity, green means disease. Billions will die.

Question 5: What do the "*balances*" represent?
Basic food being weighed out for one day's wages.

Question 6: What percentage of people will be killed by the wars and famines etc.? Or how many?
One quarter. 25%, Around 2,000,000,000 at today's population figures.

Question 7: Who are the "*souls*" seen at the opening of the fifth seal?
The martyrs of the first part of the tribulation.

Question 8: What are the kings and great men hiding from?
The "wrath of the Lamb". Towards the end of the Judgment Period.

Question 9: What happens at the 7th Seal?
There will be silence in heaven for 30 minutes. Then the 'Trumpet Judgments' will follow.

Questions & Answers for Chapter Ten – 'The Sealed Company':

Question 1: Why were the four angels holding back the four winds?
To restrain God's judgment, until He has sealed His people.

Question 2: How many Jews are sealed in total?
144,000, which is 12,000 out of each of 12 tribes.

Question 3: Why does God seal them before the Tribulation?
So that they cannot be harmed, during the 7 year period, nor "sealed" by Antichrist.

Question 4: Why does Satan hate the Jewish people?
Because they produced the "promised seed", the "Messiah", from Judah's tribe. Also, because they are a nation for whom God still has a future, on earth, in the Kingdom period.

Question 5: Why is the tribe of Judah put first?

They are the kingly tribe (Gen. chp. 49).

Question 6: Why do you think there is no tribe of Dan?

They are linked with the serpent (Gen chp. 49), and early idolatry.

Question 7: Why is Joseph listed as a tribe?

Possibly to replace Ephraim.

Question 8: Who are the multitude before the throne?

The saved of the Tribulation Period.

Question 9: What do we have in common with this company of people?

We are "washed" in the "blood of the Lamb". We are saved for eternity with Jesus Christ.

Questions & Answers for Chapter Eleven – 'The Trumpet Judgments':

Question 1: What happened before the angels blew their trumpets? And why?

Silence in heaven. Awe at the terrible judgments to come.

Question 2: What did the first trumpet judgment affect?

The trees and green grass. One third, 33% destroyed.

Question 3: What did the second trumpet judgment affect?

Sea, Sea life, shipping. One third, 33% (possibly 30,000 ships) destroyed.

Question 4: What did the fourth trumpet judgment affect?

The sky; sun, moon and stars. One third of light shut off.

Question 5: What came out of the 'pit of the Abyss' at the 5th trumpet?

A great host or army of demons.

Question 6: Who was the King over the demons?

"Abaddon" or "Apollyon". Possibly a fallen angel.

Question 7: How many are in the demon land army?

200,000,000 demons.

Question 8: What did the voice from heaven say, at the 7th trumpet?

"The kingdoms of this world have become the kingdoms of our God and of His Christ" (Rev. 11:15).

Question 9: What is the main reason for God's judgments in this period?

Because men did not repent of their wickedness, nor their worship of demons (Rev. 9:20).

Questions & Answers for Chapter Twelve – 'The War in Heaven':

Question 1: This 'parenthesis' is the middle section of the book, where does it begin and end?

It begins after the description of the 7th Trumpet judgment, and before the description of the 7 Bowl judgments begin.
Can you give the chapter and verse for both the beginning and end? *(Revelation 11:19 – 15:5).*

Question 2: There are seven 'personalities' in this centre section (Two we have not yet examined), Can you list the five that we have studied, and in the order in which they appear?

The Woman, the Dragon, the Male Son, Michael the Archangel, And the Lamb on Mount Zion.

Question 3: Why does the Dragon come between the "*woman*" and the "*man child*"?

The Dragon is the Serpent, he hates the Woman, who is Israel, and her child, who is Jesus the Messiah.

Question 4: How many names does the Devil have in this chapter?
Four; the Dragon, the Serpent, the Devil and Satan.

Question 5: Who are the leaders of the armies who fight a war in heaven?
Michael and the Dragon.

Question 6: Why is the Dragon angry at this point?
He is cast out of heaven down to earth, and he knows how little time he has left, until his judgment occurs.

Question 7: What lessons can we learn from this 'panoramic' study in the middle of the book?
God has always been in control. His purposes cannot be altered. The Devil will be defeated, Jesus must reign, as O.T. and N.T. prophecies promise He will.

Questions & Answers for Chapter Thirteen – 'The Beast out of the Sea':

Question 1: Where does the first Beast come from?
Out of the "sea".

Question 2: What and where does this "sea" represent?
The Mediterranean; the southern or 'Latin' European nations, around its shore.

Question 3: How many heads does the Beast have?
Seven heads.

Question 4: How many horns does he have?
Ten horns.

Question 5: Who is he like?
He is like his master the Dragon.

Question 6: Is there any difference between the description of the 'Dragon' and the 'Beast'?
The Dragon has his crowns on his seven heads. The "Beast" has his ten crowns on his ten heads.

Question 7: Which animals, in the passage, is he compared to?
A leopard, a bear, and a lion.

Question 8: Who does he receive his power from?
From the Dragon.

Question 9: Who sets his limits, and his final judgment?
His limits, and his final judgment are set by God.

Questions & Answers for Chapter Fourteen – 'The Beast out of Land':

Question 1: Where does the second Beast appear from?
Out of the "land".

Question 2: What does the 'land' usually represent? And why?
Often in the Bible the "land" represents the country of Israel. God promised a land to Abraham, with described boundaries (Gen. chp. 15).

Question 3: Why is this Beast so different looking?
He is meant to be deceptive. He looks like "Messiah", a counterfeit "Lamb".

Question 4: What is his role?
To direct worship to the first Beast.

Question 5: Who is he a counterfeit of?
He is a counterfeit of the Holy Spirit in his activity.

Question 6: What key event happens at the mid-point of the 7 years?
The first Beast is assassinated, and reappears, from the "Abyss".

Question 7: What, at that point, does the "False Prophet" propose?
To make an image to the first Beast, for world worship.

Question 8: What is the final choice, and between which two opposites?
To worship "Anti-Christ" or worship "Jesus Christ".

Questions & Answers for Chapter Fifteen – 'The Mark of the Beast: 666':

Question 1: Who are the 4 Personalities linked on the side of 'good'?
The Woman, the Male Son, Michael, the Lamb on Mount Zion. Also linked on the side of good are the "remnant" of believing Israelites, who will be hidden in a safe place by God.

Question 2: Who are the 3 Personalities linked on the side of 'evil'?
The Dragon, the first Beast and the False Prophet.

Question 3: What does the "False Prophet" make compulsory?
Worship of the first Beast and his image.

Question 4: What is introduced first, and why?
A "Mark"; to identify people with the Beast and worship of the Dragon.

Question 5: What can you not do without the "Mark"?
You cannot buy or sell. You have no freedom. You have no rights of your own.

Question 6: What 4 things are linked to the "Beast" (We used 'iconography' as a general term):
The Image, the Mark, the Name and the Number, which is "666".

Question 7: What is the "Number"?
The number is "six hundred and sixty and six". It may be a phrase, not just a number.

Question 8: What is God's verdict on those who have the "Mark"?
They are condemned to suffer the "wrath of God" (Rev 14:10).

Question 9: How can we be sure that the times of the "Mark" have not arrived?
True Christians cannot be deceived into taking the "mark". Not even accidentally. The "Mark" will not just be a symbol, it will be connected with voluntary worship of the Image and the Dragon. These things cannot happen until after the Church has been removed (2 Thess. chp. 2). The compulsory worship will come during the second 3.5 years, the 'Great Tribulation' period.

Questions & Answers for Chapter Sixteen – 'The Bowl Judgments':

Question 1: How many Bowl Judgments are there?
There are seven, as with the Seals and Trumpets.

Question 2: What shape are the Bowls?
They are wide bowls, not narrow necked 'vials'. God directs where they are poured.

Question 3: Who are they targeted against?
The people with the "mark", the Kingdom and the Throne of the Beast.

Question 4: What happens to the sea? And the sea-life?
The sea becomes as blood. Everything in the sea dies.

Question 5: What happens to the water sources?

The water sources become actual blood, all the rivers and fountains.

Question 6: Why does God judge in this way?

To avenge the blood of "saints and prophets"; all the martyrs of all the ages, from Abel.

Question 7: Why is the great river Euphrates dried up?

To prepare the way for the Kings from the "sun rising", from the far east.

Question 8: What is in the 'parenthesis' in Chp. 16?

One of the seven blessings (the third) of the book of Revelation. It is primarily for tribulation saints to encourage them to keep watch and be ready for the return of Messiah at His Second Coming.

Question 9: What is "*Armageddon*"?

"Armageddon" is a literal place, a 'gathering centre' for troops, in preparation for the 'last battle', both armies loyal to the "Beast" and armies of the nations (north, south and east) who are opposed to his despotic reign.

Question 10: Who controls the 'gathering' of the armies?

It is God who is in control. He 'gathers them' through lying "spirits of demons" who speak through the "mouths of the Dragon, the Beast and the False Prophet".

Questions & Answers for Chapter Seventeen – 'Mystery Babylon: The Scarlet Woman':

Question 1: There are FOUR women in the book of Revelation – Can you give their names? And the chapters where they are found?

Jezebel (Chp. 2), The Nation of Israel (Chp. 12), the "Great Whore" or "Mystery Babylon" (Chp. 17), the "Bride, the Lamb's Wife" (Chp 21).

Question 2: Who does the "*Scarlet Woman*" we have studied in Chp. 17 represent?

The system of false world religion, all combined into one in the last days, after the true Church has been removed.

Question 3: Who is the "*Beast*" she is sitting on?

The "Beast out of the Sea" of Rev. chp. 13. The "first Beast".

Question 4: Who is in control, the Woman or the Beast?

The Beast she is sitting on is in control of her. Though she thinks it is the other way around.

Question 5: Who is on supreme control?

It is God, as always, who is in supreme control.

Question 6: Can you give a verse from Chp. 17 to confirm that?

"God put it in their hearts to fulfil His will" (Rev. 17:17).

Question 7: Where does the "*Mystery Babylon*" false religion begin?

It begins in "Babil" with Nimrod, back in "Shinar".

Question 8: Can you give an O.T. Chp. reference to support that fact?

Gen. chps. 10 and 11.

Question 9: What is the end of the false religious system represented by the "*Scarlet Woman*"?

She is robbed of her wealth, she is made desolate, and burned with fire.

Question 10: Why might Satan want the false religious system out of the way?

Because he wants to create a 'spiritual vacuum' so that he can introduce the worship of the "Beast" and the "Image" and make that worship compulsory, with no other alternatives.

Questions & Answers for Chapter Eighteen – 'The Fall of Babylon':

Question 1: Do both "*Babylon*" visions happen at the same time?

No, there is a 3.5 year gap between the two visions. One comes in the centre of the 7 year period, the other at the end.

Question 2: How can we tell there is a time difference?

The phrase, "After these things" – John's time shift phrase comes between the two parts of the vision (Rev. 18:1).

Question 3: If the "*Scarlet Woman*" is a religious system, what is "*Babylon the Great*"?

It is a city, the centre of the commercial and political system of the "Beast".

Question 4: What was similar about the city and tower back in Genesis chps. 10 & 11?

The city and the tower of Babel were both a commercial and a religious centre.

Question 5: What did the 'Tower of Babel' represent?

A centre of false religion, and the worship of the heavens, the sun, moon and stars.

Question 6: Which other cities in the O.T. that God destroyed, is this city also like?

The city of Babylon is similar to Sodom and Gomorrah, and also suffers a similar judgment.

Question 7: What will happen to the future Babylon that never happened in the past?

It will be burned with fire and totally destroyed. Never to be rebuilt.

Question 8: Can you give any references from the O.T. to support that?

Jeremiah prophesied this in his prophecies (Jer. chp. 51:63-64).

Question 9: Why does God judge the future Babylon in this way?

It is part of a system of evil, it is anti-God. Because of the blood of the martyrs that were slain, and because of the "bodies and souls of men" found in it.

Questions & Answers for Chapter Nineteen – 'The Battle of Armageddon':

Question 1: Is "*Megiddo*" a real place?

Yes, "Megiddo" is a real place.

Question 2: Is it found in the O.T.? (Give an O.T. reference to prove that it is).

Megiddo is found 12 times in the O.T. The first mention is the defeat of the King of Megiddo by Joshua and the Israelites (Jos. chp. 12:21).

Question 3: Where was "*Megiddo*"?

Megiddo, the original town, was on the south side of Megiddo's valley. Probably a fortress.

Question 4: Was it just a 'walled town' or 'citadel'?

No, "Megiddo" was a town, a valley, and a fountain which flowed into a river.

Question 5: What is "*Megiddo*" most often connected with?

Megiddo is most often connected with great battles of the past.

Question 6: "*Megiddo*" is also the name for a valley. What are its approximate dimensions?

The valley is approximately 23 kilometres wide (north to south), and 32 kilometres long (west to east).

Question 7: Can you name any of the O.T. characters who had famous victories connected with "*Megiddo*"?

Some of the O.T. characters connected with Megiddo are, Joshua, Gideon, Barak and Deborah, and Elijah.

Question 8: Were there any famous defeats also connected with "*Megiddo*"?

Yes, Saul and his sons were slain on the eastern mountains, and Josiah King of Judah was slain in battle in the valley too.

Question 9: What will happen at "*Armageddon*" in the future?

The 'last battle' of the age will take place at Megiddo, the "Beast" and the "False Prophet" will be defeated and seized, by the Lord Jesus Himself, at His "Coming in Power".

Question 10: When will this take place?

It will happen at the very end of the "Great Tribulation" period, at the end of the 7 years.

Questions & Answers for Chapter Twenty – 'Christ's Coming in Power':

Question 1: Can you give three main differences between Jesus' First and Second Comings?

Jesus first coming was "lowly" His second will be a "Coming in Power". His first coming was as a babe, the second as a warrior King. His first as a rejected King, His second as a reigning and victorious Monarch.

Question 2: Many of the O.T. prophecies – looking back – have a 'time gap'. Can you name one or more?

Isaiah chp. 61:2, "the Acceptable Year of the Lord" and the "Day of Vengeance of our God", which Jesus divided in His public address in the synagogue in Nazareth (Luke 4:19). The Daniel chp. 9 'timeline' also divides into three parts.

Question 3: Something of each of these 'time-gap' prophecies was <u>not</u> fulfilled at Jesus' first coming. Can you give an example?

From Isaiah Chp. 9, "the government shall be upon His shoulder", from Isaiah chp. 41, "the Day of Vengeance of our God". From Daniel chp. 9, "He shall confirm the covenant …" is not speaking of Messiah at His first coming, but of the "Prince that shall come", which we now see is at least 1,900 years later.

Question 4: How many "*Hallelujahs*" are there in Rev. chp. 19? How many other "*Hallelujahs*" in the N.T.?

There are four "Hallelujahs" in Rev. Chp. 19. There are no other "Hallelujahs" in the N.T. All the others are in the O.T.

Question 5: How many names does Jesus have at His "*Coming in Power*"?

Jesus comes with four different names.

Question 6: Can you list some of them?

"Faithful and True", "a name no man knew", "The Word of God", and "King of Kings and Lord of Lords" (All in Rev. chp. 19).

Question 7: How many 'features' of Jesus are mentioned in Rev. chp. 19?

There are four features mentioned.

Question 8: Can you list them?

His eyes, His head, His mouth, and His thigh.

Question 9: How many 'objects of rule' are mentioned?

There are four.

Question 10: Can you list them?

A horse, a sword, a rod, and a winepress.

Question 11: Who is seized first at "*Armageddon*"? Where are they put?

The "Beast" and the "False Prophet" are taken and are cast alive into the Lake of Fire.

Questions & Answers for Chapter Twenty-One – 'The Millennial Kingdom':

Question 1: What reasons can you give for Jesus coming the second time?

Jesus is coming to fulfil the covenant promises of the O.T., and He is coming back because He promised His disciples He would, in the N.T.

Question 2: Can you name any O.T. "*covenants*" which must be finally fulfilled?

The covenant to Abraham (Gen. 15) in which he was promised a nation and a land. The covenant to David in which he was promised a king from his line, to reign forever. And the "new covenant" of Jer. chp. 31.

Question 3: We examined a list of things which must be done before the Kingdom is set up. How many can you list?

Satan must be bound, The O.T. saints must be raised, the tribulation martyrs must be raised. The living nations must be judged, the "sheep and the goats" (Matt. chp. 25), the land must be cleansed and the Millennial Temple must be built, and Jerusalem rebuilt.

Question 4: At the start of the '1,000 year kingdom', where is Satan put? For how long?

Satan is bound in the "pit of the abyss" for 1,000 years.

Question 5: What detail of the Kingdom is NOT told in O.T. prophecy?

The length of the Kingdom, 1,000 literal years.

Question 6: Who is included in the government of the Kingdom?

Jesus Christ Himself as King, David as Prince, the 12 Apostles as the rulers of the 12 Tribes, and the tribulation martyrs as part of the government.

Question 7: What will be the main characteristics of the Kingdom?

The Millennial Kingdom will be one of peace, righteous rule, and harmony between man and animals. Many people will live the full 1,000 years.

Question 8: What happens at the end of the Kingdom?

Satan is "loosed". He goes into the "four corners" of the world to find rebels, and to raise an army against the King and Jerusalem. God destroys them with fire, and Satan is sent to the Lake of Fire.

Questions & Answers for Chapter Twenty-Two – 'The Final Judgment':

Question 1: What does NOT happen at the start of the '1,000 year Kingdom'?

The 'unsaved dead' are not raised. The earth is 'cleansed' but not renewed, and the "new heaven and new earth" are not formed.

Question 2: The "first resurrection" concludes at the beginning of the Kingdom. Where does it begin?

The "first resurrection" begins with the resurrection of Jesus, on the third day after His crucifixion.

Question 3: What would be the greatest problem if there was no resurrection?

There would be no true gospel. And no true basis for salvation, if Jesus was not risen (1 Cor. 15:1-12).

Question 4: What is the "second death"?

The final judgment of all the 'wicked dead' from all ages, at the Great White Throne, and their consignment to the Lake of Fire, forever.

Question 5: Why is it contrasted with the "first resurrection"?

Those who are part of the "first resurrection" can never be touched by the "second death" (Rev. 20:6).

Question 6: Why is the judgment throne described as a "Great White Throne"?

Because of its Majesty, its Purity of judgment, and its Authority, all from the one who sits on it; Jesus Christ.

Question 7: How many books, at least, can we tell are opened?

There appear to be at least four books opened.

Question 8: Can you name them?

The Word of God, the Book of the Living, the Book of Life, and the Book of Works.

Question 9: What happens after the Last Judgment?

The old earth is dissolved, and a new earth and heavens are made.

Questions & Answers for Chapter Twenty-Three – 'The New Jerusalem':

Question 1: How many 'new things' are mentioned at the start of Rev. chp. 21?

There are 4 new things mentioned.

Question 2: Can you name them in order?
A new heaven, a new earth, a new Jerusalem, and "all things new".

Question 3: Is the *"New Jerusalem"* a real City?
Yes, it is.

Question 4: Is it the same place as Jerusalem today?
No, it is not.

Question 5: Are the dimensions symbolic, or literal?
There is no reason to believe that the dimensions are not literal.

Question 6: What shape is the *"Holy City"*?
The "Holy City" has a square base. It may be a cube, or a pyramid.

Question 7: What size is the City?
The City is 2,220 square kilometres, or 1,380 square miles.

Question 8: Would it fit on our world?
Yes, there are numerous countries in our world, today, that the New Jerusalem would fit into.

Question 9: Does it have to 'sit' on our world?
No, it doesn't. it may be a 'satellite' city, over Israel, in the Kingdom.

Question 10: Where will it rest finally?
It will rest on its foundations on the new earth, forever.

Questions & Answers for Chapter Twenty-Four – 'Jesus Coming Quickly ...':

Question 1: Is the last part of Chp. 22, a.) After the 'Kingdom Age'? b.) After the *"new heaven"*? Or during 'the Church Age'?
Neither, the last part of Revelation 22 is before the kingdom age, John goes back again in time to his position as a believer who is part of the Church.

Question 2: Who is Jesus speaking to in the last paragraph of Rev. chp. 22?
Jesus is speaking to us, the Church, to tribulation saints, and also to the unsaved readers of the book of Revelation.

Question 3: How many times does Jesus speak in the last part of Rev. chp. 22?
Jesus speaks 7 times.

Question 4: What does *"Alpha"* and *"Omega"* mean?
The beginning and the ending, the first and the last.

Question 5: How many times were angels seen, and heard, at Jesus' first coming?
Angels were sent 9 times connected with Jesus' first coming.

Question 6: Can you list some of them?
Gabriel was sent to Mary. An angel was sent to Joseph. Angels appeared to the shepherds. An angel told Joseph to take Mary and the child to Egypt, and then to bring them back. Angels came to Jesus after His temptations. An angel comforted Him at Gethsemane. Angels appeared at the tomb on resurrection morning, and angels appeared 40 days later at His ascension.

Question 7: Who is speaking right at the end of the book of Revelation?
Jesus speaks.

Question 8: Who is replying?
We, as Church Christians reply.

Question 9: Who speaks last of all?
John speaks to all his readers last of all.

Questions & Answers for Chapter Twenty-Five – 'Events that Could Happen Soon':

Question 1: What does the expression mean, 'The clock of prophecy has stopped'?

The 'clock of prophecy' refers to Daniel's 490 year 'timeline'. It 'stopped' at year 483. And 7 years are still to be counted off.

Question 2: What is the difference in "*times*" and "*seasons*"?

"Times" are to do with fixed periods, "seasons" are to do with the state of events, or the 'character' of the times.

Question 3: Which prophecies can you list, that have been fulfilled <u>since</u> Jesus' death?

Jesus' resurrection, His ascension, the descent of the Holy Spirit, the birth of the Church, the destruction of Jerusalem, and the pulling down of the Temple.

Question 4: Are there "*signs*" of Jesus' 'Second Coming' being fulfilled now?

Yes, there are possibly signs being fulfilled in our time.

Question 5: Can you list any?

Jesus spoke of them in Matt. chp. 24 & Luke chp. 21. "False Christs", "wars and rumours", "famine", "pestilence" and "earthquakes".

Question 6: What might happen in Israel, while the Church is still here?

Israel could have a priesthood established (through the breeding of a "red heifer" and the provision of 'purifying water'. They could have a "Sanctuary", possibly not a full sized Temple. They could commence sacrifices, on a 're-enactment' basis, or even for real.

Question 7: Can the "*Church*" go through the "*Great Tribulation*"?

No, the Church cannot go through the "Great Tribulation".

Question 8: Can you give any scriptural reasons why not?

Jesus said He was coming to "receive us" – take us away (John 14:6).

We will be "delivered" from the wrath coming here (1 Thess. 1:10). We will be "caught up", 'raptured' or 'snatched away' (1 Thess. 4:17). We will be "kept from the hour of trial" (Rev. 3:10).

Questions & Answers for Chapter Twenty-Six – 'Events that Must Happen ... Review':

Question 1: What is the next major event on God's Programme? (Try to use scriptural terms).

The end of the "Acceptable year of the Lord" (Isaiah 61:2), the end of the 'Church Age', the removal of the Church.

Question 2: What comes after that?   (Give a Bible ref.).

The "Day of Vengeance of our God" begins (Isa. 61:2).

Question 3: What are the time periods of prophecy that still have to be fulfilled called?

The 'tribulation' or 'Daniel's 70ᵗʰ week', a period of 7 years of judgment, which gets progressively worse.

Question 4: What happens after the Church is removed?

The removal of "restraint" allows the "Man of Sin" to have his "revelation". He will confirm the "covenant" with Israel and "many" others, and he himself will break it in the middle of the 7 years.

Question 5: What are the three 'sets' of Judgments that fall in the 'Tribulation' called?

The 7 Seal Judgments, the 7 Trumpet Judgments, and the 7 Bowl Judgments.

Question 6: What happens at the end of the 'Judgment Period'?

The 'battle of Armageddon' is set up. Jesus Christ returns in power. Satan and his "Beasts" are defeated, and their armies slain.

Question 7: What period follows after that event?

The 1,000 year 'Millennial Kingdom'.

Question 8: What happens at the end of the 1,000 Year Kingdom?
Satan is loosed, there is a last rebellion. Satan is cast into the Lake of Fire.

Question 9: What comes after that?
The last judgment, the "Great White Throne", all the unsaved dead are raised, judged, and also cast into the Lake of Fire.

Question 10: What comes last of all?
The creation of a "new heaven and a new earth". Which will have no end. God is "Alpha and Omega" forever.

JOTTINGS

Select Bibliography

Allen, J. *Daniel Reconsidered* (Cookstown, NI: Scripture Teaching Library, 2013).

Allen, J. *Revelation, What the Bible Teaches* (Kilmarnock, UK: John Ritchie Ltd., 1997). §§

Anderson, R. *The Coming Prince* (Grand Rapids, MI: Kregel Publications, 1954). §

Ariel, Y. Rabbi, *The Temple Institute* (Jerusalem, Israel: www.templeinstitute.org 1987).

Barnhouse, D. G. *Revelation, An Expositional Commentary* (Grand Rapids, MI: Zondervan Publishing, 1971).

Baron, D. Zechariah (Grand Rapids, MI: Kregel Publications, 2001).

Blanchard, J. *Does God Believe in Atheists?* (Darlington, UK: Evangelical Press, 2000).

Booth, A. E. *The Course of Time from Eternity to Eternity* (Bedford, PA: MWTB, 1978).

Bruce, F. F. *The International Bible Commentary* (Basingstoke, UK: Marshall Morgan and Scott, 1986). §

Bultema, H. *Commentary on Daniel* (Grand Rapids, MI: Kregel Publications, 1988).

Bultema, H. *Maranatha!* (Grand Rapids, MI: Kregel Publications, 1985).

Cameron, D. C. B. *Apocalypse – Facts & Fantasies* (Waterlooville, UK: Twoedged Sword Publications, 2006). §

Cameron, D. C. B. *The Blessed Hope* (Newtownards, NI: Crimond House Publishers, 2021).

Cameron, D. C. B. *Israel, The Church and Islam* (Kilmarnock, UK: John Ritchie Ltd., 2015).

Cameron, D. C. B. *The Minor Prophets and The End Times* (Kilmarnock, UK: John Ritchie Ltd., 2010). §

Cameron, D. C. B. *Rapture – Sooner Not Later* (Kilmarnock, UK: John Ritchie Ltd., 2013).

Cameron, R. *Scripture Truth About The Lord's Return* (New York, NY: Revell & Co., 1922).

Cooper, D. L. *The Rules of Interpretation* (Los Angeles, CA: Bible Research Society, 1949).

Criswell, W. A. *Expository Sermons on Revelation* (Dallas, TX: Criswell Publishing, 1995).

Dunlap, D. *The Glory of the Ages* (Port Colborne, ON: Gospel Folio Press, 2008). §§

Fruchtenbaum, A. G. *The Footsteps of the Messiah* (San Antonio, TX: Ariel Ministries, 2003). §

Fruchtenbaum, A. G. *Israelogy, The Missing Link in Systematic Theology* (San Antonio, TX: Ariel Ministries, 1994).

Gordon, S. *Great God of Heaven* (Kilmarnock, UK: John Ritchie Ltd., 2020). §§

Gordon, S. *All Hail the Lamb* (Kilmarnock, UK: John Ritchie Ltd., 2014). §§

Hendriksen, W. *I & II Thessalonians, New Testament Commentary* (Edinburgh, PA: Banner of Truth, 1991).

Hitchcock, M. *The End* (Carol Stream, IL: Tyndale House Publishers, 2012). §§

Hitchcock, M. *Who Is the Antichrist?* (Eugene OR: Harvest House Publishers, 2011).

Horovitz, D. *Times of Israel* (Jerusalem, Israel: www.timesofisrael.com 2012).

Ice, T. *Pre-Trib Research Centre* (Dallas, TX: www.pre-trib.org 2021).

Ironside, H. A. *Daniel* (Grand Rapids, MI: Kregel Publications, 2005).

Ironside, H. A. *The Minor Prophets* (Grand Rapids, MI: Kregel Publications, 2004).

Ironside, H. A. *Revelation* (Grand Rapids, MI: Kregel Publications, 2004).

Jennings, S. W. *Alpha and Omega* (Belfast, NI: Ambassador, 1996). §§

Johnstone, P. & Mandryk, J. *Operation World* (Cumbria, UK: Paternoster Press, 2005).

Ladd, G. E. *The Blessed Hope* (Grand Rapids, MI: W. B. Eerdmans Publishing, 1956).

Lahaye, T. & Ice, T. *Charting The End Times* (Eugene, ON: Harvest House Publishers, 2001). §

Larkin, C. *The Book of Daniel* (Glenside, PA: Larkin Estate, 1929).

Larkin, C. *Dispensational Truth, God's Plan and Purpose for the Ages* (Glenside PA: Larkin Est., 1920). §

Larkin, C. *The Book of Revelation* (Glenside, PA: Larkin Estate, 1919).

MacArthur, J. *Revelation 1-11, The MacArthur New Testament Commentary* (Chicago, IL: Moody Press, 1999). §

MacArthur, J. *Revelation 12-22, The MacArthur New Testament Commentary* (Chicago, IL: Moody Press, 2000). §

Martin, D. M. *1 & 2 Thessalonians, The New American Commentary* (Nashville, TN: B&H Publishing, 1995).

Mellish, N. *The Times of The Gentiles* (Port Colborne, ON: Gospel Folio Press, 2010).

Mellish, N. *Revelation from Tribulation to Triumph* (Port Colborne, ON: Gospel Folio Press, 2008).

McClain, A. J. *Daniel's Prophecy of the 70 Weeks* (Winona Lake, IN: BMH Books, 1969). §§

McClain, A. J. *The Greatness of The Kingdom* (Winona Lake, IN: BMH Books, 1974). §

McKillen, M. D. *What in the World is Happening? A Study Manual on Revelation* (Kells, NI: WITWIH, 2014).

Morris, H. M. The Revelation Record (Carol Stream, IL: Tyndale House Publishers, 1983).

Morris, J. C. *Ancient Dispensational Truth* (Taos, NM: Dispensational Publishing House, 2018).

Mounce, R. H. *The Book of Revelation* (Grand Rapids, MI: W. B. Eerdmans, 1997).

Patterson, P. *Revelation, The New American Commentary* (Nashville, TN: B&H Publishing, 2012).

Pentecost, J. D. *Things to Come* (Grand Rapids, MI: Zondervan Publishing, 1964). §

Phillips, J. *Exploring the Future* (Grand Rapids, MI: Kregel Publications, 2003). §§

Phillips, J. *Exploring Revelation* (Chicago, IL: Moody Press, 1987). §

Ritchie, J. *Impending Great Events* (London, UK: Pickering & Inglis Ltd., 1939).

Rosenthal, M. J. *The Pre-Wrath Rapture of the Church* (Nashville, TN: Thomas Nelson, 1990).

Ryrie, C. C. *The Ryrie Study Bible®, N.A.S.B. Version.* (Chicago IL: Moody Press, 1978). §§

Sauer, E. *The Dawn of World Redemption* (London, UK: Paternoster Press, 1957).

Sauer, E. *From Eternity to Eternity* (London, UK: Paternoster Press, 1957).

Scofield, C. I. *The Scofield® Reference Bible* (Oxford, UK: Oxford University Press, 1996). §

Scott. W. *Exposition of the Revelation of Jesus Christ* (London, UK: Pickering & Inglis Ltd., 1968).

Scroggie, W. G. *Know Your Bible* (London, UK: Pickering & Inglis Ltd., 1974). §§

Scroggie, W. G. *The Unfolding Drama of Redemption, Vols. I-III* (Grand Rapids, MI: Kregel Publications, 1994). §§

Shoebat, W. *God's War on Terror* (Chicago, IL: Top Executive Media, 2008).

Showers, R. E. *The Most High God* (Bellmawr, NJ: The Friends of Israel Gospel Ministry, 2006).

Showers, R. E. *What On Earth Is God Doing?* (Neptune, NJ, Loizeaux Brothers, 1973). §

Smith, T. W. *2 Thessalonians, What the Bible Teaches* (Kilmarnock, UK: John Ritchie Ltd., 1983).

Strong, J. *Exhaustive Concordance of the Bible* (Iowa Falls, IA: World Bible Publishers, 1980). §

Sweetnam, M. *To The Day of Eternity* (Cookstown, NI: Scripture Teaching Library, 2014).

Thomas, R. L. *Revelation 1-7, An Exegetical Commentary* (Chicago, IL: Moody Press, 1992).

Thomas, R. L. *Revelation 8-22, An Exegetical Commentary* (Chicago, IL: Moody Press, 1995).

Tsarfati, A. *The Day Approaching* (Eugene, OR: Harvest House Publishers, 2020).

Unger, M. F. *Unger's Bible Handbook* (Chicago, IL: Moody Press, 1966). §

Walvoord, J. F. *Daniel* (Chicago, IL: Moody Publishers, 2012). §

Walvoord, J. F. *The Prophecy Knowledge Handbook* (Wheaton, IL: Victor Books, 1990). §

Walvoord, J. F. *The Revelation of Jesus Christ* (Chicago, IL: Moody Press, 1966). §

Wilson, T. E. *1 Thessalonians, What the Bible Teaches* (Kilmarnock, UK: John Ritchie Ltd., 1983).